Lecture Notes in Computer Science 14843

Founding Editors

Gerhard Goos
Juris Hartmanis

Editorial Board Members

Elisa Bertino, *Purdue University, West Lafayette, IN, USA*
Wen Gao, *Peking University, Beijing, China*
Bernhard Steffen , *TU Dortmund University, Dortmund, Germany*
Moti Yung , *Columbia University, New York, NY, USA*

The series Lecture Notes in Computer Science (LNCS), including its subseries Lecture Notes in Artificial Intelligence (LNAI) and Lecture Notes in Bioinformatics (LNBI), has established itself as a medium for the publication of new developments in computer science and information technology research, teaching, and education.

LNCS enjoys close cooperation with the computer science R & D community, the series counts many renowned academics among its volume editors and paper authors, and collaborates with prestigious societies. Its mission is to serve this international community by providing an invaluable service, mainly focused on the publication of conference and workshop proceedings and postproceedings. LNCS commenced publication in 1973.

Jason Hemann · Stephen Chang
Editors

Trends in Functional Programming

25th International Symposium, TFP 2024
South Orange, NJ, USA, January 10–12, 2024
Revised Selected Papers

Editors
Jason Hemann
Seton Hall University
South Orange, NJ, USA

Stephen Chang
University of Massachusetts Boston
Boston, MA, USA

ISSN 0302-9743   ISSN 1611-3349 (electronic)
Lecture Notes in Computer Science
ISBN 978-3-031-74557-7   ISBN 978-3-031-74558-4 (eBook)
https://doi.org/10.1007/978-3-031-74558-4

© The Editor(s) (if applicable) and The Author(s), under exclusive license to Springer Nature Switzerland AG 2025

This work is subject to copyright. All rights are solely and exclusively licensed by the Publisher, whether the whole or part of the material is concerned, specifically the rights of translation, reprinting, reuse of illustrations, recitation, broadcasting, reproduction on microfilms or in any other physical way, and transmission or information storage and retrieval, electronic adaptation, computer software, or by similar or dissimilar methodology now known or hereafter developed.
The use of general descriptive names, registered names, trademarks, service marks, etc. in this publication does not imply, even in the absence of a specific statement, that such names are exempt from the relevant protective laws and regulations and therefore free for general use.
The publisher, the authors and the editors are safe to assume that the advice and information in this book are believed to be true and accurate at the date of publication. Neither the publisher nor the authors or the editors give a warranty, expressed or implied, with respect to the material contained herein or for any errors or omissions that may have been made. The publisher remains neutral with regard to jurisdictional claims in published maps and institutional affiliations.

This Springer imprint is published by the registered company Springer Nature Switzerland AG
The registered company address is: Gewerbestrasse 11, 6330 Cham, Switzerland

If disposing of this product, please recycle the paper.

Preface

This volume contains revised selected papers that were presented at the 25th International Symposium on Trends in Functional Programming (TFP 2024), which was held at Seton Hall University from January 10–12, 2024. TFP was co-located with the 13th International Workshop on Trends in Functional Programming in Education (TFPIE 2024), which took place on January 9, 2024.

TFP is an international forum for researchers with interests in all aspects of functional programming, taking a broad view of current and future trends in this area. It aspires to be a lively environment for presenting the latest research results and other contributions. TFP reviewing is a two-phase, single-blind process where authors may either submit a full paper for review before the symposium, or submit an extended abstract before the symposium, followed by a full paper afterwards incorporating feedback from both the pre-symposium reviews and the presentations. Each paper receives at least three reviews per round.

This year we received nineteen total submissions. Seventeen were presented at the symposium, along with three keynote talks: Benjamin C. Pierce, from University of Pennsylvania, presented "delta: Ordered Types for Stream Processing"; John H. Reppy, from the University of Chicago, presented "The Implementation of Functional Programming Languages"; and Jeremy Gibbons, from University of Oxford, presented "Turner, Bird, Eratosthenes: The Eternal Burning Thread." After the post-symposium review phase, revised versions of ten papers were selected for inclusion in these proceedings. The final selections spanned a wide variety of topics including dependent type systems, compiler optimizations, and DSL design and implementation.

In addition, TFP offers two prizes: the John McCarthy award for the best paper and the David Turner award for the best student paper. The paper "Free Monads, Intrinsic Scoping, and Higher-Order Preunification" by Nikolai Kudasov was awarded the best paper prize. The paper "Programming with Dependent Additive Pairs" by Vít Šefl was awarded the best student paper prize.

All of this was only possible thanks to the hard work of the authors, the insightful contributions of the Program Committee members, the thoughtful advice from the TFP steering committee, and the generous support of our sponsors. Funding and organizational support for the event were provided by Seton Hall University and Epic Games. We would also like to acknowledge in particular Sheila Riley, Cathy Winterfield, and Melissa Kohlman of Seton Hall University, Lenny DeGraff of the Thomas Edison National Historical Park, Dorothy Szmygiel of Gourmet Dining Catering, and Nick D'Rozario, Jennifer Turner, and Lashada Banks of Epic Games for their invaluable assistance and support. Deep thanks to everyone for making this year's symposium a success.

August 2024   Jason Hemann
                                                                                                                 Stephen Chang

Organization

Organizing Committee

Program Committee and General Chair

Jason Hemann — Seton Hall University, USA

Symposium Chair

Stephen Chang — University of Massachusetts Boston, USA

Local Arrangements

Shajina Anand — Seton Hall University, USA

Publicity Chair

Peter Achten — Radboud University, Netherlands

Program Committee

Małgorzata Biernacka	University of Wrocław, Poland
Olaf Chitil	University of Kent, UK
Yannick Forster	Inria, France
Jeremy Gibbons	University of Oxford, UK
Ralf Hinze	RPTU Kaiserslautern-Landau, Germany
Shachar Itzhaky	Technion Israel Institute of Technology, Israel
Alex Kavvos	University of Bristol, UK
Hsiang-Shang "Josh" Ko	IIS, Academia Sinica, Taiwan
Yao Li	Portland State University, USA
Erik Meijer	Facebook, USA
Koko Muroya	Kyoto University, Japan
Chandrakana Nandi	Certora Inc., USA
Amos Robinson	Australian National University, Australia
Tom Schrijvers	KU Leuven, Belgium
Vít Šefl	Charles University, Czech Republic

Peter Sestoft   ITU Copenhagen, Denmark
K. C. Sivaramakrishnan   IIT Madras, India and Tarides, India
Kristina Sojakova   Inria-Paris, France
Simon Thompson   University of Kent, UK and Eötvös Loránd
                             University, Hungary
Juliana Kaizer Vizzotto   Universidade Federal de Santa Maria, Brazil
Andy Wingo   Igalia, S.L., Spain
Brent Yorgey   Hendrix College, USA

Steering Committee

Peter Achten   Radboud University, Netherlands
Stephen Chang   University of Massachusetts Boston, USA
Jeremy Gibbons   University of Oxford, UK
Jurriann Hage   Utrecht University, Netherlands
Kevin Hammond   University of St Andrews, UK
Jason Hemann   Seton Hall University, USA
John Hughes   Chalmers University of Technology, Sweden
Pieter Koopman   Radboud University, Netherlands
Hans-Wolfgang Loidl   Heriot-Watt University, UK
Greg Michaelson   Heriot-Watt University, UK
Marco T. Morazán   Seton Hall University, USA
Wouter Swierstra   Utrecht University, Netherlands
Phil Trinder   University of Glasgow, UK
Nicolas Wu   Imperial College London, UK
Viktória Zsók   Eötvös Loránd University of Sciences, Hungary

Sponsored by Epic Games and Seton Hall University

Contents

Structural Refactorings for Exploring Dependently Typed Programming   1
   Adam D. Barwell, Christopher Brown, Mun See Chang, Constantine Theocharis, and Simon Thompson

Free Monads, Intrinsic Scoping, and Higher-Order Preunification   22
   Nikolai Kudasov

Towards a More Efficient Selection Monad   55
   Johannes Hartmann, Tom Schrijvers, and Jeremy Gibbons

Compositional Views in Compositional Images – Category: Research –   75
   Peter Achten and Pieter Koopman

Programming with Dependent Additive Pairs   92
   Vít Šefl

Context-Free Subphrase Grammars: A Grammar Formalism for Modular Syntax Definitions   112
   Björn Lötters

Polymorphism with Typed Holes   134
   Adam Chen, Thomas Porter, and Cyrus Omar

A Preliminary Type and Control-Flow Analysis for System F_ω   160
   Dongyu Wu and Matthew Fluet

Error Messages for Students Taught Using a Systematic Program Design Curriculum   195
   Shamil Dzhatdoyev, Josephine A. Des Rosiers, and Marco T. Morazán

Flattening Combinations of Arrays and Records   220
   Reg Huijben, Jordy Aaldering, Peter Achten, and Sven-Bodo Scholz

Author Index   241

Structural Refactorings for Exploring Dependently Typed Programming

Adam D. Barwell[1], Christopher Brown[1(✉)], Mun See Chang[1], Constantine Theocharis[1], and Simon Thompson[2,3]

[1] School of Computer Science, University of St Andrews, Scotland, UK
{adb23,cmb21,msc2,kt81}@st-andrews.ac.uk
[2] University of Kent, Canterbury, UK
[3] Eötvös Loránd University, Budapest, Hungary
S.J.Thompson@kent.ac.uk

Abstract. Dependent types provide users with the tools to embody specifications in types, with implementations carrying proofs that the specifications are met. One approach to developing programs in a dependently typed language develops such programs by enriching simply typed programs through a process of refactoring.

Keywords: Refactoring · Dependent Types Program Transformation

1 Introduction

Dependently typed programming languages represent a practical approach to verification in which both specifications and proofs of correctness are expressed directly in programs. These languages, including Idris [Bra21], Agda [Nor08], Coq [Coq] and Lean [dMKA+15], provide strong typing mechanisms that permit logical properties to be expressed as types, and well-typed programs will be proofs of those properties, meaning that correctness guarantees become an intrinsic part of an implementation, making programs that are correct by construction.

Despite this advantage, developing and maintaining dependently typed programs that leverage these features can represent a significant challenge. Alongside the existing tasks of designing, developing, and testing software, the programmer is now presented with the additional task of defining properties of the code as types (or predicates) and *enriching* a program to demonstrate conformance with these requirements. An exploratory approach naturally presents itself, in which the programmer first develops a simply typed prototype implementation (*i.e.* without dependent types), and then *enriches* that implementation with correctness guarantees. This enrichment is a *refactoring* [Opd92] process.

In order to meet institutional and research funder open access requirements, any accepted manuscript arising shall be open access under a Creative Commons Attribution (CC BY) reuse licence with zero embargo.

© The Author(s), under exclusive license to Springer Nature Switzerland AG 2025
J. Hemann and S. Chang (Eds.): TFP 2024, LNCS 14643, pp. 1–21, 2025.
https://doi.org/10.1007/978-3-031-74558-4_1

Refactoring techniques aim to improve the design and maintainability of software without changing its (external) functionality [Fow99]. Although much refactoring is done manually, there has been substantial interest in building tools that support the process. Refactoring tools that enable the *semi-automatic*, programmer-guided, application of refactorings have been developed for a range of functional languages [Bro08, Met, LT12] among others, and have been integrated into IDEs [Fou] and editors, initially in an *ad hoc* way and more recently by means of the Language Server Protocol [lan]. The principal advantages of refactoring tools are efficiency and the avoidance of error. Efficiency is achieved via the automatic effecting of transformations, potentially across multiple definitions and files for which it would be impractical to perform the refactoring by hand, and errors are avoided by the consistent and correct application of those transformations, which can themselves be demonstrated to be correct [ST08, TH23].

Since programs that fully leverage dependent types often exhibit tight coupling between types and values, refactoring such programs often necessitates changes that propagate across much of the codebase. Despite the obvious advantages of mechanising this process, there is currently limited refactoring tool support for dependently typed languages. Existing tool support focusses on proof-repair systems [Rin21, RYLG19, Wil20] that automatically migrate code to a new but structurally enriched type, such as the transition from lists to vectors, by means of *ornaments* [McB11]. Although these techniques represent a key component of type enrichment refactoring, they do not encompass its entirety.

In this paper, we introduce a complementary approach to refactoring dependently typed programs, building a set of refactorings that generalise the steps in an expression evaluator case study. The refactorings presented are designed to be used by the programmer in an exploratory way to transform their simply typed program into a dependently typed program in an iterative manner. In an example like this, where refactorings are applied one after another, it is often the case that a refactoring step will arise as the result of the application of another refactoring, and we will see examples of that here. In this paper, we make the following contributions:

1. We introduce a small dependently typed functional language, named Fluid, similar to a subset of Idris and based on a dependently typed lambda calculus with inductive types.
2. We introduce a number of refactorings over Fluid for dependently typed programming.
3. We implement these refactorings in a prototype refactoring tool.
4. We demonstrate these refactorings in a number of examples, and show improved safety properties over the original programs.

The implementation of Fluid and the prototype refactoring tool can be found at github.com/kontheocharis/fluid.

2 Fluid

Fluid is a small dependently typed programming language with inductive data types. The purpose of Fluid is to provide a test-bed for automatic transformations on dependently typed programs. Its syntax closely resembles that of Idris or Agda, but without elaborate features such as modules, mutually recursive definitions, or implicit parameters.

We give the syntax of Fluid in Fig. 1. A Fluid program is a sequence of declarations and type definitions. A declaration, D, is a value bound to a global name, v. Function declarations comprise a sequence of clauses that pattern match on the arguments of the function, from top to bottom. Clauses that match on a sequence of incompatible patterns can be marked as `impossible`.

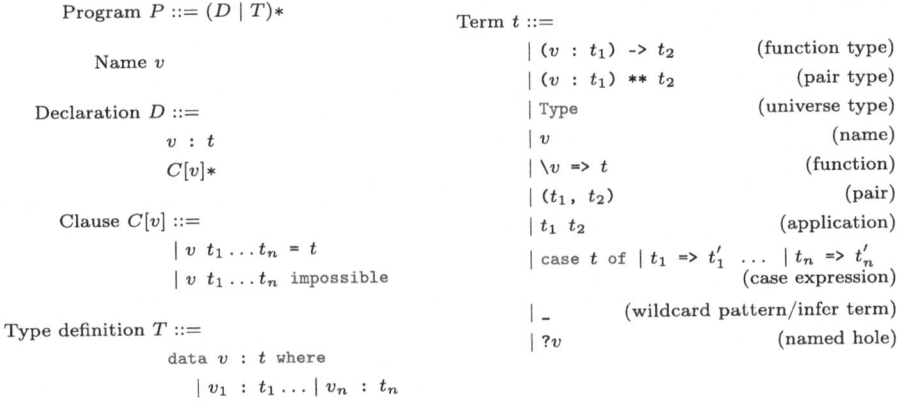

Fig. 1. The syntax of Fluid.

Type definitions in Fluid support inductive families [Dyb94], similar to those in Agda or Idris, but without implicit parameters. For clarity of presentation, Fluid does not support universe levels[1] or universe polymorphism, unlike systems such as the Calculus of Inductive Constructions (CIC) [PM15]. These features are orthogonal to the transformations we discuss in this paper.

Fluid supports named holes: in addition to being a useful tool when writing programs, holes are essential for some transformations that require additional information to be provided by the user. The symbols _::_ and [] are overloaded and used for both lists and vectors, disambiguated by context, where their type arguments are inferred from usage. For brevity, we omit the typing rules and semantics of Fluid; they closely mirror those of CIC, but with some

---

[1] A consequence of the lack of universe levels is that `Type : Type` is a valid typing judgement in Fluid. This is known to cause inconsistencies [Hur95] in the logical interpretation of the language, but that should not affect the approach that we present here.

small limitations, serving as a prototype language to demonstrate the principle of our refactoring approach. Fluid does not distinguish between Type and Prop; Fluid supports multiple declarations and arbitrary recursion, which CIC does not; and, finally, the implementation of Fluid does not force the exhaustiveness of patterns, but does ensure that `impossible` branches are correctly marked so.

3 Refactorings for Dependently Typed Programs

In this section, we describe a new catalogue of refactorings for dependently typed programs, which are motivated by the exploration of a case study in Sect. 4. This means that the refactorings have been designed to be exploratory in nature, allowing the programmer to refine their program and types by a series of steps. Each refactoring step can often arise as the result of earlier refactoring steps, and we envisage that the refactorings will typically be used as part of a sequence of transformation steps, rather than individually. The refactorings presented here do not constitute an exhaustive list, but rather a sample that is useful from a potentially wide and common class of transformations.

We illustrate each refactoring by giving examples representing code before and after their application, with high-level descriptions of the pre-conditions needed. In many cases the inverse transformations are possible with stronger pre-conditions, and are currently the target of future work. In the figures presented, we use yellow where a change has been made by the refactoring tool, red where code has been removed, green where code has been added, and blue where a hole has been introduced.

3.1 Adding an Index to a Data Type

Adding an Index to a Data Type adds an index to a specified data type. An index is a way of grouping the constructors of a data type into distinct sets – for example, grouping lists by their length yields the type of vectors, indexed by Nat. For a given data type `D : T1 -> ... -> Tn -> Type` and a requested index type I and position i, the refactoring refactors the definition of D to

`D : T1 -> ... -> Ti -> I -> ... -> Tn -> Type.`

Additional parameters of type I are added to each constructor of D and used for the indices of any inductive steps and the index of the constructor itself. All references to the type are updated for these newly added parameters.

Example. Figure 2 shows an example of an index being added to a data type, of type Nat. For each constructor, an index is added for each inductive step, as well as for the overall index of the constructor. For example, a new parameter, n2 of type Nat has been added to constructor With to capture the index in the type overall, while an additional parameter n1 of the same type has also been added to capture the index in the inductive parameter. All new parameters are fresh.

All other parts of the program that reference `Bits` must be updated to include the new index that was added. Figure 3 gives an example of such a function. Two new parameters are introduced to capture the index argument for the data type. All clauses are updated to match on the new parameters. Any references to the constructors of `Bits`, as well as recursive calls, are updated to pass in the new index parameters. Finally, all the call sites of `flip` are updated to provide proofs for the added parameters.

When there exists a unique solution for the required arguments that can be found through pattern unification, it is inserted automatically. When no such solution is found, holes are added and it is the user's responsibility to fill them. This refactoring can be viewed as producing the 'constant family' version of the original data type. As such, it is semantically equivalent to the original and the transformation process should not lead to any type errors or difference in program behaviour (modulo holes).

3.2 Specialising an Index of a Constructor

Specialising an Index of a Constructor sets the index of a specified constructor to a custom value. For a constructor `C` with return type `D t1 ... ti ... tn`, specialising the ith index to value `v` results in the return type of `C` being refactored to `D t1 ... v ... tn`. The type of `v` must match the type of `ti`. This refactoring does not update any usage sites, as this is currently intractable automatically: the user must ensure that the newly specialised index is compatible with the rest of the program.

Example. Figure 4 specialises two constructors by setting their indices to `Z` and `(S n2)` respectively. The parameter for the unused index is retained as there is a separate refactoring to remove it (Sect. 3.4).

3.3 Relating Constructor Parameters

Relating Constructor Parameters allows a new parameter to be inserted in a constructor `C` to relate some parameters via a dependent type. The input consists of the positions of the constructor parameters `t1 ... tn` to relate, and the predicate term `P` that should be used to relate them. The constructor definition

```
1  data Bits : Type where
2  | Empty : Bits
3  | With  : Bool
4           -> Bits
5           -> Bits
```

(a) Before

```
1  data Bits : Nat -> Type where
2  | Empty : (n : Nat) -> Bits n
3  | With  : Bool
4           -> (n1 : Nat) -> Bits n1
5           -> (n2 : Nat) -> Bits n2
```

(b) After

Fig. 2. Adding an index in a data type. An index of type `Nat` is added to the data type `Bits` at position 0.

```
1  flip : Bits                      1  flip : (n1 : Nat) -> Bits n1
2       -> Bits                     2       -> (n2 : Nat) -> Bits n2
3  flip Empty = Empty               3  flip _ ( Empty _) n2 = Empty n2
4  flip (With x xs) =               4  flip _ (With x n1' xs _) n2 =
5      With (not x)                 5      With (not x) ?n1
6          (flip xs)                6          (flip n1' xs ?n1) n2
```

(a) Before   (b) After

Fig. 3. Updating a usage site of the data type after adding an index.

```
1  data Bits : Nat -> Type where    1  data Bits : Nat -> Type where
2  | Empty : (n : Nat) -> Bits n    2  | Empty : (n : Nat) -> Bits Z
3  | With : Bool                    3  | With : Bool
4        -> (n1 : Nat) -> Bits n1   4        -> (n1 : Nat) -> Bits n1
5        -> (n2 : Nat) -> Bits n2   5        -> (n2 : Nat) -> Bits (S n2)
```

(a) Before   (b) After

Fig. 4. Specialising the constructors Empty and With to Z and (S n2).

is refactored to include an additional parameter P t1 ... tn, inserted in the final parameter position. Usage sites of C are updated with a hole at the position of the newly added parameter.

Example. In Fig. 5, introducing a relation between the two parameters of constructor Sat is done by inserting a new parameter of type LTE found searched. All pattern matches over the constructor Sat are modified to introduce a variable in the position of the added relation. Any applications of Sat are also transformed by introducing a hole at the relation position, allowing the programmer to complete it later.

```
1  data Solution : Type where       1  data Solution : Type where
2  | Sat : (searched : Nat)         2  | Sat : (searched : Nat)
3        -> (found : Nat)           3        -> (found : Nat)
4                                   4        -> LTE found searched
5        -> Solution                5        -> Solution
6  | Unsat : (searched : Nat) ->    6  | Unsat : (searched : Nat) ->
       Solution                              Solution
```

(a) Before   (b) After

Fig. 5. Relating the parameters searched and found in the Sat constructor of the Solution data type.

```
1  data Bits : Nat -> Type where       1  data Bits : Nat -> Type where
2  | Empty : (n : Nat) -> Bits Z       2  | Empty : Bits Z
3  | With : Bool                       3  | With : Bool
4     -> (n1 : Nat) -> Bits n1         4     -> (n1 : Nat) -> Bits n1
5     -> (n2 : Nat) -> Bits (S n2)     5     -> Bits (S n1)
```

(a) Before (b) After

Fig. 6. Collapsing the Nat indices of the data type Bits as defined previously.

3.4 Collapsing Constructor Parameters

Collapsing Constructor Parameters collapses one or more of the indices in a constructor. Alongside *Specialising an Index of a Constructor*, it can be used to refine the free indexing structure produced by *Adding an Index to a Data Type* and is a more general form of removing redundant parameters from constructors. The input is a target constructor C, a list of positions for a subset of its parameters t1 ... tn, and an optional distinguished parameter ti among those. The refactoring removes each parameter t1 ... tn from the constructor, other than ti. Occurrences of t1 ... tn in the rest of the constructor are replaced with ti. If no ti is provided, the parameters t1 ... tn are simply removed, in which case they must not be referenced elsewhere in the constructor. All usages of C are updated to remove the appropriate parameters, and all usages of the removed parameters are replaced with the retained parameter (if present). If the correct argument to the retained parameter cannot be solved through pattern unification, it is filled with a hole.

Example. Figure 6 demonstrates an example of collapsing constructor parameters in a data type. In the case of Empty, there is no target index, so the index n is removed. In the case of With, the indices n1 and n2 are collapsed to n1, with (S n2) being replaced with (S n1). In Fig. 7, a usage site of Bits is updated to remove the collapsed parameters. In the With application, the argument n1 in the output is retained only because pattern unification dictates so; in general it would be replaced with a fresh hole to ensure that the program still typechecks.

```
1  flip : (n : Nat) -> Bits n            1  flip : (n : Nat) -> Bits n
2     -> Bits n                          2     -> Bits n
3  flip Z ( Empty n) = Empty n           3  flip Z Empty = Empty
4  flip (S n) (With x n1 xs n2 ) =       4  flip (S n) (With x n1 xs) =
5     With (not x) n1                    5     With (not x) n1
6        (flip n1 xs) n2                 6        (flip n1 xs)
```

(a) Before (b) After

Fig. 7. Updating a usage site of Bits after collapsing parameters. It is assumed that some further refactoring has occurred since Fig. 3.

```
1  idx : (x : Nat)                    1  idx : (x : Nat)
2      -> (ys : List Nat)             2      -> (ys : List Nat)
3                                     3      -> Elem x ys
4      -> Maybe Nat                   4      -> Maybe Nat
5  idx x [] = Nothing                 5  idx x [] p = Nothing
6  idx x (y::ys) =                    6  idx x (y::ys) p =
7      case y == x of                 7      case y == x of
8      | True => Just x               8      | True => Just x
9      | False => idx x ys            9      | False => idx x ys ?p
```

              (a) Before   (b) After

Fig. 8. Relating the parameters x and ys of the indexing function idx with Elem.

3.5 Relating Function Parameters

Similarly to *Relating Constructor Parameters*, *Relating Function Parameters* inserts a dependent type as a new parameter to a function f to relate a number of the other function parameters. The aim of this refactoring is to constrain the valid set of input values to those that satisfy the added relation. The function f is updated to introduce pattern matching variables for the new parameters. Usage sites of f, including recursive calls, are augmented with holes for the new parameters (which is often solved by pattern unification).

Example. In Fig. 8, we introduce a new parameter of type Elem x ys to the function idx. All equations over f are updated to include a pattern variable representing the inserted parameter. The recursive call to idx in the second clause is augmented with a fresh hole that must be provided by the user.

3.6 Expanding a Pattern Variable

Expanding a Pattern Variable replaces equations containing a specified pattern variable in a function with new equations that enumerate the possible patterns for that variable, to one level of depth. This refactoring follows similar, existing, approaches, such as the Interactive Editing mode for Idris (https://idris2.readthedocs.io/en/latest/tutorial/interactive.html). The expanded equations that become *impossible* as a result of the refactoring are removed. The

```
1  count : (x : Nat)                  1  count : (x : Nat)
2      -> (ys : List Nat)             2      -> (ys : List Nat)
3      -> Elem x ys -> Nat            3      -> Elem x ys -> Nat
4                                     4  count x ys Here = ?result
5  count x ys p = ?result             5  count x ys (There p) = ?result
```

              (a) Before   (b) After

Fig. 9. Expanding pattern matching for an outer variable.

```
1  count : (x : Nat)                 1  count : (x : Nat)
2      -> (ys : List Nat)            2      -> (ys : List Nat)
3      -> Elem x ys -> Nat           3      -> Elem x ys -> Nat
4  count x ys Here = ?result         4  count x (y::ys') Here = ?result
5  count x ys (There p) = ?result    5  count x ys (There p) = ?result
```

(a) Before   (b) After

Fig. 10. Expanding pattern matching for a variable over a single equation.

```
1  count : (x : Nat)                 1  count : (x : Nat)
2      -> (ys : List Nat)            2      -> (ys : List Nat)
3      -> Elem x ys -> Nat           3      -> Elem x ys -> Nat
4  count x ys Here = ?result         4  count x (y::ys') Here = ?result
5  count x ys (There p) =            5  count x (y::ys') (There p) =
6      ?result                       6      ?result
```

(a) Before   (b) After

Fig. 11. Expanding pattern matching for a variable over all equations.

refactoring has two variants: *i)* expand patterns for a single equation; and, *ii)* expand patterns for all equations.

Example. Figure 9 expands the parameter argument p to pattern match over constructors of the Elem type. This results in two equations for both the Here and There case. A further application of this refactoring on the same function is illustrated in Fig. 10 where the parameter ys is then expanded for the equation on Line 3. All cases matching [] are impossible due to Elem relating both ys and x, and are removed by the expansion process. Finally, Fig. 11 demonstrates the second variant of the refactoring which expands *all* equations for the pattern variable selected. This results in ys being expanded to (y::ys') in the equation on Line 4. The impossible case matching [] is removed in the figure for brevity.

3.7 Eliminating Tautologous Cases

Expanding pattern variables can result in redundant case expressions, which can be eliminated. Potentially arising from the unification of pattern variables, a case expression that can match only a single clause can be safely replaced with the RHS of that clause.

A common example can be found in case expressions equivalent to if statements (Fig. 12), where arguments passed to an equality test are the same. In such cases, since the matching pattern True declares no arguments, the corresponding RHS can replace the case expression verbatim.

The *Eliminating Tautologous Cases* refactoring takes a location within a program and the name of a binary operator, say (==), representing an equality test. The location must be contained within a case expression such that its

```
1   idx : (x : Nat)                      1   idx : (x : Nat)
2       -> (xs : List Nat)               2       -> (xs : List Nat)
3       -> Elem x xs -> Maybe Nat        3       -> Elem x xs -> Maybe Nat
4   idx x (x :: ys) Here =               4   idx x (x :: ys) Here =
5       case x == x of                   5       Just x
6       | True  =>  Just x               6
7       | False => idx x ys ?h1          7
8   idx x (y :: ys) (There p) =          8   idx x (y :: ys) (There p) =
9       case y == x of                   9       case y == x of
10      | True  => Just x                10      | True  => Just x
11      | False => idx x ys ?h2          11      | False => idx x ys ?h2
```

(a) Before   (b) After

Fig. 12. Eliminating the tautology x == x in a `case` expression.

subject is of the form $x == x$, where x is a variable. The `case` expression must have at least one clause, with pattern `True`. The result, illustrated in Fig. 12, is the replacement of the `case` expression with the RHS of the `True` clause.

In principle, *Eliminating Tautologous Cases* can be generalised beyond this specific form of `case` expression. In particular, where prior refactoring stages produce a subject of the form `C e1 ... en`, where `C` is a constructor. Here, the RHS of the matching clause replaces the `case` expression, substituting the pattern variables for `e1 ... en`. Further generalisation, *e.g.* where the subject is a function call that returns a given constructor for all inputs, would require additional inspection of the called function or use of *Unfolding* [BD77]. Examples may arise as a precursor to *Eliminating* `Maybe` (Sect. 3.8).

3.8 Eliminating `Maybe`

Eliminating `Maybe` in the return type of a function `f` is a refactoring which can be applied if `f` never returns `Nothing`. Eliminating the `Nothing` cases is possible by first transforming these cases in a way that makes them `impossible` (for example through *Expanding a Pattern Variable*). The `Maybe` can then be eliminated by removing the `Just` constructs from each clause. If a clause is of the form `Just x`, it is transformed to `x`. If it is of the form `f x1 ... xn`, it is already valid since it is a recursive call. If a recursive call is being matched with a `case` expression, only the `Just` branch is retained and the `Nothing` branch is removed. In all other cases, `Maybe` cannot be eliminated. In terms of usage sites, all (non-recursive) occurrences of `f x1 ... xn` are replaced with `Just (f x1 ... xn)` since the usage sites still expect `f` to produce a `Maybe`.

Example. In Fig. 13, the return type of the function (originally `Maybe Nat`) is transformed into `Nat`. The clauses which return `Just x` are transformed into `x`. The recursive call `idx x ys p` is left untouched since it also returns `Nat` by virtue of the refactoring.

```
1  idx : (x : Nat)                  1  idx : (x : Nat)
2      -> (xs : List Nat)           2      -> (xs : List Nat)
3      -> Elem x xs                 3      -> Elem x xs
4      -> Maybe Nat                 4      -> Nat
5  idx x (x :: ys) Here = Just x    5  idx x (x :: ys) Here = x
6  idx x (y :: ys) (There p) =      6  idx x (y :: ys) (There p) =
7      case y == x of                7      case y == x of
8      | True => Just x              8      | True => x
9      | False => idx x ys p         9      | False => idx x ys p
```

           (a) Before   (b) After

Fig. 13. Eliminating the `Maybe` return type from the function `idx`.

4 A Language Evaluator

In this section, we demonstrate the refactorings in Sect. 3 on the evaluator for a small expression language in Fig. 14a. The evaluator operates in a standard way: natural numbers are treated as literals; variables are substituted for literals stored in an environment; and addition expressions are evaluated by adding the evaluated operands. The section proceeds as a series of steps that may be typically taken by a programmer to explore and enrich a program with dependent types. The goal is to use dependent types to produce a stronger version of `eval`. Presently, `eval` returns `Nothing` if a variable is not found in the environment, and will not produce a positive result for an environment that is not *covering*, *i.e.* containing all variables in a given expression. A stronger version of `eval` would remove the `Maybe` in its return type, guaranteeing a positive result for every expression and corresponding covering environment. We therefore illustrate use of the refactorings defined in Sect. 3 via the elimination of this `Maybe`.

Step 1: Introducing an Index to `Expr`. We begin by refining `Expr` so that it is indexed over a list, representing variables that are defined (or are in scope). This is achieved by applying *Adding an Index to a Data Type* (Sect. 3.1), providing the name of the type to be refactored, *i.e.* `Elem`, and both the type and name of the index, *i.e.* `List V` and `vars`, respectively. The refactored code is given in Fig. 14b. All three constructors now take an additional parameter, serving as the index `vars`. Usage sites within the type declaration, seen here in parameters to `Add`, are refactored to take an index, for which fresh parameters are introduced. Since the type signature of `eval` also represents a usage site, it now takes an additional argument. Constructor patterns are updated to include the new parameters. In the recursive calls, holes have been introduced and automatically resolved to `vars`, forced by the types of `e1` and `e2`.

Step 2: Collapse Index Variables in `Expr`. We refine the introduced index to `Expr`, enforcing the assumption that a given expression, *e*, is indexed by `vars` containing all variables occurring in *e*. This is achieved in two phases. Firstly, by ensuring that expressions of the form `Add v v1 e1 v2 e2` share their index,

```
data Expr : Type where
    | Num : (n : Nat) -> Expr
    | Var : (x : V) -> Expr
    | Add : Expr -> Expr -> Expr

lookupVar : (x : V) -> (env : List (V ** Nat)) -> Maybe Nat
lookupVar x [] = Nothing
lookupVar (MkV x) ((MkV y, val)::ys) = case isEqual x y of
    | True => Just val
    | False => lookupVar (MkV x) ys

eval : (env : List (V ** Nat)) -> Expr -> Maybe Nat
eval env (Num n) = Just n
eval env (Var x) = lookupVar x env
eval env (Add e1 e2) = case eval env e1 of
    | Nothing => Nothing
    | (Just e1') => case eval env e2 of
        | (Just e2') => Just (plus e1' e2')
        | Nothing => Nothing
```

(a) The basic language and evaluator.

```
data Expr : (vars : List V) -> Type where
    | Num : (n : Nat) -> (vars : List V) -> Expr vars
    | Var : (x : V) -> (vars : List V) -> Expr vars
    | Add : (vars1 : List V) -> Expr vars1
         -> (vars2 : List V) -> Expr vars2
         -> (vars : List V) -> Expr vars
    ...
eval : (env : List (V ** Nat)) -> (vars : List V) -> Expr vars
    -> Maybe Nat
eval env vars (Num n vars) = Just n
eval env vars (Var x vars) = lookupVar x env
eval env vars (Add vars v1 e1 v2 e2) = case eval env v1 e1 of
    | Nothing => Nothing
    | Just e1' => case eval env v2 e2 of
        | Just e2' => Just (plus e1' e2')
        | Nothing => Nothing
```

(b) Step 1: Introduce a `List Nat` index to `Expr`.

Fig. 14. The basic expression language, evaluator, and the first refactoring step.

v, with their immediate subexpressions, e1 and e2. Secondly, by relating the variable x and the index v in expressions of the form `Var x v`. In the first phase, we apply *Collapsing Constructor Parameters* (Sect. 3.4), passing as arguments: the name of the type, `Expr`; the name of the constructor, `Add`; and the indices to collapse, `vars`, `vars1`, and `vars2`. In the second phase, we apply *Relating Constructor Parameters* (Sect. 3.3), passing as arguments: the name of the type and constructor, `Expr` and `Var`; the parameters being related, `x` and `vars`; and the name of the type relating them, `Elem`. The result is given in Fig. 15a. The second and third equations of `eval` change as a consequence of both phases: in the second equation, `Var` has an additional parameter, `p`; and `Add` in the third equation has fewer parameters, reflecting the collapsing of its indices.

Step 3: Relate the Parameters of `lookupVar`. In order to successfully strengthen `eval`, we must similarly apply *Eliminating* `Maybe` (Sect. 3.8) to its helper function, `lookupVar`. To this end, we first introduce two parameters and pattern match on both in each equation. This is achieved in three phases: *i)* introducing `vars`; *ii)* introducing `p`, a membership relation; and *iii)* expanding `vars` and `p`. In the first phase, we call a standard refactoring *Introduce Function Parameter* [Li06] with arguments: function name, `lookupVar`; position where it should be added, `0`; and both the name, `vars`, and type, `List V`, of the parameter. The second phase follows similarly, introducing (`p : Elem x vars`) as the third parameter, where `x` is the variable to be found in `env`. The third phase comprises a call to *Expanding a Pattern Variable* (Sect. 3.6), specifying the name of the function and both `env` and `p` as arguments. As a consequence of the first two stages, the call sites in both `lookupVar` and `eval` are updated, introducing holes for the new arguments. We give the result of all three phases in Fig. 15b. Henceforth, we elide impossible equations for clarity. The holes `?h1`, `?h3`, and `?h4` in `lookupVar` can be filled manually by the programmer with `ys`, `ys`, and `p`, respectively. Although `?h2` is currently unsatisfied, future steps may alter this.

Step 4: Relate Environment and `Expr` index. We next relate `vars` with the given environment, `env`, in both `env` and `lookupVar`. This step comprises three phases: *i)* adding a new list parameter, `vals`; *ii)* relating `vars`, `vals`, and `env` by `p`; and *iii)* expanding the new relation, `p`. For this step, we assume the type declaration `Unzip` in Fig. 16, relating `vars` and `env`. In the first phase, we apply *Introduce Function Parameter* to introduce (`vars : List Nat`), representing the list of values in `env`. In the second phase, we apply *Relating Function Parameters* (Sect. 3.5) to introduce (`p : Unzip env vars vals`) as a function parameter. Finally, we apply *Expanding a Pattern Variable* (Sect. 3.6) on `p`, which precipitates applications on `vals`, `env`, and `vars`. Note that this step may remove equations that were previously possible, *e.g.* two equations from `lookupVar`. As in Step 4, we manually fill in the holes. The resulting code is given in Fig. 16.

Step 5: Remove `case` Expressions in `lookupVar`. We next remove the remaining hole in Fig. 16, via the removal of the tautologous `case` expression that contains it. This is achieved by applying *Eliminating Tautologous Cases* (Sect. 3.7) to the first equation of `lookupVar`. Concurrently, we may manually remove the `case` expression in the second equation since its subject will only evaluate to `False`. The resulting definition of `lookupVar` can be found in Fig. 17.

```
1  data Expr : (vars : List V) -> Type where
2      | Num : Nat -> (vars : List V) -> Expr vars
3      | Var : (x : V) -> (vars : List V) -> (p : Elem x vars)
4              -> Expr vars
5      | Add : (vars : List V) -> Expr vars -> Expr vars
6              -> Expr vars
7  ...
8  eval : (env : List (V ** Nat)) -> (vars : List V) -> Expr vars
9      -> Maybe Nat
10 eval env vars (Num n vars) = Just n
11 eval env vars (Var x vars p) = lookupVar x env
12 eval env vars (Add vars e1 e2) = case eval env vars e1 of
13     | Nothing => Nothing
14     | Just e1' => case eval env vars e2 of
15         | Just e2' => Just (plus e1' e2')
16         | Nothing  => Nothing
```

(a) Step 2: Specialise `Var` and unify index variables in `Add`.

```
1  lookupVar : (vars : List V) -> (x : V) -> (p : Elem x vars)
2              -> (env : List (V ** Nat)) -> Maybe Nat
3  lookupVar (y::ys) x (Here y ys) [] = Nothing
4  lookupVar (y::ys) x (There x ys p y) [] = Nothing
5  lookupVar (y::ys) (MkV x) (Here y ys) ((MkV z, val)::zs) =
6      case isEqual x z of
7          | True => Just val
8          | False => lookupVar ?h1 (MkV x) ?h2 zs
9  lookupVar (y::ys) (MkV x) (There x ys p y) ((MkV z, val)::zs) =
10     case isEqual x z of
11         | True => Just val
12         | False => lookupVar ?h3 (MkV x) ?h4 zs
```

(b) Step 3: Introduce parameter (`vars : List V`); relate parameters using (`Elem x vars`) in `lookupVar`; expand (`Elem x vars`) pattern variables.

Fig. 15. Refactoring Steps 2 and 3.

Step 6: Eliminate `Maybe` from `eval`. Given that `lookupVar` is incapable of returning `Nothing`, we are able to apply *Eliminating* `Maybe` (Sect. 3.8). As a result, this removes the remaining sources of `Nothing` from the base cases of `eval`. Accordingly, we are able to apply *Eliminating* `Maybe` to `eval`. The resulting definition, and final result, of `eval` is shown in Fig. 18

```
1   lookupVar : (vals : List Nat) -> (vars : List V) -> (x : V)
2            -> (q : Elem x vars) -> (env : List (V ** Nat))
3            -> (p : Unzip env vars vals) -> Maybe Nat
4   lookupVar (v::vs) (x::ys) (MkV x) (Here x ys) ((MkV x, v)::zs)
5       (ConsUZ x v zs ys vs p) = case isEqual x x of
6         | True => Just val
7         | False => lookupVar vs ys (MkV x) ?h0 zs
8   lookupVar (v::vs) (y::ys) (MkV x) (There x ys q y) ((MkV y, v)::zs)
9       (ConsUZ y v zs ys vs p) =
10          lookupVar vs ys (MkV x) q zs p
11
12  eval : (vals : List Nat)
13       -> (env : List (V ** Nat))
14       -> (vars : List V)
15       -> (p : Unzip env vars vals)
16       -> Expr vars
17       -> Maybe Nat
18  eval [] [] [] NilUZ (Num n []) = Just n
19  eval (v::vs) ((x, v)::env) (y::ys)
20      (ConsUZ x v env ys vs p) (Var x (x::ys) (Here x ys)) =
21          lookupVar (x::ys) x (Here x ys) ((k, n)::env)
22  eval (v::vs) ((y, v)::env) (y::ys) (ConsUZ y v env ys vs p)
23      (Var x (y::ys) (There x ys q y)) =
24          lookupVar (y::ys) x (There x ys q y) ((y, v)::env)
25  eval [] [] [] NilUZ (Var x [] q) =
26      lookupVar [] x q []
27  eval (v::vs) ((y,v)::env) (y::ys)
28      (ConsUZ y v env ys vs p) (Add (y::ys) e1 e2) =
29          case eval (v::vs) (e::env) (y::ys)
30              (ConsUZ y v env ys vs p) e1 of
31            | Nothing => Nothing
32            | (Just e1') =>
33                case eval (v::vs) (e::env) (y::ys)
34                    (ConsUZ y v env ys vs p) e2 of
35                  | Nothing => Nothing
36                  | (Just e2') => Just (plus e1' e2')
37  eval [] [] [] NilUZ (Add [] e1 e2) =
38      case eval [] [] [] NilUZ e1 of
39        | Nothing => Nothing
40        | (Just e1') => case eval [] [] [] NilUZ e2 of
41            | (Just e2') => Just (plus e1' e2')
42            | Nothing => Nothing
```

Fig. 16. Step 4: Introduce predicate Unzip env vars ws; expand pattern variables; manually fill remaining holes.

```
1  lookupVar : (vals : List Nat) -> (vars : List V) -> (x : V)
2          -> (q : Elem x vars) -> (env : List (V ** Nat))
3          -> (p : Unzip env vars vals) -> Maybe Nat
4  lookupVar (v::vs) (x::ys) (MkV x) (Here x ys) ((MkV x, v)::zs)
5      (ConsUZ x v zs ys vs p) = Just val
6  lookupVar (v::vs) (y::ys) (MkV x) (There x ys q y) ((MkV y, v)::zs)
7      (ConsUZ y v zs ys vs p) = lookupVar vs ps (MkV x) q ys p
```

Fig. 17. Step 5: Remove tautologous cases.

```
1  eval : (vals : List Nat) -> (env : List (V ** Nat))
2       -> (vars : List V) -> (p : Unzip env vars vals)
3       -> (Expr vars) -> Nat
4  eval [] [] [] NilUZ (Num n []) = n
5  eval (v::vs) ((x, v)::zs) (x::ys) (ConsUZ x v zs ys vs p)
6      (Var x (x::ys) (Here x ys)) = lookupVar (v::vs) (x::ys) x
7          (Here x ys) ((x, v)::zs) (ConsUZ x v zs ys vs p)
8  eval (v::vs) ((y, v)::zs) (y::ys) (ConsUZ y v zs ys vs p)
9      (Var x (y::ys) (There x xs q y)) = lookupVar (v::vs) (y::ys) x
10         (There x xs q y) ((y, v)::zs) (ConsUZ y v zs ys vs p)
11 eval (v::vs) ((y,v)::zs) (y::ys) (ConsUZ y v zs ys vs p)
12     (Add (y::ys) e1 e2) = case eval (v::vs) ((y,v)::zs) (y::ys)
13         (ConsUZ y v zs ys vs p) e1 of
14         | e1' => case eval (v::vs) ((y,v)::zs) (y::ys)
15             (ConsUZ y v zs ys vs p) e2 of
16             | e2' => plus e1' e2'
17 eval [] [] [] NilUZ (Add [] e1 e2) = case eval [] [] [] NilUZ e1 of
18     | e1' => case eval [] [] [] NilUZ e2 of
19         | e2' => plus e1' e2'
```

Fig. 18. Step 6: Eliminate Maybe.

5 Related Work

The Haskell Refactorer, HaRe [Li06,Bro08,LTR05,BLT10], is a refactoring tool for Haskell 98. The tool supports a wide number of refactorings, including *renaming, generalisation, lifting, folding,* and *clone detection* [BT10]. The refactorings are described in terms of pre-conditions, with a set of unit tests given as part of the implementation. More recently, Williams [Wil20] presents a refactoring for ML based on ornaments [McB11] that transforms functions between similar simply typed structures. Wibergh presents a preliminary catalogue of refactorings for Agda in their MSc thesis [Wib19], but to the best of our knowledge, lacks an implementation. Although the catalogue mostly comprises standard structural refactorings applied to Agda, it includes two that are closely related to our *Adding an Index to a Data Type* refactoring in Sect. 3.1. Presently, the principal difference between Wibergh's and our work lies in their respective target languages. Refactoring has also been explored in the context of security, using dependent types as a mechanism to drive the rewriting system [BBM+22].

There is a large body of work on proof-repair systems. This work typically focuses on the transformation of proofs across types, and can be used for both theorem proving and aiding developers in writing dependently typed programs [Ada15, Whi13]. For example, Ringer et al. [RYLG19] propose a refactoring plugin for Coq, allowing the automatic identification of, and transformations across, ornaments. Our work complements this technique by taking an *exploratory* approach to program enrichment, *e.g.* by facilitating development of the types and operations that are used for proof-repair. Moreover, our approach increases flexibility by enabling introduction of predicate terms (Sect. 3.5), decoupled from types, and via broadening applicability of refactorings narrowing (or widening) function scopes (Sect. 3.8). There is much work on transformations across equivalent or isomorphic data types [BP01, RPY+21, ZH15], and across different representations of the same abstract data type [CDM13, DMS12, Lam13]. Ornaments [McB11] relate data types that are structurally similar but not necessarily equivalent. Notably, ornaments have been used in transforming theorems by both Ringer et al. [RYLG19] and Williams et al. [WDR14], as discussed above. Our work goes beyond this use of ornaments, such that our approach enables the introduction and manipulation of arbitrary proof terms to functions and data types independently. Work on propagating changes precipitated by transformations to data types is studied by Robert [Rob18], where the repair functions are derived from the computed differences using elimination motives [McB00]. As before, our approach is complementary: we aim to *guide* the programmer in effecting the transformations for which Robert derives subsequent repairs. Meanwhile, Boite focuses on the specific case of propagating changes after adding constructors to data types [Boi04]. Johnsen and Lüth accommodates proof reuse by generalising theorems by abstracting their proofs [JL04].

There has been substantial work on *structural editing*, a related topic to refactoring. However, structural editing focuses on helping developers write new code, as opposite to structurally modifying existing, legacy code bases. A common problem in structural editing is the relation between linear editing and structural hierarchical representations of the program source-code. This does not apply to refactoring tooling, which must work over an abstract syntax representation of the program source. Recent work includes Hüttel et al. [HELNGS+23] who describe a new technique for structural editing, allowing type-safe copy and paste functionality. Moon et al. [MBO22] introduce `tylr` for tile-based structural editing, with the idea to eliminate the need for linear editing and instead use a tile-based representation approach, and Gopinathan [Gop22] introduces a structural editing plugin for OCaml. A recent development is to provide users with a *semantic difference* between code versions. The https://semanticdiff.com system gives one implementation of this approach, which, in particular, is able to recognise when some refactorings have taken place.

6 Conclusions and Future Work

In this paper, we introduced new refactorings for dependently typed programs, defined for the *Fluid* programming language. We presented our refactorings in the form of a small catalogue of transformations, with examples and descriptions of their general conditions. We also demonstrated our refactorings on a use case comprising a small expression language, where, through applying a series of our refactoring steps, we enriched the program to make use of dependent types via the introduction of predicates and proof terms. Using our refactorings, we were able to transform an evaluator that returned a `Maybe Nat` type to one that simply returned a `Nat`, thereby demonstrating transformations facilitating conversion of a partial function (*i.e.*that can return `Nothing`) into a total equivalent that always produces a literal. This example demonstrated that, using our refactoring approach, developers can explore the use of dependent types to develop stronger and safer programs.

Although proving correctness of the presented refactorings is outwith the scope of this paper, the question of correctness represents an interesting avenue of future work. Refactorings for dependently typed programs, as explored in this paper, suggest a greater focus on the narrowing or widening of a function's scope. Consequently, some refactorings, such as eliminating a `Maybe` type (Sect. 3.8), represent a departure from the standard refactoring correctness property of the original and refactored programs reducing to the same normal form, or set thereof. This suggests that any correctness property must account for *acceptable changes* to functionality, *e.g.*subsets of behaviours possibly identified by a simulation relation [San09]. Other future directions include exploring the use of ornaments for refactoring and the use of generic traversal libraries to aid implementation and formalisation [AAC+21].

Acknowledgements. This work was supported by UK EPSRC, EP/V006290/.

References

[AAC+21] Allais, G., Atkey, R., Chapman, J., McBride, C., McKinna, J.: A type- and scope-safe universe of syntaxes with binding: their semantics and proofs. J. Funct. Program. **31**, e22 (2021)

[Ada15] Adams, M.: Refactoring proofs with tactician. In: Bianculli, D., Calinescu, R., Rumpe, B. (eds.) SEFM 2015. LNCS, vol. 9509, pp. 53–67. Springer, Heidelberg (2015). https://doi.org/10.1007/978-3-662-49224-6_6

[BBM+22] Brown, C., Barwell, A.D., Marquer, Y., Zendra, O., Richmond, T., Gu, C.: Semi-automatic ladderisation: improving code security through rewriting and dependent types. In: PEPM, pp. 14–27. ACM (2022)

[BD77] Burstall, R.M., Darlington, J.: A transformation system for developing recursive programs. J. ACM **24**(1), 44–67 (1977)

[BLT10] Brown, C., Li, H., Thompson, S.: An expression processor: a case study in refactoring haskell programs. In: Page, R., Horváth, Z., Zsók, V. (eds.) TFP 2010. LNCS, vol. 6546, pp. 31–49. Springer, Heidelberg (2011). https://doi.org/10.1007/978-3-642-22941-1_3

[Boi04]   Boite, O.: Proof reuse with extended inductive types. In: Slind, K., Bunker, A., Gopalakrishnan, G. (eds.) TPHOLs 2004. LNCS, vol. 3223, pp. 50–65. Springer, Heidelberg (2004). https://doi.org/10.1007/978-3-540-30142-4_4

[BP01]   Barthe, G., Pons, O.: Type isomorphisms and proof reuse in dependent type theory. In: Honsell, F., Miculan, M. (eds.) FoSSaCS 2001. LNCS, vol. 2030, pp. 57–71. Springer, Heidelberg (2001). https://doi.org/10.1007/3-540-45315-6_4

[Bra21]   Brady, E.C.: Idris 2: quantitative type theory in practice. In: ECOOP. LIPIcs, vol. 194, pp. 9:1–9:26. Schloss Dagstuhl - Leibniz-Zentrum für Informatik (2021)

[Bro08]   Brown, C.M.: Tool support for refactoring haskell programs. Ph.D. thesis, University of Kent, UK (2008)

[BT10]   Brown, C., Thompson, S.J.: Clone detection and elimination for haskell. In: PEPM, pp. 111–120. ACM (2010)

[CDM13]   Cohen, C., Dénès, M., Mörtberg, A.: Refinements for free! In: Gonthier, G., Norrish, M. (eds.) CPP 2013. LNCS, vol. 8307, pp. 147–162. Springer, Cham (2013). https://doi.org/10.1007/978-3-319-03545-1_10

[dMKA+15]   de Moura, L., Kong, S., Avigad, J., van Doorn, F., von Raumer, J.: The lean theorem prover (system description). In: Felty, A.P., Middeldorp, A. (eds.) CADE 2015. LNCS (LNAI), vol. 9195, pp. 378–388. Springer, Cham (2015). https://doi.org/10.1007/978-3-319-21401-6_26

[DMS12]   Dénès, M., Mörtberg, A., Siles, V.: A refinement-based approach to computational algebra in Coq. In: Beringer, L., Felty, A. (eds.) ITP 2012. LNCS, vol. 7406, pp. 83–98. Springer, Heidelberg (2012). https://doi.org/10.1007/978-3-642-32347-8_7

[Dyb94]   Dybjer, P.: Inductive Families. For. Asp. Comp. 6(4), 440–465 (1994)

[Fou]   Eclipse Foundation. Eclipse (2023). http://www.eclipse.org/

[Fow99]   Fowler, M.: Refactoring - Improving the Design of Existing Code. Addison Wesley Object Technology Series. Addison-Wesley (1999)

[Gop22]   Kiran Gopinathan. GopCaml: A Structural Editor for OCaml (2022). https://arxiv.org/abs/2207.07423

[HELNGS+23]   Hüttel, H., Elisasen Lumholtz Nielsen, A., Gjerulf Sandberg, N., Lind Andersen, C., Mikkelsen, P.: A structure editor with type-safe copy/paste. In: IFL. ACM (2023)

[Hur95]   Hurkens, A.J.C.: A simplification of Girard's paradox. In: Dezani-Ciancaglini, M., Plotkin, G. (eds.) TLCA 1995. LNCS, vol. 902, pp. 266–278. Springer, Heidelberg (1995). https://doi.org/10.1007/BFb0014058

[JL04]   Johnsen, E.B., Lüth, C.: Theorem reuse by proof term transformation. In: Slind, K., Bunker, A., Gopalakrishnan, G. (eds.) TPHOLs 2004. LNCS, vol. 3223, pp. 152–167. Springer, Heidelberg (2004). https://doi.org/10.1007/978-3-540-30142-4_12

[Lam13]   Lammich, P.: Automatic data refinement. In: Blazy, S., Paulin-Mohring, C., Pichardie, D. (eds.) ITP 2013. LNCS, vol. 7998, pp. 84–99. Springer, Heidelberg (2013). https://doi.org/10.1007/978-3-642-39634-2_9

[lan]   Official Page for Language Server Protocol. https://microsoft.github.io/language-server-protocol/. Accessed 6 Dec 2023

[Li06]   Li, H.: Refactoring Haskell programs. Ph.D. thesis, University of Kent, UK (2006)

[LT12]   Li, H., Thompson, S.: A domain-specific language for scripting refactorings in erlang. In: de Lara, J., Zisman, A. (eds.) FASE 2012. LNCS, vol. 7212, pp. 501–515. Springer, Heidelberg (2012). https://doi.org/10.1007/978-3-642-28872-2_34

[LTR05]   Li, H., Thompson, S.J., Reinke, C.: The Haskell refactorer, HaRe, and its API. In: LDTA. ENTCS, vol. 141, pp. 29–34. Elsevier (2005)

[MBO22]   Moon, D., Blinn, A., Omar, C.: Tylr: a tiny tile-based structure editor. In: TyDe, pp. 28–37. ACM (2022)

[McB00]   McBride, C.: Elimination with a motive. In: Callaghan, P., Luo, Z., McKinna, J., Pollack, R., Pollack, R. (eds.) TYPES 2000. LNCS, vol. 2277, pp. 197–216. Springer, Heidelberg (2002). https://doi.org/10.1007/3-540-45842-5_13

[McB11]   Conor McBride. Ornamental Algebras, Algebraic Ornaments (2011). https://tinyurl.com/yc7wmb2s

[Met]   Meta. Retrie: Haskell Refactoring Made Easy. https://engineering.fb.com/2020/07/06/open-source/retrie/. Accessed 7 Dec 2023

[Nor08]   Norell, U.: Dependently typed programming in agda. In: Koopman, P., Plasmeijer, R., Swierstra, D. (eds.) AFP 2008. LNCS, vol. 5832, pp. 230–266. Springer, Heidelberg (2009). https://doi.org/10.1007/978-3-642-04652-0_5

[Opd92]   Opdyke, W.F.: Refactoring object-oriented frameworks. Ph.D. thesis, University of Illinois Urbana-Champaign, USA (1992)

[PM15]   Paulin-Mohring, C.: Introduction to the calculus of inductive constructions. In: All about Proofs, Proofs for All, vol. 55 (2015)

[Rin21]   Ringer, T.: Proof repair. Ph.D. thesis, University of Washington (2021)

[Rob18]   Robert, V.: Front-end tooling for building and maintaining dependently-typed functional programs. Ph.D. thesis, University of California, San Diego (2018)

[RPY+21] Ringer, T., Porter, R.D., Yazdani, N., Leo, J., Grossman, D.: Proof repair across type equivalences. In: PLDI, pp. 112–127. ACM (2021)

[RYLG19] Ringer, T., Yazdani, N., Leo, J., Grossman, D.: Ornaments for proof reuse in Coq. In: ITP. LIPIcs, vol. 141, pp. 26:1–26:19. Schloss Dagstuhl - Leibniz-Zentrum für Informatik (2019)

[San09]   Sangiorgi, D.: On the origins of bisimulation and coinduction. ACM Trans. Program. Lang. Syst. **31**(4), 15:1–15:41 (2009)

[ST08]   Sultana, N., Thompson, S.: Mechanical verification of refactorings. In: PEPM. ACM (2008)

[TH23]   Thompson, S.J., Horpácsi, D.: Refactoring = substitution + rewriting: towards generic, language-independent refactorings. In: Eelco Visser Commemorative Symposium. OASIcs, vol. 109, pp. 26:1–26:9. Schloss Dagstuhl - Leibniz-Zentrum für Informatik (2023)

[Coq]   The Coq Development Team. Coq (2017). https://coq.inria.fr

[WDR14]   Williams, T., Dagand, P.-É., Rémy, D.: Ornaments in practice. In: WGP, pp. 15–24. ACM (2014)

[Whi13]   Whiteside, I.: Refactoring proofs. Ph.D. thesis, University of Edinburgh, UK (2013)

[Wib19]   Wibergh, K.: Automatic Refactoring for Agda. MSc thesis, University of Gothenburg (2019)

[Wil20] Williams, A.: Refactoring functional programs with ornaments. Ph.D. thesis, Université de Paris (2020)

[ZH15] Zimmermann, T., Herbelin, H.: Automatic and transparent transfer of theorems along isomorphisms in the Coq proof assistant. In: Conference on Intelligent Computer Mathematics (2015)

Free Monads, Intrinsic Scoping, and Higher-Order Preunification

Nikolai Kudasov(✉)

Innopolis University, Innopolis, Tatarstan Republic, Russia
n.kudasov@innopolis.ru

Abstract. Type checking algorithms and theorem provers rely on unification algorithms. In presence of type families or higher-order logic, higher-order (pre)unification (HOU) is required. Many HOU algorithms are expressed in terms of λ-calculus and require encodings, such as higher-order abstract syntax, which are sometimes not comfortable to work with for language implementors. To facilitate implementations of languages, proof assistants, and theorem provers, we propose a novel approach based on the second-order abstract syntax of Fiore, data types à la carte of Swierstra, and intrinsic scoping of Bird and Patterson. With our approach, an object language is generated freely from a given bifunctor. Then, given an evaluation function and making a few reasonable assumptions on it, we derive a higher-order preunification procedure on terms in the object language. More precisely, we apply a variant of E-unification for second-order syntax. Finally, we briefly demonstrate an application of this technique to implement type checking (with type inference) for Martin-Löf Type Theory, a dependent type theory.

1 Introduction

When implementing a programming language, a proof assistant, or a theorem prover, one often relies on unification algorithms. Dealing with dependent types and/or higher-order logics requires higher-order unification (HOU) algorithms. Many such algorithms are available in the literature, most influential of which are, perhaps, Huet's preunification [14], Jensen-Pietrzykowski's full unification [15] procedures, procedures for decidable fragments [1,21,26] and a recent efficient implementation of full HOU [34].

HOU algorithms, such as mentioned above, are specified for a rather minimalistic version of λ-calculus. This is often justified by appealing to higher-order abstract syntax [29] (HOAS): any binding construction can be encoded in λ-calculus. Unfortunately, HOAS and its variants [7,35] are not always comfortable to work with as witnessed by both language implementors [8,17] and formalization researchers [12].

Thus, supporting higher-order (pre)unification either forces one to use HOAS or to implement a version of a HOU algorithm from scratch for the chosen language. This appears to be one of the main reasons for prototype implementations to omit or reduce support for type inference and demand more explicit type annotations for the user.

Second-order abstract syntax (SOAS) and second-order equational logic [11] have recently been an attractive alternative to HOAS. It has been successfully used to generate metatheory in Agda [12] and a full E-unification procedure [18] has been developed. Importantly, E-unification for SOAS is powerful enough to encode higher-order unification problems in languages with arbitrary binders.

SOAS is freely generated from a signature, which specifies the syntactic constructions available in the object language, by adding variables and parametrized metavariables. Each syntactic construction can be parametrized by a sequence of (potentially, scoped) subterms. For example, SOAS for simply typed lambda calculus [11, Example 1] is generated from a family of constructors for all types σ and τ:

$$\mathsf{app}^{\sigma,\tau} : (\sigma \Rightarrow \tau, \sigma) \to \tau \qquad \mathsf{abs}^{\sigma,\tau} : (\sigma.\tau) \to \sigma \Rightarrow \tau$$

Here, $\mathsf{app}^{\sigma,\tau}$ has two subterms of types[1] $\sigma \Rightarrow \tau$ and σ, while $\mathsf{abs}^{\sigma,\tau}$ has a single *scoped* subterm of type τ with access to a local variable of type σ.

Although it should be possible to work with intrinsically typed SOAS as in the example above, in this paper, we consider only untyped SOAS since ultimately we are interested in explicit implementations of type checking and type inference for arbitrary languages, whose type system might not be properly embeddable in the host language. For example, we consider the following SOAS for preterms in $\lambda\Pi$-calculus (i.e. well-scoped but not necessarily well-typed terms):

$$\mathsf{app} : (T, T) \to T \qquad \mathsf{abs} : (T.T) \to T \qquad \mathsf{Pi} : (T, T.T) \to T$$

Free monads [32] generate (first-order) abstract syntax trees with a monadic binding operation serving as substitution. Following Swierstra [32], we want to generate SOAS with proper variable substitution and metavariable substitutions from a signature provided by a user-defined algebraic data type (ADT). To do that, we need to be able to specify and properly handle scoped terms.

For expressions with scopes (such as let-expressions or λ-abstractions), substitution (implemented manually or via free monads) is not safe by default since a name capture might happen. To avoid this, de Bruijn indices [10] are commonly used in practice. Generalized de Bruijn indices[2] have also been used (e.g. in Epigram [25]) to keep track of scoping in types and also to allow for the lifting entire subexpressions to optimize substitutions further.

Combining free monads with intrinsic scopes via generalized de Bruijn indices we are able to generate abstract syntax with proper substitution operations. For $\lambda\Pi$-calculus the following ADT describes the signature of preterms:

---

[1] The double arrow ($\Rightarrow$) here corresponds to the function types in the object language, while single arrow ($\to$) is a part of the type signature (in the metatheory) separating types of subterms from the type of the resulting term for each of the syntactic constructors.

[2] such as implemented in the **bound** package, available at http://hackage.haskell.org/package/bound.

```
data TermF scope term
  = LambdaF scope          -- Abstraction: λx.t
  | AppF term term         -- Application: (t₁ t₂)
  | PiF term scope         -- Dependent function type: ∏ₓ:T₁ T₂
```

Here the `scope` parameter corresponds to scoped subterms, introducing local variable(s), and `term` corresponds to subterms without extra scope variables. It is possible to consider variations of our approach, supporting arbitrary indexing for bound variables and support for intrinsic typing. However, we find the suggested setting comfortable enough and defer variations for further work.

Since we can see the ADT above as a signature for SOAS, we can generate syntax for the object language (with and without metavariables), and provide higher-order preunification, adapting a version of E-unification for SOAS [18].

1.1 Related Work

Unification and Free Monads. In his 2001 pearl [31], Sheard described an efficient and modularized implementation of single-sorted first-order unification. Wren Romano has implemented this approach in Haskell as the unification-fd library. Romano's implementation also mixes well with Swierstra's data types à la carte [32]: terms with metavariables are constructed using free monads.

Axelsson and Vezzosi [4] use data types à la carte approach in their syntax for higher-order rewrite rules. However, their implementation of capture avoiding substitution explicitly demands specific syntax for variables, lambda abstractions, and applications, preventing correct treatment of other potential binding constructions. Our approach adds variables freely and does not impose any further restrictions on the syntax of the object language, allowing arbitrary binders.

Second-Order Abstract Syntax. Fiore and Szamoszvancev [12] have developed a language-formalization framework in Agda. Their approach is based on SOAS and generates Agda code for a grammar of types, operations of weakening and substitution, correctness properties, and other utilities for the formalization of an equational/rewriting theory for a given language.

Makoto Hamana [13] has developed the framework of second-order computation systems and their algebraic semantics, laying out the foundation for the SOL system, a tool to check confluence and termination of polymorphic second-order computation systems. The SOL system is implemented in Haskell and relies on the quasiquotation feature of Template Haskell to specify a second-order signature and computation rules for a second-order computation system.

Whereas the aforementioned works are focused on the metatheory of languages, we are interested more in the implementation of languages, and in particular, type checkers for dependently typed languages.

Intrinsic Scoping. Maclaurin, Radul, and Paszke have introduced the Foil [23], making it possible to have intrinsic scoping while maintaining the efficiency benefits of the Barendregt convention, as implemented in the Rapier [28], an approach to handling binders, which is implemented, in particular, in the Glasgow Haskell Compiler. It seems plausible that the Foil can be used instead of nested datatypes to ensure scope safety in the approach presented in this paper, but we leave this research for future work.

1.2 Contributions

We propose an approach to abstract syntax that relies on a combination of free monads and generalized de Bruijn indices. We argue that our approach facilitates the implementation of programming languages and proof assistants[3], in particular, of dependently typed ones, by deriving a higher-order preunification algorithm for the object language. Our specific contributions are the following:

1. In Sect. 2, we introduce *free scoped monads*, a generic data type that serves as a basis for a family of languages with well-scoped terms.
2. In Sect. 3, we propose an approach to the implementation of term reduction that mixes well with the data types à la carte approach.
3. In Sect. 4, we formulate the necessary requirements for the signature to enable higher-order preunification of terms in the object language. We adapt a version of the *E*-unification procedure for second-order abstract syntax [18] and extract the preunification component of it.
4. In Sect. 5, we demonstrate how our approach can be applied to implement type checking and type inference for Martin-Löf Type Theory [24].

2 Free Monads with Intrinsic Scoping

In this section, we merge the ideas of free monads and intrinsically scoped terms to produce free scoped monads allowing us to generate the type of well-scoped terms with correctly defined substitution. We then add metavariables, generating SOAS from a signature given by an algebraic data type (ADT) in Haskell.

Intrinsically well-scoped de Bruijn terms were introduced by Bellegarde and Hook [5], and monadic structure (substitution) for untyped terms was developed by Bird and Patterson [6]. Some later work has been done for typed terms [2,3], but those use intrinsic typing which we are not using in this paper[4].

Skipping intrinsic typing, we are not relying on dependent types in the host language, however our representation of abstract syntax still requires two important type system features. First, we require *nested* (also called *non-uniform* or *non-regular*) data types, whose definition involves a recursive component that is different from the type being defined. Second, we require higher-kinded types

---

[3] or, at the very least, prototyping of programming languages and proof assistants.
[4] We are not relying on intrinsic typing since we would like to be able to implement languages with richer type systems in weaker or differently typed host languages; for example, we would like to implement Martin-Löf Type Theory in Haskell.

in order to parametrize the signature ADT by type constructors. We are using Haskell as our language of implementation, but the reader should be aware of these requirements, if they wish to port the code to another language.

2.1 Intrinsically Well-Scoped Terms

Following Bird and Patterson [6] we start with the following definitions. First, we define a type constructor to extend the type of variables with one more name:

```
data Inc var = Z | S var
```

A scoped term is now a term defined in an extended context (i.e. over the type of variables extended with (bound) variable Z):

```
type Scope term var = term (Inc var)
```

Note that Scope is a higher-kinded type since its argument term is a type constructor.

As long as term is a Monad, we can perform substitution for the bound variable:

```
substitute :: Monad term => term a -> Scope term a -> term a
substitute u s = s >>= \x -> case x of
    Z    -> u           -- substitute bound variable
    S y  -> return y    -- keep free variable
```

Note that intrinsic scoping here makes sure that we only substitute bound variables, and free variables (as well as the rest of the structure) are left intact.

One could use Scope directly to define, for example, the type of $\lambda\Pi$-terms, parametrized over the type of free variables:

```
data Term a
  = Var a                         -- Free variable.
  | App (Term a) (Term a)         -- Application.
  | Lam (Scope Term a)            -- Abstraction.
  | Pi (Term a) (Scope Term a)    -- Function type.
```

Assuming we have Monad Term instance, and equipped with substitute, it is straightforward to define evaluation of such terms. For example, this is how evaluation to weak head normal form (WHNF) can be implemented:

```
whnf :: Term a -> Term a
whnf term = case term of
  App fun arg -> case whnf fun of
    Lam body -> whnf (substitute arg body)
    fun'     -> App fun' arg
  _ -> term
```

Compared with traditional de Bruijn indices, relying on nested data types using Scope has two great advantages. First, it is safer since ill-scoped terms are also ill-typed. Second, programming with scopes is now more type-driven and allows for more straightforward implementations (with substitute being a prime example).

Binding Multiple Variables. It will be useful to us in Sect. 2.3 to have a variation of Scope that supports binding of many variables at once:

```
data IncMany var
  = BoundVar Int  -- an Int-indexed bound variable
  | FreeVar var   -- a free variable

-- | A scope with arbitrarily many bound variables.
type IntScope term var = term (IncMany var)
```

Substitution for IntScope requires a mapping from a bound variable index to a term, but is otherwise straightforward.

```
substituteMany :: Monad term => (Int -> term var) -> IntScope term var -> term var
substituteMany f s = s >>= \x ->
  case x of
    BoundVar n -> f n
    FreeVar z -> return z
```

In this paper, we will use the regular Scope for the scopes in the object language and IntScope for metavariable substitution.

2.2 Free Scoped Monads

The use of substitute in the definition of whnf relies on a Monad instance for Term. Although we could provide it explicitly, we would rather have it for free. One common technique to get it is to reformulate Term using free monads [32]. Unfortunately, our Term is used non-uniformly in its recursive definition, which is not compatible with standard free monad definitions. To facilitate non-uniform recursion, specifically using Scope, we introduce the *free scoped monad*:

```
data FS t a
  = Pure a                           -- Free variable.
  | Free (t (Scope (FS t) a) (FS t a))  -- Some syntax, specified by t.
```

The main idea is that t in FS t a represents possible syntactic constructions of the language (similarly to generating functor in regular free monads), and it can explicitly mention both subterms and scopes. The free scoped monad is Monad a (whenever t is a Bifunctor [5]), with the bind operation (>>=) corresponding to the substitution. Importantly, unlike regular free monads [32], the substitution in free scoped monads respects bound variables.

```
instance Bifunctor t => Monad (FS t) where
  return = Pure
  Pure x >>= f = f x
  Free t >>= f = Free (bimap ((>>= traverse f)) (>>= f) t)
```

---

[5] Note that and Bifunctor some other instances can be automatically derived for a user-defined types using GHC extensions, such as DeriveFunctor, or Template Haskell utility functions like deriveBifunctor from bifunctors package.

We now reformulate our type of untyped lambda terms, defining `TermF` to specify all syntactic constructions and using `FS` to give us the type of terms:

```
data TermF scope term
  = AppF term term
  | LamF scope

type Term a = FS TermF a
type ScopedTerm a = Scope (FS TermF) a
```

The `PatternSynonyms` extensions helps us keep `whnf` implementation without any changes after the switch to free scoped monads representation:

```
pattern Var x = Pure x
pattern Lam s = Free (LamF s)
pattern App t1 t2 = Free (AppF t1 t2)
```

It will be useful to us sometimes to apply a transformation to all nodes, changing from one signature to another. For that, we introduce this function:

```
trans :: Bifunctor f => (forall x y. f x y -> g x y) -> FS f a -> FS g a
trans _phi (Pure x) = Pure x
trans phi (Free t) = Free (phi (bimap (trans phi) (trans phi) t))
```

With free scoped monads, we now have the tools to generate types of well-scoped terms. Although `FS` provides an effective mechanism to automatically get substitution for our terms, the design as presented here has some trade-offs. First, since we are using, `Scope` we are limiting ourselves to scopes that only introduce one bound variable. This can be improved by using *generalized de Bruijn indices* as implemented in the bound package [17]. In this paper, we will use a simplified version for the sake of clarity and brevity. Second, the definition of `Scope` itself can be changed to reduce the number of required traversals of the syntax tree. Again, a more elaborate version, as seen in the bound package, can be used instead. Third, we could parametrize `FS` over the scope type constructor, but that would again unnecessarily complicate the code. Finally, we could use a different formulation of `FS`, such as a Church encoding, similar to Church-encoded free monads [33] for improved asymptotic complexity of substitution.

2.3 Metavariables, SOAS, and Metavariable Substitution

For unification, we need to add metavariables to our syntax. To avoid unnecessary assumptions about the object language while keeping the expressive power of higher-order unification, we follow SOAS [11] and use parametrized metavariables. Instead of embedding metavariables directly into `FS` data type, we use data types à la carte approach [32] and extend any given bifunctor `term` with metavariables. The following datatype generates parametrized metavariables:

```
data MetaAppF v scope term = MetaAppF v [term]
```

Parametrization provides independence from object language syntax (we do not require having function application in the object language), but it also keeps all "dependencies" of a metavariable bundled with it.

Following [18], we write $M_i[t_1, t_2, \ldots, t_n]$ to mean application of metavariable M_i to terms $t_1, t_2, \ldots, t_n$. Note that $M_i[t_1][t_2]$ is invalid syntax, and it is not possible in general to partially apply a metavariable.

To add metavariables to a language, we use a variant of Swierstra's operator (:+:). Given signatures f and g, we can get a new signature Sum f g that supports constructions from both original signatures.

```
data Sum f g scope term
  = InL (f scope term)   -- inject constructions of f
  | InR (g scope term)   -- inject constructions of g
```

Now, we can extend any signature t with parametrized metavariables:

```
type SOAS v t a = FS (Sum t (MetaAppF v)) a
```

Here, SOAS stands for "Second-Order Abstract Syntax" with v being the type of metavariables, t—the term signature, and— a the type of free variables.

Metavariable Substitution. Following SOAS [11], we define substitution for parametrized metavariables by mapping each metavariable to a scoped term, with n bound variables. In the implementation, we rely on IntScope allowing arbitrarily many bound variables (not statically checked):

```
data MetaAbs t a = MetaAbs Int (IntScope (FS t) a)
```

Here, the first component of type Int represents the arity of the metavariable, which is mostly useful for pretty-printing and debugging, and is not strictly necessary for the unification algorithm. The second component is the scoped term, with (up to) n distinct bound variables used.

We represent substitution $M_i[x_1, x_2, \ldots, x_n] \mapsto t$ as a pair of metavariable M_i and the scoped term t, represented using MetaAbs for the extended language. A simultaneous substitution [11, Section 2] is represented by a list of substitutions[6]:

```
type Subst v t a = (v, MetaAbs (Sum t (MetaAppF v)) a)
newtype Substs v t a = Substs { getSubsts :: [Subst v t a] }
```

To apply Substs to a term, we merely traverse the term replacing every occurrence of that MetaAppF has a corresponding substitution:

```
applySubsts :: (Eq v, Bifunctor t) => Substs v t a -> SOAS v t a -> SOAS v t a
applySubsts substs = go where
  go term = case term of
    Pure{} -> term   -- free variables remain
```

---

[6] Here we are using a list for simplicity, but it is also possible to use other data structures, such as Data.HashMap or Data.Map.

```
    Free (InR (MetaAppF v args)) -> -- metavariables are replaced according to substs
      -- substitue metavariables in arguments
      let args' = map (applySubsts substs) args
      in case lookup v (getSubsts substs) of
           Just (MetaAbs _arity body) -> substituteMany (args' !!) body
           Nothing -> Free (InR (MetaAppF v args'))
    -- recursively traverse other syntactic constructions
    Free (InL t) -> Free (InL (bimap goScope go t))
  goScope = applySubsts (fmap S substs)
```

This concludes the definition of SOAS generated from a signature provided in a form of a `Bifunctor` in Haskell:

1. `SOAS v t a` is the type of second-order terms generated from `t`;
2. `Pure x` corresponds to a (free) variable x;
3. `Free (InR (MetaAppF v [t1, ..., tN]))` corresponds to $M[t_1, \ldots, t_N]$
4. `Free (InL t)` corresponds to some syntactic construction[7] $F(\overline{x_1}.t_1, \ldots, \overline{x_n}.t_n)$;
5. function `applySubsts` performs simultaneous metavariable substitution.

3 Term Reduction à La Carte

In this section, we organize term reduction for extensible languages following data types à la carte [32]. The motivation is twofold. On the one hand, we want to be able to specify reduction in object languages without having to deal with metavariables (indeed, it is natural for the reduction rules to be independent of metavariables). On the other hand, we want to be able to easily extend languages with new syntactic constructions (e.g. pairs and projections).

In general, assuming the constructions from the two signatures are not supposed to "interfere" with each other, we can define term reduction for each component independently. To get reduction working for terms generated from signature `Sum f g`, we need to specify reduction for `f` and `g`, however, it is important that we give that anticipating an extension[8]:

```
class Bifunctor t => Reducible t where
  reduceL :: Reducible ext
    => t (Scope (FS (Sum t ext)) a) (FS (Sum t ext) a)
    -> FS (Sum t ext) a
```

Here `reduceL` reduces a term of a language, generated by `t` extended with `ext`, assuming terms generated by `ext` are reducible. Using `reduceL` and commuting left and right languages, we get `reduceR` [9]:

```
reduceR = commute . reduceL . bimap commute commute
commute = trans $ \case
  InL x -> InR x
  InR y -> InL y
```

---

[7] Fiore and Hur call these *operators* [11, Section 2].
[8] Hence the use of `Sum` in the type signature. The importance of this definition becomes clear when we consider the instance of `Redicible` for `Sum f g`.
[9] We can also make `reduceR` a part of the `Reducible` class.

To reduce a term we use `reduceL` or `reduceR`, depending on what we find at root:

```
reduceSum :: FS (Sum t ext) a -> FS (Sum t ext) a
reduceSum t@Pure{} = t
reduceSum (Free (InL t)) = reduceL t
reduceSum (Free (InR t)) = reduceR t
```

Empty Signature. A particularly important language is an empty one:

```
data Empty scope term    -- this data type has no constructors
```

Note that language generated by `Empty` is not actually empty: free variables are always added with `FS`. Without any constructors `reduceL` is trivial:

```
instance Reducible Empty where
  reduceL e = case e of {}
```

We can express term reduction in an (unextended) object language as a special case of `reduceL`, extending it with an `Empty` signature:

```
reduce :: Reducible t => FS t a -> FS t a
reduce = trans removeEmpty . reduceSum . trans InL
  where removeEmpty (InL x) = x
        removeEmpty (InR e) = case e :: Empty of {}
```

Sum of Signatures. Combining two reducible languages with `Sum` yields a reducible language. Here, we rely on commutativity and associativity of `Sum`:

```
instance (Reducible f, Reducible g) => Reducible (Sum f g) where
  reduceL (InL t) = assoc' (reduceL (bimap assoc assoc t))
  reduceL (InR t) = from (reduceL (bimap to to t))
    where
      to = assoc . commute . assoc
      from = assoc' . commute . assoc'
```

Reducing $\lambda\Pi$-Terms. To adapt `whnf` to reduce terms in a language generated by `TermF` with arbitrary extension, we can introduce patterns for extended language:

```
pattern LamE body = Free (InL (LamF body))
pattern AppE t1 t2 = Free (InL (AppF t1 t2))
pattern ExtE t = Free (InR t)
```

Implementation of `whnf` is transferred practically letter for letter as an instance of `Reducible` for `TermF`, except now the root has type `TermF (FS (Sum TermF ext) a)` and subterms are of type `FS (Sum TermF ext) a`, so we apply `reduce` (not `reduceL`) to subterms:

```
instance Reducible TermF where
  reduceL = \case
    AppF fun arg -> case reduce fun of
      LamE body -> reduce (substitute arg body)
      fun' -> AppE fun' arg
    t -> Free (InL t)
```

Reducing with Metavariables. Parametrized metavariables reduce to themselves, however we can choose to reduce or keep their parameters, yielding two possible definitions. First one leaves parameters unevaluated:

```
-- ``lazy'' reduction (arguments remain unevaluated)
instance Reducible (MetaAppF v) where
  reduceL t = Free (InL t)
```

The second possible implementation reduces the parameters:

```
-- ``strict'' reduction (arguments are evaluated)
instance Reducible (MetaAppF v) where
  reduceL (MetaAppF m args) = Free (InL (MetaAppF m (map reduce args)))
```

Note that even though the second implementation is "strict" in the object language, using Haskell as a host language makes evaluation somewhat lazy in the sense that actual evaluation of parameters might still be delayed. This kind of lazy evaluation is used in some HOU algorithms [34] and from now we assume the second instance implementation for `MetaAppF`.

4 Higher-Order Unification

In this section, we describe a generic semi-decidable algorithm for single-sorted higher-order preunification. The algorithm stops when either the terms cannot be unified, or when the only constraints left are those between metavariables.

The algorithm is loosely based on *E*-unification for second-order abstract syntax [18], with the following important differences:

1. we forego the (**mutate**) rule [18, Definition 28], and instead assume that terms can be normalized (via `reduce`);
2. we combine the (**imitate**) and (**project**) rules [18, Definitions 24–25] into a single rule with generalized Huet-style bindings [19];
3. we implement only *pre*unification, leaving unsolved constraints between two metavariables, omitting (**eliminate**), (**identify**), and (**iterate**) rules;
4. we implement *unification* itself in an untyped setting, i.e. our implementation of higher-order unification does not (directly) take types of terms into account; technically, type information can be embedded into the terms themselves and can be used by `reduce`, but in this paper we do not make extra assumptions when generating Huet-style bindings and leave development of an algorithm for type-directed generalized Huet-style bindings for future work.

To achieve such an algorithm, we impose some constraints on the signature ADT. These constraints, formulated as type classes in Haskell, make sure that we can traverse the freely generated syntax tree, match individual nodes of that tree (enabling first-order unification), and make appropriate substitutions for metavariables (enabling higher-order unification).

4.1 Prerequisites

The unification process involves keeping track of metavariables and their values, which is a kind of effectful computation. Traversing an abstract syntax tree and making changes to the currently known values of metavariables requires not just `Bifunctor`, but `Bitraversable` instance for the generating bifunctor. Fortunately, for most practical cases, we can derive those instances automatically with common GHC extensions or Template Haskell.

Apart from `Bitraversable`, we will require object language terms to be `Reducible`, and its syntactic constructions `Unifiable`. For first-order unification, it would be enough to match individual syntactic constructions and perform unification by recursive matching.

For higher-order unification, we rely on generalized Huet-style bindings [19]. Essentially, for a given language we need to know the following information:

1. For each argument (subterm) of a syntactic construction, is there a certain shape of a term that allows further reduction? For example, given a term $\pi_1 \, \text{M}_1[]$ (where $\text{M}_1[]$ is a metavariable), we should understand that M_1 can be substituted by a tuple (M_2, M_3) (where M_2 and M_3 are fresh metavariables) to allow further reduction.
2. For parametrized metavariables, what are possible ways to construct a term that will use the parameters via reduction? For example, when unifying $\text{M}_1[(t_1, t_2)]$ with t_1, we should be able to try the substitution $\text{M}_1[x] := \pi_1 \, \text{M}_2[x]$ to find the solution $\text{M}_1[x] := \pi_1 \, x$.

First-Order Unification. For first-order unification, we need to be able to match individual nodes of the syntax tree. Similarly to Wren Romano's unification-fd package[10], we define a type class with a single method:

```
class Unifiable t where
  zipMatch :: t scope term -> t scope term -> Maybe (t (scope, scope) (term, term))
```

The method `zipMatch` takes two nodes as inputs and returns when they do not match. Otherwise, it returns a single node with subterms and subscopes paired. For example, matching `Lam t` with `Lam u` yields `Just (Lam (t, u))`, suggesting that the unification process should now proceed by going inside the lambda and attempting to unify `t` and `u`.

---

[10] In unification-fd and in our implementation the type of `zipMatch` is a little more complicated to allow for an optimization, when one of the nodes omits a subterm, and we can immediately take the necessary value from the second node. However, we decided to simplify the type here to increase readability of this paper.

```
instance Unifiable TermF where
  zipMatch (AppF f1 x1) (AppF f2 x2) = Just (AppF (f1, f2) (x1, x2))
  zipMatch (LamF body1) (LamF body2) = Just (LamF (body1, body2))
  zipMatch _ _ = Nothing
```

Implementing `Unifiable` is usually mechanical and can in fact be fully automated using GHC's Generics (as is done in unification-fd) or Template Haskell.

Higher-Order Unification. Note that, following SOAS [11], we do not require the signature to have lambda abstractions or applications as there is more than one way the user might want to introduce those. For example, application can be defined as binary or taking a list of arguments. Moreover, some theories have not one but several syntactic abstractions or applications (such as Π-types and extensions types in Riehl and Shulman's type theory with shapes [30], or μ-abstraction in Parigot's $\lambda\mu$-calculus [27]).

So instead of forcing syntax onto the user, we instead ask them to provide a basic mechanism for generating valid structural guesses (generalized Huet-style bindings) for metavariables:

```
-- | Placeholder for a subterm that may or may not contain the head.
data IsHead = HasHead | NoHead

class Unifiable t => HigherOrderUnifiable t where
  guessMetas :: t scope term -> t (scope, [t () ()]) (term, [t () ()])
  shapes :: [t IsHead IsHead]
```

The role of `guessMetas` is to provide a list of valid partial guesses for each subterm and subscope in a given node of the syntax tree. For example, given a term M_1 M_2 where M_1 and M_2 are metavariables we can guess that M_1 is a function and so should be unified with a term λM_3, where M_3 is a fresh metavariable. On the other hand, we do not have any information that would allow us to guess the structure of M_2. Each returned guess for a particular subterm or subscope has type t () (), which simply provides the general shape of the guess (e.g., that it should be a lambda abstraction). The unification algorithm will then replace each () in a guess with a fresh metavariable and continue the unification process.

Implementing this for `TermF` we get the following:

```
instance HigherOrderUnifiable TermF where
  guessMetas term = case term of
    AppF f arg -> AppF (f, [LamF ()]) (arg, [])
    _ -> bimap (,[]) (,[]) term

  shapes = [AppF HasHead NoHead]
```

Note that the type of `guessMetas` implies that a guess is based on a single syntactic construction (i.e. it cannot match a complex pattern). It also yields just one syntactic construction per guess (with placeholders for fresh metavariables).

For many type theories, one only needs to identify introduction-elimination pairs to implement `HigherOrderUnifiable`. Given an instance of `Reducible`, one can go over all possible combinations of syntactic constructions to figure out this information automatically, either using Template Haskell or GHC Generics.

4.2 Constraints

A constraint is essentially a pair of terms with metavariables that we would like to unify. Importantly, the same metavariable can be used with different parameters and in different scopes. This means that a metavariable substitution cannot depend on the bound variables (otherwise they may "leak").

Consider constraint involving λ-abstraction: $(\lambda f.\lambda x.\text{M}_1[f\ x]) \equiv (\lambda f.\lambda x.f\ x)$. Going under λ-abstraction in both terms might reduce the original constraint to $\text{M}_1[f\ x] \equiv f\ x$. However, treating f and x now as free variables is incorrect as this constraint can be satisfied with two different substitutions: $\text{M}_1[z] \mapsto f\ x$ (leaks f and x) and $\text{M}_1[z] \mapsto z$ (correct).

Since bound variables are not allowed to leak into solutions for unification problem, an appropriate simplification of the original constraint $(\lambda f.\lambda x.\text{M}_1[f\ x]) \equiv (\lambda f.\lambda x.f\ x)$ should look like $\forall f, x.(\text{M}_1[f\ x] \equiv f\ x)$. Here, f and x remain bound and are easy to avoid when generating substitutions for M_1. Fortunately, we can leverage `Scope` to manage $\forall$ quantifier and represent constraints properly:

```
data Constraint v t a
  = SOAS v t a :=: SOAS v t a         -- A unification constraint.
  | ForAll (Scope (Constraint v t) a) -- A scoped constraint.
```

The infix constructor (`:=:`) is used to construct a simple constraint with two terms. The constructor `ForAll` uses `Scope` to construct a scoped constraint. This representation does not solve the problem of leaking bound variables completely on its own, but it makes the compiler reject implementations that do not account for bound variables, as those substitutions will be impossible to lift outside of scopes.

4.3 Preunification Algorithm

In this section, we describe an algorithm for single-sorted preunification. The algorithm relies on a backtracking-capable environment and the ability to generate fresh metavariables. In Haskell, we manage those capabilities via type classes `MonadPlus` and `MonadFresh`:

```
class Monad m => MonadFresh v m | m -> v where
  freshMeta :: m v  -- Generate a fresh metavariable.
```

The main idea of the algorithm is straightforward:

1. starting with a collection of constraints,

2. attempt to simplify them into smaller constraints by using term reduction and structural guesses for metavariables, producing some flex-flex and flex-rigid constraints;
3. then take any flex-rigid constraint that could not be simplified further and try to solve it;
4. if cannot be solved—backtrack; otherwise—apply solution (substitution) to the rest of the constraints and
5. repeat until all flex-rigid constraints are resolved.

Simplifying Constraints. Simplification of one constraint follows three steps:

1. Terms are reduced using `reduce`.
2. Each term is traversed to see if any metavariables can be substituted using one of the structural guesses using `guessMetas`. If there are any potential substitutions, we apply them to both terms and repeat from step 1.
3. Finally, we `zipMatch` the two terms to break down constraint into a collection of smaller constraints.

Given a collection of constraints, we perform simplification on each of them recursively, accumulating and applying generated substitutions from `guessMeta`, until we end up with a collection of constraints that cannot be simplified any further.

Simplified constraints are expected to be

- of the form $\forall y_1 \ldots y_m.(\text{M}_i[t_1, \ldots, t_n] \equiv t)$, where t is not a metavariable application; these are called *flex-rigid* constraints;
- or of the form $\forall y_1 \ldots y_m.(\text{M}_i[t_1^i, \ldots, t_n^i] \equiv \text{M}_j[t_1^j, \ldots, t_k^j])$; these are called *flex-flex* constraints.

The third potential type of constraints, where both sides are not metavariable applications, are called *rigid-rigid* constraints. These constraints are guaranteed to be simplified in step 3 with `zipMatch`. Indeed `zipMatch`, either returns `Nothing` (which means that two nodes do not match), or it pairs syntactic subtrees to match recursively, ensuring structural recursion.

Extracting Head of a Term. If, according to `guessMetas`, there is a structural guess for some subterm position of a syntactic construction, we call a subterm in that position a *head subterm*. We say that a term h is a *head* of a term t if it is a head subterm of t or if it is a head of any head subterm of t. For example, the term $\lambda z.fz$ is the head subterm of the term $\pi_1 ((\lambda z.fz) \ x \ (\pi_2 \ y))$.

Solving Flex-Rigid Constraints. Preunification algorithm starts off with a list of constraints, reduces *rigid-rigid* constraints and solves *flex-rigid* constraints, leaving only *flex-flex* constraints to be dealt with by the user.

To solve a flex-rigid constraint $\forall y_1 \ldots y_m.(\text{M}_i[t_1, \ldots, t_n] \equiv t)$, the algorithm goes through a sequence of candidate solutions. Each candidate solution is of the form $\text{M}_i[x_1, \ldots, x_n] \mapsto T$, where T is one of the following:

- the head of t, where each variable bound by $\forall$ is replaced with a fresh metavariable application $M_k[x_1, \ldots, x_n]$;
- a bound variable of M_i: x_j;
- a candidate shape (one of shapes), where each HasHead position is filled with T' and NoHead position is filled with a fresh metavariable application $M_k[x_1, \ldots, x_n]$.

The entire algorithm is packed into a single function with the following type signature:

```
unify
  :: ( HigherOrderUnifiable t, Reducible t
     , MonadPlus m, MonadLogic m, MonadFresh v m
     , Eq a, Eq v )
  => Substs v t a
  -> [Constraint v t a]
  -> m ([Constraint v t a], Substs v t a)
```

5 Applications

In this section, we see the application of our approach to implementation of type inference for a couple of type theories. The implementation is available as part of version 0.1.0 of the proof assistant RZK[11] and contains the following relevant modules:

1. module Rzk.Free.Syntax.FreeScoped introduces the free scoped monads, Sum and utility functions as described in Sect. 2;
2. module Rzk.Free.Syntax.FreeScoped.Unification2 implements higher-order preunification as described in Sect. 4;
3. module Rzk.Free.Syntax.FreeScoped.TypeCheck implements type checking and type inference algorithms based on higher-order preunification;
4. module Rzk.Free.Syntax.Example.ULC implements untyped λ-calculus with higher-order unification;
5. module Rzk.Free.Syntax.Example.STLC implements a version of simply typed λ-calculus (STLC) with type inference via higher-order unification; this version differs from the standard STLC by allowing computation at the type level;
6. module Rzk.Free.Syntax.Example.MLTT contains the implementation of intensional Martin-Löf dependent type theory with type inference.

The type inference algorithm follows the general structure of constraint-based typechecking, where higher-order preunification is used to resolve constraints. For the typechecking preunification usually suffices, since flex-flex constraints

---
[11] see relevant modules in https://github.com/rzk-lang/rzk/tree/v0.1.0/rzk/src/Rzk/Free.

correspond to ambiguous typing which normally is considered a type error. The details of type inference algorithm can be found in Appendix A.

We now outline the key moments in the implementation of Martin-Löf type theory, more details on this and the implementation of simply typed λ-calculus can be found in Appendix B and in the corresponding implementation files.

5.1 Typed Terms

Many implementors define a single type in the host language for both terms and types in the object language [9,22]. This means that typing is treated as a relation between a term and another term. We take a similar approach, annotating every node in the syntax tree with another term, which represents the type and has annotations of its own. To achieve that, we extend the object language by modifying the generating bifunctor:

```
-- | Extending a type of types with universe.
data WithUniverse ty = BigUniverse | SomeType ty

data TyF t scope term = TyF
  { termF :: t scope term
  , typeF :: WithUniverse term
  }

-- | A typed term generated from t.
type TFS t a = FS (TyF t) a
```

We use the type `WithUniverse (TFS t a)` for type annotations, meaning that type terms themselves have type annotations. The recursive annotation stops either at variables, or at `BigUniverse`, which is an explicit universe type $\mathcal{U}_\infty$. Consider term $\lambda x.f\ x$. Adding type annotations (written $t : T$) according to `TyF` would produce the following typed term (here we assume the object language also has its own universe type $\mathcal{U}$, and f, A, B are free variables):

$$\lambda x.f\ x \qquad \text{(untyped term)}$$
$$(\lambda x.(f\ x : B)) : (A \to B : (\mathcal{U} : \mathcal{U}_\infty)) \qquad \text{(typed term)}$$

Since we have modified the type of nodes in the syntax tree, with `TFS t a`, we have type annotation *for every subterm except variables*. This makes it easy to extract types of subterms when necessary without the need to repeatedly infer types.

5.2 Typing Syntactic Constructions

To perform type inference for any given language, it is enough to know how to perform a single step: given types of parts for single syntactic construction, compute the type of the whole. An important implementation detail is to provide not just the types of the parts, but an actual computation context for that type.

In other words, TFS v t a we will have m (TFS v t a) where m is some typechecking monad. This is done to give the implementor of a particular language more control over typechecking and constraint resolution:

```
class Inferable t where
  inferF :: MonadTypecheck v t a m
    => t (m (Scope (TFS v t) a)) (m ((TFS v t a) a))
    -> m (t (Scope (TFS v t) a) ((TFS v t a) a))
```

Once we know how to perform a single step of type inference, all we need to do is traverse the entire term:

```
infer :: (Inferable t, MonadTypecheck v t a m) => FS t a -> m (TFS v t a)
infer term = case term of
  Var x -> do
    addKnownFreeVar x
    return (Var x)
  Free t -> do
    ty <- Free <$> inferTypeFor (bimap inferScope infer t)
    clarifyTypedTerm ty
```

Here, `addKnownFreeVar` adds the free variable to the `TypeInfo` state with a fresh type meta variable, if it is the first time this variable is encountered. As performing inference for a single syntactic construction may result in new meta variable substitutions, we need to apply them across known type information and, perhaps, simplify the inferred typed term. For that we use `clarifyTypedTerm`, which has a straightforward implementation that we omit here.

5.3 Martin-Löf Type Theory

Let us now apply the approach to an actual dependent type theory—intensional Martin-Löf Type Theory (MLTT). We start with a generating bifunctor:

```
data TermF scope term
  = UniverseF            -- Universe type: U
  | PiF term scope       -- Dependent product: Π_{x:T_1} T_2
  | LamF scope           -- Abstraction: λx.T_2
  | AppF term term       -- Application: (T_1 T_2)
  | SigmaF term scope    -- Dependent sum: Σ_{x:T_1} T_2
  | PairF term term      -- Pair: ⟨T_1, T_2⟩
  | FirstF term          -- First projection: π_1 T
  | SecondF term         -- Second projection: π_2 T
  | IdTypeF term term    -- Identity type: x = y
  | ReflF term           -- Reflexivity: refl_T
  | JF term term term term term term
    -- ^ Identity type eliminator: J(A, a, C, d, x, p)

-- | An MLTT term with free variables in a.
type Term a = FS TermF a
```

We note a couple of details about this particular presentation of MLTT:

1. We omit type annotations for the bound variable of λ-abstraction.
2. Both types and terms are generated with `TermF`.

In this particular implementation we use a single universe type and assume type-in-type: $\mathcal{U} : \mathcal{U}$. It is possible to introduce a hierarchy of universes $\mathcal{U}_0 : \mathcal{U}_1 : \mathcal{U}_2 : \ldots$ instead by using `UniverseF Natural` constructor.

Next step is to introduce helpful pattern synonyms. We will immediately work with typed terms, so we only create patterns for those. We remind that these can be automatically generated using Template Haskell:

```
pattern Typed ty t = Free (InL (TyF t ty))
pattern UniverseT ty     = Typed ty UniverseF
pattern PiT ty t1 t2     = Typed ty (PiF t1 t2)
pattern LamT ty body     = Typed ty (LamF body)
pattern AppT ty t1 t2    = Typed ty (AppF t1 t2)
...
pattern JT ty t1 t2 t3 t3 t4 t5 t6 = Typed ty (JF t1 t2 t3 t4 t5 t6)
```

Implementing WHNF reduction for MLTT is straightforward, we will focus here only on the case of J-eliminator:

```
instance Reducible TermF where
  reduceL = \case
    JF tA a tC d x p ->
      case reduce p of
        Refl{} -> reduce d
        p'     -> J tA a tC d x p'
    ...
```

For `Unifiable` and `HigherOrderUnifiable` we also rely on a mechanical or automatic derivation and so omit it here to save space. Finally, we define inference for individual syntactic constructions:

```
instance Inferable TermF where
  inferF term = case term of
```

To avoid infinite type annotations, we set the type of universe to be $\mathcal{U}_\infty$:

```
UniverseF -> pure (TyF UniverseF BigUniverse)
```

Inferring types for Π-types and Σ-types involves dependent type checking. Given term $\Pi_{x:A}B$, where B is a subterm that may refer to x, we have to check that both $A : \mathcal{U}$ and $B : \mathcal{U}$. Note that since B is in the scope, its inferred type, by default, might also be dependent on x. For example, in the term $\Pi_{x:A}\mathsf{refl}_x$ the algorithm would infer that refl_x has type $x = x$, which captures the variable x. To make sure the body of a Π-type is always a type, we need to unify it with $\mathcal{U}$. But for that we also need to make sure it is not dependent, so we use `nonDep`:

```
PiF inferA inferB -> do
  a <- inferA >>= shouldHaveType (UniverseT BigUniverse)
  typeOfA <- typeOf a
  b <- inScope typeOfA inferB
  typeOfB <- typeOfScope typeOfA b >>= nonDep
  typeOfB `shouldHaveType` UniverseT BigUniverse
  pure (TyF (PiF a b) (UniverseT BigUniverse))
```

Inferring the type for a dependent λ-abstraction is relatively straightforward. We generate a fresh type meta variable for the argument and infer the type of the body. In general, we should check that the inferred type is indeed a type, as many type theories, such as cubical type theory, have multiple universes. That said, in pure MLTT we can omit this check.

```
LamF inferBody -> do
  a <- freshTypeMetaVar
  typedBody <- inScope a inferBody
  b <- typeOfScope a typedBody
  typeOfScope a b >>= nonDep
    >>= shouldHaveType (UniverseT BigUniverse)
  pure $ TyF
    (LamF typedBody)
    (SomeType (PiT (UniverseT BigUniverse) a b))
```

The rest of syntactic constructors is fairly straightforward to handle similarly. Completing `Inferable` brings dependent type inference to MLTT.

6 Conclusion and Future Work

We have presented an approach to abstract syntax representation with free scoped monads and demonstrated its effectiveness for the implementation of Martin-Löf Type Theory. Our example demonstrates that the approach does not require the user to have a deep understanding of higher-order unification to enable type inference for their language.

We have also devised a few directions for future work. First, we would like to extend to full higher-order unification or, better yet, full E-unification for second-order abstract syntax [18]. Implementing generic E-unification for second-order abstract syntax would be instrumental to implementing proof assistants for type theories with non-trivial or extensible definitional equalities. In particular, we think this might be useful for the implementation of extension types in Riehl and Shulman's type theory for synthetic ∞-categories [30].

Second, we should make higher-order unification more efficient by optimizing the representation of free scoped monads, taking into account the types of unified terms, and recognizing efficient/decidable fragments of unification problems with oracles as in the work of Vukmirovic, Bentkamp, and Nummelin [34].

Acknowledgements. I am grateful to Benedikt Ahrens and Daniel de Carvalho for their invaluable feedback throughout my early work towards the implementation of typecheckers for dependently typed languages. I thank Oksana Zhirosh, Ruslan Saduov, and Benedikt Ahrens for proofreading earlier versions of this paper. I also thank the anonymous reviewer of TFP 2024 for an improvement suggestion for `Reducible`.

A A Type Inference

In this section, we describe a generic type inference algorithm for languages generated using free scoped monads. As we follow a common bottom-up constraint based type inference approach, similar to existing implementations, we do not go into all the details, and instead point out the most significant definitions and aspects.

Typed Terms

Many implementors define a single type in the host language for both terms and types in the object language [9, 22]. This means that typing is treated as a relation between a term and another term. We take a similar approach, annotating every node in the syntax tree with another term, which represents the type and has annotations of its own. To achieve that, we extend the object language by modifying the generating bifunctor:

```
-- | Extending a type of types with universe.
data WithUniverse ty = Universe | SomeType ty

data TyF t scope term = TyF
  { termF :: t scope term
  , typeF :: WithUniverse term
  }

-- | A typed term generated from t.
type TFS t a = FS (TyF t) a
```

We use the type `WithUniverse (TFS t a)` for type annotations, meaning that type terms themselves have type annotations. The recursive annotation stops either at variables, or at `Universe`, which is an explicit universe type $\mathcal{U}_\infty$. Consider term $\lambda x.f\ x$. Adding type annotations (written $t : T$) according to `TyF` would produce the following typed term (here we assume the object language also has its own universe type $\mathcal{U}$, and f, A, B are free variables):

$$\lambda x.f\ x \qquad \text{(untyped term)}$$
$$(\lambda x.(f\ x : B)) : (A \to B : (\mathcal{U} : \mathcal{U}_\infty)) \qquad \text{(typed term)}$$

Since we have modified the type of nodes in the syntax tree, with `TFS t a`, we have type annotation *for every subterm except variables*. This makes it easy to extract types of subterms when necessary without the need to repeatedly infer types.

With type inference, we also need to take into account meta variables. Extending typed terms with meta variables yields the following type:

```
type TSOAS v t a = SOAS v (TyF t) a
```

Note that the universe $\mathcal{U}_\infty$ is not available as a term, it can only be used in the type position. This, in particular, means that no variable or meta variable can be instantiated with $\mathcal{U}_\infty$.

Type Checking Context

We implement bottom-up type inference and keep track of currently available type information. As we traverse a given term and solve arising constraints, this information is updated. In this subsection, we explain what kind of type information we need to store and how we mix stateful computations with backtracking.

At any given moment in the algorithm, we are considering a subterm, possibly located inside several scopes. For the type inference algorithm, we translate nested data types with `Inc a` into `IncMany a`, effectively merging individual scopes into one.

1. Known types of free variables. Types of free variables cannot depend on any bound variables, so for each free variable we store its type as `TSOAS v t a`.
2. Known types of meta variables. Meta variables are global and, similarly to free variables, cannot depend on bound variables. So for each meta variable we store its type as `TSOAS v t a`.
3. Known types of bound variables. Types of bound variables may depend on previously introduced bound variables. We store these as a list of types:`[TSOAS v t (IncMany a)]`.
4. Known substitutions for meta variables. This is the same as in the unification algorithm with only difference being that substitutions are happening for typed terms:`Substs v (TyF t) a`.
5. Leftover unification constraints. Again, similar to the unification algorithm, each constraint has type `Constraint v (TyF t) a`.
6. A stream of fresh meta variable identifiers.

All of this is collected into a single data type:

```
data TypeInfo v t a = TypeInfo
  { typesOfFreeVars  :: [(a, TSOAS v t a)]
  , typesOfBoundVars :: [TSOAS v t (IncMany a)]
  , typesOfMetaVars  :: [(v, TSOAS v t a)]
  , metaVarSubsts    :: Substs v (TyF t) a
  , constraints      :: [Constraint v (TyF t) a]
  , freshMetaVars    :: [v]
  }
```

To go through candidate substitutions for meta variables we rely on `MonadPlus` type class. Moreover, we require the monad to obey the left distributive law, as it is essential for backtracking:

```
mplus a b >>= f  =  mplus (a >>= f) (b >>= f)
```

A well-established implementation for backtracking is Kiselyov, et al.'s `LogicT` monad transformer [16]. To deal with state and possible type errors we use `StateT` and `ExceptT` transformers [20] correspondingly.

Unfortunately, `StateT` does not mix well with non-deterministic nature of `LogicT`. In particular, neither `StateT s (LogicT m)` nor `LogicT (StateT s m)` support the left distributive law of `MonadPlus`. A common workaround is to make the state itself nondeterministic.

More specifically, we use the following data type to represent stateful computation with backtracking:

```
newtype SEL s e x = SEL
  { runSEL :: StateT (Logic s) (ExceptT e Logic) x }
```

Using `Logic s` as the type of state allows for `MonadPlus` instance that supports left distributive law:

```
instance MonadPlus (SEL s e) where
  mzero = SEL (lift (lift mzero))
  mplus (SEL l) (SEL r) = SEL $ do
    states <- get
    (x, s') <- lift $ ExceptT $ mplus
      (runExceptT (runStateT l states))
      (runExceptT (runStateT r states))
    put s'
    return x
```

We note that it is also possible to use `interleave` instead of `mplus` to force interleaving of branches in the search space. But it is also possible to leave more control on the user side, deriving `MonadLogic` instance . It is also fairly straightforward to implement `MonadState s` instance for `SEL s e`. With all those instances in place, the monad for type checking and type inference becomes merely a special case of `SEL`:

```
type TypeCheck v t a =
  SEL (TypeInfo v t a)
      (TypeError (TSOAS v t a))
```

Typing Syntactic Constructions

To perform type inference for any given language, it is enough to know how to perform a single step: given types of parts for single syntactic construction, compute the type of the whole. An important implementation detail is to provide not just the types of the parts, but an actual computation context for that type. In other words, instead of `TFS v t a` we will have `m (TFS v t a)` where `m` is some typechecking monad. This is done to give the implementor of a particular language more control over typechecking and constraint resolution:

```
class Inferable ty t where
  inferF :: MonadTypecheck v t a m
    => t (m (Scope (TFS v t) a))
         (m ((TFS v t a) a))
    -> m (t (Scope (TFS v t) a)
            ((TFS v t a) a))
```

Once we know how to perform a single step of type inference, all we need to do is traverse the entire term:

```
infer :: (Inferable t, MonadTypecheck v t a m)
      => FS t a -> m (TFS v t a)
infer term = case term of
  Var x -> do
    addKnownFreeVar x
    return (Var x)
  Free t -> do
    ty <- Free <$>
      inferTypeFor (bimap inferScope infer t)
    clarifyTypedTerm ty
```

Here, `addKnownFreeVar` adds the free variable to the `TypeInfo` state with a fresh type meta variable, if it is the first time this variable is encountered. As performing inference for a single syntactic construction may result in new meta variable substitutions, we need to apply them across known type information and, perhaps, simplify the inferred typed term. For that we use `clarifyTypedTerm`, which has a straightforward implementation that we omit here.

Unifying Types

Type checking in our implementation is merely a combination of type inference and unification:

```
typecheck term ty = infer term >>= shouldHaveType ty

shouldHaveType term expected = do
  actual <- typeOf term
  unifyWithExpected actual expected
```

Here `typeOf`, is a helper that either extracts the type annotation directly from `TyF`, or, when the term is a variable, extracts it from the `typesOfFreeVars` in current type information state.

For the unification, we take all known substitutions and constraints and run the pre-unification algorithm with `unify`, updating the type information and refining the types:

```
unifyWithExpected actual expected = do
  substs <- gets metaVarSubsts
  cs <- gets constraints
```

```
(cs', substs') <-
  unify substs ((actual :~: expected) : cs)
modify (\info -> info
  { metaVarSubsts = substs'
  , constraints = cs'
  })
clarifyTypedTerm actual
```

Fresh Type Meta Variables

Whenever a fresh type meta variable is created, we take into account all the bound variables present in scope. In other words, we generate a meta variable application with all bound variables as arguments: M$[x_1, \ldots, x_n]$. Note that we could also add all free variables, but in practice that is rarely wanted.

```
freshTypeMetaVar
  :: MonadTypecheck v t a m => m (TFS v t a)
```

Entering and Exiting Scopes

To infer types inside scopes we introduce a couple of helpers. First ,inScope one adds information about the type of a bound variable to the current state before running given computation in scope, then it exits the scope, removing information about the bound variable. Second, we introduce a helper, similar to typeOf, that figures out types for scopes.

```
inScope :: MonadTypecheck v t a m
  => TFS v t a -> m r -> m r

typeOfScope :: MonadTypecheck v t a m
  => TFS v t a
  -> Scope (TFS v t) a -> m (Scope (TFS v t) a)
```

With these helpers we are finally ready to consider implementations of specific type theories.

B Examples

B.1 Simply Typed Lambda Calculus

Here we apply our approach to an implementation of simply typed lambda calculus (STLC) with pairs. We start with a generating bifunctor:

```
data TermF scope term
  = FunF term term            -- Function type: $T_1 \to T_2$
  | LamF (Maybe term) scope   -- Abstraction: $\lambda(x:T_1).T_2$
  | AppF term term            -- Application: $(T_1\ T_2)$
  | PairTyF term term         -- Pair type: $\langle T_1, T_2 \rangle$
  | PairF term term           -- Pair: $\langle T_1, T_2 \rangle$
  | FirstF term               -- First projection: $\pi_1\ T$
  | SecondF term              -- Second projection: $\pi_2\ T$

-- | An STLC term with free variables in a.
type Term a = FS TermF a
```

We note a couple of details about this particular presentation of STLC:

1. We do not have an explicit universe type, as it is introduced automatically with `TyF`.
2. We have an optional type annotation for the bound variable of λ-abstraction. The annotation is optional to illustrate how our type inference mixes with type annotations provided by the user.
3. Both types and terms are generated with `TermF`.

Next step is to introduce helpful pattern synonyms. We will immediately work with typed terms, so we only create patterns for those. We remind that these can be automatically generated using Template Haskell:

```
pattern Typed ty t    = Free (InL (TyF t ty))
pattern FunT ty t1 t2 = Typed ty (FunF t1 t2)
pattern LamT ty body  = Typed ty (LamF body)
pattern AppT ty t1 t2 = Typed ty (AppF t1 t2)
...
```

Using these patterns we implement WHNF reduction for typed STLC terms:

```
instance Reducible TermF where
  reduce = \case
    FirstF t -> case reduce t of
      Pair f _ -> reduce f
      t' -> First t'
    SecondT t -> case reduce t of
      Pair _ s -> reduce s
      t' -> Second t'
    App fun arg -> case reduce fun of
      Lam body -> reduce (substitute arg body)
      fun' -> App fun' arg
    term -> Free (InL term)
```

First-order unification requires `Unifiable` instance, which has a straightforward implementation. Here we show the less trivial case for `LamF`:

```
instance Unifiable TermF where
  zipMatch (LamF ty1 body1) (LamF ty2 body2) = Just (LamF ty (body1, body2))
    where
      ty = case (ty1, ty2) of
        (Nothing, Nothing) -> Nothing
        (Just t1, Just t2) -> Just (t1, t2)
        (Just t, Nothing)  -> Just (t, t)
        (Nothing, Just t)  -> Just (t, t)
  ...
  zipMatch _ _ = Nothing
```

Remark 1. Since the type annotation for the bound variable is optional, it is possible that during unification we have the annotation on the left but not on the right, or vice versa. In this case we intend to keep the type annotation, so we pair it with itself. A more refined version of `Unifiable` type class, such as in Wren Romano's `unification-fd`, could handle this more gracefully, avoiding generating the unnecessary constraint of the form $t \equiv t$.

Next, for higher-order unification we need to establish structural guesses. This boils down to identifying introduction-elimination pairs of syntactic constructions:

```
instance HigherOrderUnifiable TermF where
  guessMetas term = case term of
    AppF f arg -> AppF (f, [LamF ()]) (arg, [])
    -- ^ M[z̄] t  implies  M[z̄] := λx.M'[x, z̄]
    FirstF  t  -> FirstF  (t, [PairF () ()])
    -- ^ π₁ M[z̄]  implies  M[z̄] := ⟨M₁[z̄], M₂[z̄]⟩
    SecondF t  -> SecondF (t, [PairF () ()])
    -- ^ π₂ M[z̄]  implies  M[z̄] := ⟨M₁[z̄], M₂[z̄]⟩
    _ -> bimap (,[]) (,[]) term

  shapes = [ AppF HasHead NoHead
           , FirstF HasHead, SecondF HasHead ]
```

As we mention in Sect. 4.1, the `HigherOrderUnifiable` instance can be automated entirely using either Template Haskell or GHC Generics given `Reducible` instance for the underlying bifunctor.

Finally, for type inference we specify relationships between terms and types:

```
instance Inferable t
  inferF term = case term of
```

To infer types of types, we simply need to check the types of components. For example, for the function type we only have to check that both argument and result types are indeed types:

```
    FunF inferA inferB -> do
      a <- inferA >>= shouldHaveType Universe
      b <- inferB >>= shouldHaveType Universe
      pure (TyF (FunF a b) Universe)
```

Inferring the type of a lambda abstraction requires checking the type annotation if it is exists, inferring the type of the body, and producing the final function type:

```
LamF minferA inferBody -> do
  typeOfArg <- case minferA of
    Just inferA ->
      inferA >>= shouldHaveType Universe
    Nothing -> freshTypeMetaVar
  typedBody <- inScope typeOfArg inferBody
  typeOfBody <-
    typeOfScope typeOfArg typedBody >>= nonDep
  pure $ TyF
    (LamF (typeOfArg <$ minferA) typedBody)
    (SomeType
      (FunT Universe typeOfArg typeOfBody))
```

Note the use of `nonDep`—we have to explicitly limit the inference to make sure that the type of the body does not depend on the variable bound by the lambda abstraction.

For an application term $f\ x$, we have to infer the type F of the function F and the type X of its argument x. Then, if the function type $F \equiv A \to B$, then we simply need to unify argument type X with the expected type A. Otherwise, we need to unify the type of function F with type $X \to M$, where M is a fresh type meta variable:

```
AppF inferFun inferArg -> do
  f <- inferFun   -- f : F
  x <- inferArg   -- x : X
  typeOfApp <- do
    typeOfFun <- typeOf f
    case typeOfFun of
      -- if F ≡ A → B
      FunT _ expected result -> do
        -- then X ≡ A
        shouldHaveType (SomeType expected) x
        return result
      _ -> do  -- otherwise
        result <- freshTypeMetaVar   -- M : U∞
        argType <- typeOf x
        -- F ≡ X → M
        unifyWithExpected typeOfFun
          (mkFun argType result)
        result
  return (TyF (AppF f x) (SomeType typeOfApp))
```

Completing `inferF` for the rest of syntactic constructors in `TermF` is straightforward, and we omit the implementation to save space. After all the preparation we get type inference for simply typed lambda calculus:

```
> t = LamE (LamE (Var (S Z)))   -- λx.λy.y
> infer t
LamT (SomeType
        (FunT Universe (MetaAppT Universe 1 [])
          (FunT Universe (MetaAppT Universe 2 [])
            (MetaAppT Universe 2 []))))
  (LamT (SomeType
          (FunT Universe (MetaAppT Universe 2 [])
            (MetaAppT Universe 2 [])))
    (Var (S Z)))
```

The result above corresponds to the following typed term:

$$\lambda x.(\lambda y.y : (\text{M}_2[] : \mathcal{U}_\infty) \to (\text{M}_2[] : \mathcal{U}_\infty) : \mathcal{U}_\infty)$$
$$: \text{M}_1[] \to ((\text{M}_2[] : \mathcal{U}_\infty) \to (\text{M}_2[] : \mathcal{U}_\infty) : \mathcal{U}_\infty) : \mathcal{U}_\infty \tag{1}$$

Or, omitting the $\mathcal{U}_\infty$ annotations, we get:

$$\lambda x.(\lambda y.y : \text{M}_2[] \to \text{M}_2[]) : \text{M}_1[] \to (\text{M}_2[] \to \text{M}_2[]) \tag{2}$$

Since we mix terms and types of STLC and use dependent type inference engine, our version of STLC has a couple of unique features, differentiating it from a classical STLC:

1. We explicitly prevent the type of body in a lambda abstraction to depend on the argument. For users of STLC this means that they can input terms like $\lambda A.\lambda(x : A).x$ and get a type error saying that the inferred type of $\lambda(x : A).x$, which is $A \to A$ is dependent on the bound variable A, which is not allowed in STLC.
2. We do not forbid computation in types. Indeed, a term $\lambda(f : ((\lambda x.x)A) \to B).fx$ is valid, and we can infer its type to be $(A \to B) \to B$, computing $(\lambda x.x)A \equiv A$ in the process. It is possible to add validation pass to ensure that types only consist of certain syntactic constructions, disallowing non-type terms. However, we see the ability to perform computation in types as a bonus feature for our implementation of STLC.

Overall, we had to write down definitions of `TermF`, implement WHNF reduction for STLC terms in `Reducible` and specify how to infer types in `Inferable`. Everything else could be generated automatically with Template Haskell or GHC Generics. For this fairly little effort we have gotten an implementation of a variation of STLC with type inference and computation available in types .

B.2 Martin-Löf Type Theory

Let us now apply the approach to an actual dependent type theory—intensional Martin-Löf Type Theory (MLTT). We start with a generating bifunctor:

Free Monads, Intrinsic Scoping, and Higher-Order Preunification

```
data TermF scope term
  = UniverseF              -- Universe type: $\mathcal{U}$
  | PiF term scope         -- Dependent product $\Pi_{x:T_1} T_2$
  | LamF scope             -- Abstraction: $\lambda x.T_2$
  | AppF term term         -- Application: $(T_1\ T_2)$
  | SigmaF term scope      -- Dependent sum $\Sigma_{x:T_1} T_2$
  | PairF term term        -- Pair: $\langle T_1, T_2 \rangle$
  | FirstF term            -- First projection: $\pi_1\ T$
  | SecondF term           -- Second projection: $\pi_2\ T$
  | IdTypeF term term term -- Identity type: $x = y$
  | ReflF term             -- Reflexivity: $\mathsf{refl}_T$
  | JF term term term term term term
    -- ^ Identity type eliminator: $\mathsf{J}(A, a, C, d, x, p)$

-- | An MLTT term with free variables in a.
type Term a = FS TermF a
```

Remark 2. Note that in this representation we chose to not have any type annotations for bound variables in abstraction and for the type of terms in the identity type or refl_t. We also note that it might be possible to avoid the term t in the annotation for refl_t as well, since the term t is present in the type $t = t$ of refl and can be inferred in principle.

In this implementation we use a single universe type and assume type-in-type: $\mathcal{U} : \mathcal{U}$. It is possible to introduce a hierarchy of universes $\mathcal{U}_0 : \mathcal{U}_1 : \mathcal{U}_2 : \ldots$ instead by using `UniverseF Natural` constructor.

Similarly to STLC implementation, we expect the relevant pattern synonyms to be written out in a mechanical way or derived automatically. Implementing WHNF reduction for MLTT is straightforward as it only differs from STLC in the use of J-eliminator:

```
instance Reducible TermF where
  reduceL = \case
    JF tA a tC d x p ->
      case reduce p of
        Refl{} -> reduce d
        p'     -> J tA a tC d x p'
    ...
```

For `Unifiable` and `HigherOrderUnifiable` we also rely on a mechanical or automatic derivation and so omit it here to save space. Finally, we define inference for individual syntactic constructions:

```
instance Inferable t where
  inferF term = case term of
```

To avoid infinite type annotations, we set the type of universe to be $\mathcal{U}_\infty$:

```
    UniverseF -> pure (TyF UniverseF Universe)
```

Inferring types for Π-types and Σ-types involves dependent type checking. Given term $\Pi_{x:A}B$, where B is a subterm that may refer to x, we have to check that both $A : \mathcal{U}$ and $B : \mathcal{U}$. Note that since B is in the scope, its inferred type, by default, might also be dependent on x. For example, in the term $\Pi_{x:A}\mathsf{refl}_x$ the algorithm would infer that refl_x has type $x = x$, which captures the variable x. To make sure the body of a Π-type is always a type, we need to unify it with $\mathcal{U}$. But for that we also need to make sure it is not dependent, so we use `nonDep`:

```
PiF inferA inferB -> do
  a <- inferA >>= shouldHaveType Universe
  typeOfA <- typeOf a
  b <- inScope typeOfA inferB
  typeOfB <- typeOfScope typeOfA b >>= nonDep
  typeOfB `shouldHaveType` Universe
  pure (TyF (PiF a b) Universe)
```

Inferring the type for a dependent λ-abstraction is relatively straightforward. We generate a fresh type meta variable for the argument and infer the type of the body. In general, we should check that the inferred type is indeed a type, as many type theories, such as cubical type theory, have multiple universes. That said, in pure MLTT we can omit this check.

```
LamF inferBody -> do
  a <- freshTypeMetaVar
  typedBody <- inScope a inferBody
  b <- typeOfScope a typedBody
  typeOfScope a b >>= nonDep
    >>= shouldHaveType Universe
  pure $ TyF
    (LamF typedBody)
    (SomeType (PiT Universe a b))
```

The rest of syntactic constructors is fairly straightforward to handle similarly. Completing `Inferable` brings dependent type inference to MLTT.

References

1. Abel, A., Pientka, B.: Higher-order dynamic pattern unification for dependent types and records. In: Ong, L. (ed.) TLCA 2011. LNCS, vol. 6690, pp. 10–26. Springer, Heidelberg (2011). https://doi.org/10.1007/978-3-642-21691-6_5
2. Allais, G., Atkey, R., Chapman, J., McBride, C., McKinna, J.: A type and scope safe universe of syntaxes with binding: their semantics and proofs. Proc. ACM Program. Lang. **2**(ICFP) (2018). https://doi.org/10.1145/3236785
3. Altenkirch, T., Reus, B.: Monadic presentations of lambda terms using generalized inductive types. In: Flum, J., Rodriguez-Artalejo, M. (eds.) CSL 1999. LNCS, vol. 1683, pp. 453–468. Springer, Heidelberg (1999). https://doi.org/10.1007/3-540-48168-0_32

4. Axelsson, E., Vezzosi, A.: Lightweight higher-order rewriting in Haskell. In: Serrano, M., Hage, J. (eds.) TFP 2015. LNCS, vol. 9547, pp. 1–21. Springer, Cham (2016). https://doi.org/10.1007/978-3-319-39110-6_1
5. Bellegarde, F., Hook, J.: Substitution: a formal methods case study using monads and transformations. Sci. Comput. Program. **23**(2–3), 287–311 (1994). https://doi.org/10.1016/0167-6423(94)00022-0
6. Bird, R.S., Paterson, R.: De Bruijn notation as a nested datatype. J. Funct. Program. **9**(1), 77–91 (1999). https://doi.org/10.1017/S0956796899003366
7. Chlipala, A.: Parametric higher-order abstract syntax for mechanized semantics. SIGPLAN Not. **43**(9), 143–156 (2008). https://doi.org/10.1145/1411203.1411226
8. Cockx, J.: 1001 Representations of Syntax with Binding (2021). https://jesper.sikanda.be/posts/1001-syntax-representations.html. Accessed 12 Jun 2024
9. Coquand, T., Kinoshita, Y., Nordstrom, B., Takeyama, M.: A simple type-theoretic language: Mini-TT. From Semantics to Computer Science: Essays in Honour of Gilles Kahn (2009). https://doi.org/10.1017/CBO9780511770524.007
10. de Bruijn, N.: Lambda calculus notation with nameless dummies, a tool for automatic formula manipulation, with application to the Church-Rosser theorem. Indagationes Mathematicae (Proceedings) **75**(5), 381–392 (1972). https://doi.org/10.1016/1385-7258(72)90034-0
11. Fiore, M., Hur, C.-K.: Second-order equational logic (extended abstract). In: Dawar, A., Veith, H. (eds.) CSL 2010. LNCS, vol. 6247, pp. 320–335. Springer, Heidelberg (2010). https://doi.org/10.1007/978-3-642-15205-4_26
12. Fiore, M., Szamozvancev, D.: Formal metatheory of second-order abstract syntax. Proc. ACM Program. Lang. **6**(POPL) (2022). https://doi.org/10.1145/3498715
13. Hamana, M.: Theory and practice of second-order rewriting: foundation, evolution, and SOL. In: Nakano, K., Sagonas, K. (eds.) FLOPS 2020. LNCS, vol. 12073, pp. 3–9. Springer, Cham (2020). https://doi.org/10.1007/978-3-030-59025-3_1
14. Huet, G.: A unification algorithm for typed λ-calculus. Theoret. Comput. Sci. **1**(1), 27–57 (1975). https://doi.org/10.1016/0304-3975(75)90011-0
15. Jensen, D.C., Pietrzykowski, T.: Mechanizing ω-order type theory through unification. Theor. Comput. Sci. **3**(2), 123–171 (1976). https://doi.org/10.1016/0304-3975(76)90021-9
16. Kiselyov, O., Shan, C.c., Friedman, D.P., Sabry, A.: Backtracking, interleaving, and terminating monad transformers: (Functional Pearl). SIGPLAN Not. **40**(9), 192–203 (2005).https://doi.org/10.1145/1090189.1086390
17. Kmett, E.: Bound (2015). https://www.schoolofhaskell.com/user/edwardk/bound. Accessed 12 Jun 2024
18. Kudasov, N.: E-unification for second-order abstract syntax. In: Gaboardi, M., van Raamsdonk, F. (eds.) 8th International Conference on Formal Structures for Computation and Deduction (FSCD 2023). Leibniz International Proceedings in Informatics (LIPIcs), vol. 260, pp. 10:1–10:22. Schloss Dagstuhl – Leibniz-Zentrum für Informatik, Dagstuhl, Germany (2023). https://doi.org/10.4230/LIPIcs.FSCD.2023.10
19. Kudasov, N.: Generalising huet-style projections in e-unification for second-order abstract syntax. In: UNIF 2023 - 37th International Workshop on Unification. Veena Ravishankar and Christophe Ringeissen, Rome, Italy (2023). https://inria.hal.science/hal-04128229
20. Liang, S., Hudak, P., Jones, M.: Monad transformers and modular interpreters. In: Proceedings of the 22nd ACM SIGPLAN-SIGACT Symposium on Principles of Programming Languages. POPL '95, New York, NY, USA, pp. 333–343. Association for Computing Machinery (1995). https://doi.org/10.1145/199448.199528

21. Libal, T., Miller, D.: Functions-as-constructors higher-order unification. In: Kesner, D., Pientka, B. (eds.) 1st International Conference on Formal Structures for Computation and Deduction (FSCD 2016). Leibniz International Proceedings in Informatics (LIPIcs), vol. 52, pp. 26:1–26:17. Schloss Dagstuhl–Leibniz-Zentrum fuer Informatik, Dagstuhl, Germany (2016). https://doi.org/10.4230/LIPIcs.FSCD.2016.26
22. Löh, A., McBride, C., Swierstra, W.: A tutorial implementation of a dependently typed lambda calculus. Fundamenta Informaticae **102**, 177–207 (2010). https://doi.org/10.3233/FI-2010-304
23. Maclaurin, D., Radul, A., Paszke, A.: The foil: capture-avoiding substitution with no sharp edges. In: Proceedings of the 34th Symposium on Implementation and Application of Functional Languages. IFL '22, New York, NY, USA. Association for Computing Machinery (2023). https://doi.org/10.1145/3587216.3587224
24. Martin-Löf, P.: Intuitionistic type theory, Studies in proof theory, vol. 1. Bibliopolis (1984)
25. McBride, C.: Epigram: practical programming with dependent types. In: Vene, V., Uustalu, T. (eds.) AFP 2004. LNCS, vol. 3622, pp. 130–170. Springer, Heidelberg (2005). https://doi.org/10.1007/11546382_3
26. Miller, D.: A logic programming language with lambda-abstraction, function variables, and simple unification. In: Schroeder-Heister, P. (ed.) ELP 1989. LNCS, vol. 475, pp. 253–281. Springer, Heidelberg (1991). https://doi.org/10.1007/BFb0038698
27. Parigot, M.: $\lambda\mu$-calculus: an algorithmic interpretation of classical natural deduction. In: Voronkov, A. (ed.) LPAR 1992. LNCS, vol. 624, pp. 190–201. Springer, Heidelberg (1992). https://doi.org/10.1007/BFb0013061
28. Peyton Jones, S., Marlow, S.: Secrets of the Glasgow Haskell Compiler inliner. J. Funct. Program. **12**, 393–434 (2002). https://www.microsoft.com/en-us/research/publication/secrets-of-the-glasgow-haskell-compiler-inliner/
29. Pfenning, F., Elliott, C.: Higher-order abstract syntax. In: Wexelblat, R.L. (ed.) Proceedings of the ACM SIGPLAN'88 Conference on Programming Language Design and Implementation (PLDI), Atlanta, Georgia, USA, June 22–24, 1988, pp. 199–208. ACM (1988). https://doi.org/10.1145/53990.54010
30. Riehl, E., Shulman, M.: A type theory for synthetic ∞-categories. Higher Struct. **1** (2017). https://doi.org/10.21136/HS.2017.06
31. Sheard, T.: Generic unification via two-level types and parameterized modules - functional pearl. SIGPLAN Notices - SIGPLAN **36**, 86–97 (2001). https://doi.org/10.1145/507546.507648
32. Swierstra, W.: Data types à la carte. J. Funct. Program. **18**(4), 423–436 (2008). https://doi.org/10.1017/S0956796808006758
33. Voigtländer, J.: Asymptotic improvement of computations over free monads, pp. 388–403 (2008). https://doi.org/10.1007/978-3-540-70594-9_20
34. Vukmirovic, P., Bentkamp, A., Nummelin, V.: Efficient full higher-order unification. Logical Meth. Comput. Sci. **17**(4) (2021). https://doi.org/10.46298/lmcs-17(4:18)2021
35. Washburn, G., Weirich, S.: Boxes go bananas: encoding higher-order abstract syntax with parametric polymorphism. J. Funct. Program. **18**(1), 87–140 (2008). https://doi.org/10.1017/S0956796807006557

Towards a More Efficient Selection Monad

Johannes Hartmann[1(✉)], Tom Schrijvers[2], and Jeremy Gibbons[1]

[1] Department of Computer Science, University of Oxford, Oxford, UK
{johannes.hartmann,jeremy.gibbons}@cs.ox.ac.uk
[2] Department of Computer Science, KU Leuven, Leuven, Belgium
tom.schrijvers@kuleuven.be

Abstract. This paper explores a novel approach to selection functions through the introduction of a generalised selection monad. The foundation is laid with the conventional selection monad J, defined as $(A \to R) \to A$, together with various combinators for computing new selection functions from old. However, inefficiencies in these combinators are identified. To address these issues, a specialised type K is introduced, and its isomorphism to J is demonstrated. The paper further generalises the K type to G, where performance improvements and enhanced intuitive usability are observed. The embeddings between J and G are established, offering a more efficient and expressive alternative to the well established J type for selection functions. The findings emphasise the advantages of the generalised selection monad and its applicability in diverse scenarios, paving the way for further exploration and optimisation.

Keywords: Selection monad · Functional programming · Algorithm design · Performance Optimisation · Monads

1 Introduction

The selection monad, initially introduced by Paulo Oliva and Martin Escardo [1], serves as a valuable tool for modeling selection-based algorithms in functional programming. Widely explored in the context of sequential games [2], it has been applied to compute solutions for games with perfect information and has found applications in logic and proof theory through the Double-Negation Theorem and the Tychonoff Theorem [2]. Additionally, it has been effectively employed in modeling greedy algorithms [3]. These diverse applications of the selection monad heavily rely on its monadic behavior, particularly emphasising the use of the *sequence* function for monads.

However, within the context of the selection monad, it becomes apparent that the monadic behavior of the selection monad J is needlessly inefficient. This inefficiency is scrutinised in greater detail through the examination of *sequence* function, which redundantly duplicates previously calculated work. To address this, the paper introduces two alternative types, namely K and G, for the selection monad. It establishes that the new K type is isomorphic to the existing J type, conveniently resolving the inefficiency associated with the monadic sequence function. Subsequently, the K type undergoes further generalisation into the G type. The proposition presented in this paper advocates for the adoption of the G type over the traditional J type, citing its efficiency advantages. Additionally, the G type is argued to be more intuitive for programming and, given its broader type, provides enhanced versatility for a wide array of applications involving the selection monad.

The upcoming section delves into the selection monad, with a particular focus on the type: $J_{R,A} : (A \rightarrow R) \rightarrow A$ representing selection functions [1]. The exploration of the *pair* function highlights its ability to compute a new selection function based on criteria from two existing functions. Supported by a practical example involving decision-making scenarios and individuals navigating paths, this section underscores the functionality of selection functions. An analysis of the inefficiencies in the original *pair* function identifies redundant computational work. The paper's primary contribution is outlined: an illustration and proposal for an efficient solution to enhance the performance of the *pair* function. This introductory overview sets the stage for a detailed exploration of the selection monad and subsequent discussions on optimisations.

All examples in this paper are modeled using Haskell.

2 Selection Functions

Consider the type for selection functions introduced by Paulo Oliva and Martin Escardo [1] :

```
type J r a = (a -> r) -> a
```

Now have a look at the following example. Two individuals are walking towards each other on the pavement. A collision is imminent. At this juncture, each individual must decide their next move. This decision-making process can be modeled using selection functions. The decision they need to make is either going towards the street or the wall:

```
data Decision = Street | Wall deriving (Eq, Show)
```

The respective selection functions, given a property function that tells them what decision is acceptable, select the correct one. If there are multiple optimal solutions, they select an arbitrary one. And if there is no correct one, they default to walking towards the wall.

```
s :: J Bool Decision
s p = if p Street then Street else Wall
```

When given two selection functions, a *pair* function can be defined to compute a new selection function. This resultant function selects a pair based on the criteria established by the two given selection functions:

```
pair :: J r a -> J r b -> J r (a,b)
pair f g p = (a,b)
```

```
  where
    a = f (\x -> p (x, g (\y -> p (x,y))))
    b = g (\y -> p (a,y))
```

To apply the *pair* function, a property function *pred* is needed that will judge two decisions and return $True$ if a crash is avoided and $False$ otherwise.

```
pred :: (Decision, Decision) -> Bool
pred (d1, d2) = d1 /= d2
```

The *pair* function, merges the two selection functions into a new one that calculates an overall optimal decision.

```
ghci> pair s s pred
(Street,Wall)
```

Examining how the *pair* function is defined reveals that the first element a of the pair is determined by applying the initial selection function f to a newly constructed property function. Intuitively, selection functions can be conceptualised as entities containing a collection of objects, waiting for a property function to assess their underlying elements. Once equipped with a property function, they can apply it to their elements and select an optimal one.

Considering the types assigned to selection functions, it is evident that an initial selection function f remains in anticipation of a property function of type $(A \to R)$ to determine an optimal A. The *pair* function is endowed with a property function p of type $((A, B) \to R)$. By using this property function, a property function for f can be derived by using the second selection function g to select a corresponding B and subsequently applying p to assess (A, B) pairs as follows: $(\lambda x \to p(x, g(\lambda y \to p(x, y))))$. Upon the determination of an optimal A, a corresponding B can then be computed as $g(\lambda y \to p(a, y))$. In this case, the *pair* function can be conceptualised as a function that constructs all possible combinations of elements within the provided selection function and subsequently identifies the overall optimal one. It might feel intuitive to consider the following modified *pair* function that seems to be more symmetric.

```
pair' :: J r a -> J r b -> J r (a,b)
pair' f g p = (a,b)
  where
    a = f (\x -> p (x, g (\y -> p (x,y))))
    b = g (\y -> p (f (\x -> p (x,y)), y))
```

However, applying this modified *pair'* to our previous example this results in a overall non optimal solution.

```
ghci> pair' p1 p2 pred
(Wall,Wall)
```

This illustrates how the original *pair* function keeps track of its first decision when determining its second element. It is noteworthy that, in the example, achieving a satisfying outcome for both pedestrians is only possible when they consider the direction the other one is heading. The specific destination does not matter, as long as they are moving in different directions. Consequently, the original *pair* function can be conceived as a function that selects the optimal solution while retaining awareness of previous solutions, whereas our modified *pair'* does not.

An issue with the original *pair* function might have been identified by the attentive reader. There is redundant computational work involved. Initially, all possible pairs are constructed to determine an optimal first element A, but the corresponding B that renders it an overall optimal solution is overlooked, resulting in only A being returned. Subsequently, the optimal B is recalculated based on the already determined optimal A when selecting the second element of the pair. The primary contribution of this paper will be to illustrate and propose a solution to this inefficiency.

2.1 Sequence

The generalisation of the *pair* function to accommodate a sequence of selection functions is the initial focus of exploration. In the context of selection functions, a *sequence* operation is introduced, capable of combining a list of selection functions into a singular selection function that, in turn, selects a list of objects [2]:

```
sequence  :: [J r a] -> J r [a]
sequence [] p      = []
sequence (e:es) p = a : as
  where
    a  = e (\x -> p (x : sequence es (p . (x:))))
    as = sequence es (p . (a:))
```

Here, similar to the *pair* function, the sequence function extracts elements for the resulting list through the corresponding selection functions. This extraction is achieved by applying each function to a newly constructed property function that possesses the capability to foresee the future, thereby constructing an optimal future based on the currently examined element.

However, a notable inefficiency persists, exacerbating the issue observed in the *pair* function. During the determination of the first element, the *sequence* function calculates an optimal remainder of the list, only to overlook it and redundantly perform the same calculation for subsequent elements. This inefficiency in *sequence* warrants further investigation for potential optimisation in subsequent sections of this paper.

2.2 Selection Monad J

The formation of a monad within the selection functions unfolds as follows [1]:

```
(>>=) :: J r a -> (a -> J r b) -> J r b
(>>=) e f p = f (e (p . flip f p)) p
```

```
return :: a -> J r a
return x p = x
```

These definitions illustrate the monadic structure inherent in selection functions. The Haskell standard library already incorporates a built-in function for monads, here referred to as *sequence'*, defined as:

```
sequence' :: [J r a] -> J r [a]
sequence' []        = return []
sequence' (ma:mas)  = ma >>=
                      \x -> sequence' mas >>=
                      \xs -> return (x:xs)
```

Notably, in the case of the selection monad, this built-in *sequence'* function aligns with the earlier provided *sequence* implementation specific to the *J* type.

2.3 Illustration of Sequence in the Context of Selection Functions

To illustrate the application of the *sequence* function within the domain of selection functions, consider a practical scenario [3]: the task of cracking a secret password. In this hypothetical situation, a black box property function *p* is provided that returns whether the correct password is entered. Additionally, knowledge is assumed that the password is six characters long. Consider the following example:

```
p :: String -> Bool
p "secret" = True
p _        = False
```

Suppose access is available to a *maxWith* function that given a list of *A* values, returns the *A* value that produces a maximum *R* value through a given property function *p* of type $A \to R$. It is defined as:

```
maxWith :: Ord r => [a] -> J r a
maxWith xs p = snd (maximumBy (compare `on` fst)
                              (map (\x -> (p x , x)) xs))
```

With these resources, a selection function denoted as *selectChar* can be constructed, which, given a property function that evaluates each character, selects a single character satisfying the specified property function:

```
selectChar :: J Bool Char
selectChar = maxWith ['a'..'z']
```

It's worth noting that the use of *maxWith* is facilitated by the ordered nature of booleans in Haskell, where *True* is considered greater than *False*. Leveraging this selection function, the sequence function can be employed on a list comprising six identical copies of *selectChar* to successfully crack the secret password. Each instance of the selection function focuses on a specific character of the secret password:

```
ghci> sequence (replicate 6 selectChar) p
"secret"
```

This illustrative example is showcasing the application of the *sequence* function on a real-world problem like cracking a password. Notably, there is no need to explicitly specify a property function for judging individual characters; rather, this property function is constructed within the monads bind definition, and its utilisation is facilitated through the application of the *sequence* function. Additionally, attention should be drawn to the fact that this example involves redundant calculations. After determining the first character of the secret password, the system overlooks the prior computation of the entire password and initiates the calculation anew for subsequent characters.

2.4 Efficiency Issues

Lets examine this inefficiency in more detail. When the *sequence* function is used by the selection monad, an exhaustive search of all possible combinations of the values underlying the selection functions is executed. For the analisys of this inefficiency it is assumed that the $maxWith$ function precisely applies the property function p once to each of its elements. The efficiency of the *sequence* function is scrutinised to determine how often the property function p is invoked during the calculation of a solution.

Given that *sequence* operates as an exhaustive search resembling a tree search with a branching factor of K, the number of times the property function p is called for a tree of depth n can be expressed as $T(n) = F(n) + T(n-1)$, where $F(n) = K * T(n-1)$. Substituting $F(n)$ into $T(n)$ yields $T(n) = K * T(n-1) + T(n-1)$. This simplifies to $T(n) = (K+1)^n$. While an exhaustive search on a tree can be performed with K^n calls of p, the *sequence* function duplicates some of the work by forgetting previously computed results.

To address this specific inefficiency within the selection monad, concerning the pair and sequence functions, two new variations of the selection monad will be introduced. Initially, an examination of a new special K type will reveal its isomorphism to the selection monad J. Subsequently, an exploration of the generalisation of this K type to the G type will be presented with a view to enhancing its intuitive usability. Remarkably, it will be demonstrated that the J monad can be embedded into this general G type.

3 Special K

The following type K is to be considered:

```
type K r a = forall b. (a -> (r,b)) -> b
```

Selection functions of type J are in anticipation of a property function capable of judging their underlying elements, and a similar operation is performed by the new K type. The property function of the K type also assesses its elements by transforming them into R values. Additionally, it converts the A into any B and returns that B along with its judgment R.

```
pairK :: K r a -> K r b -> K r (a,b)
pairK f g p = f (\x ->
                g (\y -> let (r, z) = p (x,y)
                         in (r, (r,z))))
```

The previously mentioned inefficiency is now addressed by the definition of *pairK*. This is achieved by examining every element x in the selection function f. For each element, a corresponding result is extracted from the second selection function g. Utilising the additional flexibility provided by the new K type, the property function for g is now constructed differently. Instead of merely returning the result z along with the corresponding R value, a duplicate of the entire result pair calculated by p is generated and returned. As this duplicate already represents the complete solution, the entire result for an optimal x can now be straightforwardly yielded by f, eliminating the need for additional computations.

The *sequenceK* for this special K type can be defined as follows:

```
sequenceK :: [K r a] -> K r [a]
sequenceK [] p       = (snd . p) []
sequenceK (e:es) p = e (\x -> sequenceK es
                       (\xs -> let (r,y) = p (x:xs)
                               in (r,(r,y))))
```

This *sequenceK* implementation employs the same strategy as the earlier *pairK* function. It essentially generates duplicates of the entire solution pair, returning these in place of the result value. The selection function one layer above then unpacks the result pair, allowing the entire solution to be propagated. The efficiency issues previously outlined are addressed by these novel *pairK* and *sequenceK* functions. It will be further demonstrated that this K type is isomorphic to the preceding J type. This essentially empowers the transformation of every problem previously solved with the J type into the world of the K type. Subsequently, the solutions can be computed more efficiently before being transformed back to express them in terms of J.

3.1 Special K Is Isomorphic To J

To demonstrate the isomorphism between the new Special K type and the J type, two operators are introduced for transforming from one type to the other:

```
j2k :: J r a -> K r a
j2k f p = snd (p (f (fst . p)))
```

When provided with a selection function $f : J_{R,A}$, the *j2k* operator constructs an entity of type $K_{R,A}$. For a given f of type $(A \to R) \to A$ and p of type $\forall B.(A \to (R, B))$, the objective is to return an entity of type B. This is achieved by initially extracting an A from f using the constructed property function $(fst \circ p)$. Subsequently, p is applied to A, yielding an (R, B) pair, from which the B is obtained by applying *snd* to the pair.

The transformation of a selection function of type K into a selection function of type J is accomplished as follows:

```
k2j :: K r a -> J r a
k2j f p = f (\x -> (p x, x))
```

Given a selection function f of type $\forall B.(A \to (R, B)) \to B$ and a p of type $(A \to R) \to A$, an A can be directly extracted from f by constructing a property function that utilises p to obtain an R value while leaving the corresponding x of type A untouched. To validate that these two operators indeed establish an isomorphism between $J_{R,A}$ and $K_{R,A}$, the following equations must be proven: $(k2j \circ j2k)f = f$ and $(j2k \circ k2j)g = g$.

Proof (J to K Embedding).

$$(k2j \circ j2k)f$$
$= \{ \text{Apply definitions} \}$
$$(\lambda g\, p_2 \to g(\lambda x \to (p_2\, x, x)))(\lambda p_1 \to snd(p_1(f(fst \circ p_1))))$$
$= \{ \text{Simplify} \}$
$$f$$

The proof utilises the direct application of lambda expressions and the definitions of fst and snd for simplification. The proof for the second isomorphism involves the initial requires the use of the free for the special K type [5]:

Theorem 1 (Free Theorem for K). *Given the following functions with their corresponding types:*

$g : K_{R,A}$
$h : B_1 \to B_2$
$p : A \to (R, B_1)$
$*** : (A \to A') \to (B \to B') \to (A, B) \to (A', B')$

It follows:
$$h(g\, p) = g((id *** h) \circ p)$$

where $***$ is the obvious operator.

The free theorem essentially asserts that a function h of type $B_1 \to B_2$, when applied to the result of a selection function, can also be incorporated into the property function and applied to each individual element. This follows from the generalised type of K, where the only means of generating B_1 values is through the application of p. Therefore, it becomes inconsequential whether h is applied to the final result or to each individual intermediate result. Note that $***$ is the operator that given two functions $f : A \to A'$ and $g : B \to B'$ returns a function of type $(A, B) \to (A', B')$, where f is applied to the first element of the tuple and g is applied to the second element of the tuple.

With the free theorem for K, the remaining portion of the isomorphism can now be demonstrated as follows:

Proof (K to J Embedding). The equality $(j2k \circ k2j)g = g$ is established through the following steps:

$$(j2k \circ k2j)g$$
$$= \{ \text{ Apply definitions and simplify } \}$$
$$\lambda p \to snd(p(g(\lambda x \to ((fst \circ p)x, x))))$$
$$= \{ \text{ Free Theorem for } K \}$$
$$\lambda p \to g(\lambda x \to ((fst \circ p)x, (snd \circ p)x))$$
$$= \{ \text{ Simplify } \}$$
$$g$$

The monad definitions and *sequence* definition for the new K type can be derived from this isomorphism. While the definition of K achieves the desired performance improvements, it necessitates significant copying of data structures, which are subsequently deconstructed and discarded at a higher layer. This necessity significantly complicates the associated definitions for *sequence* and *pair*, making them challenging to handle and less intuitive.

For these reasons, we will now introduce another type G, which returns the entire tuple rather than merely the result value, appears more intuitive. This shift is elaborated upon in the following section, where G is observed to facilitate similar performance improvements while simplifying the definitions. This method also removes the need for unnecessary data copying. Nevertheless, it is disclosed that G is not isomorphic to J and K but rather these can be embedded into G. In contrast, an investigation into a specific precondition allowing for G to be embedded into J or K is presented.

4 General G

Consider the more general type G, derived from the previous special K type:

```
type G r a = forall b. (a -> (r,b)) -> (r,b)
```

Unlike its predecessor, G returns the entire pair produced by the property function, rather than just the result value. The implementation of *pairG* for the new G type no longer necessitates the creation of a copy of the data structure. It suffices to return the result of the property function's application to the complete pair:

```
pairG :: G r a -> G r b -> G r (a,b)
pairG f g p = f (\x -> g (\y -> p (x,y)))
```

In terms of readability, the definition of *pairG* is significantly more concise, with the essence of the *pair* function being conveyed without unnecessary boilerplate code. Every element x of type A within f is inspected and evaluated by the given property function p for all y of type B within g. The optimal pair of (A, B) values is returned by the resulting pair selection function according to the provided property function. Furthermore, *sequenceG* is defined as follows:

```
sequenceG :: [G r a] -> G r [a]
sequenceG [] p     = p []
sequenceG (e:es) p = e (\x -> sequenceG es
                             (\xs -> p (x:xs)))
```

Following a similar pattern, this *sequenceG* function builds all possible futures for each element within e. Once an optimal list of elements is found, this list is simply returned along with the corresponding R value.

4.1 Relationship Between General G and Special K

With the following operators, selection functions of type K can be embedded into G.

```
g2k :: G r a -> K r a
g2k f = snd . f

k2g :: K r a -> G r a
k2g f p = f (\x -> let (r,y) = p x in (r, (r,y)))
```

Similar to the free theorem for the K type, it is equally possible to derive the free theorem [5] for the new G type:

Theorem 2 (Free Theorem for G). *Given the following functions with their corresponding types:*

$g : G_{R,A}$
$f : B_1 \to B_2$
$p : A \to (R, B_1)$
$*** : (A \to A') \to (B \to B') \to (A, B) \to (A', B')$

It follows:

$$((id *** f) \circ g)p = g((id *** f) \circ p)$$

where $***$ is the obvious operator.

This theorem communicates a concept similar to the free theorem for K. It suggests that the outcome remains unchanged whether a function f is applied directly to the final result of a selection function or within the selection function's property function. This idea is now adapted to include the behavior of the G type, which also returns the R value.

By using the free theorem for G, it becomes clear that selection functions designed for the K type can be directly embedded into the G structure:

Theorem 3 (K to G Embedding). *Given:*
$f : K_{R,A}$
The following embedding of f into G follows:

$$(k2g \circ g2k)f = f$$

The proof for this embedding is straight forward utilising the free theorem for G:

Proof (K to G Embedding). Assuming that for:
$$f : K_{R,A}$$
It can be reasoned:

$\quad (g2k \circ k2g)f$
$= \quad \{$ Definitions and rewrite $\}$
$\quad \lambda p \rightarrow (snd \circ f)(\lambda x \rightarrow \text{ let } (r,y) = p\,x \text{ in } (r,(r,y)))$
$= \quad \{$ Free theorem of G $\}$
$\quad \lambda p \rightarrow f(\lambda x \rightarrow \text{ let } (r,y) = p\,x \text{ in } (r, snd(r,y)))$
$= \quad \{$ Simplify $\}$
$\quad f$

Further, to establish that selection functions of type G can be embedded into the K type a specific precondition is introduced, under which this embedding is possible:

Theorem 4 (G to K Embedding). *Assuming that for:*
$$g : G_{R,A}$$
$$\forall p : \forall B.A \rightarrow (R,B), \exists x : A \text{ such that: } g\,p = p\,x$$
It follows:
$$(k2g \circ g2k)g = g$$

The essential condition is that the selection function g should not modify the R value after p has been applied to its elements. Given this precondition, the embedding can be proven as follows:

Proof (G to K Embedding). It can be reasoned:

$\quad (k2g \circ g2k)g$
$= \quad \{$ Definitions and rewrite $\}$
$\quad \lambda p \rightarrow snd(g(\lambda x \rightarrow \text{ let } (r,y) = p\,x \text{ in } (r,(r,y))))$
$= \quad \{$ Assumption $\}$
$\quad \lambda p \rightarrow snd(\exists x. \text{ let } (r,y) = p\,x \text{ in } (r,(r,y)))$
$= \quad \{$ Exists commutes $\}$
$\quad \lambda p \rightarrow \exists x. \text{ let } (r,y) = p\,x \text{ in } snd(r,(r,y))$
$= \quad \{$ Assumption $\}$
$\quad \lambda p \rightarrow g(\lambda x \rightarrow \text{ let } (r,y) = p\,x \text{ in } snd(r,(r,y)))$
$= \quad \{$ Simplify $\}$
$\quad g$

5 G Forms a Monad

The formation of the monad for G follows a straightforward definition:

```
bindG :: G r a -> (a -> G r b) -> G r b
bindG e f p = e (\x -> f x p)
```

Each element x of type A underlying e is assesed by using f. This process yields a pair consisting of the R value, which serves as the basis for judgment, and the result value of type C. As the pair is already of the correct type, a straightforward return suffices. The return for the G type is defined as follows:

```
returnG :: a -> G r a
returnG x p = p x
```

The proofs substantiating the monad laws may be found in the appendix. Exploring the alignment of these monad definitions with those of J or K, respectively, is our next objective. The aim is to ensure that the behavior of the G monad aligns with that of the J and K monads. Therefore, consider the following two operators that transform between G selection functions and J selection functions:

```
j2g :: J r a -> G r a
j2g f p = p (f (fst . p))

g2j :: G r a -> J r a
g2j f p = snd (f (\x -> (p x, x)))
```

Utilising these operators, it can be shown that the G monad definition aligns with the J monad definition in the case that the G selection functions fulfill the previously introduced precondition for the embedding. This is achieved by proving the following theorem:

Theorem 5 (G Monad Embedding). *Given:*
  $f : G_{R,A}$
  $g : a \to G_{R,B}$
  $\forall p : \forall B. A \to (R, B), \exists x : A$ *such that:* $g\,p = p\,x$
It follows:
$$j2g(g2j\ f \ggg g2j \circ g) = bindG\,f\,g$$

To derive the monad definitions from the embedding operators, it is convenient to introduce the following two lemmas:

Lemma 1. *Given:*
  $f : (R, B_1) \to (R, B_2)$
  $g : G_{R,A}$
  $p : A \to (R, B_1)$
It follows:
$$fst \circ f \circ p = fst \circ p \implies (f \circ g)p = g(f \circ p)$$

This lemma asserts that given a function f acting upon the result of a selection function of type $G_{R,A}$, it is possible to apply f to each element of $G_{R,A}$ within the property function, provided f solely transforms the B value without affecting the R value.

Proof (Lemma 1). Assuming that for:
  (1) $f : (R, B_1) \to (R, B_2), g : G_{R,A}, p : A \to (R, B_1)$
  (2) $\forall p : \forall B. A \to (R, B), \exists x : A$ such that $g\, p = p\, x$
  (3) $fst \circ f \circ p = fst \circ p$
It can be reasoned:

$\quad f(g\, p)$
$= \quad \{$ Assumption (2) $\}$
$\quad \exists x. f(p\, x)$
$= \quad \{$ Rewrite as tuple $\}$
$\quad \exists x.((fst \circ f \circ p)x, (snd \circ f \circ p)x)$
$= \quad \{$ Assumption (3) $\}$
$\quad \exists x.((fst \circ p)x, (snd \circ f \circ p)x)$
$= \quad \{$ Rewrite as lambda $\}$
$\quad \exists x.(\lambda(r, y) \to (r, (snd \circ f)(r, y)))p\, x$
$= \quad \{$ Assumption (2) $\}$
$\quad (\lambda(r, y) \to (r, (snd \circ f)(r, y)))g\, p$
$= \quad \{$ Free Theorem for G $\}$
$\quad g((\lambda(r, y) \to (r, (snd \circ f)(r, y))) \circ p)$
$= \quad \{$ Rewrite $\}$
$\quad g(\lambda x \to ((fst \circ p)x, (snd \circ f \circ p)x))$
$= \quad \{$ Assumption (3) $\}$
$\quad g(\lambda x \to ((fst \circ f \circ p)x, (snd \circ f \circ p)x))$
$= \quad \{$ Simplify $\}$
$\quad g(f \circ p)$

To further simplify the calculation the following lemma is introduced:

Lemma 2. *Let q be a function that applies p to obtain the R value while preserving the original value. If this original value is subsequently utilised to compute the (R, Z) values using p, then g can be invoked directly with p.*
Given:
  $p :: A \to (R, B)$
  $g :: K_{R,A}$

It follows:

$$(p \circ snd)(g\, q) = g\, p \text{ where } q = \lambda x \to ((fst \circ p)x, x)$$

To prove Lemma 2, Lemma 1 is utilised:

Proof (Lemma 2).

$(p \circ snd)(g\ q)$
$=$ { Definition of q }
$(p \circ snd)(g\ (\lambda x \to ((fst \circ p)x, x)))$
$=$ { Lemma 1 }
$g(\lambda x \to (p \circ snd)((fst \circ p)x, x))$
$=$ { Simplify }
$g\ p$

To apply Lemma 1, the following condition from Lemma 1 must be fulfilled:

$(fst \circ p \circ snd)(\lambda x \to ((fst \circ p)x, x))$
$=$ { Simplify }
$\lambda y \to (fst(p(snd((\lambda x \to ((fst \circ p)x, x))y))))$
$=$ { Simplify }
$\lambda y \to (fst(p(snd((fst \circ p)y, y))))$
$=$ { Simplify }
$\lambda x \to (fst \circ p)x$
$=$ { Simplify }
$fst \circ (\lambda x \to ((fst \circ p)x, x))$

Now it is possible calculate the $bindG$ implementation for G with the $j2g$ and $g2j$ operators and the previously introduced theorems:

Proof (G Monad behaves similar to J).

$j2g(g2j\ f \ggg g2j \circ g)$
$=$ { Definition of $J_{\ggg}$ }
$j2g((\lambda f\ g\ p \to g(f(p \circ flip\ g\ p))p)(g2j\ f)(g2j \circ g))$
$=$ { simplify }
$j2g(\lambda p \to g2j(g(g2j\ f(p \circ (\lambda x \to g2j(g\ x)p))))p)$
$=$ { Definition of j2k and rewrite }
$\lambda p \to p(g2j(g(g2jf(\lambda x \to fst((p \circ snd)((g\ x)(\lambda x \to ((fst \circ p)x, x)))))))$
$(fst \circ p))$
$=$ { Lemma 1 }
$\lambda p \to p(g2j(g(g2jf(\lambda x \to fst(((g\ x)(\lambda x \to (p \circ snd)((fst \circ p)x, x)))))))$
$(fst \circ p))$
$=$ { Definition of j2g and rewrite }
$\lambda p \to p(snd(g(snd(f(\lambda x \to (fst(g\ x\ p), x))))(\lambda x \to ((fst \circ p)x, x))))$
$=$ { Lemma 2 }
$\lambda p \to g(snd(f(\lambda x \to (fst(g\ x\ p), x))))p$
$=$ { Rewrite }
$\lambda p \to (\lambda y \to g(snd\ y)p)(f(\lambda x \to (fst(g\ x\ p), x)))$
$=$ { Lemma 1 }
$\lambda p \to f((\lambda y \to g(snd\ y)p) \circ (\lambda x \to (fst(g\ x\ p), x)))$
$=$ { Simplify }

$$\lambda p \to f(\lambda x \to g\ x\ p)$$

This shows that all G selection functions fulfilling the precondition behave the same when transformed to K or J selection functions.

6 Performance Analysis

In this section, the performance of the J, K, and G monads will be compared. All three are designed to perform an exhaustive search, exploring the complete problem space to select the best possible solution. The comparison will focus on the number of calls to the property function p, as well as the time taken for each of the monads to calculate a solution.

Given the following $maxWith$ functions for each of the monad types:

```
maxWithJ :: Ord r => [a] -> J r a
maxWithJ xs f = snd (maximumBy (compare `on` fst)
                    (map (\x -> (f x , x)) xs))

maxWithK :: Ord r => [a] -> K r a
maxWithK xs f =
snd (maximumBy (compare `on` fst) (map f xs))

maxWithG :: Ord r => [a] -> G r a
maxWithG xs f = maximumBy (compare `on` fst) (map f xs)
```

6.1 Runtime Analysis

Initially, the runtime, while exploring a particular search space for each type, will be compared. For this purpose, the following basic property functions will be utilised. These functions simply sum up the elements of a given list of integers.

```
pJ :: [Int] -> Int
pJ = sum

pK :: [Int] -> (Int, [Int])
pK x = (sum x, x)
```

A list of selection functions for each type is further defined. A list of integers is searched by each individual selection function, which then selects the integer that will maximise a given property function.

```
js :: [J Int Int]
js = replicate 6 (maxWithJ [1..10])

ks :: [K Int Int]
ks = replicate 6 (maxWithK [1..10])

gs :: [G Int Int]
gs = replicate 6 (maxWithG [1..10])
```

Considering a list of selection functions with a length of 6, where each selection function explores 10 possible elements, the search space size is 10^6. This search space can be conceptualised as a tree with a depth n of 6 and a branching factor K of 10. By employing the respective *sequence* function for each type, along with the corresponding property function, an initial analysis of runtime and space complexity was conducted within GHCi.

```
ghci> sequence js pJ
[10,10,10,10,10,10]
(3.69 secs, 1,612,913,328 bytes)

ghci> sequenceK ks pK
[10,10,10,10,10,10]
(2.85 secs, 2,431,196,064 bytes)

ghci> sequenceG gs pK
(60,[10,10,10,10,10,10])
(1.56 secs, 869,778,256 bytes)
```

The results obtained from GHCi already demonstrate a significant improvement in performance for the G and K monad. It further highlights the space efficiency of the G monad over the J and K monad, while further showing the significant memory overhead of the K type, that is due to the nested duplications of the final solution.

For a more robust performance analysis, the runtime of each type was tested with increasing depth of the search tree, i.e., longer lists of selection functions. This analysis was performed on the compiled version of the code with the -O2 optimisation flag enabled to utilise any potential performance improvements the compiler offers.

Figure 1 plots the runtime of the compiled Haskell code for each monad J, K, and G as they navigate an increasingly complex search space. The graph demonstrates a consistent trend where the G monad outperforms the others J and K types. As the depth of the search tree increases, the gap in performance becomes even more pronounced, clearly showcasing the efficiency and effectiveness of the generalised selection monad approach.

Additionally, by employing Haskell's trace debug option, the frequency with which the property function was invoked for each monad was tallied. Through this method, verification was achieved that for the J monad, its property function is indeed called $(K+1)^n$ times. Conversely, owing to the performance enhancements, the K and G monads necessitate only K^n calls to their property function, where K represents the branching factor and n the depth of the search tree being explored.

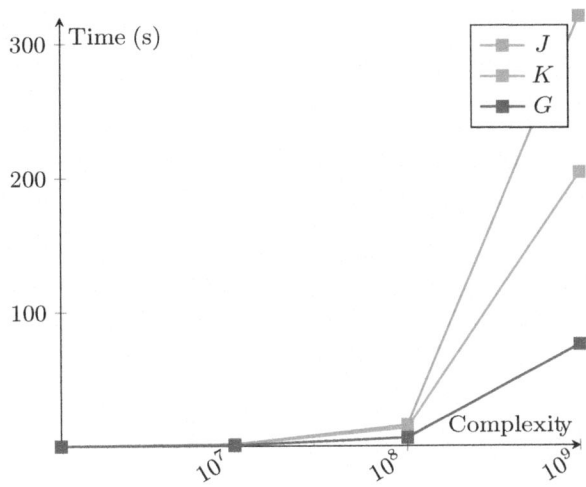

Fig. 1. Runtime of J, K, and G with increasing complexity

7 Related and Future Work

The exploration of the selection monad, particularly the J type, has been predominantly focused on sequential games with total information [2]. This line of research has primarily employed a minimax algorithm to calculate optimal strategies for these games, showcasing the utility of the J monad in navigating complex decision-making processes. Beyond this, the selection monad's applications have extended into logic, proof theory [2], and algorithm design. Notably, within algorithm design, the J monad can also be utilised in modeling greedy algorithms [3].

When considering the implementation of greedy algorithms via the J monad, it is important to acknowledge that the performance optimisations proposed in this paper do not extend to these algorithms. The reason is that the greedy algorithm approach is already optimal when applied through the J type, without unnecessarily duplicating any computations. However, this revelation paves the way for further research into the modeling of greedy algorithms using the new G type. Investigating this could determine if the efficiencies intrinsic to the G monad might present any benefits for greedy algorithms, given their already optimal performance under the J type.

Jules Hedges contributions have laid a solid foundation in understanding the monad transformer for the conventional J selection monad [4]. This work has illuminated the potential for integrating selection functions into more intricate computational constructs. Future research should consider extending these insights to the G type through the development of a corresponding monad transformer. Such endeavors could reveal new applications, potentially enhancing the computational efficiency and expressiveness of functional programming paradigms that leverage selection monads.

The advent of the G type marks a progression by mitigating redundant computations, thus yielding performance enhancements in specific scenarios. Nonetheless, it is imperative to maintain a measured perspective on the impact of these advancements. The efficiency improvements offered by the G monad do not tackle the intrinsic challenge of exponential time complexity that is a hallmark of exhaustive search strategies. Although reducing unnecessary computations is a noteworthy optimisation, the broader issue of exhaustive search strategies' computational demands remains largely unchanged. Future research might explore the feasibility of incorporating alpha-beta pruning into the minimax algorithm, potentially offering a strategy to mitigate the computational intensity of exhaustive searches.

8 Conclusion

This paper presents a compelling case for the adoption of the new general selection monad type G over the conventional J type in the realm of functional programming, particularly within the context of selection functions. The introduction of the G monad marks a significant advancement in the field, offering not only performance improvements but also a more intuitive and practical approach to monad, pair, and sequence implementations.

The core argument for transitioning to the G monad stems from its utility and intuitive nature, which, though it may require a slight learning curve, ultimately provides a more efficient and user-friendly programming experience. The performance enhancements associated with the G monad are not merely theoretical but have practical implications for the execution of complex algorithms and the overall computational efficiency.

Furthermore, the G monad's design facilitates a more intuitive understanding and implementation of monad, pair, and sequence constructs for selection functions, which are central to functional programming paradigms. This intuitiveness, coupled with the performance gains, makes the G type an attractive alternative to the J type.

A pivotal finding of this research is that all G constructs meeting the specific precondition can be seamlessly embedded into the J type. This implies that any model or algorithm previously framed within the J type can be transitioned to, or represented in, the G framework without loss of functionality. Consequently, it is advocated that future research and development in the selection monad domain pivot towards the G type. This shift is recommended not only because of the aforementioned performance and usability benefits but also to harness the full potential of the G type's more advanced and efficient approach to handling selection functions.

In light of these findings, it is proposed that ongoing and future work in the selection monad sphere should utilise the advantages of the presented G type. This involves translating existing work from the J framework to the G framework, thus leveraging the G type's advantages to foster a more efficient, intuitive, and robust functional programming environment. The transition to the G type represents a forward-thinking approach to functional programming, promising improvements in both the development and execution of complex computational tasks.

Appendix

Proof Monad Laws for G

Proof (Left identity).

```
  return a >>= h
= (flip ($)) a >>= h
= (\p -> p a) >>= h
= \p' -> (\p -> p a) ((flip h) p')
= \p' -> ((flip h) p') a
= \p' -> h a p'
= h a
```

Proof (Right identity).

```
  m >>= return
= \p -> m ((flip return) p)
= \p -> m ((flip (flip ($))) p)
= \p -> m (($) p)
= \p -> m p
= m
```

Proof (Associativity).

```
  (m >>= g) >>= h
= \p -> (m >>= g) ((flip h) p)
= \p -> (\p' -> m ((flip g) p')) ((flip h) p)
= \p -> (m ((flip g) ((flip h) p)))
= \p -> m ((\y x -> g x y) ((flip h) p))
= \p -> m ((\x -> g x ((flip h) p)))
= \p -> m ((\p' x -> (g x) ((flip h) p')) p)
= \p -> m ((flip (\x p' -> (g x) ((flip h) p'))) p)
= \p -> m ((flip (\x -> (\p' -> (g x) ((flip h) p')))) p)
= \p -> m ((flip (\x -> g x >>= h)) p)
= m >>= (\x -> g x >>= h)
```

References

1. Escardó, M., Oliva, P.: Selection functions, bar recursion and backward induction. Math. Struct. Comput. Sci. **20**(2), 127–168 (2010)
2. Escardó, M., Oliva, P.: What sequential games, the Tychonoff Theorem and the double-negation shift have in common. In: Proceedings of the third ACM SIGPLAN workshop on Mathematically Structured Functional Programming, pp. 21–32 (2010)

3. Hartmann, J., Gibbons, J.: Algorithm design with the selection monad. In: Swierstra, W., Wu, N. (eds.) Trends in Functional Programming: 23rd International Symposium, TFP 2022, Virtual Event, March 17–18, 2022, Revised Selected Papers, pp. 126–143. Springer International Publishing, Cham (2022). https://doi.org/10.1007/978-3-031-21314-4_7
4. Hedges, J.: Monad transformers for backtracking search. In: Levy, P.B., Krishnaswami, N. (eds.) Mathematically Structured Functional Programming. EPTCS, vol. 153, pp. 31–50 (2014)
5. Wadler, P.: Theorems for free! In: Proceedings of the Fourth International Conference on Functional Programming Languages and Computer Architecture, pp. 347–359 (1989)

Compositional Views in Compositional Images – Category: Research –

Peter Achten(✉) and Pieter Koopman

Institute for Computing and Information Sciences, Radboud University Nijmegen,
Nijmegen, The Netherlands
{P.Achten,pieter}@cs.ru.nl

Abstract. The iTask SVG Image library uses a combinator approach to specify the layout of graphical elements. These graphics can be made interactive, by associating callback functions with images. The type system is used to make sure that the callback functions operate on view-model values of the correct type. A long-standing open problem with the library is how to deal with interactive images that work on different view-model values. This is a highly desirable feature because it allows code reuse and modularization. A solution should not 'pollute' the set of image combinators with view-model plumbing combinators. It should also not alter the design philosophy that considers images as being layers of images on top of a host image. We propose a solution to this problem by recursively applying editor task customization to images.

Keywords: model-view · graphics · interaction

1 Introduction

The iTasks system [24,25,27] is a general purpose framework to create multi-user web applications. An iTask application runs as a web server application that users can connect with via web browser clients. The iTasks system is implemented as an embedded domain-specific language in the pure, lazy, strongly typed, functional programming language Clean [16]. The key design goal of the iTask system is that the code required for multi-user web applications is generated automatically, using the host language features such as generic programming, dynamic types, and efficient rewriting using uniqueness types. The server application runs in native code, and on each web client application, a WebAssembly and Javascript image is running [26].

The principle building blocks in iTasks are *tasks*, of parameterized type (Task m). The type parameter m models the information that the task shares with its environment to represent its current state. *Editor tasks* are the chief component for programmers to create interactive tasks. Ordinarily, a (graphical) user interface for an editor task is automatically generated via generic programming techniques [7,18,21]. Other tasks can inspect the current value of a task, and tasks can share their task value with other tasks, and allow manipulations, via shared data sources.

There are several ways to customize the user interface. The easiest way is to equip the editor task with an asymmetric lens [2,19] from the task-model of type m to a view-model of type v for which a more suitable generic instance is available. The hardest way is to use the Editor interface, which gives the programmer access to write arbitrary Javascript code [23]. The middle road is what this paper is about: to use an *SVG editor task* [6]. It features a compositional image library, based on the W3C Scalable Vector Graphics standard [11], and uses a combinator approach, inspired by the seminal Functional Geometry approach by Henderson [17] and the comprehensive Racket image library [1]. In SVG editor tasks, callback functions do not operate directly on the task-model value but instead on the view-model value of the custom view. It uses a model-view customization [22]: the model, say of type m, corresponds with the task-value, and the view, say of type v, corresponds with the view-value at the client side. Callback functions are pure functions on the view-model of type v. To enforce matching types of callback functions in the rendered views, the image type is parameterized with the type of the view-model: Image v.

As an example, consider a task of type (Task Time) (Time is available in iTask as a record of three integer values to keep track of the hours, minutes, and seconds). So the task-model type is Time. Suppose we want to render time graphically, and give the user the choice to select whether it should be rendered with an analog clock face or a digital clock face. So the view-model type is (Time,Bool) and the type of the corresponding image is (Image (Time,Bool)). The choice of clock face does not concern the task, so user events selecting the face should stay local at the client side. Callback functions can be added anywhere in the image, and because of the type parameter of the image, these callback functions work on view-model values of type (Time,Bool).

For the programmer, it suffices to define the connection between the task-model value of type m and the client-view value of type v and its rendering of type (Image v) with three pure functions, collected in a structure of type (SVGEditor m v)[1]:

```
:: SVGEditor m v
= { initView    :: m -> v
  , renderImage :: m v *TagSource -> Image v
  , updModel    :: m v -> m
  }
```

In the existing approach, images are compositional, but this is not true for the single view-model type v. It is enforced on all parts of the compositional image, of type (Image v). This severely hampers code reuse and modularization.

For instance, in the previous example, the image that represents the toggle that the user can press to alter the clock face must have type (Image (Time,Bool)). However, the toggle really should have view-model type Bool and its image should have type (Image Bool). Moreover, such a toggle should be reusable in other contexts, letting the context define how the view-model of the toggle interacts with the view-model of the context.

---

[1] *TagSource and Image v are explained in Sect. 2.

We eliminate the existing restriction by making view-models compositional.
The key idea is that within an (Image v) created by a (SVGEditor m v), we recursively allow an (Image w) created by a (SVGEditor v w). In this way, the 'current' view-model of type v serves as model for another view of type w obtained via (initView v), that is rendered independently via (renderImage v w), interacts independently, and in which new values w' get updated into v again via (updModel v w').

Although the initView and updModel operations are reminiscent of asymmetric lenses [2,19], it is important to observe that the challenge here is not an instance of the *view update problem* in which changes to a view need to be incorporated into the model *without touching some identified complement* of the model. In general, the updModel function can alter the model in such a way that the changed view that caused the change is irretrievable from the updated model. This violates the *PutGet* law, which, translated to the above names, demands that initView (updModel m v) = v holds for all possible values m and v. Examples of such violations are when a user creates an invalid view value that is rejected or altered in the model, or when the model value makes a state transition. We show an example in the case study in Sect. 4, and discuss this further in Sect. 6.

To preserve type safety, callback functions should still be associated correctly with the view-model of the associated type. This is obtained for free when recursively allowing SVGEditors. To preserve the compositional nature of images, it should not matter from which view-model they originate. To obtain compositional images, we need to erase the view value types as soon as these are no longer required. This has become possible in a completely new implementation of SVG editor tasks [3].

With the enhanced image library the application programmer can develop interactive image components, concerning themselves only with the appropriate view-model data types, rendering, and behaviour. The SVGEditor takes care of logically connecting their view-model with the view-model of their context. The design is clean, i.e.: we take care that the image API is not 'polluted' with view-model plumbing combinators that steer the programmer away from thinking of interactive, compositional images as image stacks on top of image hosts.

The remainder of this paper is structured as follows. In Sect. 2 we give an overview of a representative snapshot of the image API. We show how to extend the image API to allow for recursively nested images that have their own view-model in Sect. 3. We show how to use this extension in a case study in Sect. 4. The implementation is discussed in Sect. 5. We discuss related work and alternative designs in Sect. 6. The conclusions are presented in Sect. 7.

2 Compositional Images

A representative snapshot of the API of compositional and interactive images in shown in Fig. 1. Conceptually, every image is infinitely wide and perfectly transparent. Instead of pixel, the unit of measure is px^2 of type Span. Instead

---

[2] Browser SVG renderers usually map (px 1.0) to one pixel.

```
:: Image v           // Image is an abstract data type
:: ImageTag          // identify a (sub) image (see tag function)
:: Span              // measure, unit is px
:: FontDef           // font family, height, and attributes
:: *TagSource        :== *[TagRef]
:: *TagRef           :== *(ImageTag, *ImageTag)
:: XYAlign           :== (XAlign, YAlign)
:: XAlign             = AtLeft  | AtMiddleX | AtRight
:: YAlign             = AtTop   | AtMiddleY | AtBottom
:: Host             v = NoHost  | Host (Image v)
:: SyncWithServer     = SyncWithServer | NoSyncWithServer
:: OnClickAttr    v = {onNclick   ::        Int v -> (SyncWithServer,v)}
:: OnKeyDownAttr  v = {onkeydown  :: Keyboard v -> (SyncWithServer,v)}

px               :: Real     -> Span
imagexspan       :: ImageTag -> Span
imageyspan       :: ImageTag -> Span
normalFontDef    :: String   Real                              -> FontDef
empty            :: Span     Span                              -> Image v
ellipse          :: Span     Span                              -> Image v
rect             :: Span     Span                              -> Image v
text             :: FontDef  String                            -> Image v
overlay          :: [XYAlign] [(Span, Span)] [Image v] (Host v) -> Image v
tag              :: *ImageTag       (Image v)                  -> Image v
class        (<@<) attr infixl 2 :: (Image v) (attr v)         -> Image v
instance (<@<) OnClickAttr, OnKeyDownAttr
```

Fig. 1. A representative snapshot of the image API

of bounding boxes for layout, we use *span boxes*. Just as bounding boxes, span boxes have a width and height, but unlike bounding boxes, span boxes allow graphical content to appear anywhere in the image, relative to the span box[3]. Images are either basic (empty, ellipse, rect, text) or an overlay of images. Basic images can be tuned (<@<) via attributes to control their stroke, fill, colour, and so on. All images can be made interactive via the mouse (OnClickAttr) and keyboard (OnKeyDownAttr), and decide whether the event should be handled only locally on the client (NoSyncWithServer) or should be synchronised with the server (SyncWithServer). These callback functions manipulate the same view-model type v that is passed along every (Image v).

Image composition is defined by (overlay aligns offsets imgs h), which is a stack of images imgs[4] on top of a host image (h = Host img) or no host image (h = NoHost). The span box of the overlay is the span box of img, if available, or

---

[3] x-axes increase to the right, y-axes increase downwards.
[4] $imgs_{i+1}$ is rendered on top of $imgs_i$.

the bounding box of the span boxes of imgs. The relative layout of imgs_i is first determined by aligns_i[5] and then fine-tuned with offsets_i[6].

Defining the image layout sometimes requires you to refer to the span box width and height of images that are used in the composition. The functions imagexspan and imageyspan use an ImageTag value for this purpose. Any image can get a fresh and unique tag value, using the tag function. The uniqueness type attribute * [8] prevents conflicting uses of the same tag, but an image tag can still be dangling if its unique counterpart does not tag an image. ImageTags are drawn from *TagSource, which is available only via the renderImage function of an SVGEditor. The labels come in pairs: one uniquely attributed value and its non-unique counterpart that can be used arbitrarily many times.

The image library lets you design the individual images that occur in the ensemble. These images can be composed in any way in any layout. This is not true for the view-model and the callback functions: this has to be the same for the individual images and its compositions.

3 Compositional Images with Compositional Views

In the iTask framework, SVG editor task customization occurs at the task level (Fig. 2). The task, say of type (Task m), resides at the server side. We abstract from its task structure (the left triangle), and focus on its task-model value (the circle at its top). Suppose it has task-model value m_0 of type m (1), then the editor task with generically generated user interface is created by (updateInformation [] m_0) which has type (Task m). If we create a custom look and feel view_v :: SVGEditor m v, for some existentially quantified view-model type v, then this task is customized by (updateInformation [toUpdateOption view_v] m_0). This customized task still has type (Task m), but it is rendered at the client side as an image of type (Image v) (right triangle). First, the task model value is made available at the client side (2). Second, view_v.toView (3) computes the matching view-model value v_0 of type v. Third, view_v.renderImage (4) computes the image from m_0 and v_0. We abstract from its image structure (the right triangle). From the image an SVG rendering is generated (5) which the end-user sees and interacts with. When the user generates an event within the SVG, the corresponding callback function is retrieved from the image structure img_v and is applied to v_0 to compute the next view-model value v_1 (6). If the callback function decides that this change should remain local, then at the client side the model value gets updated, but the server side is not informed. If the change should be synchronized with the server, then the new view-model value is sent to the server (7). In either case, at the corresponding side, view_v.updModel updates the model value m_0 with v_1, resulting in a new task-model value m_1, a new view-model value v_2 and image.

Task customization remains untouched in the proposed extension. We extend the image API of Fig. 1 with just one new function:

---

[5] The default alignment is (AtLeft,AtTop).
[6] The default offset is (px 0.0,px 0.0).

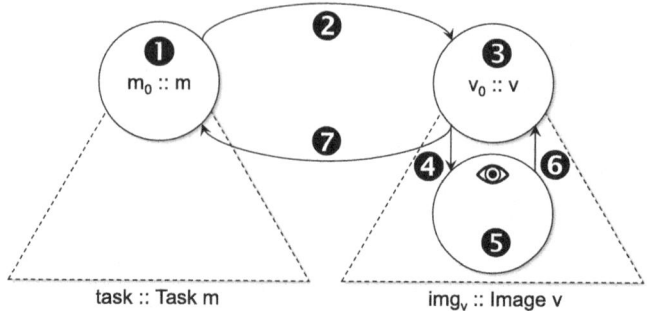

Fig. 2. Customizing a task with an Image

```
svg :: (SVGEditor v w) -> Image v
```

The key idea is to recursively apply the model-view customization defined by a $view_w$ of type (SVGEditor v w), but now to the view-model of type v of an (Image v) instead of the task-model of a task. This gives a view-model of type w and its corresponding image of type (Image w) with callback functions on the existentially quantified type w. This customized image still has type (Image v), but it is rendered as an image of type (Image w). Because it has type (Image v), it can be combined with other parts of the image of the same type.

Figure 3 shows the recursive application of such a SVG editor abstraction $view_w$ inside an image. As before, an SVG rendering of the image of type (Image v) is generated at the client side (1). New is that part of this SVG rendering (2) is generated via (svg $view_w$) (6) within the image of type (Image v). When (svg $view_w$) is encountered, ($view_w$.toView v_0) computes the local view-model value w_0 (3) and stores it at the client side (4). The user interface is computed by $view_w$.renderImage from v_0 and w_0 (5). The SVG rendering (6) of the $view_w$ is used within the SVG rendering of $view_v$. When the user generates an event within that part of the SVG, the corresponding callback function is

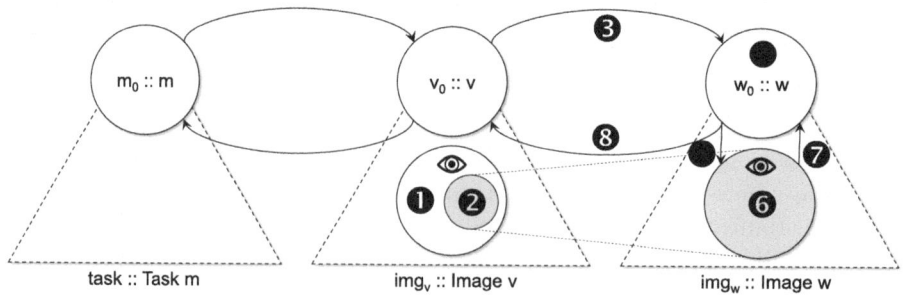

Fig. 3. Customizing a task with an Image

retrieved from the image structure img_w and applied to w_0 to compute the next view-model value w_1 (7). Next, $view_w$.updModel updates v_0 with w_1, resulting in v_1. If the callback function decides that this change needs to be synchronized with the server, then this cascade of changes is propagated higher-up, ultimately to the task at the server side, resulting in a new task-model value and new images.

4 Case Study

In this section we show how to use the new form of compositionality. We create a stateful interactive image:

> *The user can alter two independent integer counter elements as long as their sum is below some threshold value. As soon as the threshold value is reached or exceeded, the interactive image steps into a display of the sum of the chosen values.*

We proceed in a bottom-up style: once an image element has been introduced, it is used without changes.

Let us start with three helper images:

- space r creates an invisible rectangular white space of width and height r.
- isosceles_triangle b h creates an isosceles triangle with a base of width b and height h, with a downward pointing tip.
- display h x uses the Courier font of height h to show x as a string.

Their definitions are (| toString a is a type class constraint):

```
space :: Real -> Image v
space r = empty (px r) (px r)

isosceles_triangle :: Real Real -> Image v
isosceles_triangle b h = polygon [(px 0.0, px 0.0),(px b, px 0.0),(px (b / 2.0),
  px h)]

display :: Real a -> Image v | toString a
display h x = text (normalFontDef "Courier" h) (toString x)
```

These work for any image context because of their polymorphic type (Image v).

Next, we turn the triangle into an interactive image:

- step edge diff creates an isosceles triangle of base length edge and height $\frac{edge}{4}$ that reacts to mouse clicks: a single mouse click adds diff to the integer view value, but keeps the change local on the client (NoSyncWithServer), and a (double/triple) mouse click synchronizes the current integer view value with the server (SyncWithServer).

The definition is:

```
step :: Real Int -> Image Int
step edge diff = isosceles_triangle edge (edge / 4.0)
                    <@< {onNclick = \c v = if (c == 1) (NoSyncWithServer, v + diff)
                                                      ( SyncWithServer,  v)
                        }
```

With these elements, we construct an integer counter:

- value n is a display of the number (initially n), and next to it, above each other, two steppers to increase and decrease the integer view value.

The definition is (beside and above are special cases of overlay and place an image stack beside each other and above each other respectively; flipy flips an image along the x-axis):

```
value :: Int -> Image Int
value n = beside (repeat AtMiddleY) [] ?None []
              [ display 20.0 n
              , space 2.0
              , above [] [] ?None []
                    [ flipy (step 12.0 1)
                    , space 2.0
                    , step 12.0 -1
                    ] NoHost
              ] NoHost
```

42⬥

The screenshot to the right shows the value image for view value 42.

We model the state and state transition of the interactive image with an algebraic data type Model and function accept:

```
:: Model = Offer Int Int | Result Int

accept :: Model -> Model
accept (Offer a b) = if (a + b < threshold) (Offer a b) (Result (a + b))
accept result      = result
```

The accept rule remains in the Offer state until the components exceed threshold, and remains in the Result state afterwards.

The interactive image creates a different rendering based on the Model value. For this, we define one function:

- render m generates two interactive value images to independently alter the two integer view values during the Offer state, and switches to a display of the obtained sum in the Result state.

To do this, render distinguishes the two cases:

```
render :: Model -> Image Model
render (Offer _ _)
  = above [] [] ?None []
      [svg {initView   = \(Offer a _)  = a
           ,renderImage = \_ a _        = value a
           ,updModel    = \(Offer _ b) a = accept (Offer a b)
           }
      ,space 2.0
      ,svg {initView   = \(Offer _ b)  = b
           ,renderImage = \_ b _        = value b
           ,updModel    = \(Offer a _) b = accept (Offer a b)
           }
      ] NoHost
render (Result _)
  = svg {initView   = \(Result sum) = sum
        ,renderImage = \_ sum _      = display sum
        ,updModel    = \m _          = m
        }
```

42⇕

57⇕

100

In the Offer state, the new svg image function is used to 'connect' one value image with the first integer component, and another value image with the second integer component. The screenshot shows the result of render for the model value (Offer 42 57). In the Result state, the sum value is shown via the display. In the screenshot we have used threshold value 100.

5 Implementation of Compositional Views

In this section we discuss the implementation of the extension of the image API.

We first give an overview of the current implementation that was sketched in Sect. 3 (Fig. 2). Recall that at the server side and client side an equivalent code base is available, executed natively at the server side and running WebAssembly and Javascript at the client side (Sect. 1). For performance reasons, the server side computes a serialized version of the SVG representation of the custom image and sends it to the client, and the client uses the Javascript DomParser to create the client side user interface. The serialized version is generated in four steps: *(i)* the renderImage function creates a deep embedding of itself, *(ii)* the deep embedding is transformed into a shallow embedding that calculates the entire layout of the image, *(iii)* an SVG friendly representation of the image is generated, *(iv)* the SVG friendly representation is serialized. The client side handles events. It has obtained the task-model value from the server at the initialisation message, and stores this value along with the view-model value that it computes, using toView. The client side uses the result of step *(i)* to retrieve the callback function from the image with the least amount of overhead. The callback function is applied to the locally available view-model value. The new view-model value is stored and applied to the task-model value using updModel which is also stored at the client side. The client is fully able to compute a new serialized version if the event should be handled without informing the server, otherwise it simply sends the new task-model value to the server.

The following changes need to be implemented:

- The Image API functions generate a deep embedding of the renderImage function. This deep embedding is type parameterized with the view type because we need to find callback functions when client events must be handled. This changes the deep embedding and locating callback functions (Sect. 5.1).
- Knowing where to find a callback function, it needs to be evaluated when its corresponding event has occurred at the client side. The callback function might be operating on a different, nested, view value, so this has to be kept track of (Sect. 5.2).
- The SVG image that is generated on the client side has no need of the (nested) view values after computing the (sub) images. At every recursive occurrence of a nested image, the proper SVG image is computed and used (Sect. 5.3).

5.1 Deep Image Embedding

The image functions (Fig. 1) immediately return a deep embedding of themselves (Figs. 4 and 5) to efficiently extract the callback function in case of an event. The image functions and data structures have the same strictness properties. Moreover, we use lazy lists, so the list elements are not evaluated when they are not needed. Hence, creating this deep embedding of a renderImage function is a cheap operation.

```
empty               x y        = Empty'    x y
ellipse             x y        = Ellipse'  x y
rect                x y        = Rect'     x y
text           font str        = Text' font str
overlay aligns offs imgs h = Overlay' aligns offs imgs h
instance (<@<) OnClickAttr
tag            t img       = Tag'      t img
where       (<@<) img f = Attr' (ImgEventhandlerOnClickAttr   f) img
instance (<@<) OnKeyDownAttr
where       (<@<) img f = Attr' (ImgEventhandlerOnKeydownAttr f) img
```

Fig. 4. Implementation of Image API functions

The deep embedding of images gets extended with an existentially quantified (E.w:) data constructor SVGEditor', limiting the scope of w to inside the data constructor. The key purpose of the deep image embedding is to identify callback functions via the ImgNodePath from the root of the image embedding to the attribute data constructor that contains the actual function. We extend the path directive with ViaSVG which identifies the use of an SVGEditor.

```
:: Image v
 = Empty`    Span      Span
 | Ellipse`  Span      Span
 | Rect`     Span      Span
 | Text`     FontDef   String
 | Tag`      ImageTag              (Image v)
 | Overlay`  [XYAlign] [(Span, Span)] [Image v] (Host v)
 | Attr`     (ImageAttr` v)        (Image v)
// new:
 | E.w : SVGEditor` (SVGEditor v w)
:: ImageAttr` v
 = HandlerAttr`               (ImgEventhandler v)
:: ImgEventhandler v
 = ImgEventhandlerOnClickAttr    (OnClickAttr    v)
 | ImgEventhandlerOnKeydownAttr (OnKeyDownAttr  v)
:: ImgNodePath :== [ViaImg]
:: ViaImg        = ViaChild Int    // ViaChild i: visit child image with index @i
                 | ViaHost         // ViaHost: visit host image
                 | ViaAttr         // ViaAttr: visit attribute image
// new:
                 | ViaSVG          // ViaSVG: visit SVGEditor
```

Fig. 5. Deep embedding of image API

5.2 Finding and Applying a Callback Function

Without integrated SVGEditors, obtaining the callback function from the deep image embedding is a matter of 'following' the path directives in the ImgNodePath:

```
getImgEventhandler :: (Image` v) ImgNodePath -> ?(ImgEventhandler v)
```

With integrated SVGEditors this straightforward approach is not possible. Instead, while navigating the deep image embedding via the ImgNodePath we keep track of the current view-model value, and switch to the next one whenever an SVGEditor is encountered. Furthermore, we need to pass around any arguments that have been generated at the client side callback function (encoded below as ImgEventhandlerArgs). This leads to a function of the following signature:

```
:: ImgEventhandlerArgs
 = ImgEventhandlerOnNClickArg Int
 | ImgEventhandlerOnKeydownArg Keyboard

appImgEventhandler :: ImgEventhandlerArgs (Image v) v ImgNodePath
                      -> ?(SyncWithServer,v)
```

The relevant parts of the new function concern handling the found callback function and switching to a new view when handling an SVGEditor. When the empty ImgNodePath arrives at the callback function, it is applied to the arguments and the view-model value.

```
appImgEventhandler args (Attr' (HandlerAttr' f) _) v []
  = appEventHandler args f v
where
  appEventHandler :: ImgEventhandlerArgs (ImgEventhandler v) v
                     -> ?(SyncWithServer,v)
  appEventHandler (ImgEventhandlerOnNClickArg  n)
                  (ImgEventhandlerOnClickAttr   {onNclick =f}) v = ?Just (f n v)
  appEventHandler (ImgEventhandlerOnKeydownArg k)
                  (ImgEventhandlerOnKeydownAttr {onkeydown=f}) v = ?Just (f k v)
  appEventHandler _ _ _ = ?None
```

In case of an `SVGEditor` view, the corresponding view-model value `w` is computed using `view.initView`, and the corresponding image is rendered using `view.renderImage`. The function `freshImageTags` generates a stream of `ImageTag` value pairs. If a new view-model value `w'` is returned, then it is used to update the context view-model using `view.updModel`.

```
appImgEventhandler args (SVGEditor' view) v [ViaSVG : p]
  = case appImgEventhandler args img w p of
      ?Just (sync,w') = ?Just (sync, view.updModel v w')
      _               = ?None
where
  w   = view.initView v
  img = view.renderImage v w (freshImageTags -1)
```

5.3 Model View Agnostic Image Representation

The deep representation that we have discussed up until now (Fig. 5) is used to locate a callback function and its (local) model view value, if an event occurs at the client side. The (local) model view types are only relevant there, and are no longer needed afterwards. The second phase of the implementation erases this type information, and yields an SVG friendly image representation of type `Img` (Fig. 6).

Every image item receives a unique identification number (`uniqId`). Basic images are a basic `host` image without `overlays`. An `overlay` has a possibly empty `host` image and with `overlays`. We will not discuss the `BasicImgAttr` further.

The algorithm is reported in detail in [3]. The part that is of interest here has signature:

```
toImg :: (Image v) v ImgNodePath ImgTagNo -> (Img,ImgTagNo)
```

The algorithm proceeds by case distinction on the first argument. The second argument is new, and keeps track of the 'current' model view value. The third argument keeps track of the location of callback functions, as described in Sect. 5.2. The fourth argument provides the unique identification number. The algorithm handles the former `Image` data constructors as before, and `SVGEditor'` recursively:

```
toImg (SVGEditor' svg) v p no = toImg img w [ViaSVG:p] (no-1)
```

```
:: Img
 = { uniqId    :: !ImgTagNo
   , host      :: !HostImg
   , overlays  :: ![Img]
   , offsets   :: ![(Span,Span)]
   }
:: HostImg
 = BasicHostImg !BasicImg !(SetBy BasicImgAttr)
 | CompositeImg !Img
:: BasicImg
 = EmptyImg
 | EllipseImg
 | RectImg
 | TextImg !FontDef !String
```

Fig. 6. Model view agnostic representation of images

where w   = svg.initView v
      img = svg.renderImage v w (freshImageTags no)

6 Discussion and Related Work

In the introduction we observed that the initView and updModel functions of an SVGEditor have the same signatures as the get and put operations of asymmetric lenses. In general, interactive images are not an instance of the *view update problem* for which lenses have been developed. The case study (Sect. 4) demonstrates this: putting an integer value from one of the integer counters can alter the Model value to change from the Offer case into the Result case, making it impossible to get back the integer value that caused the change. This violates the lens *PutGet* law. This is not an uncommon pattern. For instance, in the Ligretto card game case study [6] a similar situation occurs when one of the players creates an empty Ligretto pile by placing one of the row cards on one of the middle card piles. The Ligretto game makes a state transition to a final game state.

Another challenge of interactive tasks is that view value changes of components can induce changes to view values 'outside' of their composition [23]. Their case study analyses the compositional structure of list editors in which the user can dynamically add, remove, and move around editable list elements. For instance, changing the number of elements changes the summary label of the list editor. Their solution is to equip all customizable editor tasks with a read and write interface, possibly of different type, yielding *directional composable editors*. A collection of built-in editors is provided (e.g. buttons, sliders, integer editors), each one with their particular read and write interface. Combinators are introduced to alter the read and write interface, as well as combinators to combine these editors. Finally, to allow for one component affect other components, a loopback combinator is introduced with which the programmer specifies whether local changes need to be propagated back into the composite editor structure.

Directional composable editors are available in the iTask system, and SVG editor tasks are actually a special case. Nevertheless, we have not adopted this approach to equip images with a read and write interface. The main reason is that this would 'pollute' the image API, and force the programmer to mix layout combinators with logic. Also the goal is different: the editor tasks are at the task level, so these are tasks with task values, and the provided solution shows how to compose them. Interactive images are a custom interface to one task, so one task value, and it is clear that this task value is associated with the task instead of interactive, stateful, image components. Nevertheless, for future research it is interesting to investigate the design space.

Similar concerns can be raised when adopting approaches such as the seminal work on *Fudgets* [9] that inspired many approaches that utilize a mix of combinators for combining logic with layout. An entirely different view on images is taken by the school of *functional reactive programming*, started with Pan [12], enhancing it with interaction, resulting in Fran [13] and, finally, amongst others, Yampa [10,20]. Characteristic to these approaches is to consider images as functions from coordinates to a well-defined range (Pan and Fran), animations as functions from continuous time to images, and interactive applications as functions from discrete events to animations (Yampa). A recurring theme in their work is that specifications are functions from a continuous domain to a discrete domain. The implementation 'samples' these functions. This differs greatly from our approach that advocates a 'structurally-analytic' view on image specifications and embedding in TOP to define behavior.

Compositionality of interactive applications with state was one of the key design decisions of the Object IO system [4]. Also this area of the design space chose to offer combinators that deal with local and shared state, and mix it with interactive components [5]. This approach has in common with the earlier mentioned composable editors that it is natural to introduce stateful components that are hidden from their context via the type system, using existentially quantified states. When comparing these approaches to the compositional images, one can characterize the older approaches as a bottom-up and stateful approach, i.e. the programmer carefully introduces state in the interactive components, making sure that the callback functions have matching types, whereas in the compositional images actually something similar happens regarding the callback functions, except that instead of explicit state, functions are used to access the proper parts of the parent level image view.

In the above approach, the library designer has a lot of control in the whereabouts of state. That does come at a price, having to introduce combinators that deal with the application logic or making certain that the information is available at the right location in the interactive image. Another approach to manipulate (local) state is via references to state. State references do not have this problem, and their use is much more 'free-style' programming. Examples are MVars in Haskell and Shared Data Sources (SDS's) in the iTask system. We have not adopted them to equip images with state via them. The main reason is that the image API is purely functional, and callback functions are 'just' pure functions altering a view value. Incorporating references would turn these callback functions into callback actions, for instance in a monadic style, because one needs to read and write to the referenced states. The implementation is challenging as well when arbitrary browser clients are reading and writing arbitrary Shared Data Sources. Nevertheless, for future research it is interesting to investigate the design space.

Another way of controlling updates to a context is provided with *Functional-Forms* [14,15]. In this approach, the context corresponds with the top level image view-model, and updates on components of the view-model are transformed to updates on the top level view-model. Each component identifies which part of the context it updates. In this sense, the approach is less compositional than the one we have presented: in our approach a component only specifies its behaviour on its local view-model, and the `initView` and `updModel` define its relation to the local view-model of the parent. To use the component in another context, we only need to alter these two functions, whereas in FunctionalForms, the component itself needs to adapt to its new context.

7 Conclusions

We propose a solution to a long-standing open problem with the iTask SVG Image library: how to combine interactive images that rely on different view model values without introducing view model plumbing combinators and without moving away from the design philosophy of the image library. The solution is based on incorporating the task customization of SVG editors into the compositional image library. The application programmer can now develop interactive images that operate on arbitrary view model (types), and use them in any image by defining how the local view model depends on the context and how changes to that view model affect the context. This greatly increases code reuse and modularization.

Acknowledgements. The authors thank the anonymous reviewers for their constructive feedback.

References

1. image.rkt, November 2023. https://docs.racket-lang.org/teachpack/2htdpimage.html
2. Abou-Saleh, F., Cheney, J., Gibbons, J., McKinna, J., Stevens, P.: Introduction to Bidirectional Transformations, pp. 1–28. Springer, Cham (2018). https://doi.org/10.1007/978-3-319-79108-1_1
3. Achten, P.: Mix and match deep and shallow embeddings for interactive web based SVG content. In: The 35th Symposium on Implementation and Application of Functional Languages (2023). Under submission

4. Achten, P., Plasmeijer, R.: The ins and outs of Concurrent Clean I/O. J. Funct. Program. **5**(1), 81–110 (1995)
5. Achten, P., Plasmeijer, R.: The implementation of interactive local state transition systems in Clean. In: Koopman, P., Clack, C. (eds.) Proceedings of the 11th International Workshop on the Implementation of Functional Languages, IFL 1999. LNCS, vol. 1868, pp. 115–130. Springer, Cham (2000). https://doi.org/10.1007/10722298_7
6. Achten, P., Stutterheim, J., Domoszlai, L., Plasmeijer, R.: Task oriented programming with purely compositional interactive scalable vector graphics. In: Tobin-Hochstadt, S. (ed.) Proceedings of the 26nd 2014 International Symposium on Implementation and Application of Functional Languages, IFL 2014, pp. 7:1–7:13. ACM, New York, NY, USA (2014). https://doi.org/10.1145/2746325.2746329
7. Alimarine, A., Plasmeijer, R.: A generic programming extension for Clean. In: Arts, T., Mohnen, M. (eds.) Selected Papers of the 13th International Workshop on the Implementation of Functional Languages, IFL 2001, Stockholm, Sweden. LNCS, vol. 2312, pp. 168–186. Springer, Cham (2002). https://doi.org/10.1007/3-540-46028-4_11
8. Barendsen, E., Smetsers, S.: Conventional and uniqueness typing in graph rewrite systems (extended abstract). In: Shyamasundar, R. (ed.) Proceedings of the Conference on the Foundations of Software Technology and Theoretical Computer Science, FSTTCS 1993, Bombay, India. LNCS, vol. 761, pp. 41–51. Springer, Cham (1993). https://doi.org/10.1007/3-540-57529-4_42
9. Carlsson, M., Hallgren, T.: Fudgets - a graphical user interface in a lazy functional language. In: Proceedings of the 6th International Conference on Functional Programming Languages and Computer Architecture, FPCA 1993, Kopenhagen, Denmark (1993)
10. Courtney, A., Elliott, C.: Genuinely functional user interfaces. In: Proceedings of the 5th Haskell Workshop, Haskell 2001, September 2001
11. Dahlström, E., et al.: Scalable vector graphics (SVG) 1.1 (second edition). Technical report. REC-SVG11-20110816, W3C Recommendation 16 August 2011 (2011)
12. Elliot, C.: Functional images. In: Gibbons, J., de Moor, O. (eds.) The Fun of Programming, pp. 131–150. Palgrave Macmillan (2003)
13. Elliot, C., Hudak, P.: Functional reactive animation. In: Proceedings International Conference on Functional Programming, ICFP 1997, pp. 263–273, Netherlands, Amsterdam, June 1997
14. Evers, S., Achten, P.M., Kuper, J.: A functional programming technique for forms in graphical user interfaces. In: Grelck, C., Huch, F., Michaelson, G., Trinder, P. (eds.) Proceedings of the 16th International Symposium on the Implementation and Application of Functional Languages, IFL 2004. LNCS, vol. 3474, pp. 35–51. Springer, Cham (2004). https://doi.org/10.1007/11431664_3
15. Evers, S., Achten, P.M., Plasmeijer, M.J.: Disjoint forms in graphical user interfaces. In: Loidl, H.W. (ed.) Proceedings of the 5th Symposium on Trends in Functional Programming, TFP 2004, pp. 113–128, Munich, Germany (2004)
16. van Groningen, J., van Noort, T., Achten, P., Koopman, P., Plasmeijer, R.: Exchanging sources between Clean and Haskell: a double-edged front end for the Clean compiler. In: Gibbons, J. (ed.) Haskell 2010: Proceedings of the Third ACM Haskell Symposium on Haskell, pp. 49–60. ACM (2010)
17. Henderson, P.: Functional geometry. In: Friedman, D., Wise, D. (eds.) Conference Record of the 1982 ACM Symposium on LISP and Functional Programming, pp. 179–187. ACM Press, Pittsburgh, Pennsylvania (1982). http://www.ecs.soton.ac.uk/~ph/funcgeo.pdf

18. Hinze, R.: A new approach to generic functional programming. In: Reps, T. (ed.) Proceedings of the 27th International Symposium on Principles of Programming Languages, POPL 2000, Boston, MA, USA, pp. 119–132. ACM Press (2000)
19. Hofmann, M., Pierce, B.C., Wagner, D.: Symmetric lenses. In: Ball, T., Sagiv, M. (eds.) Proceedings of the 38th ACM SIGPLAN-SIGACT Symposium on Principles of Programming Languages, POPL 2011, Austin, TX, USA, pp. 371–384. ACM (2011)
20. Hudak, P., Courtney, A., Nilsson, H., Peterson, J.: Arrows, robots, and functional reactive programming. In: Jeuring, J., Peyton Jones, S. (eds.) Proceedings of the 4th International Summer School on Advanced Functional Programming, AFP 2003, Oxford, UK. LNCS, vol. 2638, pp. 159–187. Springer, Cham (2003). https://doi.org/10.1007/978-3-540-44833-4_6
21. Jansson, P., Jeuring, J.: PolyP—a polytypic programming language extension. In: Conference Record of POPL 1997: The 24th ACM SIGPLAN-SIGACT Symposium on Principles of Programming Languages, pp. 470–482. ACM Press (1997)
22. Krasner, G., Pope, S.: A cookbook for using the model-view-controller user interface paradigm in Smalltalk-80. J. Object-Oriented Program. 1(3), 26–49 (1988)
23. Lijnse, B., Plasmeijer, R.: Typed directional composable editors in iTasks. In: Proceedings of the 32nd Symposium on Implementation and Application of Functional Languages, IFL 2020, pp. 115–126. Association for Computing Machinery, New York, NY, USA (2021). https://doi.org/10.1145/3462172.3462197
24. Plasmeijer, M.J., Achten, P.M., Koopman, P.W.M.: iTasks: executable specifications of interactive work flow systems for the web. In: Proceedings of the 12th International Conference on Functional Programming, ICFP 2007, pp. 141–152. ACM Press, Freiburg, Germany, 1–3 October 2007
25. Plasmeijer, R., Lijnse, B., Michels, S., Achten, P., Koopman, P.: Task-oriented programming in a pure functional language. In: Proceedings of the 2012 ACM SIGPLAN International Conference on Principles and Practice of Declarative Programming, PPDP 2012, pp. 195–206. ACM, Leuven, Belgium, September 2012
26. Staps, C., Van Groningen, J., Plasmeijer, R.: Lazy interworking of compiled and interpreted code for sandboxing and distributed systems. In: Stutterheim, J., Chin, W.N. (eds.) Implementation and Application of Functional Languages (IFL 2019), 25–27 September 2019, Singapore, Singapore, p. 12. ACM, New York, NY, USA (2019). https://doi.org/10.1145/3412932.3412941
27. Steenvoorden, T.J.: TopHat. Task-oriented programming with style. Ph.D. thesis (2022). https://repository.ubn.ru.nl/handle/2066/253701

Programming with Dependent Additive Pairs

Vít Šefl[✉]

Charles University, Prague, Czech Republic
sefl@ksvi.mff.cuni.cz

Abstract. Linear logic gives us additive pairs in the form of the additive conjunction. Intuitionistic type theory gives us dependent pairs in the form of the dependent sum type. What happens when we combine these two kinds of pairs together? And is this new pair type useful in practice? To answer these questions, we employ quantitative type theory, which can describe both substructural and dependent types simultaneously. In our previous work, we introduced dependent additive pairs. In this work, we show how these pairs can be used in three completely different scenarios: folding data structures using linear recursion schemes, computing resource-aware proofs, and defining additive versions of inductive and coinductive types. Each of these scenarios is then illustrated by an implementation in the Janus language.

Keywords: Dependent types · Linear types · Quantitative type theory · Additive pairs

1 Introduction

Many programming languages use type systems. Their main purpose is to detect a wide variety of bugs before the program is even run. Throughout the years, type systems have become quite sophisticated, supporting features such as subtyping, parametric polymorphism, or metatypes. Today, some of the most expressive type systems are based on *dependent type theories*, such as the Martin-Löf type theory [11]. As the name suggests, a dependent type is a type which can depend on a value. A standard example is a vector: a list that contains its length in its type. Dependent types can be exploited to express very detailed properties of programs, which can then be automatically checked by the computer.

However, dependent types are poorly suited to describe how a program uses its values. In particular, any value can be freely duplicated or discarded. A programmer might want to ensure that a value representing an important resource, such as an open file, is not simply discarded. *Substructural type systems* seek to address this issue by restricting certain operations on variables. The most well known subclass of substructural type systems are linear type systems. In these systems, variables are typically split into two subsets: unrestricted and linear. The key restriction is that linear variables must be used exactly once. Other restrictions give rise to different systems, such as affine type systems.

Quantitative type theory (QTT) [3] is a recent attempt at combining dependent and substructural types into a single theory. In QTT, variables are not split into subsets. Instead, each variable is associated with an element of a semiring, so called *multiplicity*, which keeps track of how that particular variable is used. If the same variable occurs in different contexts, semiring operations are used to combine its constituent multiplicities into a single value.

Different semirings give rise to various kinds of substructural systems. A single-element semiring results in a system in which all variables are unrestricted. The usual semiring on natural numbers results in a system where multiplicity tracks exact usage of a given variable, with 1 corresponding to linear use. The zero-one-many semiring avoids unnecessarily precise multiplicities while still supporting irrelevant, linear, and unrestricted variables.

In QTT, multiplicities can also appear in some types. These indexed types replace the need for multiple versions of each connective, as is the case in linear logic. For example, instead of having linear $(A \multimap B)$ and unrestricted $(A \to B)$ functions, QTT has a single (dependent) function type $(x \overset{\sigma}{:} A) \to B$. Linear and unrestricted functions can be obtained by choosing a suitable value for σ. However, since the value of σ can be arbitrary, each element of the semiring thus gives rise to a different variant of the function type. In the $\mathbb{N}$ semiring, each number n gives a function that must use its parameter exactly n times.

Substructural types can be further classified as either *multiplicative* or *additive*. Multiplicative types split resources. When introducing a new value, the resources are divided into groups and each group is used to construct a part of the value. When eliminating a value, each part must be used to ensure no resources are discarded. Additive types preserve resources. When introducing a new value, each part of the value has access to all resources. When eliminating a value, only one part must be used to ensure no resources are duplicated.

Since QTT supports both dependent and substructural types, it gives us a unique opportunity to explore dependent versions of multiplicative and additive types. One example is the previously mentioned function type $(x \overset{\sigma}{:} A) \to B$. Another example is the dependent additive pair $(x : A) \& B$, which is a generalization of the additive conjunction found in linear logic. This pair type, introduced in our previous work [14], is the main focus of this work.

1.1 Goals

The primary objective of this work is to identify and describe practical uses of dependent additive pairs. In particular, we seek problems in resource-aware programming that are best solved by these pairs. The solutions should make use of both the type dependency and the additive nature of this type. More generally, we also seek novel applications of these pairs where the type dependency can be useful but is not strictly necessary.

A secondary objective is to provide an implementation of each solution in a language capable of expressing dependent additive pairs, which will demonstrate the correctness of our solutions and allow the reader to easily verify our claims.

1.2 Contributions

To achieve the stated goals, we identify three distinct and novel scenarios that are best solved by dependent additive pairs. Firstly, we implement a linear *paramorphism*, which is a recursion scheme that allows access to both the recursive result and the remainder of the structure. Secondly, we show how to compute resource-aware proofs, which demonstrate that a witness satisfies a given property while allowing their resources to be shared. Thirdly, we define additive versions of inductive lists and coinductive streams and implement linear versions of commonly used operations. Finally, we provide implementation in the Janus language [14].

2 Quantitative Type Theory

2.1 Semirings

QTT uses positive semirings to keep track of variable usage. A semiring is a tuple $(S, +, \cdot, 0, 1)$ where S is a set, $+$ and $\cdot$ are binary operations on S, 0 and 1 are elements of S such that $(S, +, 0)$ is a commutative monoid, $(S, \cdot, 1)$ is a monoid, $\cdot$ distributes over $+$, and $0a = 0 = a0$. A positive semiring further satisfies the following two properties: if $a + b = 0$ then $a = 0$ and $b = 0$, if $ab = 0$ then $a = 0$ or $b = 0$.

Without semiring positivity, we could have variables that are used nonzero times in two different contexts but their overall usage is still zero. A similar issue can occur with nested contexts, which are handled by semiring multiplication.

In this work, we use the zero-one-many semiring. Its elements are 0, 1, and ω, which represents more than one use. The definitions of addition and multiplication follow from these two equations: $\omega \cdot \omega = \omega$ and $\forall \rho.\ \rho + \omega = \omega$.

2.2 Syntax

An overview of the syntax of the particular QTT flavor used in this work is given below.

$$\pi, \sigma ::= 0 \mid 1 \mid \omega$$
$$\Gamma ::= \cdot \mid \Gamma, x \stackrel{\sigma}{:} M$$
$$M, N, O ::= x \mid \mathcal{U}$$
$$\mid \lambda x.\ M \mid MN \mid (x \stackrel{\sigma}{:} M) \to N$$
$$\mid (M, N) \mid \text{let}_\sigma\ (x, y) = M \text{ in } N \mid (x \stackrel{\sigma}{:} M) \otimes N$$
$$\mid () \mid \text{let } () = M \text{ in } N \mid \mathbf{1}$$
$$\mid \text{inl } M \mid \text{inr } M \mid \text{case}_\sigma\ M \text{ of } \{\text{inl } x \to N; \text{inr } y \to O\} \mid M \oplus N$$
$$\mid \text{case } M \text{ of } \{\} \mid \bot\ \textit{(no introduction)}$$
$$\mid \langle M, N \rangle \mid \text{fst } M \mid \text{snd } M \mid (x : M)\ \&\ N$$
$$\mid \langle \rangle \mid \top\ \textit{(no elimination)}$$

Going from top to bottom, we have multiplicities π, σ; contexts Γ; and terms M, N, O. When unambiguous, the empty context $\cdot$ is omitted. Contexts can be scaled and added together. Context addition is not used in this work and we thus only define scaling by π:

$$\pi(\cdot) = \cdot \qquad \pi(\Gamma, x \overset{\sigma}{:} M) = \pi\Gamma, x \overset{\pi\sigma}{:} M$$

A term can be a variable or the universe constant $\mathcal{U}$, representing the type of types. Each of the remaining lines then describes introduction, elimination, and formation (in this order) of all the types present in the system: dependent function, dependent multiplicative pair, multiplicative unit, additive sum, additive zero, dependent additive pair, and additive unit.

We also need a modified typing judgment that takes into account the multiplicities:

$$\Gamma \vdash M \overset{\sigma}{:} N$$

That is, given the context Γ, we can show that the term M is usable exactly σ times and has the type N. A key restriction is that σ must be either 0 or 1. The judgment thus only communicates whether the term M can be used in a computationally relevant context.

For further details, we encourage the reader to check the original presentation given by Atkey [3]. However, there are some notable differences worth emphasizing. Firstly, types and terms are not separated and instead of the **El** decoder, we have the universe constant $\mathcal{U}$. The boolean type has been replaced with three additive types: sum, unit, and pair. And finally, the multiplicative pair and additive sum eliminators contain multiplicity annotations.

2.3 Weakening

As currently presented, the ω multiplicity is only applicable when a variable is used at least twice in a relevant context. However, we would like to associate ω with unrestricted use. The system must be able to treat other multiplicities as ω, which can be accomplished by adding an ordering to the semiring and using a weakening rule, as described by McBride [12]. In particular, $\sigma \leq \pi$ means that a variable with σ uses may be treated as a variable with π uses.

Unsurprisingly, such ordering needs to be reflexive, transitive and must respect the semiring operations. A suitable ordering is $0 \leq \omega$ and $1 \leq \omega$. Since we want 1 to represent linear use, $0 \leq 1$ must not hold.

Contexts can also be ordered. If the contexts Γ_1 and Γ_2 only differ in multiplicities ($0\Gamma_1 = 0\Gamma_2$), we define $\Gamma_1 \leq \Gamma_2$ as a pointwise extension of the semiring ordering $\leq$. In other words, $\Gamma_1 \leq \Gamma_2$ iff the multiplicity of each variable in Γ_1 is less than or equal to the multiplicity of the same variable in Γ_2. The weakening rule then states that if the typing judgment holds in a typing context Γ_1, it also holds in any greater typing context Γ_2:

$$\frac{\Gamma_1 \vdash M \overset{\sigma}{:} T \qquad \Gamma_1 \leq \Gamma_2}{\Gamma_2 \vdash M \overset{\sigma}{:} T} \text{ WEAK}$$

2.4 Annotated Eliminators

While weakening works well in most cases, there is an issue with its interaction with eliminators of some types. Consider the following judgment:

$$p \overset{\omega}{:} (\_ \overset{1}{:} \mathbb{N}) \otimes \mathbb{N} \vdash \text{let } (x, y) = p \text{ in } (x + x) \overset{1}{:} \mathbb{N}$$

If we remove the multiplicities, we obtain a judgment that is valid in an intuitionistic setting. One of the goals of weakening in the system is the ability to treat ω as unrestricted use, turning that fragment of the system into a regular intuitionistic type theory.

However, adding weakening does not make this judgment valid. Atkey's elimination rule for multiplicative pairs states that while checking the subterm $x + x$, the variables x and y must be added to the typing context with multiplicity 1, which prevents y from being discarded and x from being duplicated. Notice that the weakening rule *can* be used to treat the single use of p in the eliminator as ω to match the multiplicity of p in the typing context. The problem is thus the inability of the eliminator to use p multiple times.

In theory, we could have only a single copy of p in the typing context and use the exponential modality for the elements of the pair, but such solution is not very flexible since the programmer must know ahead of the time where all such values will be required.

Instead, the eliminator is extended with a multiplicity annotation [14] which lets it consume the eliminated pair ω times. To ensure resource correctness, this multiplicity is propagated to the freshly bound variables. At that point, the weakening rule may be applied, allowing us to treat the zero uses of y as ω uses. The following judgment is now valid:

$$p \overset{\omega}{:} (\_ \overset{1}{:} \mathbb{N}) \otimes \mathbb{N} \vdash \text{let}_\omega (x, y) = p \text{ in } (x + x) \overset{1}{:} \mathbb{N}$$

Apart from the dependent multiplicative pair $(x \overset{?}{:} S) \otimes T$, this annotation may also be added to the eliminator of the additive sum $S \oplus T$. However, in the case of additive sums, the annotation cannot be 0 as the eliminator provides computationally relevant information.

3 Dependent Additive Pairs

An additive pair consists of two elements that have access to the same resources. This property can lead to seemingly unsound resource use. Consider the following judgment:

$$x \overset{1}{:} T \vdash \langle x, x \rangle \overset{1}{:} T \mathbin{\&} T$$

Each element is forced to use the variable x and yet x is still considered linear. The trick lies in the elimination: only one element of the additive pair can be extracted and the other must necessarily be discarded. The end result is that the variable x is indeed used once.

In the original presentation of QTT, an additive pair $S \mathbin{\&} T$ is represented by a function from booleans to either S or T. A similar encoding can be used in our presentation, since booleans are a special case of the more general additive sum type. Indeed, we can define the boolean type $\mathbf{2}$ as $\mathbf{1} \oplus \mathbf{1}$. An additive pair $S \mathbin{\&} T$ is then defined by the following term:

$$S \overset{0}{:} \mathcal{U}, T \overset{0}{:} \mathcal{U} \vdash (b \overset{1}{:} \mathbf{2}) \to \mathbf{case}_1\ b\ \mathbf{of}\ \{\mathbf{inl}\ () \to S; \mathbf{inr}\ () \to T\} \overset{0}{:} \mathcal{U}$$

Introduction and elimination follow immediately from this definition. Note that in a computationally relevant context, the units contained in the additive sum need to be eliminated as well. For brevity, this step is not explicitly written out and is only implied by using () in place of the bound variable.

Notice that the resource use matches our expectations. The eliminator of additive sums has a property similar to the additive pair introduction: each branch of the case analysis has access to the same resources. Resource soundness of the pair elimination comes from the fact that function application counts as a use of that function. In particular, if we wish to extract both elements of such a pair, we need to apply the function twice and thus use it twice. As an example, we can implement an operation to swap the elements of the pair.

$$p \overset{1}{:} S \mathbin{\&} T \vdash \lambda b.\ \mathbf{case}_1\ b\ \mathbf{of}\ \{\mathbf{inl}\ () \to p\ (\mathbf{inr}\ ()); \mathbf{inr}\ () \to p\ (\mathbf{inl}\ ())\} \overset{1}{:} T \mathbin{\&} S$$

However, this approach has two major downsides. Firstly, dependent type theories often lack a function extensionality principle, which complicates reasoning about functions. Proving that two additive pairs are the same thus becomes quite difficult. Adding function extensionality as an axiom presents other problems. Using a different notion of equality, such as in observational type theory [2] or homotopy type theory [16], might be possible but is out of the scope of this work.

The second, bigger problem is that this encoding is incapable of expressing type dependency between S and T. Since the two alternatives of the additive sum type elimination are independent, neither type has access to a value of the other type.

Instead of using an encoding, dependent additive pairs are built into the system as one of its base types. Formation, introduction and elimination are defined by the following rules:

$$\dfrac{0\Gamma \vdash S \overset{0}{:} \mathcal{U} \quad 0\Gamma, x \overset{0}{:} S \vdash T \overset{0}{:} \mathcal{U}}{0\Gamma \vdash (x:S) \mathbin{\&} T \overset{0}{:} \mathcal{U}}\ \&\text{-F} \qquad \dfrac{\Gamma \vdash M \overset{\pi}{:} S \quad \Gamma \vdash N \overset{\pi}{:} T[M/x]}{\Gamma \vdash \langle M, N \rangle \overset{\pi}{:} (x:S) \mathbin{\&} T}\ \&\text{-I}$$

$$\dfrac{\Gamma \vdash M \overset{\pi}{:} (x:S) \mathbin{\&} T}{\Gamma \vdash \mathbf{fst}\ M \overset{\pi}{:} S}\ \&\text{-E}_1 \qquad \dfrac{\Gamma \vdash M \overset{\pi}{:} (x:S) \mathbin{\&} T}{\Gamma \vdash \mathbf{snd}\ M \overset{\pi}{:} T[\mathbf{fst}\ M/x]}\ \&\text{-E}_2$$

In the dependent additive pair $(x : S)\,\&\,T$, the type T can refer to the value of the first element via the variable x. As expected, the introduction rule gives both elements of the pair access to the entire context Γ.

Notice that the second elimination rule uses both **fst** M and **snd** M, seemingly resulting in unsound resource use. However, because the first element is accessed in a computationally irrelevant context, resource soundness is not affected. The behavior of these eliminators is as follows:

$$\textbf{fst } \langle M, N \rangle \rightsquigarrow M$$
$$\textbf{snd } \langle M, N \rangle \rightsquigarrow N$$

4 Programming with Dependent Additive Pairs

In this section, we discuss three distinct scenarios that benefit from the use of dependent additive pairs. We restrict ourselves to linear uses of these pairs. Indeed, in the presence of weakening, additive and multiplicative pairs are mostly interchangeable.

Each definition found in this section is also implemented in Janus. Janus is a language based on the extended QTT mentioned in Sect. 2. It comes with a type checker and an interactive evaluator, which are implemented in Haskell and their source code is available online [15]. It is provided as a Cabal package and can be built and run with any recent version of `ghc` and `cabal`.

The examples are provided as `.jns` files and are available online.[1] These files can be loaded into Janus with the `:load` command, which performs type checking and adds the new definitions to the context. The user may then evaluate them or query their type using the `:type` command. If querying a type is not sufficient, the `.jns` files contain very detailed type information.

4.1 Linear Folds

In functional programming, operations that eliminate values of recursively defined data types are typically called *folds*. Consider the case of a singly-linked list type: **List**. The constant **Nil** represents an empty list, **Cons** introduces a non-empty list. We can define a simple fold operation with these two equations:

$$\textbf{fold } f\ z\ \textbf{Nil} = z$$
$$\textbf{fold } f\ z\ (\textbf{Cons } x\ xs) = f\ x\ (\textbf{fold } f\ z\ xs)$$

These simple folds are sometimes called *catamorphisms*. In categorical terms, a catamorphism is a unique homomorphism out of an initial algebra. Since we are in a dependent setting, we would like to give this operation a fully dependent

---

[1] https://github.com/vituscze/dependent-additive-pairs.

type. If we use a dependent function $P : \mathbf{List}\ A \to \mathcal{U}$ (also known as a *motive*) to describe the return type, we obtain the following:

$$A : \mathcal{U}, P : \mathbf{List}\ A \to \mathcal{U} \vdash \mathbf{fold} : (f : (x : A) \to (r : P\ ?) \to P\ (\mathbf{Cons}\ x\ ?)) \to$$
$$(z : P\ \mathbf{Nil}) \to (l : \mathbf{List}\ A) \to P\ l$$

However, we are unable to specify the type of f. The type of r as well as the type of the result need to mention the list xs, which is not available at this point. The only way to solve this problem is to add an additional parameter to f. We get different versions of **fold** depending on how this extra parameter is used. Since we are also in a substructural setting, we can specify and enforce this usage. Let us analyze the previous equations to see how the other parameters are used.

We can see that if the function f consumes the elements and the recursive results linearly, the whole list is also consumed linearly. The value z is also used exactly once. The only input that is not used linearly is the function f itself, which can be used any number of times, including zero. However, thanks to weakening, the ω multiplicity can be used to describe this usage. In this case, the additional parameter is not used in a relevant context. We obtain a resource-aware version of the previous type.

$$A \stackrel{0}{:} \mathcal{U}, P \stackrel{0}{:} (l \stackrel{0}{:} \mathbf{List}\ A) \to \mathcal{U} \vdash \mathbf{fold} \stackrel{1}{:}$$
$$(f \stackrel{\omega}{:} (x \stackrel{1}{:} A) \to (xs \stackrel{0}{:} \mathbf{List}\ A) \to (r \stackrel{1}{:} P\ xs) \to P\ (\mathbf{Cons}\ x\ xs)) \to$$
$$(z \stackrel{1}{:} P\ \mathbf{Nil}) \to (l \stackrel{1}{:} \mathbf{List}\ A) \to P\ l$$

If we allow the function f to use the additional parameter, we obtain a *paramorphism*. More generally, a paramorphism is a generalized catamorphism which allows the combining function access to both the recursive result and the remaining structure. We can again express this fact using two equations:

$$\mathbf{para}\ f\ z\ \mathbf{Nil} = z$$
$$\mathbf{para}\ f\ z\ (\mathbf{Cons}\ x\ xs) = f\ x\ (xs, \mathbf{para}\ f\ z\ xs)$$

In a substructural setting, we have an additional decision to make regarding the function f. If f uses both elements of the pair, we need to use a multiplicative pair. In this case, the variable xs is used twice and thus the list cannot be consumed linearly. If f uses exactly one of the elements of the pair, we need to use an additive pair. The variable xs is now used exactly once and the list can be consumed linearly. However, we cannot guarantee that the value z is used once. We obtain the following type:

$$A \stackrel{0}{:} \mathcal{U}, P \stackrel{0}{:} (l \stackrel{0}{:} \mathbf{List}\ A) \to \mathcal{U} \vdash \mathbf{para} \stackrel{1}{:}$$
$$(f \stackrel{\omega}{:} (x \stackrel{1}{:} A) \to (p \stackrel{1}{:} (xs : \mathbf{List}\ A)\ \&\ P\ xs) \to P\ (\mathbf{Cons}\ x\ (\mathrm{fst}\ p))) \to$$
$$(z \stackrel{\omega}{:} P\ \mathbf{Nil}) \to (l \stackrel{1}{:} \mathbf{List}\ A) \to P\ l$$

These linear paramorphisms are useful whenever only a part of the structure needs to be traversed. Examples include various insertion and deletion operations. A deletion operation can be linear as long as the deleted element is returned alongside the remaining structure.

The original **fold** can be implemented using **para** quite easily. However, since catamorphisms are also the eliminators of inductive types, it should be possible to implement **para** in terms of **fold**. Since the combining function does not have access to the rest of the list, it has to reconstruct it. The reconstructed list and recursive result are stored in an additive pair. The following definition demonstrates the desired semantics:

$$\textbf{para} = \lambda f\ z\ l.\ \textbf{snd}\ (\textbf{fold}\ (\lambda x\ xs\ p.\ \langle \textbf{Cons}\ x\ (\textbf{fst}\ p), f\ x\ p \rangle)\ \langle \textbf{Nil}, z \rangle\ l)$$

However, this definition requires some changes to satisfy the type checker. We have two choices for the motive P: $\lambda\_.\ (l' : \textbf{List}\ A) \& P\ l'$, or $\lambda l.\ (\_ : \textbf{List}\ A) \& P\ l$. The first one fails when applying the final **snd** because the first element is *not* the list l. The second one fails when applying f because xs and **fst** p are different lists. In both cases, the type checker is not convinced that the original and the reconstructed list are the same.

The motive offers us a hint. Notice we are either ignoring the lambda parameter or the first element of the pair. However, to use both of these, we will need an identity type. In particular, we need the following constants for the formation and introduction:

$$A \overset{0}{:} \mathcal{U}, x \overset{0}{:} A, y \overset{0}{:} A \vdash x \equiv y \overset{0}{:} \mathcal{U}$$
$$A \overset{0}{:} \mathcal{U} \vdash \textbf{refl} \overset{1}{:} (x \overset{0}{:} A) \to x \equiv x$$

We use *based path induction* [13] as the eliminator.

$$A \overset{0}{:} \mathcal{U}, x \overset{0}{:} A, y \overset{0}{:} A \vdash \textbf{J} \overset{1}{:} (P \overset{0}{:} (y' \overset{0}{:} A) \to (\_ \overset{0}{:} x \equiv y') \to \mathcal{U}) \to$$
$$(f \overset{1}{:} P\ x\ (\textbf{refl}\ x)) \to (p \overset{1}{:} x \equiv y) \to P\ y\ p$$

The new motive contains the additive pair and the proof that the original and reconstructed list are the same:

$$\textbf{Triple} = \lambda l.\ (p \overset{1}{:} (l' : \textbf{List}\ A) \& P\ l') \otimes (\textbf{fst}\ p \equiv l)$$

Of course, the fold now needs to construct this proof as it goes and then use it at the very end. The latter can be accomplished by using the identity $l' \equiv l$ to rewrite the type of the result from Pl' to Pl. The following function uses the proof contained in **Triple**l to produce Pl.

$$\textbf{extract} = \lambda t.\ \textbf{let}_1\ (p, q) = t\ \textbf{in}\ \textbf{J}\ (\lambda l'\ \_.\ P\ l')\ (\textbf{snd}\ p)\ q$$

For the former, we start with the proof **Nil** ≡ **Nil**. The inductive step asks us to prove **Cons**x(**fst** p) ≡ **Cons**xl given **fst** $p \equiv l$, which is accomplished by using the congruence property. That is, if $p \overset{1}{:} x \equiv y$ then **cong**$fp \overset{1}{:} f\ x \equiv fy$. Putting it all together, we obtain the following:

para = $\lambda f\ z\ l.$ extract (fold ($\lambda x\ xs\ t.$ let$_1$ $(p, q) = t$ in
$(\langle$**Cons** x (**fst** $p), f\ x\ p\rangle,$ **cong** $(\lambda l.\ $**Cons** $x\ l)\ q))\ (\langle$**Nil**$, z\rangle,$ **refl Nil**$)\ l)$

This definition is now correct and matches the type given earlier. The type of **para** is thus justified. Note that in practice, paramorphisms would not be defined in terms of catamorphisms, as the need to reconstruct the structure removes one of their main benefits.

While we focused on list paramorphisms here, this definition can be generalized to any tree-like structure. For example, the combining function for a binary tree paramorphism would have the following type:

$$(x \overset{1}{:} A) \to (l \overset{1}{:} (t : \mathbf{Tree}\ A)\ \&\ P\ t) \to (r \overset{1}{:} (t : \mathbf{Tree}\ A)\ \&\ P\ t) \to$$
$$P\ (\mathbf{Node}\ x\ (\mathbf{fst}\ l)\ (\mathbf{fst}\ r))$$

4.2 Resource-Aware Proofs

Dependent type theories use dependent pairs to express existential quantification. The first element of such a pair is typically called a *witness*, as it is a value that witnesses the inhabitation of the type of the second element.

In some cases, the witness can be computationally relevant. This kind of witness is typically found in operations that prove some correctness properties as their output. There are also cases where the witness is mainly used to specify the type of the second element, even though it might carry computationally relevant information itself. This use case can be found whenever the indices of dependent types cannot (or should not) be specified.

In the intersection of these two cases are operations that compute a relevant witness *and* a relevant dependent value that hides one or more of its indices. Consider a **filter** operation on vectors. Instead of using a natural number as the witness, we could use an entire **List**.

$$A : \mathcal{U}, n : \mathbb{N} \vdash \mathbf{filter} : (p : A \to \mathbf{2}) \to (xs : \mathbf{Vec}\ A\ n) \to$$
$$(l : \mathbf{List}\ A) \times \mathbf{Vec}\ A\ (\mathbf{length}\ l)$$

The list and the vector have the same length. But since the length of the list is not a part of its type, the length of the vector is still effectively hidden. However, the user has a much more interesting choice: if the hidden index is no longer necessary, the witness still carries all the useful information.

Partition. The **filter** example does not quite fit into our substructural setting. The input list cannot be used linearly since its elements might be discarded.

Instead of using a different example, we will adjust the **filter** operation as it allows us to demonstrate a couple of useful techniques.

First of all, if we want the operation to be linear, it also needs to return the elements that have been filtered out, ideally in a separate list. Such operation is sometimes called **partition**. Since the lists contain different elements, they need to be in a multiplicative pair.

$$A \stackrel{0}{:} \mathcal{U} \vdash \textbf{partition} \stackrel{1}{:} (p \stackrel{\omega}{:} (a \stackrel{1}{:} A) \to \mathbf{2}) \to (l \stackrel{1}{:} \textbf{List } A) \to$$
$$(\_ \stackrel{1}{:} \textbf{List } A) \otimes \textbf{List } A$$

The first problem we encounter is that applying the predicate p consumes the element of the list, leaving us with nothing to put into the result. Changing the multiplicity of the first parameter to zero would solve this issue, but predicates that are not allowed to inspect their input are generally not useful.

Instead, we require the predicate to also return a new version of the input, such as $p \stackrel{\omega}{:} (a \stackrel{1}{:} A) \to (\_ \stackrel{1}{:} \mathbf{2}) \otimes A$. With this change, implementing **partition** is easy. Now, suppose we want to also return a description of the resulting partition. We can use the following type:

$$A \stackrel{0}{:} \mathcal{U}, xs\ ys\ zs \stackrel{0}{:} \textbf{List } A \vdash \textbf{Union } xs\ ys\ zs \stackrel{0}{:} \mathcal{U}$$
$$A \stackrel{0}{:} \mathcal{U}, xs\ ys\ zs \stackrel{0}{:} \textbf{List } A \vdash \textbf{Left } \stackrel{1}{:} (x \stackrel{1}{:} A) \to (u \stackrel{1}{:} \textbf{Union } xs\ ys\ zs) \to$$
$$\textbf{Union } (\textbf{Cons } x\ xs)\ ys\ (\textbf{Cons } x\ zs)$$
$$A \stackrel{0}{:} \mathcal{U}, xs\ ys\ zs \stackrel{0}{:} \textbf{List } A \vdash \textbf{Right } \stackrel{1}{:} (x \stackrel{1}{:} A) \to (u \stackrel{1}{:} \textbf{Union } xs\ ys\ zs) \to$$
$$\textbf{Union } xs\ (\textbf{Cons } x\ ys)\ (\textbf{Cons } x\ zs)$$
$$A \stackrel{0}{:} \mathcal{U} \vdash \textbf{Stop } \stackrel{1}{:} \textbf{Union Nil Nil Nil}$$

Union $xs\ ys\ zs$ is a proof that the lists xs and ys can be interleaved to obtain the list zs. The introductions **Left** and **Right** are used to express whether the first element of the result came from the first or the second list. The elimination is left out as it will not be needed in this case. Since the type of the result is quite large, it might be useful to split it into a couple of auxiliary definitions.

$$\textbf{Result}_1 = \lambda A.\ (\_ \stackrel{1}{:} \textbf{List } A) \otimes \textbf{List } A$$
$$\textbf{Result}_2 = \lambda A\ zs\ r_1.\ \textbf{let}_0\ (xs, ys) = r_1\ \textbf{in Union } xs\ ys\ zs$$
$$\textbf{Result} = \lambda A\ zs.\ (r_1 : \textbf{Result}_1\ A)\ \&\ \textbf{Result}_2\ A\ zs\ r_1$$
$$\textbf{Pred} = \lambda A.\ (x \stackrel{1}{:} A) \to (\_ \stackrel{1}{:} \mathbf{2}) \otimes A$$

With that, we can state the full type of the **partition** operation as follows:

$$A \stackrel{0}{:} \mathcal{U} \vdash \textbf{partition} \stackrel{1}{:} (p \stackrel{\omega}{:} \textbf{Pred } A) \to (l \stackrel{1}{:} \textbf{List } A) \to \textbf{Result } A\ l$$

Programming with Dependent Additive Pairs   103

Since the type of the result depends on the input list, we need to use the dependent **fold** defined earlier. The base case has the type **Result** A **Nil** and only has a single valid value: $\langle(\textbf{Nil}, \textbf{Nil}), \textbf{Stop}\rangle$. The inductive case can be broken down into three steps. Firstly, we define auxiliary functions that add the new element to one of the **Result**$_1$ lists.

$$\textbf{add}'_\textbf{l} = \lambda x\ r_1.\ \textbf{let}_1\ (l, r) = r_1\ \textbf{in}\ (\textbf{Cons}\ x\ l, r)$$
$$\textbf{add}'_\textbf{r} = \lambda x\ r_1.\ \textbf{let}_1\ (l, r) = r_1\ \textbf{in}\ (l, \textbf{Cons}\ x\ r)$$

Secondly, we use these definitions to add the new elements to the whole **Result**. However, since the first element does not reduce to a pair, the type of the second element remains some form of **Result**$_2$, rather than reducing to **Union**. We can fix this by inspecting the first element to force reduction.

$$\textbf{add}_\textbf{l} = \lambda x\ r.\ \langle\textbf{add}'_\textbf{l}\ x\ (\textbf{fst}\ r), \textbf{let}_0\ (\_, \_) = \textbf{fst}\ r\ \textbf{in}\ \textbf{Left}\ x\ (\textbf{snd}\ r)\rangle$$

However, this definition has a problem similar to the one before. This time it is the term **snd** r whose type does not reduce. Without access to dependent pattern matching [9], we need to eliminate into a function type. That way, the type of the argument reduces and can be given to **Left**. The resulting function is then applied to **snd** r.

$$\textbf{add}_\textbf{l} = \lambda x\ r.\ \langle\textbf{add}'_\textbf{l}\ x\ (\textbf{fst}\ r), (\textbf{let}_0\ (\_, \_) = \textbf{fst}\ r\ \textbf{in}\ \lambda r_2.\ \textbf{Left}\ x\ r_2)\ (\textbf{snd}\ r)\rangle$$
$$\textbf{add}_\textbf{r} = \lambda x\ r.\ \langle\textbf{add}'_\textbf{r}\ x\ (\textbf{fst}\ r), (\textbf{let}_0\ (\_, \_) = \textbf{fst}\ r\ \textbf{in}\ \lambda r_2.\ \textbf{Right}\ x\ r_2)\ (\textbf{snd}\ r)\rangle$$

We can easily check that all auxiliary definitions have the expected types:

$$\ldots \vdash \textbf{add}'_\textbf{l}\ \textbf{add}'_\textbf{r}\ \vdots\ (x \vdots A) \to (r_1 \vdots \textbf{Result}_1\ A) \to \textbf{Result}_1\ A$$
$$\ldots \vdash \textbf{add}_\textbf{l}\ \textbf{add}_\textbf{r}\ \vdots\ (x \vdots A) \to (r \vdots \textbf{Result}\ A\ xs) \to \textbf{Result}\ A\ (\textbf{Cons}\ x\ xs)$$

Finally, we can apply the predicate and then use $\textbf{add}_\textbf{l}$ or $\textbf{add}_\textbf{r}$ depending on the result.

$$\textbf{step} = \lambda p\ x\ r.\ \textbf{let}_1\ (b, x') = p\ x\ \textbf{in}$$
$$\textbf{case}_1\ b\ \textbf{of}\ \{\textbf{inl}\ () \to \textbf{add}_\textbf{l}\ x'\ r; \textbf{inr}\ () \to \textbf{add}_\textbf{r}\ x'\ r\}$$

However, both $\textbf{add}_\textbf{l}\ x'\ r$ and $\textbf{add}_\textbf{r}\ x'\ r$ produce **Result** A (**Cons** $x'\ xs$) as we were forced to use x', which does not match **Result** A (**Cons** $x\ xs$) required by **fold**. The problem is that the predicate is allowed to return any value and thus we cannot assume that x and x' are the same. We can force it to return the same value by adding the identity type to the definition of **Pred**.

$$\textbf{Pred} = \lambda A.\ (x \vdots A) \to (\_ \vdots 2) \otimes (x' \vdots A) \otimes (x' \equiv x)$$

The proof can be extracted with a second **let** term. It can then be used to rewrite the type of the result, which is done by using the substitutivity of the identity type. In particular, if $v \stackrel{!}{:} P\ x$ and $p \stackrel{!}{:} x \equiv y$ then $\mathbf{subst}\ P\ p\ v \stackrel{!}{:} P\ y$. We can now fix the **step** function.

$$\mathbf{step} = \lambda p\ x\ r.\ \mathbf{let}_1\ (b, s) = p\ x\ \mathbf{in}\ \mathbf{let}_1\ (x', q) = s\ \mathbf{in}$$
$$\mathbf{subst}\ (\lambda x.\ \mathbf{Result}\ A\ (\mathbf{Cons}\ x\ xs))\ q$$
$$(\mathbf{case}_1\ b\ \mathbf{of}\ \{\mathbf{inl}\ () \to \mathbf{add}_\mathbf{l}\ x'\ r; \mathbf{inr}\ () \to \mathbf{add}_\mathbf{r}\ x'\ r\})$$

And finally, we can put it all together to implement the **partition** operation itself.

$$\mathbf{partition} = \lambda p\ l.\ \mathbf{fold}\ (\mathbf{step}\ p)\ \langle(\mathbf{Nil}, \mathbf{Nil}), \mathbf{Stop}\rangle\ l$$

It should be noted that the reduction behavior of $\mathbf{Result}_2$ might not be desirable in some situations. Even though it will eventually reduce to a **Union**, the type checker cannot see that without eliminating the pair first. In cases like this, it is generally recommended to move the computation to the indices of the type. We can define projections **Fst** and **Snd** for the multiplicative pair that may be used in types. We can then define another version of $\mathbf{Result}_2$.

$$\mathbf{Result}_2 = \lambda A\ zs\ r_1.\ \mathbf{Union}\ (\mathbf{Fst}\ r_1)\ (\mathbf{Snd}\ r_1)\ zs$$

We have implemented **partition** for both versions, but here we only present the one that does not require additional auxiliary definitions to function.

Insertion. As mentioned previously, many insertion operations may be implemented by using a paramorphism. We can reuse the **Union** type to implement a sorted list insertion operation that also produces a resource-aware proof. In particular, if the list l is the result of inserting a new element x into the list xs, we expect $\mathbf{Union}\,xs(\mathbf{Cons}\,x\,\mathbf{Nil})l$ to hold. We shall abbreviate $\mathbf{Cons}\,x\,\mathbf{Nil}$ as $[x]$. We begin with a couple of auxiliary definitions.

$$\mathbf{Result} = \lambda A\ x\ xs.\ (l : \mathbf{List}\ A)\ \&\ \mathbf{Union}\ xs\ [x]\ l$$
$$\mathbf{Cmp} = \lambda A.\ (x \stackrel{!}{:} A) \to (y \stackrel{!}{:} A) \to$$
$$(b \stackrel{!}{:} \mathbf{2}) \otimes (x' \stackrel{!}{:} A) \otimes (y' \stackrel{!}{:} A) \otimes (\_ \stackrel{!}{:} x' \equiv x) \otimes (y' \equiv y)$$

As before, we use the identity type to make sure the comparison function returns the same values it was given. We can now state the full type of a dependent **insert** operation.

$$A \stackrel{0}{:} \mathcal{U} \vdash \mathbf{insert} \stackrel{!}{:} (c \stackrel{\omega}{:} \mathbf{Cmp}\ A) \to (x \stackrel{!}{:} A) \to (xs \stackrel{!}{:} \mathbf{List}\ A) \to \mathbf{Result}\ A\ x\ xs$$

The base case is seemingly trivial: we only need to insert x into the empty list. However, because **para** requires the base case to have multiplicity ω, simply using

$[x]$ would require $x \overset{\omega}{:} A$. We instead eliminate into a linear function. The function can be discarded and thus the ω multiplicity is not a problem. In particular, we use the following motive:

$$A \overset{0}{:} \mathcal{U} \vdash \lambda xs.\ (x \overset{1}{:} A) \to \mathbf{Result}\ A\ x\ xs \overset{0}{:} (xs \overset{0}{:} \mathbf{List}\ A) \to \mathcal{U}$$

The base case is then trivial.

$$\mathbf{base} = \lambda x.\ \langle [x], \mathbf{Right}\ x\ \mathbf{Stop} \rangle$$

The inductive case is more interesting. If the inserted element x is smaller than or equal to y (according to the comparison function), we have found the insertion point and no further recursion is necessary. Recall that a paramorphism gives us access to an additive pair r containing the rest of the list and the recursive result. We ignore the recursive result and return $\mathbf{Cons}\ x\ (\mathbf{Cons}\ y\ (\mathbf{fst}\ r))$. We also need to construct a proof of the following type:

$$\mathbf{Union}\ (\mathbf{Cons}\ y\ (\mathbf{fst}\ r))\ [x]\ (\mathbf{Cons}\ x\ (\mathbf{Cons}\ y\ (\mathbf{fst}\ r)))$$

Clearly, x must have come from the $\mathbf{Right}$ list. We then need a simple lemma to show that $\mathbf{Union}\ l\ \mathbf{Nil}\ l$ holds for any l. The proof consists of a $\mathbf{Left}$ for each element of l and a $\mathbf{Stop}$ at the end.

$$\mathbf{lem} = \lambda l.\ \mathbf{fold}\ (\lambda x\ xs\ r.\ \mathbf{Left}\ x\ r)\ \mathbf{Stop}\ l$$

Putting it all together, we obtain the $\mathbf{done}$ function that handles the non-recursive case.

$$\mathbf{done} = \lambda x\ y\ r.\ \langle \mathbf{Cons}\ x\ (\mathbf{Cons}\ y\ (\mathbf{fst}\ r)), \mathbf{Right}\ x\ (\mathbf{lem}\ (\mathbf{Cons}\ y\ (\mathbf{fst}\ r))) \rangle$$

If x is greater than y, we must recursively insert x into the sublist by using the second element of the additive pair, giving us a new list and also a proof.

$$\cdots \vdash \mathbf{snd}\ r\ x \overset{1}{:} (l : \mathbf{List}\ A)\ \&\ \mathbf{Union}\ (\mathbf{fst}\ r)\ [x]\ l$$

Of course, we need to add the element y back to the list and return the list $\mathbf{Cons}\ y\ (\mathbf{fst}\ (\mathbf{snd}\ r\ x))$. Additionally, we need to construct a proof of the following type:

$$\mathbf{Union}\ (\mathbf{Cons}\ y\ (\mathbf{fst}\ r))\ [x]\ (\mathbf{Cons}\ y\ (\mathbf{fst}\ (\mathbf{snd}\ r\ x)))$$

The element y must have come from the $\mathbf{Left}$ list this time. The remaining proof obligation is satisfied by using the second element of $(\mathbf{snd}\ r)\ x$, the induction hypothesis. The following $\mathbf{go}$ function handles the recursive case:

$$\mathbf{go} = \lambda x\ y\ r.\ \langle \mathbf{Cons}\ y\ (\mathbf{fst}\ (\mathbf{snd}\ r\ x)), \mathbf{Left}\ y\ (\mathbf{snd}\ (\mathbf{snd}\ r\ x)) \rangle$$

Combining the functions **done** and **go** gives us a single step of the insertion. Note that we use a shortcut to represent the use of four $\mathbf{let}_1$ eliminations required to unpack the result of the comparison $c\ x\ y$.

$$\mathbf{step} = \lambda c\ y\ r\ x.\ \mathbf{let}_1\ (b, (x', (y', (p_x, p_y)))) = c\ x\ y\ \mathbf{in}$$
$$\mathbf{case}_1\ b\ \mathbf{of}\ \{\mathbf{inl}\ () \to \mathbf{done}\ x'\ y'\ r; \mathbf{inr}\ () \to \mathbf{go}\ x'\ y'\ r\}$$

The result of this function has the type **Result** $A\ x'$ (**Cons** y' (**fst** r)), which does not match the type required by **para**. As before, we use the proofs p_x and p_y to rewrite this type. However, we now need to use the **subst** operation twice.

$$\mathbf{step} = \lambda c\ y\ r\ x.\ \mathbf{let}_1\ (b, (x', (y', (p_x, p_y)))) = c\ x\ y\ \mathbf{in}$$
$$\mathbf{subst}\ (\lambda x.\ \mathbf{Result}\ A\ x\ (\mathbf{Cons}\ y\ (\mathbf{fst}\ r)))\ p_x$$
$$(\mathbf{subst}\ (\lambda y.\ \mathbf{Result}\ A\ x'\ (\mathbf{Cons}\ y\ (\mathbf{fst}\ r)))\ p_y$$
$$(\mathbf{case}_1\ b\ \mathbf{of}\ \{\mathbf{inl}\ () \to \mathbf{done}\ x'\ y'\ r; \mathbf{inr}\ () \to \mathbf{go}\ x'\ y'\ r\}))$$

And finally, we have everything needed to define the dependent **insert** operation itself.

$$\mathbf{insert} = \lambda c\ x\ xs.\ \mathbf{para}\ (\mathbf{step}\ c)\ \mathbf{base}\ xs\ x$$

Notice that the linearity of **insert** provides some guarantees for free. In particular, we know that the value x must be present in the list. Similarly, none of the elements of the original list could be discarded or duplicated. The computed proof makes these guarantees explicit, allowing their further use in other proofs. Additionally, it shows that the insertion does not change the relative positions of the original elements.

4.3 Inductive and Coinductive Types

So far we have seen additive pairs used with other data types. Let us consider what happens when these pairs are used to define a data type. Going back to the **List** type, we can see that its definition does not explicitly mention pairs. However, inductive types can be represented as least fixed points. **List** A is the least fixed point of the following type function:

$$\mathbf{ListF} = \lambda X.\ \mathbf{1} \oplus (\_ \overset{!}{:} A) \otimes X$$

This representation reveals the implicit use of a pair type. If we replace the multiplicative pair with an additive pair and compute the new fixed point we obtain the following type:

$$A \overset{0}{:} \mathcal{U} \vdash \mathbf{List}^+\ A \overset{0}{:} \mathcal{U}$$
$$A \overset{0}{:} \mathcal{U} \vdash \mathbf{Nil}^+ \overset{!}{:} \mathbf{List}^+\ A$$
$$A \overset{0}{:} \mathcal{U}, p \overset{!}{:} (\_ : A)\ \&\ \mathbf{List}^+\ A \vdash \mathbf{Cons}^+\ p \overset{!}{:} \mathbf{List}^+\ A$$

If additive pairs represent a choice between two resources, an additive list represents a choice between n resources, where n is not known ahead of time. However, before we even attempt to define the eliminator, we quickly run into an issue. In a linear context, we cannot create a list with a single element.

$$A \overset{0}{:} \mathcal{U}, x \overset{1}{:} A \not\vdash \mathbf{Cons}^+ \langle x, \mathbf{Nil}^+ \rangle \overset{1}{:} \mathbf{List}^+ \ A$$

The second element of the pair discards x. We could fix it by also changing the multiplicative unit $\mathbf{1}$ to the additive unit $\top$. However, we would be treating symptoms rather than the cause, which is that a choice between zero resources does not make sense. We therefore want nonempty lists, which can be accomplished by replacing $\mathbf{Nil}^+$ with $\mathbf{Last}^+$. $\mathbf{Last}^+ \ x$ represents a list with a single element x. Let us analyze the behavior of the eliminator so that we can assign the correct multiplicities.

$$\mathbf{fold}^+ \ f \ z \ (\mathbf{Last}^+ \ x) = z \ x$$
$$\mathbf{fold}^+ \ f \ z \ (\mathbf{Cons}^+ \ p) = f \ \langle \mathbf{fst} \ p, \mathbf{fold}^+ \ f \ z \ (\mathbf{snd} \ p) \rangle$$

The function f is discarded in one case and duplicated in the other and thus needs the ω multiplicity. However, the function z also needs ω, as it is discarded in the second case.

$$A \overset{0}{:} \mathcal{U}, P \overset{0}{:} \mathcal{U} \vdash \mathbf{fold}^+ \overset{1}{:} (f \overset{\omega}{:} (\_ \overset{1}{:} (\_ : A) \& P) \to P) \to$$
$$(z \overset{\omega}{:} (\_ \overset{1}{:} A) \to P) \to (l \overset{1}{:} \mathbf{List}^+ \ A) \to P$$

Additive lists admit some common list operations, such as $\mathbf{map}^+$. However, unlike the normal $\mathbf{map}$, we can guarantee that the mapped function is used linearly. Notice that since the combining function given to $\mathbf{fold}^+$ is used ω times, referencing the mapped function inside it would not count as linear use. Instead, we eliminate into a function type and thread the mapped function through the entire fold. That is, instead of the usual type $\mathbf{List} \ B$ we eliminate into the type $(f \overset{1}{:} (\_ \overset{1}{:} A) \to B) \to \mathbf{List} \ B$. The result is then applied to the mapped function.

$$\mathbf{map}^+ = \lambda f \ l. \ \mathbf{fold}^+ \ (\lambda p \ f. \ \mathbf{Cons}^+ \ \langle f \ (\mathbf{fst} \ p), \mathbf{snd} \ p \ f \rangle)$$
$$(\lambda x \ f. \ \mathbf{Last}^+ \ (f \ x)) \ l \ f$$

A linear operation that can be implemented on additive lists but not normal lists is **replicate**. Since we are using nonempty lists, we need to ensure that **replicate** is not used with zero, or generate a list one element longer. We also need to define natural numbers, though for this example only the non-dependent eliminator **rec** with the usual semantics will suffice.

$$P \overset{0}{:} \mathcal{U} \vdash \mathbf{rec} \overset{1}{:} (f \overset{\omega}{:} (\_ \overset{1}{:} P) \to P) \to (z \overset{1}{:} P) \to (n \overset{1}{:} \mathbb{N}) \to P$$

Like before, the replicated value needs to be threaded through, this time in an additive pair.

$$\mathbf{replicate} = \lambda n\, x.\, \mathbf{fst}\ (\mathbf{rec}\ (\lambda p.\ \langle \mathbf{Cons}^+\ \langle \mathbf{snd}\ p, \mathbf{fst}\ p \rangle, \mathbf{snd}\ p \rangle)$$
$$\langle \mathbf{Last}^+\ x, x \rangle\ n)$$

Many linear operations that can be implemented only on additive lists generate the list from a single seed value. Types that are defined using these unfolding operations are called coinductive types. As the name suggests, they are dual to inductive types. If an inductive type corresponds to a least fixed point, a coinductive type corresponds to a greatest fixed point. Values of such types are potentially infinite.

While inductive definitions need to exhibit termination, the same cannot be required of coinductive definitions, which may produce infinite values and thus do not always terminate. Instead, coinductive definitions need to exhibit *productivity*. A productive definition always produces a new piece of the final value after a finite amount of time. Coinductive types thus naturally lend themselves to describing processes that always progress but might not terminate, such as a Turing machine simulation.

In a linear setting, an infinite value makes sense only if each of its elements uses the same finite resources. Coinductive types thus naturally lend themselves to definitions using additive pairs. Let us consider infinite **Stream**s as an example. When defining a coinductive type, the eliminators are regarded as primary.

$$A \overset{0}{:} \mathcal{U} \vdash \mathbf{Stream}\ A \overset{0}{:} \mathcal{U}$$
$$A \overset{0}{:} \mathcal{U}, s \overset{1}{:} \mathbf{Stream}\ A \vdash \mathbf{head}\ s \overset{1}{:} A$$
$$A \overset{0}{:} \mathcal{U}, s \overset{1}{:} \mathbf{Stream}\ A \vdash \mathbf{tail}\ s \overset{1}{:} \mathbf{Stream}\ A$$

Introduction is defined by specifying what happens when an eliminator is applied to it. Just like the behavior of eliminators of inductive types can be expressed using pattern matching, we can express the behavior of this introduction using copattern matching [1].

$$\mathbf{head}\ (\mathbf{unfold}\ f\ s) = \mathbf{fst}\ (f\ s)$$
$$\mathbf{tail}\ (\mathbf{unfold}\ f\ s) = \mathbf{unfold}\ f\ (\mathbf{snd}\ (f\ s))$$

No matter which eliminator is used, the seed value s is used exactly once. The generating function f is duplicated in the second case and thus needs to have the ω multiplicity. We obtain the following type for the introduction:

$$S \overset{0}{:} \mathcal{U}, A \overset{0}{:} \mathcal{U} \vdash \mathbf{unfold} \overset{1}{:} (f \overset{\omega}{:} (\_ \overset{1}{:} S) \to (\_ : A)\ \&\ S) \to (s \overset{1}{:} S) \to \mathbf{Stream}\ A$$

Some of the operations defined on additive lists earlier can be expressed much more naturally using streams. For example, we can define **repeat**, an infinite version of **replicate**. If we want to create streams that consist of more than one distinct value, we can use its generalization, the **iterate** operation.

$$\mathbf{repeat} = \lambda a.\ \mathbf{unfold}\ (\lambda a.\ \langle a, a \rangle)\ a$$
$$\mathbf{iterate} = \lambda f\ a.\ \mathbf{unfold}\ (\lambda a.\ \langle a, f\ a \rangle)\ a$$

We also expect streams to support a mapping operation. Just like before, the mapped function cannot be directly referenced in the generating function. However, unlike before, we do not have full control over the output of **unfold** and thus cannot use a function type. Since we need both the stream and the function to be accessible, we must use a multiplicative pair. That is, instead of the usual seed type **Stream**A, we use $(f \stackrel{!}{:} (\_ \stackrel{!}{:} A) \to B) \otimes \mathbf{Stream}\ A$.

$$\mathbf{map_s} = \lambda f\ s.\ \mathbf{unfold}\ (\lambda p.\ \mathbf{let}_1\ (f, s) = p\ \mathbf{in}\ \langle f\ (\mathbf{head}\ s), (f, \mathbf{tail}\ s) \rangle)\ (f, s)$$

While we focused on the standard infinite streams here, coinductive types can also contain type dependencies. In that case, the type of at least one eliminator mentions the other eliminators and a dependent additive pair is required to specify the type of the generating function in the introduction.

5 Related Work

Some type systems split variables into multiple subsets that restrict how these variables can be used. Type dependency can also be added to these systems. An early example of such a dependent theory is Cervesato and Pfenning's Linear Logical Framework [7]. LLF splits the typing context into two parts: linear and intuitionistic. One major downside of this approach is that a dependent type may only refer to variables from the intuitionistic context. A more recent example of this split-context system is given by Krishnaswami et al. [10].

Semirings have also been used before to keep account of variable usage. One such example is given by Brunel et al. [6]. Semiring annotations are used with the exponential modality, which is then generalized into a full *coeffect* system. The typing context is not split. Unlike in QTT, it contains linear and *discharged* variables, which carry the semiring annotations.

The key insight behind QTT is provided by McBride [12]. In his type system, semiring zero represents computational irrelevance. Types are then treated as computationally irrelevant and variable occurrences there do not count towards the total multiplicity, which allows types to depend on any kind of variable. This idea is further reinforced by providing a type-erasing translation which also removes the computationally irrelevant parts.

QTT itself is described by Atkey [3]. This work addresses a problem with inadmissible substitution as well as extending the theory with dependent multiplicative pairs and booleans. A categorical model is also provided. Note that other additive types are only available via encoding involving booleans and function types.

A graded dependent type system, an approach similar to QTT, is given by Choudhury et al. [8]. The key difference is that types are not forced to use the semiring zero for all variables. This change gives a finer control over resources at the type level and also places fewer restrictions on the semiring.

QTT forms the basis of some programming languages. Idris 2 is a purely functional, general purpose programming language developed by Brady et al. [5] and based on the zero-one-many flavor of QTT. Brady [4] provides compelling examples of combining dependent and substructural types to increase the type safety of programs, such as dependent session types: a two party communication channels that enforce a protocol at the type level.

QTT has been extended with dependent additive pairs and annotated eliminators in our previous work [14]. Multiplicity annotations help resolve a few undesirable interactions between weakening and eliminators of the sum and pair types. This extended theory serves as the basis of the Janus language.

6 Conclusion

The most important aspect of additive types is that they extend resource handling with the notion of choice. This choice comes in two different flavors: *external* choice, which happens during introduction; and *internal* choice, which happens during elimination.

External choice is typically provided by an additive sum. This type is commonly found in substructural systems and has many well-documented use cases. Internal choice is less common, typically provided by an additive pair. Many substructural systems either do not support this type at all or only support it via an inconvenient encoding, which cannot express any form of type dependency.

In this work, we showed that additive pairs in general and dependent additive pairs in particular are not only an interesting theoretical construct but also a practical tool for solving problems in resource-aware programming. Specifically, we identified three distinct kinds of problems that are best solved by these pairs, and successfully implemented solutions in the Janus language. We hope this work inspires further adoption of both dependent and ordinary additive pairs in QTT and other substructural systems, as well as a wider use of these pairs in this style of programming.

References

1. Abel, A., Pientka, B., Thibodeau, D., Setzer, A.: Copatterns: programming infinite structures by observations. In: Proceedings of the 40th Annual ACM SIGPLAN-SIGACT Symposium on Principles of Programming Languages, POPL 2013, pp. 27–38. Association for Computing Machinery, New York (2013). https://doi.org/10.1145/2429069.2429075
2. Altenkirch, T., McBride, C., Swierstra, W.: Observational equality, now! In: Proceedings of the 2007 Workshop on Programming Languages Meets Program Verification, PLPV 2007, pp. 57–68. Association for Computing Machinery, New York (2007). https://doi.org/10.1145/1292597.1292608

3. Atkey, R.: Syntax and semantics of quantitative type theory. In: Proceedings of the 33rd Annual ACM/IEEE Symposium on Logic in Computer Science, LICS 2018, pp. 56–65. Association for Computing Machinery, New York (2018). https://doi.org/10.1145/3209108.3209189
4. Brady, E.: Idris 2: quantitative type theory in practice. In: Møller, A., Sridharan, M. (eds.) 35th European Conference on Object-Oriented Programming (ECOOP 2021). Leibniz International Proceedings in Informatics (LIPIcs), vol. 194, pp. 9:1–9:26. Schloss Dagstuhl – Leibniz-Zentrum für Informatik, Dagstuhl, Germany (2021). https://doi.org/10.4230/LIPIcs.ECOOP.2021.9
5. Brady, E., et al.: Idris 2 (2023). https://github.com/idris-lang/Idris2
6. Brunel, A., Gaboardi, M., Mazza, D., Zdancewic, S.: A core quantitative coeffect calculus. In: Shao, Z. (ed.) ESOP 2014. LNCS, vol. 8410, pp. 351–370. Springer, Heidelberg (2014). https://doi.org/10.1007/978-3-642-54833-8_19
7. Cervesato, I., Pfenning, F.: A linear logical framework. Inf. Comput. **179**(1), 19–75 (2002). https://doi.org/10.1006/inco.2001.2951
8. Choudhury, P., Eades, H., Eisenberg, R., Weirich, S.: A graded dependent type system with a usage-aware semantics. Proc. ACM Program. Lang. 5(POPL) (2021). https://doi.org/10.1145/3434331
9. Coquand, T.: Pattern matching with dependent types. In: Nordström, B., Pettersson, K., Plotkin, G. (eds.) Proceedings of the 1992 Workshop on Types for Proofs and Programs, pp. 71–83. Båstad, Sweden (1992)
10. Krishnaswami, N.R., Pradic, P., Benton, N.: Integrating linear and dependent types. In: Proceedings of the 42nd Annual ACM SIGPLAN-SIGACT Symposium on Principles of Programming Languages, POPL 2015, pp. 17–30. Association for Computing Machinery, New York (2015). https://doi.org/10.1145/2676726.2676969
11. Martin-Löf, P.: An intuitionistic theory of types: predicative part. In: Rose, H., Shepherdson, J. (eds.) Logic Colloquium '73, Studies in Logic and the Foundations of Mathematics, vol. 80, pp. 73–118. Elsevier (1975). https://doi.org/10.1016/S0049-237X(08)71945-1
12. McBride, C.: I got plenty o' nuttin'. In: Lindley, S., McBride, C., Trinder, P., Sannella, D. (eds.) A List of Successes That Can Change the World. LNCS, vol. 9600, pp. 207–233. Springer, Cham (2016). https://doi.org/10.1007/978-3-319-30936-1_12
13. Paulin-Mohring, C.: Inductive definitions in the system Coq rules and properties. In: Bezem, M., Groote, J.F. (eds.) TLCA 1993. LNCS, vol. 664, pp. 328–345. Springer, Heidelberg (1993). https://doi.org/10.1007/BFb0037116
14. Šefl, V., Svoboda, T.: Additive types in quantitative type theory. In: Ciabattoni, A., Pimentel, E., de Queiroz, R.J.G.B. (eds.) Logic, Language, Information, and Computation, pp. 250–262. Springer, Cham (2022). https://doi.org/10.1007/978-3-031-15298-6_16
15. Svoboda, T., Šefl, V.: Janus (2023). https://github.com/svobot/janus
16. The Univalent Foundations Program: Homotopy Type Theory: Univalent Foundations of Mathematics. Institute for Advanced Study (2013). https://homotopytypetheory.org/book

Context-Free Subphrase Grammars
A Grammar Formalism for Modular Syntax Definitions

Björn Lötters[(✉)]

Technische Hochschule Mittelhessen (University of Applied Sciences), Wiesenstr. 14,
35390 Giessen, Hesse, Germany
bjoern.loetters@mni.thm.de

Abstract. In this paper, we propose *Context-Free Subphrase Grammars*, a grammar formalism that is as powerful as Chomsky's Context-Free Grammars, but without their notorious lack of modularity. The key to this improvement is an alternative approach to precedence that naturally applies to arbitrary production rules using a notion of *subphrase structure*. We provide evidence that our formalism is complete and sound with respect to Context-Free Grammars, and demonstrate how it can be used to define syntax in a modular way by means of a small example.

Keywords: Context-Free Grammars · Context-Free Languages · Modular Grammar Formalism · Operator Precedence

1 Introduction

Context-Free Grammars (CFGs) as proposed by Chomsky [5] appear everywhere in computer science: Be it to describe the syntax of a programming language, the text protocol of a web application or to process natural languages. They provide an intuitive yet powerful means to describe *Context-Free Languages* (CFLs) [13], the class of formal languages recognized by push-down automatons [11]. Software tools like Bison [8], ANTLR [16], SDF [10] and GF [17] witness their success story. In face of this, their notorious lack of *modularity*, as we can observe it with the grammar in (1), is all the more surprising.

$$
\begin{aligned}
E &\to E + T \mid T \\
T &\to T * F \mid F \\
F &\to (\ E\ ) \mid x
\end{aligned}
\quad (1)
$$

Here, we describe a language of arithmetic terms with the usual precedence between addition and multiplication. For this purpose, the grammar makes use of the well-known operator-precedence climbing method. The lack of modularity now becomes apparent when we try to add a new operator to the language. To see this, let us consider an exponentiation operator $a \mathbin{\hat{}} b$, which binds more tightly than multiplication. In order to take this precedence into account, we must not only add two *new* productions $P \to F \mathbin{\hat{}} P \mid F$, but we are also forced to replace any occurrence of F with P in the *existing* productions of T. It is this replacement that contradicts the idea of a modular system and which comes with a lack of several other design principles we know from software engineering (such as composability, reusability, scalability and extensibility).

But why is that? The central problem here is that precedence manifests as a close relation between the constituents of the language, while CFGs offer no way to abstract over such a relation. A widespread solution to this deficiency is therefore not to model the precedence with the grammar at all. Instead, it is left ambiguous, and additional disambiguation rules are used to solve this issue separately [1,10]. The example in (2) illustrates this, using the notion of precedence grammars proposed by Aasa [1] and used for Agda's mixfix operators [6,15].

$$\begin{aligned} &E \rightarrow E + E \quad &&1 \quad \textit{left associative} \\ &E \rightarrow E * E \quad &&2 \quad \textit{left associative} \\ &E \rightarrow (\,E\,) \ \mid x \end{aligned} \qquad (2)$$

In this case, the aforementioned modularity concerns are indeed solved, as the grammar itself does not encode the precedence anymore. The resulting ambiguities are then resolved using the concept of *tree filters*. These filter out all those derivation trees that do not respect the intended precedence and associativity, leaving the overall derivation process unambiguous again.

However, as elegant as this solution is, it comes at its own price: These additional disambiguation rules are not an integral part of the underlying grammar formalism and as such it is not only hard to formally reason about the language being described. We also claim that this solution is counter-intuitive in the general case for arbitrary productions. In the words of Aasa [1] herself, "there is no adequate definition of what it means for a production in a grammar to have higher precedence than another production". While tree filters seem to provide appropriate formal semantics, grammars do not only describe *trees*. First and foremost, we use grammars to describe the *sets of strings* we call languages. The central question that drives our research is therefore:

> How can we apply the notion of precedence to CFGs in a natural language-oriented fashion to finally improve on their lack of modularity?

In this paper, we answer the question above and propose *Context-Free Subphrase Grammars* (CFSGs): a novel grammar formalism that is as powerful as CFGs but improves on their lack of modularity in a language-oriented way. This is made possible by an alternative interpretation of precedence that is not based on tree filters but on the notion of *subphrases*. In detail, our contributions are:

– An alternative approach to precedence using *subphrases* in Sect. 2
– A formalization of *Context-Free Subphrase Grammars* (CFSGs) in Sect. 3
– Evidence about the meta-theoretic properties of CFSGs and in particular their *completeness* and *soundness* with respect to CFGs in Sect. 4

In Sect. 5 we showcase our formalism by means of a small but representative example. We furthermore highlight and compare the most relevant work in Sect. 6 and give a brief excerpt of future work in Sect. 7, before we finally conclude our findings in Sect. 8.

2 The Notion of Subphrases

Before we dive into the actual CFSG formalism in Sect. 3, let us first develop an intuition for subphrases and their connection to precedence in this section. For this purpose, we briefly recall the term *phrase* and clarify what we mean by a *subphrase* in Sect. 2.1. Followed by that, we motivate an alternative approach to precedence in Sect. 2.2 by examining the traditional one using tree filters. Section 2.3 finally shows how we can use the notion of subphrases to approach precedence in a more natural and language-oriented way.

2.1 Terminology

Chomsky [5] himself referred to his grammar formalisms as so-called *phrase structure grammars*. This is because we can use them to describe the structure of the different phrases in a language. Take, for example, the phrase structure of the English sentence *the dog likes this food* in Fig. 1.

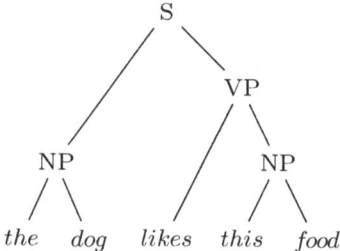

Fig. 1. An exemplary phrase structure

Here, the sentence is hierarchically decomposed into different parts, which we call *phrases*. For example, at the topmost level it consists of the noun phrase (NP) *the dog* and the verb phrase (VP) *likes this food*. This verb phrase is, in turn, a composition of the verb *likes* and the noun phrase (NP) *this food*. Note, that we use the term *phrase* in a broader sense here and consider the sentence (S) itself a phrase as well. It is this hierarchical decomposition which also gives rise to the notion of *subphrases*. That is, we call any phrase which is part of another phrase a subphrase. Hence, the noun phrase (NP) *this food* is a subphrase of the verb phrase (VP) *likes this food*. Just like set inclusion, this kind of relation between phrases is reflexive as well as transitive, which is why the noun phrase (NP) *this food* is also a subphrase of itself and the sentence (S) *the dog likes this food*.

2.2 The Traditional Approach to Precedence

When we first learn about precedence in elementary school, we are given examples such as $1 + 2 * 3$ and are told that the 2 is tied to the multiplication and not to the addition. That is, multiplication *precedes* addition. Such a conflict resolution is necessary because both infix operators compete for the exact same argument here, which manifests as the grammatical ambiguity in (2).

While this intuition of precedence promises to solve the ambiguity issues, it surprisingly fails to naturally apply to less common examples, let alone arbitrary phrases. What, for example, is "a noun phrase binds more tightly than a verb phrase" supposed to mean? At this point, the traditional explanation attempt resorts to the concept of tree filters (cf. [1,3]). That is, whenever a production binds less tightly than another production, it is not allowed to occur as a subtree in a derivation tree of the other production. We can observe this very well by comparing the two derivation trees in Fig. 2. Here, the usual precedence between addition and multiplication prohibits the subtree with + at its top to occur as a child of *.

Fig. 2. An example for a valid and invalid derivation tree

The problem with this traditional approach is its dissonance with the idea of grammars being rewrite systems. As such, they focus on the pure rule-based *generation* of strings, whereas tree filters are not about the generation of strings, but rather the *filtration* of derivation trees. This additional second layer makes it more difficult to reason about the language, as we have to keep in mind not only the strings generated by the production rules of a grammar. We are therefore interested in a shift towards a more language-oriented, generative approach to precedence, as we explore in next subsection.

2.3 An Interpretation of Precedence Using Subphrases

For a language-oriented approach to precedence, it is beneficial to first understand the actual effect of precedence on a language. To this end, we examine the languages presented in (3), which describe the sets of words derivable from the respective non-terminals of the introductory grammar in (1).

$$\begin{aligned}
\mathcal{L}(E) &= \{\, a + b \mid a \in \mathcal{L}(E), b \in \mathcal{L}(T) \,\} \cup \mathcal{L}(T) \\
\mathcal{L}(T) &= \{\, a * b \mid a \in \mathcal{L}(T), b \in \mathcal{L}(F) \,\} \cup \mathcal{L}(F) \\
\mathcal{L}(F) &= \{\, (\,a\,) \mid a \in \mathcal{L}(E) \phantom{, b \in \mathcal{L}(F)} \,\} \cup \{\, x \,\}
\end{aligned} \qquad (3)$$

Upon closer inspection, one thing catches the eye in particular: We can observe an inclusion hierarchy $\mathcal{L}(E) \supseteq \mathcal{L}(T) \supseteq \mathcal{L}(F)$ that resembles our initial precedence relation. This is due to the concept of *safe substitution*, as it is introduced by the unary productions $E \to T$ and $T \to F$ in the grammar.

But this is not the only observable effect of precedence: When we consider the source set $\mathcal{L}(T)$ for the right operand b in the first equation, it becomes apparent that this set has not been chosen at random. It reflects the idea of the operator-precedence *climbing* method and refers to the greatest proper subset according to the aforementioned inclusion hierarchy. More intuitively, it can also be seen as the language of the next precedence level.

It is these two observations which lead us to the central idea of our work: Why not leverage the easy-to-understand concept of language inclusion to model precedence? We therefore propose two extensions to CFGs:

1. Similar to the idea of subtyping in type theory, we introduce a new rule scheme that captures the notion of subphrases: *subphrase rules*. We therefore write $T \sqsubseteq E$ (which can be read as "T is a subphrase of E") instead of $E \to T$ to state that any T-phrase is also an E-phrase.
2. In order to make use of the emerging *subphrase relation* $\sqsubseteq$, we generalize non-terminal symbols to *non-terminal expressions*. In particular, we introduce the expression $E \downarrow$ which denotes the *greatest proper subphrase* of E or, respectively, the greatest proper subset in the inclusion hierarchy.

As a consequence of the above extensions our introductory grammar from (1) can now be rewritten as shown in (4). Here, we use subphrase rules to include $\mathcal{L}(F)$ in $\mathcal{L}(T)$ and $\mathcal{L}(T)$ in $\mathcal{L}(E)$. At the same time, we also use this inclusion hierarchy to abstractly refer to the respective next greater precedence level, which is $E \downarrow$ in case of E and $T \downarrow$ in case of T. Due to this indirection, our initial modularity concerns are now solved as well. For example, if we consider the extension example from the introduction again, we can see how the addition of the exponentiation operator in (5) does not force us to correct existing production rules. Whenever we change the subphrase relation by adding new subphrase rules, the interpretation of $T \downarrow$ changes accordingly and without further ado.

$$
\begin{aligned}
E &\to E + E \downarrow \\
T &\sqsubseteq E \\
T &\to T * T \downarrow \\
F &\sqsubseteq T \\
F &\to (\,E\,) \quad | \ x
\end{aligned}
\qquad (4) \qquad
\begin{aligned}
P &\to P \downarrow * P \\
P &\sqsubseteq T \\
F &\sqsubseteq P
\end{aligned}
\qquad (5)
$$

And it is not only that: As we will see in the next section, our subphrase relation induces a special kind of lattice which we call *subphrase lattice*. It shows great similarity with the precedence graphs proposed by Danielsson et al. [6] for Agda's mixfix operators and provides a strong theoretical foundation for the semantics of CFSGs. The underlying idea is to form so-called lower-sets of non-terminal symbols. That is, sets which are "downward closed" with respect to the subphrase relation and which can be ordered by set inclusion. Consider, for example, the subphrase lattice in Fig. 3 that corresponds to the grammar in (4).

As we can see here, the interpretation of a non-terminal expression such as $[\![E \downarrow]\!]$ simply corresponds to an element of the subphrase lattice. In the other

$\{\top, E, T, F, \bot\} \longrightarrow \supseteq \longrightarrow \{E, T, F, \bot\} \longrightarrow \supseteq \longrightarrow \{T, F, \bot\} \longrightarrow \supseteq \longrightarrow \{F, \bot\} \longrightarrow \supseteq \longrightarrow \{\bot\}$

with $[\![E \downarrow]\!]$, $[\![T \downarrow]\!]$, $[\![T \downarrow]\!]$ labels on the arrows.

Fig. 3. The subphrase lattice of the grammar in (4)

direction, we furthermore obtain a notion of the *greatest* $\top$ and *least subphrase* $\bot$ or, respectively, a least and greatest precedence level. And since lattices give rise to two dual binary operations, we also obtain a notion of the *least common superphrase* (the join operation) and the *greatest common subphrase* (the meet operation). In other words, these correspond to the greatest common preceding and the least common subsequent precedence level. At this point it is worth paying attention to the contrary wording: Whenever we say that X binds more tightly than Y (i.e., X has a higher precedence than Y), this means that X is a subphrase of Y (or Y is a superphrase of X). Conversely, whenever X has a lower precedence than Y, this means that Y is a subphrase of X.

These insights illustrate how introducing a lattice can enrich our understanding of the connection between subphrases and precedence. With this in mind, let us now transition to the next section, where we formalize CFSGs and the aforementioned concepts.

3   Context-Free Subphrase Grammars

Within this section we properly formalize *Context-Free Subphrase Grammars* (CFSGs). For this purpose, we first define an abstract syntax for our grammar formalism in Sect. 3.1. In contrast to CFGs, not every instance of CFSGs is well-formed, which is why we give a proper definition of well-formedness in Sect. 3.2. We then define the semantics of our grammar formalism in terms of the derivation relation in Sect. 3.3.

3.1   Abstract Syntax

The abstract syntax of our grammar formalism is given by the productions in Fig. 4. Just like CFGs, it is based on a vocabulary that consists of a finite set of terminal symbols $\mathbb{T}$ and a finite set of non-terminal symbols $\mathbb{N}$ with $\mathbb{T} \cap \mathbb{N} = \varnothing$. As there might be situations where we consider vocabularies of different grammars, we may write $G_{\mathbb{T}}$ to disambiguate the set of terminal symbols $\mathbb{T}$ of the grammar G from others (likewise for other grammar-dependent sets).

Upon closer inspection one syntactic particularity stands out here: The set of non-terminal symbols $\mathbb{N}$ is itself based on a finite set of variable symbols $\mathbb{V}$ with $\bot, \top \notin \mathbb{V}$ and a finite set of so-called domain symbols $\mathbb{D}$. This leaves non-terminal symbols as two-dimensional identifiers and goes back to an important observation: One grammar may describe the union of *multiple* languages. The challenge with this observation is that all these languages may come with their own subphrase structure, whereas the naive union of subphrase relations does not always produce the desired results. Ultimately, this would leave CFSGs as a proper subclass of CFGs. In order to achieve our goal of an equally powerful grammar formalism, we therefore need the ability to define *multiple* subphrase relations per CFSG. For this reason, each domain symbol a ∈ $\mathbb{D}$ identifies another subphrase relation.[1]

t		**terminal symbol**	$\mathbb{T}$
a, b, c		**variable symbol**	$\mathbb{V}$
a, b, c		**domain symbol**	$\mathbb{D}$
$X, Y, Z ::=$		**non-terminal symbol**	$\mathbb{N}$
	a^{a}	variable	
	$\top^{\text{a}}$	top	
	$\bot^{\text{a}}$	bottom	
$E ::=$		**non-terminal expression**	$\mathbb{E}$
	X	non-terminal symbol	
	$X \downarrow$	proper subphrase	
	$E_1 \sqcup E_2$	least common superphrase	
	$E_1 \sqcap E_2$	greatest common subphrase	
$S ::=$		**symbol expression**	
	t	terminal	
	E	non-terminal	
$R ::=$		**rule**	
	$X \to S_1 \dots S_n$	production	
	$X \sqsubseteq Y$	subphrase	
$G ::=$		**grammar**	
	$\to$ a	start domain	
	$G; R$	rule	

Fig. 4. The abstract syntax of our formalism

However, due to the introduction of multiple subphrase relations, we must now be careful not to accidentally mix them. Because of this, we partition the set of non-terminal symbols $\mathbb{N}$ such that each variable symbol $a \in \mathbb{V}$ identifies a non-terminal symbol $a^{\text{a}} \in \mathbb{N}$ with respect to the domain symbol a. Consequently, we consider a^{a} and a^{b} two different non-terminal symbols and say that a^{a} is a non-terminal symbol of domain a. Besides this partition, we must also take care to disallow expressions such as $a^{\text{a}} \sqcup b^{\text{b}}$ which use unrelated non-terminal

---

[1] The term *domain symbol* originates from the observation that most trivial *domain*-specific languages expose just one subphrase structure and can hence be identified by this symbol.

symbols in relation. This leads us to the notion of well-formedness we present in the next subsection.

3.2 Well-Formedness

Not any syntactic instance of our grammar formalism is well-formed. The introduction of multiple subphrase relations makes CFSGs as expressive as CFGs (as shown in Sect. 4), but also more complex. This is because we may neither put nor use two non-terminal expressions of different domains in relation. In order to identify such ill-defined constructions, we use the notion of well-formedness from Fig. 5.

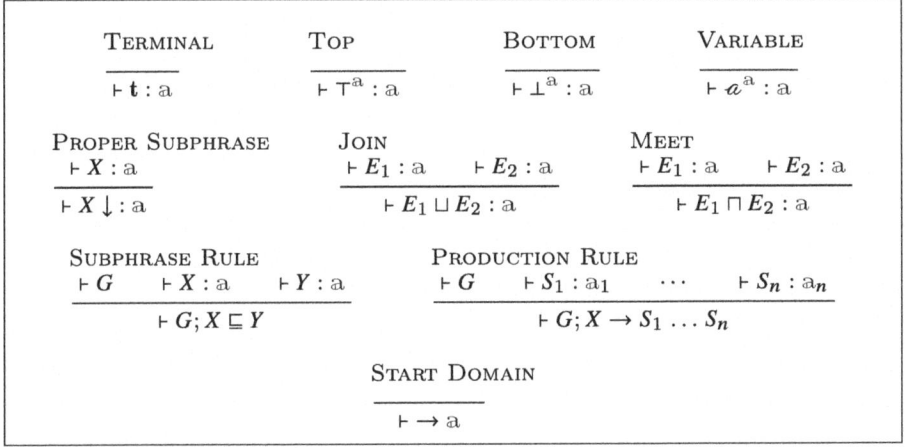

Fig. 5. Well-formedness for our formalism

The rules we present here use the following judgements:

- We write $\vdash G$ to state that G is a well-formed grammar.
- We write $\vdash X : \mathrm{a}$ to state that $X \in \mathbb{N}$ is a well-formed non-terminal symbol of domain $\mathrm{a} \in \mathbb{D}$.
- We write $\vdash E : \mathrm{a}$ to state that $E \in \mathbb{E}$ is a well-formed non-terminal expression of domain $\mathrm{a} \in \mathbb{D}$.

While non-terminal and terminal symbols are always well-formed, let us pay special attention to the rules JOIN, MEET and SUBPHRASE RULE. It is these which effectively rule out any ill-formed construction by ensuring that we do not mix different domains in one non-terminal expression or subphrase rule. All remaining rules merely propagate the well-formedness property and therefore require no special attention.

3.3 Semantics

In this subsection we define the semantics of CFSGs by providing a proper definition of the language that is described by a grammar. As our notion of subphrases plays a vital role here, we also provide a definition for subphrase relations as well as the subphrase lattices induced by them. However, due to lack of space, we leave out most of the foundations on lattices and order theory. For details, please refer to standard literature such as [4] or [7]. Unless specified otherwise, the definitions that follow in the rest of this subsection assume a well-formed grammar $G = \to \mathrm{s}; R_1; \ldots; R_n$ with the start domain $\mathrm{s} \in \mathbb{D}$ and a sequence of n rules $R_1, \ldots, R_n$.

Since our definition of well-formedness ensures that we may not put or use non-terminal expressions of different domains in relation, we begin with the convenient partition of $\mathbb{N}$ and $\mathbb{E}$ in Definition 1.

Definition 1 (Domain Partition of $\mathbb{N}$ and $\mathbb{E}$). *Let $\mathbb{N}_\mathrm{a} = \{\, X \in \mathbb{N} \mid X : \mathrm{a}\, \}$ be the set of non-terminal symbols of domain $\mathrm{a} \in \mathbb{D}$. Likewise, we refer to $\mathbb{E}_\mathrm{a} = \{\, E \in \mathbb{E} \mid E : \mathrm{a}\, \}$ as the set of non-terminal expressions of domain $\mathrm{a} \in \mathbb{D}$.*

The Subphrase Relation. A central aspect of our grammar formalism is the so-called *subphrase relation* given in Definition 2. Just like the subtype relation in type theory, it captures the idea of safe substitution. As previously noted, such a subphrase relation exists for each domain $\mathrm{a} \in \mathbb{D}$, which leaves it as a relation between the non-terminal symbols $\mathbb{N}_\mathrm{a}$.

Definition 2 (Subphrase Relation). *Let $\sqsubseteq_\mathrm{a} \subseteq \mathbb{N}_\mathrm{a} \times \mathbb{N}_\mathrm{a}$ denote the reflexive and transitive closure of the below relation. We then call $\sqsubseteq_\mathrm{a}$ the subphrase relation of domain a.*

$$\{\, (X,Y) \in \mathbb{N}_\mathrm{a} \times \mathbb{N}_\mathrm{a} \mid \exists i : R_i = X \sqsubseteq Y \,\}$$
$$\cup \; \{\, (X, \top^\mathrm{a}) \mid X \in \mathbb{N}_\mathrm{a} \,\}$$
$$\cup \; \{\, (\bot^\mathrm{a}, X) \mid X \in \mathbb{N}_\mathrm{a} \,\}$$

We can easily convince ourselves, that this definition of the subphrase relation renders the symbols $\top^\mathrm{a}$ and $\bot^\mathrm{a}$ as the actual greatest and least subphrase. Besides this, it is important to note that this reflexive and transitive relation is actually a *pre-order* and not a *partial-order*. This is due to the lack of *antisymmetry*. However, it is often recognized that such a pre-order induces a partial-order by establishing the following equivalence in Definition 3.

Definition 3 (Equivalence of Non-Terminal Symbols). *Let $\sim_\mathrm{a} \subseteq \mathbb{N}_\mathrm{a} \times \mathbb{N}_\mathrm{a}$ be the equivalence relation we obtain by $X \sim_\mathrm{a} Y \iff X \sqsubseteq_\mathrm{a} Y \wedge Y \sqsubseteq_\mathrm{a} X$.*

For this reason, we identify non-terminal symbols up to this equivalence and consider the relation in Definition 2 a partial-order. We leave out the proof for the correctness of this identification at this point. The intuition is, however, that X and Y describe the same language as we can always substitute X for Y and vice versa, which is due to $X \sqsubseteq_\mathrm{a} Y$ and $Y \sqsubseteq_\mathrm{a} X$.

The Subphrase Lattice. With the subphrase relation for a given domain symbol $a \in \mathbb{D}$ at hand, we can now define the aforementioned subphrase lattice. As we already pointed out in Sect. 2.3, the elements of this lattice are sets of non-terminal symbols which are "downward closed" with respect to the subphrase relation. The intuition behind these so-called lower-sets is driven by the question: What are the production rules we can apply, given a specific non-terminal expression? In case of a non-terminal symbol the answer seems to be straightforward, as we can apply all the production rules associated with it.

However, the situation is slightly different in the general case for non-terminal expressions such as the $T \downarrow$ in (4) from Sect. 2.3. These cannot occur on the left-hand side of a production rule and are therefore never associated with production rules in a direct sense. In order for them to be productive at some point, they must consequently "evaluate" to something that is instead associated with production rules. Since this does not necessarily have to be just one single non-terminal symbol, we finally arrive at the definition of the lower-sets we call *subphrase closures* in Definition 4.

Definition 4 (Subphrase Closure). *Let $S \subseteq \mathbb{N}_a$ be an arbitrary subset of $\mathbb{N}_a$. We define the lower-set of S as $\downarrow S = \{ Y \in \mathbb{N}_a \mid \exists X \in S : Y \sqsubseteq_a X \}$ and call it the subphrase closure of S.*

On the basis of these subphrase closures we can now turn our attention to the actual *subphrase lattice* in Definition 5. In the literature, this lattice is also known as *stone* [21] or *superalgebraic lattice* [9]. What makes it special amongst other things is its *complete distributivity* [4,7], which means that arbitrary joins distribute over arbitrary meets.

Definition 5 (Subphrase Lattice). *Let $\mathbb{S}_a \subseteq \mathcal{P}(\mathbb{N}_a) \setminus \emptyset$ be the family of all subphrase closures over $\mathcal{P}(\mathbb{N}_a) \setminus \emptyset$ ordered by set inclusion. We call $\mathbb{S}_a$ the subphrase lattice of domain $a \in \mathbb{D}$.*

Thanks to $\mathbb{N}_a$ being finite, we know that the subphrase lattice $\mathbb{S}_a$ is finite as well. Moreover, due to Definition 2 we also know that $\downarrow \top^a$ must be the top element of $\mathbb{S}_a$ and since we exclude the empty set $\emptyset$ in Definition 5 this leaves $\downarrow \bot^a = \{ \bot^a \}$ as the bottom element of $\mathbb{S}_a$. In other words, these two subphrase closures correspond to the least and greatest precedence level, whereas all other precedence levels live between them. When visualized as a Hasse diagram, this structure therefore shows great similarity with a precedence graph. Using the denotation in Definition 6 we can now use this subphrase lattice to assign each non-terminal expression in $E \in \mathbb{E}_a$ appropriate semantics.

Definition 6 (Denotation of Non-Terminal Expressions). *We refer to $[\![E]\!] : \mathbb{S}_a$ as the denotation of the non-terminal expression $E \in \mathbb{E}_a$ in domain* a ∈ 𝔻. It is defined inductively over the abstract syntax of E as follows.

$$[\![X]\!] = \downarrow \{ X \}$$
$$[\![X \downarrow]\!] = ([\![X]\!] \setminus \{ X \}) \cup [\![\bot^a]\!]$$
$$[\![E_1 \sqcup E_2]\!] = [\![E_1]\!] \cup [\![E_2]\!]$$
$$[\![E_1 \sqcap E_2]\!] = [\![E_1]\!] \cap [\![E_2]\!]$$

While $[\![X]\!]$ simply denotes the *principal ideal* with X as its *principal element*, it is a known fact that $[\![E_1 \sqcup E_2]\!]$ and $[\![E_1 \sqcap E_2]\!]$ also denote lower-sets [4,7]. It trivially follows that $[\![X \downarrow]\!]$ must be a lower-set as well (Proposition 1).

Proposition 1. *Given* $X \in \mathbb{N}_a$, *it holds that* $(([\![X]\!] \setminus \{ X \}) \cup [\![\bot^a]\!]) \in \mathbb{S}_a$.

Another important aspect is captured by Proposition 2 where we use the notation $a \rightarrowtail b$ to say that a covers b. It states that $X \downarrow$ is the immediately following subphrase of X that is not X itself and as long as we do not hit the bottom $\bot^a$. Thanks to this, we can be sure that our definition of the greatest proper subphrase $X \downarrow$ indeed matches the intuition of "climbing down" the precedence hierarchy by one level at the time.

Proposition 2. *Given* $X \in \mathbb{N}_a$, *it holds that* $X \neq \bot^a \implies [\![X]\!] \rightarrowtail [\![X \downarrow]\!]$

The Described Language. With all the groundwork in place, we can now define what it means to derive strings with our formalism. In this context, we consider a string to be an element of the set $(\mathbb{T} \cup \mathbb{E})^*$ and a word to be a string of the subset $\mathbb{T}^*$. We use small Greek letters such as α and β for strings where ϵ denotes the empty string and small Latin letters such as v and w for words. The concatenation of two strings is either written as $\alpha\beta$ or, more explicitly, as $\alpha \cdot \beta$.

The derivation of a string is determined by the application of production rules given in Definition 7 and the substitution of subphrases given in Definition 8. Because the meaning of double arrows is quite overloaded in computer science and mathematics, we stick to the convention of using short arrows $\Rightarrow$ to denote derivation and long arrows $\Longrightarrow$ to denote logical consequence here.

Definition 7 (Application of a Production Rule). *The application of production rules is defined by the relation* $\Rightarrow_P \subseteq (\mathbb{T} \cup \mathbb{E})^* \times (\mathbb{T} \cup \mathbb{E})^*$ *below.*

$$\alpha \, X \, \beta \Rightarrow_P \alpha \, S_1 \ldots S_m \, \beta \quad \Longleftrightarrow \quad \exists i : R_i = X \rightarrow S_1 \ldots S_m$$

Note, how the application of production rules is just the same as it is for CFGs. As a consequence, we can never apply a production rule to a non-terminal expression such as $X \downarrow$ in a direct sense. Instead, we have to substitute them with one of their subphrases until we finally reach a non-terminal symbol. This is captured by the relation in Definition 8 below.

Definition 8 (Substitution by a Subphrase). *The substitution by a subphrase is defined by the relation* $\Rightarrow_S \subseteq (\mathbb{T} \cup \mathbb{E})^* \times (\mathbb{T} \cup \mathbb{E})^*$ *below.*

$$\alpha \, E_1 \, \beta \Rightarrow_S \alpha \, E_2 \, \beta \quad \Longleftrightarrow \quad [\![E_2]\!] \subseteq [\![E_1]\!]$$

With these two relations we can now pay attention to the direct derivation relation in Definition 9. Intuitively, it corresponds to the set of all possible derivation steps we can perform with respect to a given grammar. We therefore say a string α *directly yields* a string β or β is *directly derived* from α if $\alpha \Rightarrow \beta$ holds.

Definition 9 (Direct Derivation Relation). *Let $\Rightarrow$ denote the direct derivation relation. It is defined as the union $\Rightarrow_P \cup \Rightarrow_S$.*

By completing the above relation by all transitive and reflexive steps we finally obtain the derivation relation $\Rightarrow^*$. Analogously to the direct derivation relation, we say a string α *yields* a string β or β is *derived* from α if $\alpha \Rightarrow^* \beta$ holds.

Similarly to the CFG formalism, we can now advance to the language that is described by a CFSG in Definition 10. It is simply the set of words that can be derived from the start non-terminal symbol $\top^s$. A noteworthy aspect here is that any top symbol $\top^a$ is not only the greatest (sub-) phrase of its domain $a \in \mathbb{D}$, but it also behaves just like the start symbol of a CFG. This leads us to the question: From a dual perspective, what can we say about the bottom symbol $\bot^a$ then? Most interestingly, the bottom symbol behaves just like an end symbol. That is, while *any subphrase* can be *derived* from the top symbol $\top^a$ including itself, the bottom symbol $\bot^a$ *yields no subphrase* but itself. In practice, this often means that $\mathcal{L}(\bot^a) = \emptyset$ and hence $\bot^a$ terminates any derivation. Yet, it is not forbidden to associate production rules with $\bot^a$, which is why this is not universally true.

Definition 10 (Language of G). *Let $\mathcal{L}(\alpha) = \{ w \in \mathbb{T}^* \mid \alpha \Rightarrow^* w \}$ be the language described by the string $\alpha \in (\mathbb{T} \cup \mathbb{E})^*$ with respect to G. The language described by G is then given as $\mathcal{L}(G) = \mathcal{L}(\top^s)$.*

In order to conclude this section, let us finally pay attention to Definition 11. It defines what we call the sublanguage lattice.

Definition 11 (Sublanguage Lattice). *Let $\mathcal{L}_a$ be a surjective map with $\mathcal{L}_a(S) = \bigcup_{X \in S} \mathcal{L}(X)$ where $S \in \mathbb{S}_a$. We then call $\mathbb{L}_a = \{ \mathcal{L}_a(S) \mid S \in \mathbb{S}_a \}$ ordered by set inclusion the sublanguage lattice of domain a.*

Due to the lack of space, we do not provide full evidence for $\mathbb{L}_a$ being a lattice here. The idea, however, is to show that $\mathcal{L}_a$ is an order- and join-preserving map. This leaves $\mathbb{L}_a$ as a finite join-semilattice and hence as a finite lattice (cf. [4,7]). That aside, what is much more interesting here, is that this sublanguage lattice reflects our initial observation in (3). To see this, let us consider the Hasse diagram of the sublanguage lattice shown in Fig. 6. It is induced by the subphrase lattice in Fig. 3 from Sect. 2.3. Mainly due to $\mathcal{L}_a$ being an order-preserving map, the inclusive property of the subphrase lattice is preserved and exactly matches our intuition of modeling language inclusion.

$$\begin{array}{rl}
\{\mathsf{T}^{\mathrm{a}}, E^{\mathrm{a}}, T^{\mathrm{a}}, F^{\mathrm{a}}, \bot^{\mathrm{a}}\} = & [\![\mathsf{T}^{\mathrm{a}}]\!] \\
& | \\
\{E^{\mathrm{a}}, T^{\mathrm{a}}, F^{\mathrm{a}}, \bot^{\mathrm{a}}\} = & [\![E^{\mathrm{a}}]\!] \\
& | \\
\{T^{\mathrm{a}}, F^{\mathrm{a}}, \bot^{\mathrm{a}}\} = & [\![T^{\mathrm{a}}]\!] \\
& | \\
\{F^{\mathrm{a}}, \bot^{\mathrm{a}}\} = & [\![F^{\mathrm{a}}]\!] \\
& | \\
\{\bot^{\mathrm{a}}\} = & [\![\bot^{\mathrm{a}}]\!]
\end{array}
\quad \mathcal{L}_{\mathrm{a}}
\quad
\begin{array}{l}
\mathcal{L}(E^{\mathrm{a}}) = \ldots \cup \mathcal{L}(T^{\mathrm{a}}) \\
\ | \\
\mathcal{L}(T^{\mathrm{a}}) = \ldots \cup \mathcal{L}(F^{\mathrm{a}}) \\
\ | \\
\mathcal{L}(F^{\mathrm{a}}) = \ldots \\
\ | \\
\mathcal{L}(\bot^{\mathrm{a}}) = \emptyset
\end{array}$$

Fig. 6. The sublanguage lattice of the subphrase lattice in Fig. 3

4 Meta Theory

Within this section we investigate some meta theoretical properties of our formalism. In particular, we will see that CFSGs generate exactly the class of CFLs. That is, they are *sound* and *complete* with respect to CFGs. In order to show this, we will introduce two normal forms that ultimately lead to a correspondence between CFSGs and CFGs.

4.1 Expression-Free Normal Form

If we consider the major difference between CFSGs and CFGs we must realize that it is the existence of *proper non-terminal expressions* such as $X \downarrow$ (see Definition 12). Without these, there would be no need for subphrase rules like $Y \sqsubseteq X$ and we could as well represent them by unary production rules such as $X \to Y$.

Definition 12 (Proper Non-Terminal Expression). *Let $\mathbb{P} = \mathbb{E} \setminus \mathbb{N}$ denote the set of proper non-terminal expressions of some grammar G. Just like with $\mathbb{N}$ and $\mathbb{E}$ we partition $\mathbb{P}$ and write $\mathbb{P}_{\mathrm{a}} = \{E \in \mathbb{P} \mid E : \mathrm{a}\}$ for the set of proper non-terminal expressions of domain $\mathrm{a} \in \mathbb{D}$.*

Based on this observation let us introduce the *Expression-Free Normal Form* (EFNF) in Definition 13. Any grammar exhibiting this normal form does not contain proper non-terminal expressions, which is a first milestone towards our goal to remove all subphrase rules from a CFSG.

Definition 13 (Expression-Free Normal Form). *Let $G = \to \mathsf{s}; R_1; \ldots; R_n$ be a well-formed grammar. We say G is in Expression-Free Normal Form (EFNF) if and only if $\forall i : R_i = X \to S_1 \ldots S_m \implies S_1 \notin \mathbb{P} \land \cdots \land S_m \notin \mathbb{P}$ holds.*

Note, that the EFNF only requires the absence of proper non-terminal expressions in a CFSG. This does not exclude proper non-terminal expressions from occurring as the result of a subphrase substitution. However, as we show in

Lemma 1, there is actually no need to derive proper non-terminal expressions when a grammar exhibits the EFNF.

Lemma 1 (Expression-Free Derivation). *Let G be a grammar in EFNF with $s \in \mathbb{D}$ as its start domain. Then there is a $X, Y \in \mathbb{N}_a$ for any $E_1, E_2 \in \mathbb{P}_a$ and $a \in \mathbb{D}$ such that the following holds for all $\alpha, \beta \in (\mathbb{T} \cup \mathbb{E})^*$ and $w \in \mathcal{L}(G)$.*

$$\mathsf{T}^s \Rightarrow^* \alpha \; E_1 \; \beta \Rightarrow_S \alpha \; E_2 \; \beta \Rightarrow^* w$$
$$\implies \mathsf{T}^s \Rightarrow^* \alpha \; X \; \beta \Rightarrow_S \alpha \; Y \; \beta \Rightarrow^* w$$

Proof. Assume the derivation $\mathsf{T}^s \Rightarrow^* \alpha \; E_1 \; \beta \Rightarrow_S \alpha \; E_2 \; \beta \Rightarrow^* w$ of the word w. Since proper non-terminal expressions are never associated with production rules, there must be a non-terminal symbol $Y \in \mathbb{N}_a$ with $[\![Y]\!] \subseteq [\![E_2]\!]$. Moreover, because G is in EFNF there is no such production rule $Z \to \gamma \; E_1 \; \delta$ with $Z \in \mathbb{N}$ and $\gamma, \delta \in (\mathbb{T} \cup \mathbb{E})^*$ which could have led to $\mathsf{T}^s \Rightarrow^* \alpha \; E_1 \; \beta$. As a consequence, there must be a non-terminal symbol $X \in \mathbb{N}_a$ with $[\![E_1]\!] \subseteq [\![X]\!]$. Since $[\![E_2]\!] \subseteq [\![E_1]\!]$ holds by assumption, we know that $[\![Y]\!] \subseteq [\![X]\!]$ must hold as well and therefore $\mathsf{T}^s \Rightarrow^* \alpha \; X \; \beta \Rightarrow_S \alpha \; Y \; \beta \Rightarrow^* w$ is indeed a derivation of w. □

Due to the EFNF and Lemma 1 we can now restrict our direct derivation relation $\Rightarrow \subseteq (\mathbb{T} \cup \mathbb{E})^* \times (\mathbb{T} \cup \mathbb{E})^*$ to its greatest subset over $(\mathbb{T} \cup \mathbb{N})^* \times (\mathbb{T} \cup \mathbb{N})^*$. That is, we can derive any word $w \in \mathcal{L}(G)$ described by a grammar G in EFNF with non-terminal symbols only. Thanks to this, we also know that the subphrase relation $\sqsubseteq_a$ for any $a \in \mathbb{D}$ is indeed superfluous now. We only need it to perform the substitution of $X \in \mathbb{N}_a$ with $Y \in \mathbb{N}_a$ in a derivation such as $\alpha \; X \; \beta \Rightarrow_S \alpha \; Y \; \beta$ where $\alpha, \beta \in (\mathbb{T} \cup \mathbb{N})^*$. However, this kind of substitution can also be performed by the unary production rule $X \to Y$. If we were able to translate any CFSG to an equivalent grammar in EFNF, we could therefore remove all of its subphrase rules in a next step. But what do we mean by *equivalent* here? Definition 14 provides an answer to this question.

Definition 14 (Weak Equivalence of Grammars). *Let G_1, G_2 be two well-formed grammars. We write $G_1 \equiv G_2$ and say that G_1 and G_2 are (weakly) equivalent when $\mathcal{L}(G_1) = \mathcal{L}(G_2)$ holds.*

With this in mind, we can now pay attention to Lemma 2 below. It reflects the fact that non-terminal expressions are just a tool to improve the modularity of our grammars. We can therefore always decide to sacrifice modularity by "evaluating" them ahead of derivation time.

Lemma 2 (Existence of the EFNF). *Let G be a well-formed grammar. Then there is an equivalent grammar G' in EFNF.*

Before we prove the above lemma, let us take note of the observation in Corollary 1. Because of this, we know that the language described by a non-terminal expression can be expressed as the language union $\bigcup_{X \in [\![E]\!]} \mathcal{L}(X)$.

Corollary 1 (Congruency of $\mathcal{L}_a$). *Let $E \in \mathbb{E}_a$ be a non-terminal expression of some domain $a \in \mathbb{D}$ and grammar G. It then holds that $\mathcal{L}_a([\![E]\!]) = \mathcal{L}(E)$.*

Proof (Lemma 2). Let G be a well-formed grammar. Due to Corollary 1 we know that we can replace any proper non-terminal expression $E \in G_\mathbb{P}$ with a fresh non-terminal symbol $\mathscr{O}^\text{b}$ as long as there is a production rule $\mathscr{O}^\text{b} \to X$ for each $X \in [\![E]\!]$. Because $\mathscr{O}^\text{b}$ being a fresh symbol, we also know that $G_{\mathbb{N}_\text{b}} = \{\top^\text{b}, \mathscr{O}^\text{b}, \bot^\text{b}\}$ with $\mathcal{L}(\top^\text{b}) = \mathcal{L}(\mathscr{O}^\text{b})$ and $\mathcal{L}(\bot^\text{b}) = \varnothing$. As a consequence, $\mathcal{L}(\mathscr{O}^\text{b}) = \mathcal{L}(E)$ holds. By repetitively applying this transformation to G we can obtain an equivalent grammar G' in EFNF. □

4.2 Subphrase-Free Normal-Form

We can now advance to our second normal form called the *Subphrase-Free Normal Form* (SFNF) in Definition 15. It is based on the idea that there is no need for subphrase substitutions if we can achieve the same results using the application of production rules only. As a result, we may remove all the subphrase rules from a grammar in SFNF without affecting its language.

Definition 15 (Subphrase-Free Normal-Form). *Let $G = \to \mathbb{s}; R_1; \ldots; R_n$ be a grammar in EFNF. We say G is in Subphrase-Free Normal Form (SFNF) if $\forall \alpha, \beta \in (\mathbb{T} \cup \mathbb{N})^* : \alpha \Rightarrow_S \beta \implies \alpha \Rightarrow_P \beta$ holds.*

Note, how we restrict α and β to elements of $(\mathbb{T} \cup \mathbb{N})^*$ here. As we mentioned before, we know that this subset of $\Rightarrow_S$ suffices to generate the language and consequently it also suffices to embed this subset in $\Rightarrow_P$ only.

Lastly, with Lemma 3 we can now convince ourselves that the SFNF indeed exists for any CFSG and therefore opens the path to soundness and completeness theorems in the next subsection.

Lemma 3 (Existence of the SFNF). *Let $G = \to \mathbb{s}; R_1; \ldots; R_n$ be a grammar in EFNF. Then there is an equivalent grammar G' in SFNF.*

Proof. In order to transform G into an equivalent grammar G' that exhibits the SFNF, we must embed any element $(\alpha\ X\ \beta, \alpha\ Y\ \beta) \in (G_\mathbb{T} \cup G_\mathbb{N})^* \times (G_\mathbb{T} \cup G_\mathbb{N})^*$ where $\alpha\ X\ \beta \Rightarrow_S \alpha\ Y\ \beta$ holds in $\Rightarrow_P$. We can easily achieve this if we add a production rule $X \to Y$ for each $X, Y \in G_{\mathbb{N}_\text{a}}$ and $\mathbb{a} \in G_\mathbb{D}$ with $Y \sqsubseteq_\text{a} X$ to G. □

4.3 Soundness and Completeness

Within this section we finally substantiate our claim that CFSGs are exactly as powerful as Chomsky's [5] CFGs. In order to do this, we prove that CFSGs are sound (Theorem 1) and complete (Theorem 2) with respect to CFGs. But before we actually do that, let us briefly recall the notion of CFGs in Definition 16.

Definition 16 (Context-Free Grammar). *Let $G = (\Sigma, N, P, S)$ be a Context-Free Grammar (CFG) where Σ is a finite set of terminal symbols, N is a finite set of non-terminal symbols with $N \cap \Sigma = \varnothing$, $S \in N$ is the start non-terminal symbol and $P \subseteq N \times (\Sigma \cup N)^*$ is a finite set of production rules. Moreover, we use a dotted arrow to denote the direct derivation relation $\dashrightarrow \subseteq (\Sigma \cup N)^* \times (\Sigma \cup N)^*$ and $\dashrightarrow^*$ for its reflexive and transitive closure. The language of G is then defined as $\mathcal{L}(G) = \{w \in \Sigma^* \mid S \dashrightarrow^* w\}$.*

With this definition in mind, we can now advance to Theorem 1. It is the most important statement about our formalism, as it states that there is an equivalent CFG for any CFSG. The idea here is to normalize the CFSG to a grammar in SFNF whose production rules then correspond to a CFG.

Theorem 1 (Soundness). *Let G_1 be a well-formed CFSG. Then there is a CFG G_2 such that $\mathcal{L}(G_1) = \mathcal{L}(G_2)$.*

Proof. Because of Lemma 2 and Lemma 3 we know there must be a CFSG $G' = \to \mathsf{s}; R_1; \ldots; R_n$ in SFNF which is equivalent to G_1. Due to the SFNF of G', we can now choose $G_2 = (G'_{\mathbb{T}}, G'_{\mathbb{N}}, P, \top^s)$ to be a well-formed CFG with $P = \{ (X, S_1 \ldots S_m) \mid X \to S_1 \ldots S_m \in \{R_1, \ldots, R_n\} \}$. For the same reason it holds for all $\alpha, \beta \in (G'_{\mathbb{T}} \cup G'_{\mathbb{N}})^*$ and $w \in G'^*_{\mathbb{T}}$ that $\top^s ::\!\!\Rightarrow^* \alpha ::\!\!\Rightarrow \beta ::\!\!\Rightarrow^* w$ is a derivation using G_2 if and only if $\top^s \Rightarrow^*_P \alpha \Rightarrow_P \beta \Rightarrow^*_P w$ is a derivation using G', from which follows that $\mathcal{L}(G_1) = \mathcal{L}(G') = \mathcal{L}(G_2)$. □

Now that we know that CFSGs are sound, we can also show that they are exactly as powerful as CFGs. This is formalized by Theorem 2. The idea behind this is to lift any non-terminal symbol X of a CFG to a non-terminal symbol X^X of the corresponding CFSG. While this automatically introduces a non-terminal symbol $\top^X$ and $\bot^X$ as well, the language is unaffected by this circumstance. This is because no production rule of the CFG is aware of $\top^X$ and $\bot^X$ and consequently they are never introduced by the application of production rules.

Theorem 2 (Completeness). *Let $G_1 = (\Sigma, N, P, S)$ be a CFG. Then there is a CFSG G_2 in SFNF such that $\mathcal{L}(G_1) = \mathcal{L}(G_2)$.*

Proof. Let $\mathbb{T} = \Sigma$ and $\mathbb{V} = \mathbb{D} = N$. We can now choose $G_2 = \to S; R_1; \ldots; R_n$ such that the following equation holds (where we require $\top, \bot \notin \Sigma \cup N$).

$$\begin{aligned}
\{R_1, \ldots, R_n\} &= \{ X^X \to \phi(\gamma) \mid X \to \gamma \in P \} & \phi(\epsilon) &= \epsilon \\
&\cup \{ \top^X \to X^X \mid X \in N \} & \phi(\mathbf{t} \cdot \alpha) &= \mathbf{t} \cdot \phi(\alpha) \\
&\cup \{ X^X \to \bot^X \mid X \in N \} & \phi(X \cdot \alpha) &= X^X \cdot \phi(\alpha)
\end{aligned}$$

Clearly, G_2 is in SFNF as we neither introduce proper non-terminal expressions nor subphrase rules. Moreover, it holds for any $X \in N$ that nothing yields $\top^X$ and $\bot^X$ never yields anything. Consequently, we know that for all $\alpha, \beta \in (\Sigma \cup N)^*$ and all $w \in \Sigma^*$ the derivation $S ::\!\!\Rightarrow^* \alpha ::\!\!\Rightarrow \beta ::\!\!\Rightarrow^* w$ using G_1 holds if and only if the corresponding derivation $S^S \Rightarrow^*_P \phi(\alpha) \Rightarrow_P \phi(\beta) \Rightarrow^*_P w$ using G_2 holds as well. Since $\top^S \Rightarrow_P S^S$ holds by construction, we know $\forall w \in \mathcal{L}(G_1) : \top^S \Rightarrow^*_P w$ and $\mathcal{L}(G_1) = \mathcal{L}(G_2)$ must be true as well. □

5 An Example

In this section we illustrate how CFSGs can be used to define syntax in a modular way. For this purpose, let us consider the syntax of the small language Λ in (6).

$$\begin{array}{ll} \to \Lambda\ ; \\ Abs^\Lambda \to \lambda\ x\ .\ Abs^\Lambda\ ; \\ App^\Lambda \sqsubseteq Abs^\Lambda\ ; & (6) \\ App^\Lambda \to App^\Lambda\ App^\Lambda \downarrow\ ; \\ \bot^\Lambda \to x \mid (\ \top^\Lambda\ ) \end{array} \qquad \begin{array}{l} \top^\Lambda \Rightarrow_S App^\Lambda \Rightarrow_P App^\Lambda\ App^\Lambda \downarrow \\ \Rightarrow_P App^\Lambda\ App^\Lambda \downarrow\ App^\Lambda \downarrow \\ \Rightarrow_S^* \bot^\Lambda\ \bot^\Lambda\ \bot^\Lambda \\ \Rightarrow_P^* f\ x\ (\ \top^\Lambda\ ) \Rightarrow_S f\ x\ (\ Abs^\Lambda\ ) \qquad (7) \\ \Rightarrow_P f\ x\ (\ \lambda\ z\ .\ Abs^\Lambda\ ) \\ \Rightarrow_S f\ x\ (\ \lambda\ z\ .\ \bot^\Lambda\ ) \\ \Rightarrow_P f\ x\ (\ \lambda\ z\ .\ z\ ) \end{array}$$

Although this grammar just describes the syntax of the lambda calculus, it already demonstrates the features of CFSGs very well. Here, we use the symbol $\bot^\Lambda$ as the greatest precedence level to refer to variables (represented by x) and expressions enclosed by parentheses. Conversely, we use the symbol $\top^\Lambda$ as the lowest precedence level to abstractly refer to arbitrary expressions of Λ. Since applications should bind more tightly than abstractions (i.e., $\lambda x.f\ x = \lambda x.(f\ x)$), we define App^Λ as a subphrase of Abs^Λ. Moreover, applications should be left associative, which is why the production rule of App^Λ is left recursive, using the non-terminal expression $App^\Lambda \downarrow$ to refer to an argument that binds more tightly than App^Λ itself. Altogether, one possible derivation of an expression such as $f\ x\ (\lambda z.z)$ would look as shown in (7).

$$\begin{array}{ll} Add^\Lambda \sqsubseteq Abs^\Lambda\ ; & Or^\Lambda \sqsubseteq Abs^\Lambda\ ; \\ Add^\Lambda \sqsubseteq Sub^\Lambda\ ; & Or^\Lambda \to Or^\Lambda \vee Or^\Lambda \downarrow\ ; \\ Add^\Lambda \to Add^\Lambda + Add^\Lambda \downarrow\ ; & And^\Lambda \sqsubseteq Or^\Lambda \\ Sub^\Lambda \sqsubseteq Add^\Lambda\ ; & And^\Lambda \to And^\Lambda \wedge And^\Lambda \downarrow\ ; \qquad (8) \\ Sub^\Lambda \to Sub^\Lambda - Sub^\Lambda \downarrow\ ; \\ Mul^\Lambda \sqsubseteq Add^\Lambda\ ; & App^\Lambda \sqsubseteq Mul^\Lambda\ ; \\ Mul^\Lambda \to Mul^\Lambda * Mul^\Lambda \downarrow\ ; & App^\Lambda \sqsubseteq And^\Lambda \end{array}$$

In order to extend our grammar at this point, all we have to do is to add production and subphrase rules. No deletions or corrections of existing rules are necessary. This is demonstrated by the grammar extension in (8). Here, we embed two new (sub-) languages in our language Λ. One for arithmetic expressions and another one for logical expressions. Although these two languages are small, we believe their algebraic character is representative enough for most of the equally algebraic *Domain-Specific Languages* (DSLs) that occur in practice.

What we can observe at this example is the advantage of using a partial-order over a total-order, as it is implicitly enforced by Aasa's precedence grammars due to the use of discrete numbers (cf. grammar in (2)). While both Add^Λ and Or^Λ bind more tightly than Abs^Λ and less tightly than App^Λ, we do not relate them directly. As a consequence, we cannot mix these two branches without the use of parentheses. Although this might seem conservative in some situations, this gives the user of a language more certainty about the interpretation of expressions and prevents unintended interactions between languages of different authors. The corresponding (simplified) subphrase lattice $\mathbb{S}_\Lambda$ as well as its induced sublanguage lattice $\mathbb{L}_\Lambda$ in Fig. 7 both reflect this fact.

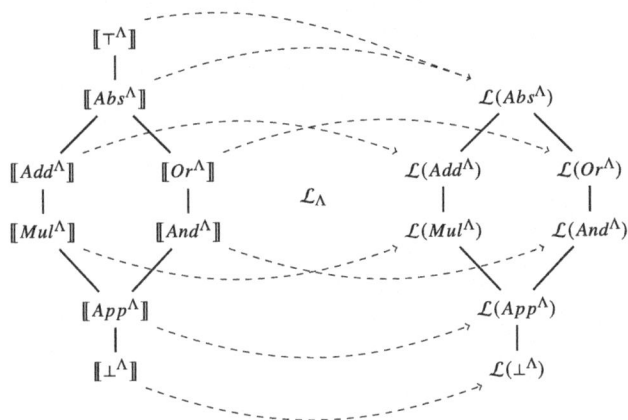

Fig. 7. The simplified subphrase lattice $\mathbb{S}_\Lambda$ and its sublanguage lattice $\mathbb{L}_\Lambda$

Note how the choice of using just one single subphrase lattice is a design decision: We could just as well have used two more subphrase lattices, one for each sublanguage. The specific advantages and disadvantages of this design space are part of our ongoing research and promise new ways to encapsulate sublanguages.

6   Related Work

Our approach to precedence using the notion of subphrases is, to the best of our knowledge, a novel one that has not yet been proposed by others. Nevertheless, there is a huge amount of related work on operator precedence in a broader sense. Besides the early work on operator-precedence grammars and operator-precedence parsing (cf. [2]), Aasa's [1] work on precedence grammars is a noteworthy foundation. These grammars formalize what is known as *mixfix operators* in theorem provers such as Agda and have been extended with directed acyclic precedence graphs by Danielsson et al. [6]. If we consider the close connection between directed acyclic graphs and lattices, this last work is probably the closest to ours.

Yet, we do not propose a new approach to precedence as an end in itself but to solve another problem: The notorious lack of modularity of CFGs. From this perspective, the work of Wintner [22] and Johnstone et al. [12] is also relevant and should be noted here. Both attempt to fix the lack of modularity from seemingly different directions. Wintner seeks for modularity insofar he solves the problem that the naive union of two CFGs G_1 and G_2 does not generate the union $\mathcal{L}(G_1) \cup \mathcal{L}(G_2)$ of their languages. For this reason, he proposes to assign CFGs an alternative semantics that is composable and fully-abstract, and which eventually leads to a notion of modules. Johnstone et al. approach modularity by the introduction of a module system that resembles that of a programming language and which allows fine-grained control over the composition of production rules using import statements. In this way, they solve the aforementioned problem with the naive union of two CFGs insofar the user has to specify how grammars should be composed. Both approaches compare to ours in that we also introduce the concept of abstract interfaces that can be considered as modules (i.e., the subphrase relations).

Lastly, there are two noteworthy frameworks which offer the development of grammars in a modular but more comprehensive sense: The *Syntax Definition Formalism* (SDF) [10,19] and the *Grammatical Framework* (GF) [17]. Both offer an extensive toolchain for grammatical engineering and allow the definition of modules as well as the disambiguation using precedence and similar techniques. However, as with all other aforementioned approaches, both frameworks interpret precedence in the traditional way. Furthermore, with our present work we focus on a natural and fundamental solution, while these frameworks constitute a comprehensive extension on top of classical CFGs. In case of the GF this even goes beyond a plain syntax definition formalism, as it can be considered a dependently typed programming language.

7 Future Work

As with any new formalism, there is a lot of work to be done in order to explore the potential and the limitations of CFSGs. Some open questions and directions for future research are:

- *Ambiguity* – In which way do CFSGs introduce ambiguities on top of corresponding CFGs and how can we solve them? Initial analyses of this subject indicate that most of the ambiguities are introduced by the transitivity of the subphrase closures. A conceivable way of disambiguation would therefore be the application of a transitive reduction.
- *Parsing Problem* – Since any CFSG can be translated to an equivalent CFG, we can apply generalized parsing techniques such as Tomita's [18,20] *Generalized LR Parsers* (GLRs) to them. However, it would be interesting to investigate whether there is a more direct approach to the parsing problem, applying known techniques directly to CFSGs. Regarding the runtime complexity, we are confident that the translation to CFGs can be performed within the worst-time complexity $O(n^3)$ of the GLR technique.
- *Strong Equivalence* – At the moment, we provide evidence that CFSGs are sound and complete with respect to CFGs and a naive language equality.

However, in connection with the first and next point, it would be important to show that the parse trees of a CFSG are isomorphic to those of its corresponding CFG.
- *Semantics* – How can we define the dynamic semantics of a language described by a CFSG? First experiments showed that Knuth's [14] attribute grammars can be applied to our formalism as well. The technical challenge here is to handle the aforementioned transitivity in the correct way. On top of this, we are also interested in how we can assign static semantics (e.g., types) to a CFSG. Due to the connection of grammars and type systems to logic, we suspect some connection between subphrases and subtyping or, more generally, subsumption.
- *Closure Properties* – Do CFSGs exhibit the same closure properties as CFGs? For example, are CFSGs closed under union, concatenation and Kleene closure?
- *Low Priority Pre- and Postfix Operators* – Although CFSGs are equally expressive as CFGs, there is no non-terminal expression that supports low priority pre- and postfix operators in a modular way yet. For example, how can we express phrases such as $a + \mathbf{if}\ b\ \mathbf{then}\ 1\ \mathbf{else}\ 2$ without sacrificing modularity?

8 Conclusion

In this paper, we propose *Context-Free Subphrase Grammars* (CFSGs) as a solution to the lack of modularity *Context-Free Grammars* (CFGs) are known for. We achieve this by a novel interpretation of precedence using the concept of subphrases we present in Sect. 2. Unlike the traditional approach, our solution relies on the intuitive concept of language inclusion rather than tree filters. In this way, our notion of precedence can be applied to arbitrary production rules in a natural and language-oriented manner. In Sect. 3, we provide a proper formalization of CFSGs and demonstrate how the semantics of subphrase relations match our intuition of language inclusion. Followed by that, we show in Sect. 4 that CFSGs are sound and complete with respect to CFGs. This implies that CFSGs are an equally powerful grammar formalism capable of generating the entire class of *Context-Free Languages* (CFLs). As a result, our formalism is not only an alternative to CFGs, but also opens the design space for the modular development of CFLs without sacrificing much of the simplicity and elegance of CFGs.

Acknowledgments. The author would like to express his sincere gratitude to all those who have supported and helped throughout this work, even if they may not agree with all the interpretations and conclusions of the final paper.

Disclosure of Interests. The author has no competing interests to declare that are relevant to the content of this paper.

References

1. Aasa, A.: Precedences in specifications and implementations of programming languages. Theoret. Comput. Sci. **142**(1), 3–26 (1995). https://doi.org/10.1016/0304-3975(95)90680-J
2. Aho, A.V., Sethi, R., Ullman, J.D.: Compilers, Principles, Techniques, and Tools, 1 edn. Addison-Wesley, Boston (1986)
3. Amorim, L.E.D.S., Steindorfer, M.J., Visser, E.: Deep priority conflicts in the wild: a pilot study. In: Proceedings of the 10th ACM SIGPLAN International Conference on Software Language Engineering, SLE 2017, pp. 55–66. Association for Computing Machinery, New York (2017). https://doi.org/10.1145/3136014.3136020
4. Birkhoff, G.: Lattice Theory. Colloquium Publications, American Mathematical Society (1948)
5. Chomsky, N.: On certain formal properties of grammars. Inf. Control **2**(2), 137–167 (1959). https://doi.org/10.1016/S0019-9958(59)90362-6
6. Danielsson, N.A., Norell, U.: Parsing mixfix operators. In: Scholz, S.-B., Chitil, O. (eds.) IFL 2008. LNCS, vol. 5836, pp. 80–99. Springer, Heidelberg (2011). https://doi.org/10.1007/978-3-642-24452-0_5
7. Davey, B.A., Priestley, H.A.: Introduction to Lattices and Order, 2 edn. Cambridge University Press, Cambridge (2002). https://doi.org/10.1017/CBO9780511809088
8. Demaille, A., Eggert, P.: Bison. https://www.gnu.org/software/bison/
9. Erné, M., Gehrke, M., Pultr, A.: Complete congruences on topologies and downset lattices. Appl. Categorical Struct. **15**, 163–184 (2007). https://doi.org/10.1007/s10485-006-9054-3
10. Heering, J., Hendriks, P.R.H., Klint, P., Rekers, J.: The syntax definition formalism SDF-reference manual-. SIGPLAN Not. **24**(11), 43–75 (1989). https://doi.org/10.1145/71605.71607
11. Hopcroft, J.E., Motwani, R., Ullman, J.D.: Introduction to Automata Theory, Languages, and Computation, 3 edn. Addison-Wesley, Boston (2006)
12. Johnstone, A., Scott, E., van den Brand, M.: Modular grammar specification. Sci. Comput. Program. **87**, 23–43 (2014). https://doi.org/10.1016/j.scico.2013.09.012
13. Kats, L.C., Visser, E., Wachsmuth, G.: Pure and declarative syntax definition: paradise lost and regained. In: OOPSLA 2010. Association for Computing Machinery, New York (2010). https://doi.org/10.1145/1869459.1869535
14. Knuth, D.E.: Semantics of context-free languages. Math. Syst. Theory **2**(2), 127–145 (1968). Correction: 5(1): 95-96 (1971)
15. Norell, U.: Towards a practical programming language based on dependent type theory. Ph.D. thesis, Chalmers University of Technology (2007)
16. Parr, T.: The Definitive ANTLR 4 Reference, 2 edn. Pragmatic Bookshelf (2013)
17. Ranta, A.: Grammatical framework. J. Funct. Program. **14**(2), 145–189 (2004). https://doi.org/10.1017/S0956796803004738
18. Scott, E., Johnstone, A.: Right nulled GLR parsers. ACM Trans. Program. Lang. Syst. **28**(4), 577–618 (2006). https://doi.org/10.1145/1146809.1146810
19. de Souza Amorim, L.E., Visser, E.: Multi-purpose syntax definition with SDF3. In: de Boer, F., Cerone, A. (eds.) SEFM 2020. LNCS, vol. 12310, pp. 1–23. Springer, Cham (2020). https://doi.org/10.1007/978-3-030-58768-0_1
20. Tomita, M.: An efficient context-free parsing algorithm for natural languages. In: Proceedings of the 9th International Joint Conference on Artificial Intelligence - Volume 2, IJCAI 1985, pp. 756–764. Morgan Kaufmann Publishers, San Francisco (1985)

21. Weaver, N.: Lipschitz Algebras. World Scientific (1999). https://doi.org/10.1142/4100
22. Wintner, S.: Modular context-free grammars. Grammars **5**(1), 41–63 (2002). https://doi.org/10.1023/A:1014216630973

Polymorphism with Typed Holes

Adam Chen[1]([✉]), Thomas Porter[2], and Cyrus Omar[2]

[1] Stevens Institute of Technology, Hoboken, USA
achen19@stevens.edu
[2] University of Michigan, Ann Arbor, USA
{thomasjp,comar}@umich.edu

Abstract. Live programming environments aim to provide rapid and continuous feedback to developers, but this can be challenging when a program is incomplete. Hazel is a live programming environment that aims to solve this problem by using expression and type holes to stand for missing terms or mark erroneous terms. Hazel is based on the Hazelnut Live calculus presented in prior work.

This paper starts by presenting Polymorphic Hazelnut Live, an extension of Hazelnut Live to support explicit System F-style polymorphism. We show, with mechanized proofs in Agda, that this extended system satisfies the key metatheoretic properties necessary for live programming with typed holes. We compare the type system of Polymorphic Hazelnut Live to other systems that combine gradual typing (i.e. the theory of type holes) with polymorphism, discussing subtleties related to parametricity and the gradual guarantee.

Finally, we present a method to integrate a form of implicit type application into the Hazel architecture. We propose a system in which the programmer may omit explicit type applications, and the editor (rather than downstream tools like a typechecker or compiler) implicitly inserts and fills them, allowing the user to see and override these implicit type applications as needed.

1 Introduction

Live programming environments seek to provide programmers with continuous feedback by analyzing and evaluating programs as they are being edited [24]. Some common examples of live programming environments are Jupyter Notebooks [11] (which integrate with several languages such as Julia, Python, and R), spreadsheets [26], and editor-integrated debuggers [13]. However, one challenge to the live model is that in most languages, incomplete programs do not have formal structure or meaning. Many IDEs therefore either exhibit gaps in liveness or rely on heuristic error recovery methods to reason about incomplete programs. This creates many situations where a programmer may receive incomplete or incorrect information about their code as they are in the process of editing it. In these cases, they must finish their edit then wait for the tool's analysis to update.

The Hazel programming language and environment seeks to solve this problem of reasoning about incomplete programs by defining a formal semantics for expressions that can contain *holes* in types, expressions, and patterns (collectively, terms). Empty holes stand for missing terms, while non-empty holes serve as marked membranes around erroneous terms. The Hazel editor inserts these holes automatically [15], and Hazel is unique in assigning rich static and dynamic meaning to every editor state [19].

Hazel is based on the Hazelnut Live calculus, which defines a static and dynamic semantics for programs with expression and type holes [18]. Hazelnut Live combines and extends ideas from contextual modal type theory [16] and the gradually typed lambda calculus [21]. Section 2.1 provides more background on the details of Hazel and its calculi.

The problem that motivates this work is that Hazelnut Live did not consider abstraction over types, which is key for practical typed functional programming. Our contributions in this paper are to:

- extend the theory of Hazelnut Live to include explicit polymorphism,
- extend the existing Hazel implementation to support polymorphic programming with typed holes,
- define a novel weakening of parametricity that is shown to hold of the system,
- prove the static gradual guarantee for the system, and
- propose an editor service that combines some of the strengths of explicit and implicit polymorphism.

Section 3 presents *Polymorphic Hazelnut Live*, a polymorphic extension of Hazelnut Live. Section 4 establishes that Polymorphic Hazelnut Live retains the key metatheoretic properties of Hazelnut Live, suitably modified to account for type variables, including type safety (in the presence of holes), and discusses the important metatheoretic properties that were not previously considered for Hazel but that have been studied in the literature, namely parametricity [9] and the gradual guarantee [22]. Type holes are known to weaken parametricity. We review this active research area and discuss a weakening of parametricity that holds of our system. Section 5 describes our mechanization of these metatheoretic properties in Agda and the implementation of polymorphism in the Hazel programming environment. In practice, it is cumbersome to explicitly apply type abstractions and most major functional languages support implicitly inferred type applications. Section 6 approaches the problem of implicit type application in a unique way – by outlining an in-progress edit-time implicit type application system for Hazel, whereby users can see and intervene in the implicit application when desired rather than relying on invisible implicit type application logic.

2 Background

2.1 The Hazel Programming Environment

Hazel is a live functional programming environment that provides gapless editor support; that is, all editor states, including those corresponding to incomplete

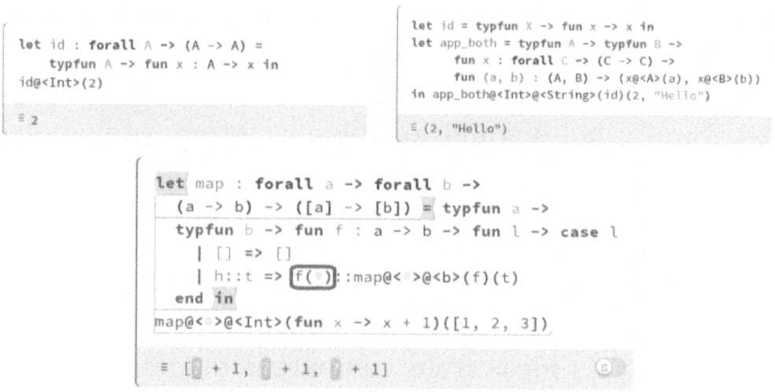

136   A. Chen et al.

Fig. 1. Screenshots of the current Hazel UI showing off polymorphic functions, including the polymorphic identity, a rank-2 polymorphic function, and a polymorphic map featuring both type and expression holes (expression hole is the argument of the outlined application).

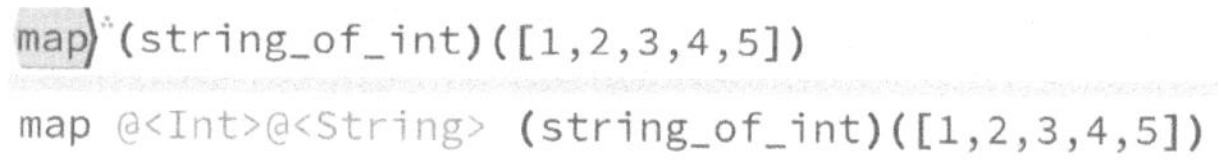

Fig. 2. Mockup of a hypothetical Hazel UI showing a folded (above) and unfolded (below) automatically inserted type application. Such an editor service fits into the existing Hazel architecture and would allow polymorphic functions to be used as if they were implicit.

programs, are endowed with static and dynamic meaning. Figure 1 displays some examples of polymorphic code in the Hazel editor and shows typed expression holes within polymorphic code. Figure 2 displays a hypothetical Hazel interface for a editor service that would insert type applications automatically, and would recover some benefits of implicit polymorphism. A reader who is more interested in the user-centered aspect of Hazel and less in its formal theory may wish to jump directly to the discussion of this feature, in Sect. 6.

2.2 The Theory of Hazel

The theory of Hazel is organized into several calculi, somewhat analogous to compiler phases. The Hazel grammar is shown in Fig. 3, including types and three different kinds of expressions. b stands for any base types of the language, and c for any constants. We have simplified the presentation slightly by removing

$$\text{Type } \tau ::= b \mid \tau \to \tau \mid {?}$$
$$\text{HExp } e ::= c \mid x \mid \lambda x : \tau.\, e \mid \lambda x.\, e \mid e\, e \mid (\!|\,|\!)$$
$$\text{IHExp } d ::= c \mid x \mid \lambda x : \tau.\, d \mid \lambda x.\, d \mid d\, d \mid (\!|\,|\!) \mid (\!|d|\!) \mid d\langle \tau \Rightarrow \tau \rangle \mid d\langle \tau \Rightarrow {?} \not\Rightarrow \tau \rangle$$

Fig. 3. Simplified Hazel grammar.

information carried by the holes in the different calculi and other constructs not relevant to this work (such as abstract data types, etc.).

To illustrate the main components of the theory of Hazel, we provide an example rule for dealing with function applications at each major stage of Hazel in Fig. 4.

Parsing with Holes. Hazel users enter code using an editor that inserts holes automatically to ensure that every editor state contains a well-formed expression with holes, e. The Hazelnut calculus [19] defined an edit action calculus that inserts these holes, which has since evolved to a support more natural keyboard-driven input [15].

In Hazelnut, the resulting expression is guaranteed to be both syntactically and statically valid. However, in the newer editor calculus with flexible keyboard-driven input, the resulting expression is only guaranteed to be syntactically valid, and may still have static errors. To address this, Zhao et al. [28] describe the *marked lambda calculus*, a system that restores static correctness by inserting marks, or nonempty holes, into syntactically valid programs. We further discuss this procedure in Sect. 6, but do not include it in our presentation.

Elaboration. After marking, the program is syntactically and statically valid. *Hazelnut Live* is a system for endowing Hazel with dynamic semantics. It operates by bidirectionally elaborating external (hole) expressions (HExp) into internal (holes) expressions (IHExp). We will identify the external expressions of Hazelnut Live with the marked expressions of the marked lambda calculus. In Hazelnut Live, all holes also carry a unique name, and internal holes carry a finite substitution of terms in for variables.

The elaboration judgment forms are $\Gamma \vdash e \Rightarrow \tau \leadsto d \dashv \Delta$ and $\Gamma \vdash e \Leftarrow \tau_1 \leadsto d : \tau_2 \dashv \Delta$. Note that in the analytic case a type τ_2 is output as well, which must be consistent with the input τ_1. During elaboration, casts between types are inserted to enable dynamic type checks that are necessary due to missing type information, i.e. type holes, in the original program. Elaboration also produces a hole context Δ, which maps the program's empty and nonempty holes to their contexts and expected types, and associates each hole occurrence with a sequence of substitutions that has been applied to it. This facilitates the *fill-and-resume* operation, by which a reduced program with holes can be refined (by filling an empty hole with an expression) and reduction can be resumed.

These internal expressions d are typed via a type assignment judgment of form $\Delta; \Gamma \vdash d : \tau$. This type assignment judgment is not bidirectional, unlike for external expressions. The hole context is an input to this judgment, as it assigns types to holes. Figure 4 contains the elaboration and internal typing rules for applications, ESAP and TALAM.

Evaluation. Internal expressions are evaluated via a stepping relation of form $d \mapsto d'$, and the resulting normal form, if it exists, is reported back to the end user. The stepping relation is defined via contextual semantics, meaning redexes and evaluation contexts are defined (not shown here), with a transition

SAP
$$\frac{\Gamma \vdash e_1 \Rightarrow \tau \quad \tau \blacktriangleright_\to \tau_1 \to \tau_2 \quad \Gamma \vdash e_2 \Leftarrow \tau_1}{\Gamma \vdash e_1\, e_2 \Rightarrow \tau_2}$$

ESAP
$$\frac{\Gamma \vdash e \Rightarrow \tau_1 \quad}{\tau \blacktriangleright_\to \tau_1 \to \tau_2 \quad \Gamma \vdash e_1 \Leftarrow \tau_2 \to \tau \leadsto d_1 : \tau_1' \dashv \Delta_1 \quad \Gamma \vdash e_2 \Rightarrow \tau_2 \leadsto d_2 \dashv \tau_2'\Delta_2}$$
$$\overline{\Gamma \vdash e_1\, e_2 \Rightarrow \tau \leadsto (d_1\langle \tau_1' \Rightarrow \tau_2 \to \tau\rangle)\,(d_2\langle \tau_2' \Rightarrow \tau_2\rangle) \dashv \Delta_1 \cup \Delta_2}$$

TALAM
$$\frac{\Delta;\Gamma \vdash d_1 : \tau_2 \to \tau \quad \Delta;\Gamma \vdash d_2 : \tau_2}{\Delta;\Gamma \vdash d_1\, d_2 : \tau}$$

ITLAM
$$\frac{[d_2 \text{ final}]}{(\lambda x : \tau.\, d_1)\,(d_2) \longrightarrow [d_2/x]d_1}$$

Fig. 4. Example rules for function application expressions. SAP synthesizes a type for the external expression ($\blacktriangleright_\to$ expands the gradual type to a function type if need be), TAAP assigns a type to the internal expression, and ITLAM describes how it reduces. The brackets on ITLAM indicate that the hypothesis may be omitted for a non-deterministic evaluation system.

relation $d \longrightarrow d'$ defined on redexes. Figure 4 contains the transition relation corresponding to beta reduction, ITLAM.

Note that having a gradually typed, user-facing language that elaborates into an internal cast calculus is typical of gradually typed systems [22]. The transitions include standard features like beta reduction, holes blocking reduction, and tracking casts to catch dynamic type errors. Casts are decomposed as much as possible, until they are between top-level type formers applied only to holes (ground types), with inconsistencies at this level resulting in a failed cast, representing a dynamic type error.

2.3 Polymorphic Gradual Typing

The gradually typed lambda calculus is an extension to the simply typed lambda calculus [4] that adds the gradual type (commonly notated as a question mark: ?) to the simply typed lambda calculus, with type equivalence giving way to a (non-transitive) consistency relation between types: the unknown type is consistent with every type [21]. Gradual typing offers a compromise between an untyped and a simply typed calculus; indeed, any untyped term may be embedded into the gradually typed calculus by typing everything at the gradual type. This offers programmers the flexibility to work outside of the type system when they deem it beneficial to do so, and the benefits of allowing this are exemplified in the success of TypeScript [3]. Siek et al. [22] later formalized some properties that hold of the gradually typed lambda calculus that make working in a gradually typed system intuitive for programmers. These properties are collectively known as the gradual guarantee, and are the gold standard properties that are desirable for extensions of the gradually typed lambda calculus. Informally, the gradual guarantee states that removing parts of type annotations from a program cannot introduce new static or dynamic errors.

System F [8,20] is another extension to the simply typed lambda calculus that adds type functions and polymorphic types. System F has become the go-to model for polymorphic functions, with restrictions of System F becoming the type systems for widely-used functional programming languages such as Haskell, OCaml, F#, and more. One of the reasons System F is so powerful is the strong metatheoretic property of parametricity [9]. Informally, parametricity asserts that a polymorphic function should behave in analogous ways no matter what type the function is instantiated at. This means that one cannot perform computations based on types, and indeed, parametric systems allow for identical evaluation after type erasure [14], which can also be used as a run-time optimization.

There have been several attempts to combine the gradually typed lambda calculus with System F. λB, presented by Ahmed et al. [2], was the first system to add the gradual type to a cast calculus based on System F while preserving parametricity. They achieved this by using type bindings as opposed to type substitutions. In effect, this means that if a polymorphic functions error on any instantiation, then it will error on all instantiations, even if it makes sense to successfully evaluate some of the instantiations. (We will argue that this behavior is undesirable and investigate what metatheoretic properties hold without type bindings.) This also introduces some run-time overhead. System F_G, presented by Igarashi et al. [10], presents a user-facing gradually typed calculus that compiles to a cast calculus, akin to the gradually typed lambda calculus. System F_G is shown to both be parametric as well as satisfy the gradual guarantee – albeit for a modified notion of precision for polymorphic types. Parametric and gradual system PolyG$^\nu$, presented by New et al. [17], requires explicit sealing and unsealing of type variables. The system is based on the intuition that parametricity arises from disallowing computation on types. Gradual System F (GSF) is a system presented by Labrada et al. [12], which, like System F_G, also exhibits parametricity as well as the gradual guarantee. Similarly to the previous systems, this is accomplished with the use of type bindings. However unlike System F_G, a more intuitive notion of precision is defined. Out of the previously presented systems, GSF is the most similar to the one we will present. It is also worth noting the work of Xie et al. [27], who define a system that uses subtyping to provide implicit polymorphism. Notably, their system violates the gradual guarantee due to the necessity of an oracle for some ambiguous instantiations.

3 The System

We extend the types, external expressions, and internal expressions of Hazelnut Live with type variables, universal types, polymorphic abstraction, and type application (Fig. 5).

$$\begin{array}{l}\text{Type } \tau ::= \ldots \mid \alpha \mid \forall \alpha.\, \tau \\ \text{HExp } e ::= \ldots \mid \Lambda\alpha.\, e \mid e\, [\tau] \\ \text{IHExp } d ::= \ldots \mid \Lambda\alpha.\, d \mid d\, [\tau]\end{array}$$

Fig. 5. Syntax extension of polymorphic Hazel.

With the introduction of the new type form, we define a corresponding matching judgment for expanding the gradual type into a forall form where necessary (Fig. 6). Note that the gradual type is identified with the type hole and is denoted ?.

3.1 Gradually Typed Calculus

We extend the bidirectional typing rules as shown in Fig. 8. We augment typing judgments with type variable contexts Σ, which are sets of type variables in scope. Notably, type functions may be typed both analytically and synthetically. Type functions admit both analytic and synthetic rules. This is a deviation from Dunfield and Krishnaswami's "bidirectional recipe" [6], which prescribes only the analysis rule for type abstractions, since they are introduction forms. We include both rules because doing so improves the expressiveness of the system (for example, the type of the polymorphic identity function $\Lambda\alpha.\, \lambda x : \alpha.\, x$ may be synthesized).

Rule STAP has as a premise $\Sigma \vdash \tau_1$, the well-formedness of τ_1 with respect to Σ. This new judgment is defined in Fig. 7 and must also be inserted as a premise into existing rules for terms involving types, namely ascriptions and annotated lambdas. The well-formedness judgment ensures that all type variables appearing in a term are either bound or appear in the type variable context.

It is at this stage that marking would occur. As previously mentioned, we do not include this process in our presentation; we assume the user provides an expression that is already well typed in the gradually typed calculus. We discuss how our system may be extended to include marking and the use of marking to simulate a form of implicit polymorphism in Sect. 6.

3.2 Elaboration and Cast Calculus

We extend the typed elaboration rules as shown in Fig. 9. Type function applications are elaborated analogously to function applications. The function is cast to the output of the matched type judgment to accommodate the gradual type, and the function is analyzed against this type. Note that to ensure elaboration unicity (further discussed in Appendix A), EATLAM cannot be applied when the function body is a hole, although disallowing type functions in subsumption achieves the same effect. An implicit change from Hazelnut Live is that hole contexts must now assign to each hole a type variable context Σ in addition to a type τ and context Γ.

3.3 Dynamics and Final Forms

Figure 10 contains the type assignment rules for the internal cast calculus. They are the standard System F typing rules, with the addition of the hole context. No matched forall premise is necessary in TATAP because a cast to a forall type has been inserted before the type application during elaboration.

The universal type creates a new ground type case (Fig. 11). The matched ground judgment is used in the ITGROUND and ITEXPAND instruction transitions, which are not presented here as they are not directly modified. The ground type judgment is used to simplify the range of final forms, presented in Fig. 12. We add new value, boxed value, and indeterminate form cases for type functions and casts between universal types. Each normal form is exactly one of these three kinds of final form.

The operational semantics is presented as a contextual semantics. Evaluation contexts must be extended to allow for the new syntactic forms. Since type functions are values, all that is required is to extend evaluation contexts into type function application (omitted from figures as this is standard).

Finally, we add new transition rules. Type functions applied to a type are evaluated by type substitution, as in System F. Note that previous work [2, 10, 12, 17] avoided this approach, instead choosing to keep a partial mapping from type variables to types. A discussion of the decision to eschew this development and its implications for parametricity and graduality is contained in Sect. 4. In contrast with merely extending GTLC with System F rules, we must add an additional rule that allows type function application to move past casts. The rule is analogous to the rule for term functions.

The instruction transitions are shown in Fig. 13. The bracketed d final premise may be omitted to have an unspecified evaluation strategy. Choosing to including it for eager evaluation creates a deterministic evaluation useful for implementations of the system. Finally, the step relation $d \mapsto d'$ is defined by performing instruction transitions in an evaluation context; this is typical of contextual semantics, and we introduce no modifications to the original presentation, so it is not reproduced here.

$\boxed{\tau \triangleright_\forall \forall \alpha.\, \tau'}$ τ has matched forall type $\forall \alpha.\, \tau'$

$$\frac{}{?\triangleright_\forall \forall\alpha.\,?} \text{MFHOLE} \qquad \frac{}{\forall\alpha.\,\tau \triangleright_\forall \forall\alpha.\,\tau} \text{MFFORALL}$$

Fig. 6. Matched forall types.

$\boxed{\Sigma \vdash \tau}$ τ is well-formed in type variable context Σ

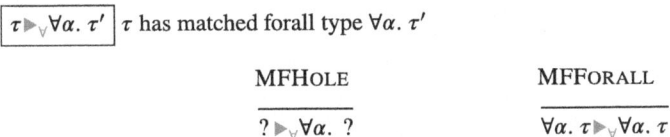

Fig. 7. Well-formedness rules.

$\boxed{\Sigma; \Gamma \vdash e \Rightarrow \tau}$ Expression e synthesizes type τ in context $\Sigma; \Gamma$

$$\text{STLAM} \quad \frac{\Sigma, \alpha; \Gamma \vdash e \Rightarrow \tau}{\Sigma; \Gamma \vdash \Lambda\alpha.\, e \Rightarrow \forall\alpha.\, \tau}$$

$$\text{STAP} \quad \frac{\Sigma \vdash \tau_1 \quad \Sigma; \Gamma \vdash e \Rightarrow \tau_2 \quad \tau_2 \blacktriangleright_\forall \forall\alpha.\, \tau_3}{\Sigma; \Gamma \vdash e\,[\tau_1] \Rightarrow [\tau_1/\alpha]\tau_3}$$

$\boxed{\Sigma; \Gamma \vdash e \Leftarrow \tau}$ Expression e analyzes against type τ in context $\Sigma; \Gamma$

$$\text{ATLAM} \quad \frac{\tau_1 \blacktriangleright_\forall \forall\alpha.\, \tau_2 \quad \Sigma, \alpha; \Gamma \vdash e \Leftarrow \tau_2}{\Sigma; \Gamma \vdash \Lambda\alpha.\, e \Leftarrow \tau_1}$$

Fig. 8. Bidirectional typing rules.

$\boxed{\Sigma; \Gamma \vdash e \Rightarrow \tau \leadsto d \dashv \Delta}$ e synthesizes type τ and elaborates to d with hole context Δ

$$\text{ESTLAM} \quad \frac{\Sigma, \alpha; \Gamma \vdash e \Rightarrow \tau \leadsto d \dashv \Delta}{\Sigma; \Gamma \vdash \Lambda\alpha.\, e \Rightarrow \forall\alpha.\, \tau \leadsto \Lambda\alpha.\, d \dashv \Delta}$$

$$\text{ESTAP} \quad \frac{\Sigma \vdash \tau_1 \quad \Sigma; \Gamma \vdash e \Rightarrow \tau_2 \quad \tau_2 \blacktriangleright_\forall \forall\alpha.\, \tau_3 \quad \Sigma; \Gamma \vdash e \Leftarrow \forall\alpha.\, \tau_3 \leadsto d : \tau_4 \dashv \Delta}{\Sigma; \Gamma \vdash e\,[\tau_1] \Rightarrow [\tau_1/\alpha]\tau_3 \leadsto d\langle\tau_4 \Rightarrow \forall\alpha.\, \tau_3\rangle\,[\tau_1] \dashv \Delta}$$

$\boxed{\Sigma; \Gamma \vdash e \Leftarrow \tau_1 \leadsto d : \tau_2 \dashv \Delta}$ e analyzes against τ_1 and elaborates to d of consistent type τ_2 with hole context Δ

$$\text{EATLAM} \quad \frac{e \neq (\!|\!|)^u \quad e \neq (\!|e'|\!)^u \quad \tau_1 \blacktriangleright_\forall \forall\alpha.\, \tau_2 \quad \Sigma, \alpha; \Gamma \vdash e \Leftarrow \tau_2 \leadsto d : \tau_3 \dashv \Delta}{\Sigma; \Gamma \vdash \Lambda\alpha.\, e \Leftarrow \tau_1 \leadsto \Lambda\alpha.\, d : \forall\alpha.\, \tau_3 \dashv \Delta}$$

Fig. 9. Elaboration rules from external expressions to internal expressions.

$\boxed{\Delta; \Sigma; \Gamma \vdash d : \tau}$ d is assigned type τ

$$\text{TATLAM} \quad \frac{\Delta; \Sigma, \alpha; \Gamma \vdash d : \tau}{\Delta; \Sigma; \Gamma \vdash \Lambda\alpha.\, d : \forall\alpha.\, \tau}$$

$$\text{TATAP} \quad \frac{\Sigma \vdash \tau_1 \quad \Delta; \Sigma; \Gamma \vdash d : \forall\alpha.\, \tau_2}{\Delta; \Sigma; \Gamma \vdash d\,[\tau_1] : [\tau_1/\alpha]\tau_2}$$

Fig. 10. Type assignment for internal expressions.

$\boxed{\tau \text{ ground}}$ τ is a ground type $\qquad$ $\boxed{\tau \blacktriangleright_{\text{ground}} \tau'}$ τ has matched ground type τ'

$$\text{GFORALL} \quad \frac{}{\forall\alpha.\, ?\text{ ground}}$$

$$\text{MGFORALL} \quad \frac{\forall\alpha.\, \tau \neq \forall\alpha.\, ?}{\forall\alpha.\, \tau \blacktriangleright_{\text{ground}} \forall\alpha.\, ?}$$

Fig. 11. Ground and matched ground rules.

$\boxed{d \text{ val}}$ d is a value $\qquad$ $\boxed{d \text{ boxedval}}$ d is a boxed value

$$\frac{}{\Lambda\alpha.\, d \text{ val}} \text{VTLAM} \qquad \frac{\forall\alpha_1.\, \tau_1 \neq \forall\alpha_2.\, \tau_2 \quad d \text{ boxedval}}{d\langle\forall\alpha_1.\, \tau_1 \Rightarrow \forall\alpha_2.\, \tau_2\rangle \text{ boxedval}} \text{VTLAM}$$

$\boxed{d \text{ indet}}$ d is indeterminate

$$\frac{d \neq d'\langle\forall\alpha_1.\, \tau_1 \Rightarrow \forall\alpha_2.\, \tau_2\rangle \quad d \text{ indet}}{d\,[\tau]\text{ indet}} \text{ITAP} \qquad \frac{\forall\alpha_1.\, \tau_1 \neq \forall\alpha_2.\, \tau_2 \quad d \text{ indet}}{d\langle\forall\alpha_1.\, \tau_1 \Rightarrow \forall\alpha_2.\, \tau_2\rangle \text{ indet}} \text{ICASTFORALL}$$

Fig. 12. Final form rules.

$\boxed{d \longrightarrow d'}$ d takes an instruction transition to d'

$$\frac{}{(\Lambda\alpha.\, d)\,[\tau] \longrightarrow [\tau/\alpha]d} \text{ITTLAM} \qquad \frac{[d \text{ final}]}{d\langle\forall\alpha_1.\, \tau_1 \Rightarrow \forall\alpha_2.\, \tau_2\rangle\,[\tau] \longrightarrow d\,[\tau]\langle[\tau/\alpha_1]\tau_1 \Rightarrow [\tau/\alpha_2]\tau_2\rangle} \text{ITTAPCAST}$$

Fig. 13. Instruction transitions.

4 Metatheoretic Properties

Our system conserves all of the typing properties that held of the original system (c.f. Theorems 3.1 through 3.14 in [18]), up to the inclusion of an additional type variable context. Notably, we show type safety of the system:

Theorem 1 (Type Safety). *The system presented in Sect. 3 is type safe:*

1. *Progress: If $\emptyset \vdash \Delta$ and $\Delta; \emptyset; \emptyset \vdash d : \tau$ then either d indet, d boxedval, or there exists an IHExp d' such that $d \mapsto d'$.*
2. *Preservation: If $\emptyset \vdash \Delta$, $\Delta; \emptyset; \emptyset \vdash d : \tau$ and $d \mapsto d'$ then $\Delta; \emptyset; \emptyset \vdash d' : \tau$.*

We also show the properties of elaboration and properties of complete terms that hold of Hazelnut Live. The full statements and explanations of these theorems can be found in Appendix A.

We now discuss the two key metatheoretic properties of this work: parametricity and the gradual guarantee.

4.1 Parametricity

As mentioned before, previous systems obeyed additional restrictions in order to preserve parametricity. These stem from the approach of Ahmed et al. [1], which showed that substitution typing is not parametric, but the approach of using type bindings is. The example to show this presented in Igarashi et al. is thus:

$$f = \Lambda\alpha.\ \lambda x : \mathsf{num}.\ x\langle\mathsf{num} \Rightarrow ? \Rightarrow \alpha\rangle$$

Noting that
$$f\ [\mathsf{num}]\ 1 \ \mapsto^*\ 1$$
$$f\ [\mathsf{bool}]\ \mathsf{true} \mapsto^* \mathsf{true}\langle\mathsf{num} \Rightarrow ? \not\Rightarrow \mathsf{bool}\rangle$$

where 1 boxedval, and $\mathsf{true}\langle\mathsf{num} \Rightarrow ? \not\Rightarrow \mathsf{bool}\rangle$ indet. Indeterminate forms correspond to blame/errors in other calculi. Using type bindings would instead result in:

$$f\ [\mathsf{num}]\ 1 \mapsto^* 1\langle\mathsf{num} \Rightarrow ? \not\Rightarrow \alpha\rangle$$

We argue that creating errors from otherwise sensibly executable programs is against the spirit of live programming with holes, and we would like to avoid doing so. In live programming, we would like to explore the implications of filling the type holes, where it is helpful to not prematurely error. Igarashi et al. further note that type bindings carry overhead, and they introduce static and gradual type variables to allow for substitution typing when no cast to the gradual type exists. Our system does not contain the labels on type variables; they complicate decisions for the programmer, and also complicate the definition of consistency, which must now allow for quasi-polymorphic functions to appear in places expecting polymorphic functions. We furthermore argue that in our setting, since expressions can be holes that might be filled in later, it is impossible to know *a priori* whether a static type variable label is appropriate.

Since the approach of using type bindings (also used in systems such as GSF) only enforces parametricity by introducing unnecessary error states, we instead focus on weakening parametricity. We follow the construction of parametricity presented by Crary [5]. We define equality up to type annotations similarly:

Definition 1. $d_1 =_0 d_2$ *whenever d_1 and d_2 differ only in syntactic types. Namely, this means that types in lambda annotations, type function applications, and casts may vary, and only such types may vary.*

We define a similar relation for external expressions. We say that a program (term) is *complete* if it does not contain any expression or type holes. If a program is complete and well-typed, all of its casts are identity casts. This can be intuitively thought of as an embedding in System F, which is parametric. We formalize this intuition in the following theorem:

Theorem 2. *Suppose e_1 complete and e_2 complete and $\Sigma; \Gamma \vdash e_1 \Rightarrow \tau_1 \leadsto d_1 \dashv \emptyset$ and $\Sigma; \Gamma \vdash e_2 \Rightarrow \tau_2 \leadsto d_2 \dashv \emptyset$ and $e_1 =_0 e_2$.*
If $d_1 \mapsto^* v_1$ and v_1 val then there exists v_2 such that $d_2 \mapsto^* v_2$ and v_2 val and $v_1 =_0 v_2$.

Corollary 1. *If $\mapsto$ is confluent and $d_1 \mapsto^* v_1$ and $d_2 \mapsto^* v_2$ and v_1 val and v_2 final then v_2 val and $v_1 =_0 v_2$.*

We actually have too strong of a hypothesis here; we merely need $d_1 =_0 d_2$ to prove the result, but we focus on external expressions to emphasize that is what the programmer sees and has control over. Note also that the evaluation of all complete terms terminates in a val (this is not proven of the original system, but should also hold from embedding in System F). And so, the hypothesis of the theorem is satisfied by any well-typed, complete expression.

The theorem is proven by formalizing the intuition that all casts are identity casts. We define a relation $='_0$ that also requires that casts must be identity casts, and is thus a sub-relation of $=_0$. We show that if two terms are $=_0$ and are complete, well-typed programs, then they must be $='_0$. We show that if $d_1 ='_0 d_2$ and $d_1 \mapsto d'_1$ then there exists a d'_2 such that $d'_1 ='_0 d'_2$ and $d_2 \mapsto d'_2$. Thus we can push the relation through the entire evaluation of d_1. Since it relates values to values, then when we reach the end of d_1's trace, we have a v_2 that is a value. (2) follows from (1) by using the unique normal form property (which follows from confluence); the final (normalized) value of d_2 must be unique and so v_2 must be identical to the existentially quantified normal value from (1). We do not show confluence of the system in this work, so we leave it as a hypothesis in the theorem.

In short, this theorem asserts that if we do not deal with graduality then we are able to ensure full parametricity. However, to motivate the use of substitution in our *gradual* system, we also make a guarantee about possibly incomplete terms when using eager evaluation semantics (by which we mean requiring the argument to a beta reduction to be final)[1].

Definition 2. *$d_1 =_{casts} d_2$ when d_1 and d_2 differ only in syntactic types and presence of casts. More formally, we say $=_{casts}$ is the smallest congruence that contains $=_0$, and for all types τ_1, τ_2, $d_1 =_{casts} d_2$ implies $d_1 \langle \tau_1 \Rightarrow \tau_2 \rangle =_{casts} d_2$ and $d_1 =_{casts} d_2 \langle \tau_1 \Rightarrow \tau_2 \rangle$*

Theorem 3. *If $\Delta; \emptyset; \emptyset \vdash d_1 : \tau_1$ and $\Delta; \emptyset; \emptyset \vdash d_2 : \tau_2$ and $d_1 =_{casts} d_2$ and $d_1 \mapsto^* v_1$ and v_1 boxedval then there exists v_2 such that $d_2 \mapsto^* v_2$ and either (v_2 boxedval and $v_1 =_{casts} v_2$) or v_2 indet.*

---

[1] The reason this is required is that if the argument to a function loops infinitely, if it is lazily evaluated it may be completely thrown away (consider the function $\lambda x\ :?.\ \lambda y\ :?.\ y$), whereas if the beta reduction cannot happen due to a failing cast in the function, the argument *will* be continually reduced.

Corollary 2. *If $\mapsto$ is confluent and $\Delta; \emptyset; \emptyset \vdash d_1 : \tau_1$ and $\Delta; \emptyset; \emptyset \vdash d_2 : \tau_2$ and $d_1 =_{casts} d_2$ and $d_1 \mapsto^* v_1$ and $d_2 \mapsto^* v_2$ and v_1 boxedval and v_2 boxedval then $v_1 =_{casts} v_2$.*

We remark that $=_0$ is a subrelation of $=_{casts}$, so we may have $d_1 =_0 d_2$ in the hypothesis instead. The theorem is proven via induction on the evaluation of d_1. Namely, we show two lemmas:

Lemma 1 (Stepwise Parametricity Lemma). *If $\Delta; \emptyset; \emptyset \vdash d_1 : \tau_1$ and $\Delta; \emptyset; \emptyset \vdash d_2 : \tau_2$ and $d_1 =_{casts} d_2$ and $d_1 \mapsto d_1'$ then there exists a d_2' such that $d_2 \mapsto^* d_2'$ and either $d_1' = d_2'$ or d_2' indet.*

Lemma 2 (One-sided Parametricity Lemma). *If $d_1 =_{casts} d_2$ and d_1 boxedval then there exists a d_2' such that $d_2 \mapsto^* d_2'$ and $d_1 =_{casts} d_2'$ and d_2' final.*

Lemma 1 allows us to use the trace of d_1 as a target for induction until d_1 boxedval. We find a sequence of steps for d_2 that preserve $=_{casts}$; the difficulty here is that we may have to do some sequence of cast reductions before applying the appropriate beta reduction. We proceed by induction on the syntactic sub-expression of d_2 that corresponds to the sub-expression of d_1 that is reduced (picked such that the outer form of the sub-expression is not a cast). We show that we either perform the same beta reduction (in the absence of casts), or we can find a sequence of cast reductions that reduce an ordering[2] and thus we may proceed inductively.

Once this process has finished, Lemma 2 may be applied to show that the evaluation of d_2 terminates, and thus we have the desired final result. The proof of this proceeds similarly to the previous Lemma, noting that d_2 cannot beta reduce due to the $=_{casts}$ constraint and for any trailing casts, there is a sequence of cast reductions that reduces the syntactic size of d_2.

Together, these two properties establish that modulo successful termination, even gradual terms behave in a parametric manner. Existing systems that possess parametricity uniformly introduce cast errors to do so, so we have effectively proven our claim that the difference between those systems and ours is that we raise fewer cast errors on otherwise successfully executing programs.

4.2 Gradual Guarantee

The gradual guarantee specifies how the static and dynamic semantics of a gradual language should behave relative to a precision relation between programs. This relation captures the operation of filling in holes – a program is made

---

[2] The exact ordering is to, for each natural number n up to the number of function applications, count the number of casts in the function position of n function applications. Then lexicographically order them from largest to smallest n with syntactic size at the end. Such a bizarre ordering must be used as the ITApCast rule increases the number of casts and the size of the term, but moves a cast from the function position to argument and external positions.

more precise by replacing its empty holes with other terms. We shall consider a precision relation on types, external expressions, internal expressions, and hole contexts, all of which we denote $\sqsubseteq$.

Intuitively, the gradual guarantee states that making a program less precise results in more permissive type checking (the *static* gradual guarantee) and a less precise evaluated result (the *dynamic* gradual guarantee). Another way to phrase the static gradual guarantee is that deleting parts of a program, e.g. type annotations, cannot introduce new static errors. We take the formal statement of the gradual guarantee from Siek et al. [22] and adapt it to our notation:

Definition 3. *We say* $d \Uparrow$ *when there does not exist a* v *such that* $d \mapsto^* v$ *and* v final *(in other words, d diverges).*

Definition 4. *The Gradual Guarantee is a collection of four properties:*
Suppose $e \sqsubseteq e'$ *and* $\emptyset; \emptyset \vdash e \Rightarrow \tau \leadsto d \dashv \Delta$.

1. *There exists a* τ' *such that* $\emptyset; \emptyset \vdash e' \Rightarrow \tau'$ *with* $\tau \sqsubseteq \tau'$.
2. *There exist a* d' *and a* Δ' *such that* $\emptyset; \emptyset \vdash e' \Rightarrow \tau' \leadsto d' \dashv \Delta'$ *with* $\Delta \sqsubseteq \Delta'$ *and* $\Delta, \Delta'; \emptyset, \emptyset \vdash d \sqsubseteq d'$.
3. *If* $d \mapsto^* v$ *with* v boxedval *then* $d' \mapsto^* v'$ *with* v' boxedval *and* $v \sqsubseteq v'$.
   If $d \Uparrow$ *then* $d' \Uparrow$.
4. *If* $d' \mapsto^* v'$ *with* v' boxedval *then* $d \mapsto^* v$ *such that either* v boxedval *and* $v \sqsubseteq v'$ *or* v indet.
   If $d' \Uparrow$ *then* $d \Uparrow$ *or* $d \mapsto^* v$ *with* v indet.

Of course, what the guarantee establishes depends on the definitions of the various precision relations. Recall that our setting is that of a live programming environment. Thus we would like increased precision to coincide with the intuitive idea of the programmer filling holes in the program. Thus we do not want a definition similar to System F_G's definition, but rather one closer to GSF's definition.

We omit the rules for precision for types and for external expressions, since they are completely straightforward and do not depart from previous presentations of precision in gradual languages, such as for the Gradually Typed Lambda Calculus (GTLC) of Siek et al. The precision relation holds between two syntactic constructs with the same head if it holds between their corresponding children, and anything is more precise than a hole. Using these straightforward definitions, we can prove the following theorem:

Theorem 4. *Our system satisfies Property 1 of Definition 4.*

This property, the static gradual guarantee, states that a less precise term synthesizes a less precise type. It is amenable to direct proof by induction, strengthened to include contexts and both analytic and synthetic typing. We have completed such a proof in our Agda mechanization as discussed in Sect. 5.

The remaining components of the gradual guarantee are not proven for our system, and we leave them to future work. However, there are some features of the system that seem necessary in order to hope for these properties to hold.

Firstly, in order to satisfy Property 2 of Definition 4, a less precise term must analytically elaborate with a less precise type. This is broken with the standard subsumption rule found in Hazelnut Live, in which terms elaborate their synthesized type, even if it is less precise than the analyzed type, so long as the two are consistent. Therefore we consider a modified subsumption rule in Fig. 14. It employs the meet between types, which is the greatest lower bound of types with respect to the aforementioned precision relation, and is a partial function defined only on consistent types. With the new rule, subsumption elaborates with a type that is more precise than both the analyzed and synthesized type, supporting graduality. In order to retain the properties of typed elaboration and elaboration unicity, the rule must insert a cast and must not apply to type functions. It is with this version of the subsumption rule that we have proven the theorems in this paper.

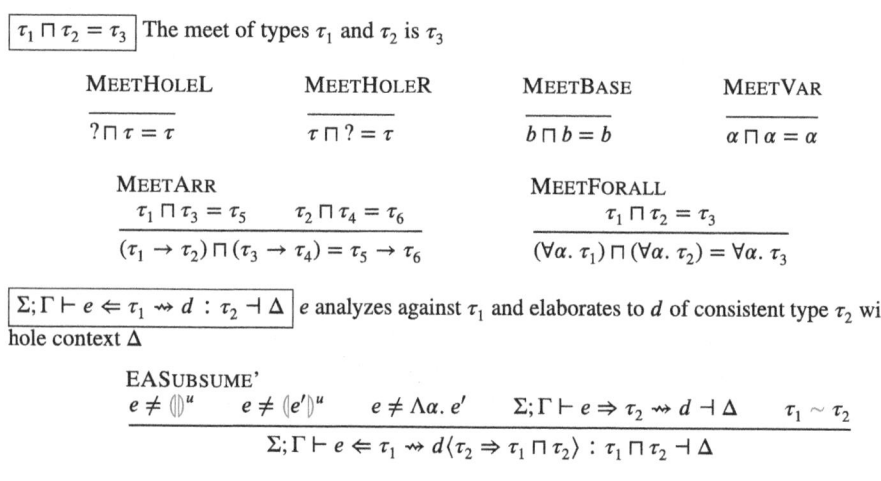

Fig. 14. Modified subsumption rule.

Properties 2–4 of Definition 4 depend on the precision relation for internal expressions, which is considerably more subtle than that for external expressions and types. Siek et al. define an appropriate definition of internal precision for the GTLC, and prove the gradual guarantee for this system. We adapt this relation to our system. The rules that do not involve casts or the empty hole are analogous to the rules for external expressions, so are elided. The remaining rules are provided in Fig. 15. The rules involving casts correspond directly to the rules for term precision for the GTLC's cast calculus. Since internal holes carry type information, a term is only more precise than a hole if its assigned type is more precise than the hole's contextually assigned type. Since internal precision involves type assignment, it depends on a pair of contexts, one for each side of the relation, which may share a type context since the different contexts need only vary by term precision.

We define $\Gamma \sqsubseteq \Gamma'$ to hold when Γ and Γ' have equal domains and for all x such that $x : \tau \in \Gamma$ and $x : \tau' \in \Gamma'$, $\tau \sqsubseteq \tau'$. We define $\Delta \sqsubseteq \Delta'$ to hold when for all u such that $u :: \tau[\Sigma; \Gamma] \in \Delta$ and $u :: \tau'[\Sigma; \Gamma'] \in \Delta'$, $\tau \sqsubseteq \tau'$ and $\Gamma \sqsubseteq \Gamma'$.

$\boxed{\Delta, \Delta'; \Sigma; \Gamma, \Gamma' \vdash d \sqsubseteq d'}$ d in context $\Delta; \Sigma; \Gamma$ is more precise than d' in context $\Delta'; \Sigma; \Gamma'$

$\cdots$

PIEHOLE
$$\frac{\Delta; \Sigma; \Gamma \vdash d : \tau \quad u :: \tau'[\Sigma'; \Gamma''] \in \Delta' \quad \tau \sqsubseteq \tau'}{\Delta, \Delta'; \Sigma; \Gamma, \Gamma' \vdash d \sqsubseteq (\!|\;|\!)_\sigma^u}$$

PICAST
$$\frac{\Delta, \Delta'; \Sigma; \Gamma, \Gamma' \vdash d \sqsubseteq d' \quad \tau_1 \sqsubseteq \tau_1' \quad \tau_2 \sqsubseteq \tau_2'}{\Delta, \Delta'; \Sigma; \Gamma, \Gamma' \vdash d\langle \tau_1 \Rightarrow \tau_2 \rangle \sqsubseteq d'\langle \tau_1' \Rightarrow \tau_2' \rangle}$$

PIFAILEDCAST
$$\frac{\Delta'; \Sigma; \Gamma' \vdash d' : \tau \quad \tau_2 \sqsubseteq \tau}{\Delta, \Delta'; \Sigma; \Gamma, \Gamma' \vdash d\langle \tau_1 \Rightarrow ? \not\Rightarrow \tau_2 \rangle \sqsubseteq d'}$$

PIREMOVECAST
$$\frac{\Delta, \Delta'; \Sigma; \Gamma, \Gamma' \vdash d \sqsubseteq d' \quad \Delta'; \Sigma; \Gamma' \vdash d' : \tau' \quad \tau_1 \sqsubseteq \tau' \quad \tau_2 \sqsubseteq \tau'}{\Delta, \Delta'; \Sigma; \Gamma, \Gamma' \vdash d\langle \tau_1 \Rightarrow \tau_2 \rangle \sqsubseteq d'}$$

PIADDCAST
$$\frac{\Delta, \Delta'; \Sigma; \Gamma, \Gamma' \vdash d \sqsubseteq d' \quad \Delta; \Sigma; \Gamma \vdash d : \tau \quad \tau \sqsubseteq \tau_1 \quad \tau \sqsubseteq \tau_2}{\Delta, \Delta'; \Sigma; \Gamma, \Gamma' \vdash d \sqsubseteq d'\langle \tau_1 \Rightarrow \tau_2 \rangle}$$

Fig. 15. Precision between internal expressions

Having adapted internal precision from the GTLC to our system, the gradual guarantee is fully defined. We have proven the static gradual guarantee, but it remains to be seen whether the rest of the properties hold, as they do for the GTLC. The updated subsumption rule is necessary for typed elaboration to behave monotonically on types.

5 Implementation

5.1 Agda Mechanization

This paper is accompanied by an Agda mechanization of the system and proofs of most of the theorems[3]. The mechanization is based on that of Hazelnut Live, with a few differences. This mechanization uses de Bruijn indices to represent both term and type bindings, and uses an ordered, combined context rather than independent term and type contexts. It also does not include hole names or hole contexts, and therefore does not capture the formalism for the *fill-and-resume* operation of Hazelnut Live, since the present work does not extend that part of the theory. The mechanization uses the updated subsumption rule for

---

[3] The code is available at https://github.com/hazelgrove/hazelnut-polymorphism-agda/.

elaboration, EASUBSUME'. Due to the absence of hole contexts and the new subsumption rule, the analytic elaboration rules for holes can be removed entirely, as can the premises disallowing holes in the subsumption elaboration rule. Matched arrow and matched forall judgments are implemented using the meet operation.

The following theorems have been proven: all parts of Theorem 5, Theorem 1, and Theorem 6, along with the parametricity theorems (Theorems 2 and 3) and the static gradual guarantee (Theorem 4). The repository indicates where to find the proof of each theorem.

5.2 Implementation

We have fully implemented the polymorphic system into the Hazel programming environment[4]. Notably, the implementation coexists with other extensions to Hazelnut Live, such as algebraic data types, recursion, type aliases, etc.; the combination of all of these features has not been formalized. Hazel is implemented in ReasonML and uses js_of_ocaml [25] to compile to a website.

Refer again to Fig. 1 for the appearance of the Hazel user interface. The user-facing gradually typed calculus is input via a gradual structure editor that uses obligations (see Tylr [15], the basis for Hazel's input system[5]); for example, inserting a `typfun` creates an obligation for a `->` and inserts the appropriate expression hole. Type function application is denoted with `@< >`.

6 Towards Implicit Polymorphism

For practical programming purposes, it is burdensome to write explicit type applications for each use of a polymorphic term. Therefore, many general-purpose functional languages adopt implicit polymorphism, in which the type applications are left out of the concrete syntax, and the instantiated types are statically inferred. There exist bidirectional calculi for implicit polymorphism, such as in Dunfield and Krishnaswami [7], which we could have chosen to gradualize in the same manner as we did for System F above.

Instead we propose to take advantage of the structured editing capabilities of Hazel. The widespread practice of implicit language features represents a compromise between the interests of the language user and the language developer. Compared to explicit features, the user benefits by typing and seeing less code, and by achieving more flexible code, at the cost of language transparency, consistency, and control. The implementer benefits by maintaining the same user interface and language architecture, only needing to insert an instantiation phase in the language processing pipeline, at the cost of increased language complexity.

We believe that by improving the programming environment architecture, this compromise can in turn be improved. Hazel is a gapless editor, meaning that at every point in time, syntactic information, static information, and all

---

[4] The Hazel project is described, with a link to the source code, at https://hazel.org.
[5] In short, there is an indication for necessary syntactic forms that must be added before a valid editor state can be reached.

downstream services are maintained by the editor. In this context we propose a system of implicit polymorphism in which the editor maintains appropriate type applications in the visible surface syntax of the program. This improves the transparency and regularity of the language while retaining the ease of editing and flexibility of implicit systems.

For example, this system would ideally insert the $[A]$ and $[B]$ type applications into the program below, supposing that $f : A \to B$ and $l : A$ list.

$map\ [A]\ [B]\ (f)\ (l)$

These type applications could be folded by default to avoid cluttering the screen with useless information. Despite this diminution of the type application forms, the proposed strategy is distinct from usual implicit schemes because the persisted program will retain the inferred type applications, and because the user will be able to see and edit the type arguments if needed. Figures 16, 17, 18 and 19 display mock ups of various editor states in a hypothetical version of Hazel with implicit polymorphism.

6.1 Mark Insertion

Zhao et al. [28] describe the "mark insertion" component of the Hazel architecture. Hazel programs begin as unmarked expressions e, corresponding exactly to the external expressions in Hazelnut Live except that they do not contain nonempty holes. Next comes a bidirectionally typed mark insertion phase, with judgment forms $\Sigma; \Gamma \vdash e \looparrowright \check{e} \Rightarrow \tau$ and $\Sigma; \Gamma \vdash e \looparrowright \check{e} \Leftarrow \tau$. Each unmarked expression e is mapped to a corresponding marked expression $\check{e}$, which is identical to e except for the presence of annotated nonempty holes called marks. Both unmarked and marked expressions have typing rules, and the mark insertion phase inserts the minimal marks needed to produce a well-typed result, essentially sectioning off ill-typed subexpressions with informatively annotated nonempty holes. After mark insertion comes the elaboration and evaluation stages of Hazelnut Live.

Figure 20 contains the mark insertion rules for the polymorphic fragment. The other mark insertion rules are similarly related to the basic typing rules. For each typing rule, there is a mark insertion rule that inserts no marks in the case that the premises of the typing rule are met. Each check in the premise of a typing rule gives rise to an additional mark insertion rule which inserts an appropriate mark when the check fails.

Mark insertion should satisfy certain metatheoretic properties. These properties include totality and unicity, which mean that the insertion operation is a total function on unmarked expressions. Mark insertion should only generate well-typed terms, and erasing marks from the marked term should recover the original term. The mark insertion process should not affect terms that already type check, and should insert at least one mark into terms that do not type check. These properties hold of the original marked lambda calculus, but do not all hold of our polymorphic extension. The reason is that a mark inserted around a type abstraction in analytic position may not be well typed. Considering the mark

```
let map : forall X -> forall Y -> (X -> Y) -> [X] -> [Y] = ◦ in
map)˄(string_of_int)([1,2,3,4,5])
```
EXP Variable reference : forall X -> forall Y -> (X -> Y) -> [X] -> [Y] with X as Int , Y as String

Fig. 16. Hypothetical behavior: when a type application insertion succeeds, the type arguments are listed along with the type of the polymorphic term. An ellipsis mark indicates folded code and provides a way to examine it.

```
let map : forall X -> forall Y -> (X -> Y) -> [X] -> [Y] = ◦ in
map @<Int>@<String> (string_of_int)([1,2,3,4,5])
```
🔍 Automatically inserted type application

Fig. 17. Hypothetical behavior: when the ellipsis mark is selected, it expands to reveal the explicit type applications and arguments that have been inserted by the editor. If this code is edited by the user, it becomes fully explicit and is colored accordingly.

```
let map : forall X -> forall Y -> (X -> Y) -> [X] -> [Y] = ◦ in
map)˄(string_of_int)([true, false])
```
EXP Variable reference : forall X -> forall Y -> (X -> Y) -> [X] -> [Y] with X unsolved , Y as String

Fig. 18. Hypothetical behavior: when a type application insertion fails, the conflicted type arguments are indicated. The ellipsis mark signals an error.

```
let map : forall X -> forall Y -> (X -> Y) -> [X] -> [Y] = ◦ in
map @<⌊⌋>@<String> (string_of_int)([true, false])
```
TYP conflicting constraints Bool Int

Fig. 19. Hypothetical behavior: the editor displays the conflicting required refinements of the unfillable type argument hole. If the user hovers over or selects one of the refinements, it will be applied to the hole, resulting in errors elsewhere in the code.

$\boxed{\Sigma; \Gamma \vdash e \leftrightsquigarrow \check{e} \Rightarrow \tau}$ e is marked into $\check{e}$ and synthesizes type τ

$$\text{MKSTypeLam} \quad \frac{\Sigma, \alpha; \Gamma \vdash e \leftrightsquigarrow \check{e} \Rightarrow \tau}{\Sigma; \Gamma \vdash \Lambda\alpha.\, e \leftrightsquigarrow \Lambda\alpha.\, \check{e} \Rightarrow \forall\alpha.\, \tau}$$

$$\text{MKSTypeAp1} \quad \frac{\Sigma; \Gamma \vdash e \leftrightsquigarrow \check{e} \Rightarrow \tau \quad \tau \blacktriangleright_\forall \forall\alpha.\, \tau_1}{\Sigma; \Gamma \vdash e\,[\tau_2] \leftrightsquigarrow \check{e}\,[\tau_2] \Rightarrow \tau_1[\tau_2/\alpha]}$$

$$\text{MKSTypeAp2} \quad \frac{\Sigma; \Gamma \vdash e \leftrightsquigarrow \check{e} \Rightarrow \tau_1 \quad \tau_1 \blacktriangleright_\forall}{\Sigma; \Gamma \vdash e\,[\tau_2] \leftrightsquigarrow (\!|\check{e}|\!)^{\Rightarrow}_{\blacktriangleright_\forall}\,[\tau_2] \Rightarrow ?}$$

$\boxed{\Sigma; \Gamma \vdash e \leftrightsquigarrow \check{e} \Leftarrow \tau}$ e is marked into $\check{e}$ and analyzes against type τ

$$\text{MKATypeLam1} \quad \frac{\tau_1 \blacktriangleright_\forall \forall\alpha.\, \tau_2 \quad \Sigma, \alpha; \Gamma \vdash e \leftrightsquigarrow \check{e} \Leftarrow \tau_2}{\Sigma; \Gamma \vdash \Lambda\alpha.\, e \leftrightsquigarrow \Lambda\alpha.\, \check{e} \Leftarrow \tau_1}$$

$$\text{MKATypeLam2} \quad \frac{\tau \blacktriangleright_\forall \quad \Sigma, \alpha; \Gamma \vdash e \leftrightsquigarrow \check{e} \Leftarrow ?}{\Sigma; \Gamma \vdash \Lambda\alpha.\, e \leftrightsquigarrow (\!|\Lambda\alpha.\, \check{e}|\!)^{\Leftarrow}_{\blacktriangleright_\forall} \Leftarrow \tau}$$

Fig. 20. Mark insertion rules

to be a nonempty hole, it can only analyze against a type if its contents synthesizes a type, and in the case of a type abstraction, this only holds if its body synthesizes a type. Since our language includes unannotated lambda abstractions, which do not have a type synthesis rule, this case is possible. Concretely, judgements such as:

$$\Sigma; \Gamma \vdash (\!|\Lambda\alpha.\ \lambda x.\ e|\!)_{\blacktriangleright_\forall}^{\Leftarrow} \Leftarrow \tau$$

do not hold, even if the term is the output of the marking process. To address this, additional typing and elaboration rules for marked type abstractions would need to be added.

6.2 Type Application Insertion

The mark insertion phase currently uses the bidirectional typing flow to insert marks into a Hazel program where there would otherwise be a static error. Type applications may be inserted by enriching this operation, so that some static errors are addressed not by inserting a mark, but by inserting a type applications with a type hole as the argument. Specifically, when a polymorphic term is found, but is inconsistent with the expected type or type former, a type application may be inserted rather than a mark. The new rules for these insertions at type applications are given in Fig. 21. These rules replace the previous rules for applications presented in Zhao et al. Rules for type application insertion at projections and at subsumptions are omitted for brevity.

$\boxed{\Sigma;\Gamma \vdash e \leadsto \check{e} \Rightarrow \tau}$ Synthetic marking judgment

$$\begin{array}{c}
\text{INSERTSAP1}\\
\dfrac{\Sigma;\Gamma \vdash e_1 \leadsto \check{e}_1 \Rightarrow \tau_1 \quad \tau_1 \blacktriangleright_\to \tau_2 \to \tau_3 \quad \Sigma;\Gamma \vdash e_2 \leadsto \check{e}_2 \Leftarrow \tau_2}{\Sigma;\Gamma \vdash e_1\, e_2 \leadsto \check{e}_1\, \check{e}_2 \Rightarrow \tau_3}
\end{array}$$

$$\begin{array}{c}
\text{INSERTSAP2}\\
\dfrac{\Sigma;\Gamma \vdash e_1 \leadsto \check{e}_1 \Rightarrow \tau_1 \quad \tau_1 \blacktriangleright_{\not\to} \quad \forall^\square(\tau_1) \blacktriangleright_\to \tau_2 \to \tau_3 \quad \Sigma;\Gamma \vdash e_1\,[?]\, e_2 \leadsto \check{e}_3 \Rightarrow \tau_4}{\Sigma;\Gamma \vdash e_1\, e_2 \leadsto \check{e}_3 \Rightarrow \tau_4}
\end{array}$$

$$\begin{array}{c}
\text{INSERTSAP3}\\
\dfrac{\Sigma;\Gamma \vdash e_1 \leadsto \check{e}_1 \Rightarrow \tau \quad \forall^\square(\tau) \blacktriangleright_{\not\to} \quad \Sigma;\Gamma \vdash e_2 \leadsto \check{e}_2 \Leftarrow ?}{\Sigma;\Gamma \vdash e_1\, e_2 \leadsto (\!|\check{e}_1|\!)_{\blacktriangleright_{\not\to}}^{\Rightarrow}\, \check{e}_2 \Rightarrow ?}
\end{array}$$

Fig. 21. Implicit insertion.

These type application insertion rules are derived from the mark insertion rules in Zhao et al. The rules that have been updated are those with a premise of the form $\tau \blacktriangleright_\to \tau_1 \to \tau_2$, $\tau \blacktriangleright_{\not\to}$, $\tau \blacktriangleright_\times \tau_1 \times \tau_2$, $\tau \blacktriangleright_{\not\times}$, $\tau \sim \tau_1$, or $\tau \not\sim \tau_1$, where

τ and none of the other types involved are synthesized from a subexpression of the expression being marked. These conditions correspond to an opportunity to insert a type application that may avoid a failed type matching or consistency check, and thereby avoid a mark insertion.

The mark insertion rule for conditionals involves a consistency check between the types synthesized from the branches of the conditional. It is possible to write valid type application insertion rules for conditionals, but it is not clear what should be done in the case of inconsistent polymorphic branches.

In order to gauge when it is appropriate to insert a type application, we introduce a prenex erasure operation $\forall^{\Box}(\tau)$, which erases all leading $\forall$. constructors of τ and replaces their bound variables with ?. If a type matching or consistency check fails on the originally synthesized type, the check is retried on the prenex erased type. This new check corresponds to whether, according to the structure of the type, it may be possible to pass the type matching or consistency check after type applications are inserted around the subexpression.

The new rules are designed so that the new mark and type application insertion operation retains most desirable metatheoretic properties of the original mark insertion operation. The combined insertion phase should still be a total function, generate well-typed terms, and not affect terms which already type check. However, it is no longer the case that the operation's only effect is the insertion of marks. The new rules ought to ensure that erasing all marks and some subset of the type applications recovers the original term, and that the insertion operation applied to a term that does not type check produces a term that includes either a mark or a type application. These properties remain conjectural for the new system, but they should be straightforward to prove.

6.3 Type Arguments

The type application insertion process described above simply inserts type holes as arguments, which is not satisfactory for handling type errors that arise from implicit polymorphic code. Therefore we propose a static phase for instantiating type arguments, which occurs after mark and type application insertion and before elaboration into the internal calculus. Ideally this phase would simply reuse type hole inference machinery from mark insertion, which uses constraints on type holes generated during the mark insertion phase to generate the possible fillings for the type holes that appear in the program. To simulate implicit instantiation, when the constraints for an inserted type hole contain no conflicts, the editor would automatically fill the hole accordingly. When there are conflicts, the same user interface that appears in Zhao et al. would be used to convey this information to the user, who could then select an option for filling the hole.

Unfortunately, the type hole inference technique dose not directly generalize to the polymorphic setting. As the type level of System F is isomorphic to the untyped lambda calculus, the constraints on type holes comprise general higher-order unification problems, the solution of which is not decidable. For example, the code below generates the higher order unification problem $?^1\,(?^3) = ?^2$, where application between types is defined so as to obey the obvious beta rule.

let $f :?^1 = (\!|\!)$ in let $x :?^2 = f\ [?^3]$ in $(\!|\!)$

However, this is a rather unnatural example. In many cases, a programmer is applying a polymorphic library function, like map, the type of which is completely known, in the sense of containing no metavariables (holes). This suggests the following algorithm: perform standard unification, eagerly simplifying constraints by applying (language level, not meta-level) substitutions into types that are free of metavariables. All other substitutions are stuck, but may become unstuck as metavariables are solved. Constraints involving perpetually stuck substitutions would never be used, the fact of which is a manifestation of the incompleteness of the algorithm, but many useful cases, like the application of polymorphic library functions, could be solved.

7 Related and Future Work

Fill and Resume. Hazelnut Live presented a notion of fill-and-resume. That is, that a program could be evaluated, after which the programmer fills in (i.e. replaces) a hole with a valid expression. Then, because program evaluation is pure, the operation of program reduction commutes with replacing the hole, so the evaluator can replace the corresponding hole(s) in the evaluated expression, and continue evaluating. This required a notion of tracking substitutions that occurred in the closure around holes, and replaying those substitutions on the newly provided expression. This has a very close connection to contextual modal type theory, with the hole context tracking contexts. These substitutions were a part of the cast calculus, and their validity was checked via substitution typing, which is used as a premise to type assignment on holes.

We do not argue for the correctness of fill-and-resume in this work, but we conjecture it to still be valid. This is because our system is still pure, so evaluation should still commute with hole filling. There are subtle issues with naively extending substitution typing. It is clear the substitutions must now also track type substitutions. Term substitutions that happen after a type substitution may have their typing affected, and it is not immediately obvious how to account for this with a static typing judgment. An analogous problem does not exist in the original formulation, since substituting in sub-terms does not change the type of a term, which is all that is tracked in the substitution typing.

Thus, we leave proving validity of fill-and-resume with corresponding substitution typing judgments as future work.

Implicit Polymorphism. We have described a system for allowing polymorphic terms to be used without an explicit type application, as with implicit polymorphism. Yet this editor service does not address implicit polymorphism on a theoretical level, and may fail to catch type errors that a truly implicit system can. As seen in Xie et al. [27], implicit polymorphism may force instantiations that cause errors that may be resolved with additional typing information, violating the gradual guarantee. As far we know, the problem of a gradually parametric implicit polymorphic system has yet to be solved. We are interested in whether such a system exists, and whether the solution to this problem relates to the problems described previously and could be adapted to type hole inference.

References. References see popular use even in functional programming languages, such as the ML family of languages. However, references have not yet been implemented into the Hazel programming environment, nor has there been development on the theory of how references interact with expression holes. Siek et al. [23] have shown that references can work with the gradually typed lambda calculus. We are unaware of any work that adds references to a polymorphic gradually typed calculus.

It appears that combining graduality, polymorphism, hole expressions, and references creates unique problems; for example, type $\forall \alpha.\ \alpha$ ref can be populated with $\Lambda \alpha.\ \text{ref}(\emptyset)$, but cannot be populated in a system without expression holes. Such examples that create a new reference with each type function application may preclude future attempts at type erasure run-time semantics, which are otherwise a promising optimization as shown in Igarashi et al.

Acknowledgements. The authors would like to thank the referees and attendees of TFP 2024 for their insightful feedback about earlier drafts of this work. Adam Chen would like to acknowledge Eric Koskinen for helping with the opportunity and logistics for working on a project outside of the topic of their funded work. We would also like to acknowledge Kevin Li and Yuchen Jiang for the preliminary implementation of type functions and polymorphic types in the Hazel codebase. This work was partially funded through the NSF grant #CCF-2238744.

A Type Safety Theorems

Our system conserves all of the typing properties that held of the original system (c.f. Theorems 3.1 through 3.14 in [18]). To begin with, the bidirectional typing allows for unique elaboration to a term of a consistent type:

Theorem 5. *The following properties hold:*

- *Elaborability: any term typable by the bidirectional system has an elaboration.*
  1. *If $\Sigma; \Gamma \vdash e \Rightarrow \tau$ then there exist d and Δ such that $\Sigma; \Gamma \vdash e \Rightarrow \tau \leadsto d \dashv \Delta$.*
  2. *If $\Sigma; \Gamma \vdash e \Leftarrow \tau$ then there exist d, τ', and Δ such that $\Sigma; \Gamma \vdash e \Leftarrow \tau \leadsto d : \tau' \dashv \Delta$.*
- *Elaboration Generality: the converse of the above is true.*
  1. *If $\Sigma; \Gamma \vdash e \Rightarrow \tau \leadsto d \dashv \Delta$ then $\Sigma; \Gamma \vdash e \Rightarrow \tau$.*
  2. *If $\Sigma; \Gamma \vdash e \Leftarrow \tau \leadsto d : \tau' \dashv \Delta$ then $\Sigma; \Gamma \vdash e \Leftarrow \tau$.*
- *Elaboration Unicity: elaboration of terms is unique.*
  1. *If $\Sigma; \Gamma \vdash e \Rightarrow \tau_1 \leadsto d_1 \dashv \Delta_1$ and $\Sigma; \Gamma \vdash e \Rightarrow \tau_2 \leadsto d_2 \dashv \Delta_2$ then $\tau_1 = \tau_2$, $d_1 = d_2$, and $\Delta_1 = \Delta_2$.*
  2. *If $\Sigma; \Gamma \vdash e \Leftarrow \tau \leadsto d_1 : \tau_1 \dashv \Delta_1$ and $\Sigma; \Gamma \vdash e \Leftarrow \tau \leadsto d_2 : \tau_2 \dashv \Delta_2$ then $\tau_1 = \tau_2$, $d_1 = d_2$, and $\Delta_1 = \Delta_2$.*

- *Typed Elaboration:* the elaboration is consistent with the type assignment system.
  1. *If* $\Sigma; \Gamma \vdash e \Rightarrow \tau \leadsto d \dashv \Delta$ *then* $\Delta; \Sigma; \Gamma \vdash d : \tau$.
  2. *If* $\Sigma; \Gamma \vdash e \Leftarrow \tau \leadsto d : \tau' \dashv \Delta$ *then* $\Delta; \Sigma; \Gamma \vdash d : \tau'$ *with* $\tau \sim \tau'$.
- *Type Assignment Unicity:* type assignment assigns a unique type.
  If $\Delta; \Sigma; \Gamma \vdash d : \tau$ *and* $\Delta; \Sigma; \Gamma \vdash d : \tau'$ *then* $\tau = \tau'$

In short, these properties show that elaboration defines a unique embedding from the user-facing gradually typed calculus into the typed cast calculus. Thus it is sufficient to state type safety solely in terms of the cast calculus. We repeat that we prove that the system with the instruction transitions defined in Fig. 13 is type safe:

Theorem 1 (Type Safety). *The system presented in Sect. 3 is type safe:*

1. *Progress: If* $\emptyset \vdash \Delta$ *and* $\Delta; \emptyset; \emptyset \vdash d : \tau$ *then either* d indet, d boxedval, *or there exists an* IHExp d' *such that* $d \mapsto d'$.
2. *Preservation: If* $\emptyset \vdash \Delta$, $\Delta; \emptyset; \emptyset \vdash d : \tau$ *and* $d \mapsto d'$ *then* $\Delta; \emptyset; \emptyset \vdash d' : \tau$.

Recall that a program (term) is *complete* if it does not contain any expression or type holes. Complete programs are elaborated into internal expressions with only identity casts and without type or expression holes. This fragment of internal expressions is equivalent to System F, and therefore recovers its properties such as strong normalization. These properties are formalized in the following theorem that our system conserves from Hazelnut Live [18]:

Theorem 6. *The following properties about complete programs hold:*

1. *Complete Elaboration: If* Γ complete, e complete, *and* $\Gamma; \Sigma \vdash e \Rightarrow \tau \leadsto d \dashv \Delta$ *then* τ complete, d complete, *and* $\Delta = \emptyset$.
2. *Complete Preservation: If* d complete, $\Delta; \Sigma; \Gamma \vdash d : \tau$, *and* $d \mapsto d'$ *then* d' complete *and* $\Delta; \Sigma; \Gamma \vdash d' : \tau$
3. *Complete Progress: If* d complete *and* $\Delta; \Sigma; \Gamma \vdash d : \tau$ *then either* d val *or there exists an* IHExp d' *such that* $d \mapsto d'$.

Complete elaboration states that a complete program in the user-facing gradually typed calculus elaborates into a complete program in the cast calculus. Complete preservation states that the step relation preserves completeness as well as typing, and complete progress states that every complete term is a val or can step.

References

1. Ahmed, A., Findler, R.B., Siek, J.G., Wadler, P.: Blame for all. In: Ball, T., Sagiv, M. (eds.) Proceedings of the 38th ACM SIGPLAN-SIGACT Symposium on Principles of Programming Languages, POPL 2011, Austin, TX, USA, 26–28 January 2011, pp. 201–214. ACM (2011). https://doi.org/10.1145/1926385.1926409

2. Ahmed, A., Jamner, D., Siek, J.G., Wadler, P.: Theorems for free for free: parametricity, with and without types. Proc. ACM Program. Lang. **1**(ICFP), 39:1–39:28 (2017). https://doi.org/10.1145/3110283
3. Bierman, G.M., Abadi, M., Torgersen, M.: Understanding typescript. In: Jones, R.E. (ed.) ECOOP 2014 - Object-Oriented Programming - 28th European Conference, Uppsala, Sweden, 28 July–1 August 2014, Proceedings. LNCS, vol. 8586, pp. 257–281. Springer, Cham (2014). https://doi.org/10.1007/978-3-662-44202-9_11
4. Church, A.: A formulation of the simple theory of types. J. Symb. Log. **5**(2), 56–68 (1940). https://doi.org/10.2307/2266170
5. Crary, K.: A simple proof technique for certain parametricity results. In: Rémy, D., Lee, P. (eds.) Proceedings of the Fourth ACM SIGPLAN International Conference on Functional Programming (ICFP 1999), Paris, France, 27–29 September 1999, pp. 82–89. ACM (1999). https://doi.org/10.1145/317636.317787
6. Dunfield, J., Krishnaswami, N.: Bidirectional typing. ACM Comput. Surv. **54**(5), 98:1–98:38 (2022). https://doi.org/10.1145/3450952
7. Dunfield, J., Krishnaswami, N.R.: Complete and easy bidirectional typechecking for higher-rank polymorphism. CoRR abs/1306.6032 (2013). http://arxiv.org/abs/1306.6032
8. Girard, J.Y.: Interpretation fonctionelle et elimination des coupures dans l'aritmetique d'ordre superieur (1972). https://api.semanticscholar.org/CorpusID:117631778
9. Harper, R.: Practical Foundations for Programming Languages, 2nd edn. Cambridge University Press, Cambridge (2016). https://www.cs.cmu.edu/%7Erwh/pfpl/index.html
10. Igarashi, Y., Sekiyama, T., Igarashi, A.: On polymorphic gradual typing. Proc. ACM Program. Lang. **1**(ICFP), 40:1–40:29 (2017). https://doi.org/10.1145/3110284
11. Kluyver, T., et al.: Jupyter notebooks - a publishing format for reproducible computational workflows. In: Loizides, F., Schmidt, B. (eds.) Positioning and Power in Academic Publishing: Players, Agents and Agendas, 20th International Conference on Electronic Publishing, Göttingen, Germany, 7–9 June 2016, pp. 87–90. IOS Press (2016). https://doi.org/10.3233/978-1-61499-649-1-87
12. Labrada, E., Toro, M., Tanter, É.: Gradual system F. J. ACM **69**(5), 38:1–38:78 (2022). https://doi.org/10.1145/3555986
13. McCauley, R., et al.: Debugging: a review of the literature from an educational perspective. Comput. Sci. Educ. **18**(2), 67–92 (2008). https://doi.org/10.1080/08993400802114581
14. Mishra-Linger, N., Sheard, T.: Erasure and polymorphism in pure type systems. In: Amadio, R.M. (ed.) Foundations of Software Science and Computational Structures, 11th International Conference, FOSSACS 2008, Held as Part of the Joint European Conferences on Theory and Practice of Software, ETAPS 2008, Budapest, Hungary, 29 March–6 April 2008, Proceedings. LNCS, vol. 4962, pp. 350–364. Springer, Cham (2008). https://doi.org/10.1007/978-3-540-78499-9_25
15. Moon, D., Blinn, A., Omar, C.: Gradual structure editing with obligations. In: IEEE Symposium on Visual Languages and Human-Centric Computing, VL/HCC 2023, Washington, DC, USA, 3–6 October 2023, pp. 71–81. IEEE (2023). https://doi.org/10.1109/VL-HCC57772.2023.00016
16. Nanevski, A., Pfenning, F., Pientka, B.: Contextual modal type theory. ACM Trans. Comput. Log. **9**(3), 23:1–23:49 (2008). https://doi.org/10.1145/1352582.1352591

17. New, M.S., Jamner, D., Ahmed, A.: Graduality and parametricity: together again for the first time. Proc. ACM Program. Lang. 4(POPL), 46:1–46:32 (2020). https://doi.org/10.1145/3371114
18. Omar, C., Voysey, I., Chugh, R., Hammer, M.A.: Live functional programming with typed holes. Proc. ACM Program. Lang. 3(POPL), 14:1–14:32 (2019). https://doi.org/10.1145/3290327
19. Omar, C., Voysey, I., Hilton, M., Aldrich, J., Hammer, M.A.: Hazelnut: a bidirectionally typed structure editor calculus. In: Castagna, G., Gordon, A.D. (eds.) Proceedings of the 44th ACM SIGPLAN Symposium on Principles of Programming Languages, POPL 2017, Paris, France, 18–20 January 2017, pp. 86–99. ACM (2017). https://doi.org/10.1145/3009837.3009900
20. Reynolds, J.C.: Towards a theory of type structure. In: Robinet, B.J. (ed.) Programming Symposium, Proceedings Colloque sur la Programmation, Paris, France, 9–11 April 1974. LNCS, vol. 19, pp. 408–423. Springer, Cham (1974). https://doi.org/10.1007/3-540-06859-7_148
21. Siek, J., Taha, W.: Gradual typing for functional languages, January 2006
22. Siek, J.G., Vitousek, M.M., Cimini, M., Boyland, J.T.: Refined criteria for gradual typing. In: Ball, T., Bodík, R., Krishnamurthi, S., Lerner, B.S., Morrisett, G. (eds.) 1st Summit on Advances in Programming Languages, SNAPL 2015, 3–6 May 2015, Asilomar, California, USA. LIPIcs, vol. 32, pp. 274–293. Schloss Dagstuhl - Leibniz-Zentrum für Informatik (2015). https://doi.org/10.4230/LIPICS.SNAPL.2015.274
23. Siek, J.G., Vitousek, M.M., Cimini, M., Tobin-Hochstadt, S., Garcia, R.: Monotonic references for efficient gradual typing. In: Vitek, J. (ed.) ESOP 2015. LNCS, vol. 9032, pp. 432–456. Springer, Heidelberg (2015). https://doi.org/10.1007/978-3-662-46669-8_18
24. Tanimoto, S.L.: A perspective on the evolution of live programming. In: Burg, B., Kuhn, A., Parnin, C. (eds.) Proceedings of the 1st International Workshop on Live Programming, LIVE 2013, San Francisco, California, USA, 19 May 2013, pp. 31–34. IEEE Computer Society (2013). https://doi.org/10.1109/LIVE.2013.6617346
25. Vouillon, J., Belat, V.: From bytecode to javascript: the js_of_ocaml compiler. Softw. Pract. Experience 44(8), 951–972 (2014). https://doi.org/10.1002/spe.2187
26. Wakeling, D.: Spreadsheet functional programming. J. Funct. Program. 17(1), 131–143 (2007). https://doi.org/10.1017/S0956796806006186
27. Xie, N., Bi, X., D. S. Oliveira, B.C., Schrijvers, T.: Consistent subtyping for all. ACM Trans. Program. Lang. Syst. 42(1), 2:1–2:79 (2020). https://doi.org/10.1145/3310339
28. Zhao, E., Maroof, R., Dukkipati, A., Pan, Z., Omar, C.: Total type error localization and recovery with holes. Proc. ACM Program. Lang. 8(POPL), 2041–2068 (2024). https://doi.org/10.1145/3632910

A Preliminary Type- and Control-Flow Analysis for System F_ω

Dongyu Wu and Matthew Fluet

Rochester Institute of Technology, Rochester, NY 14623, USA
dw1823@g.rit.edu, mtf@cs.rit.edu

Abstract. A type- and control-flow analysis is a program analysis that yields both type-flow information, approximating the types that may instantiate type variables, and control-flow information, approximating the values (especially λ- and Λ-expressions) that may be bound to variables. Moreover, each of the flows informs the other; control-flow establishes the types that may instantiate Λ-bound type variables by determining the Λ-expressions that flow to a type-application expression, while type-flow filters control-flow by rejecting the flow of values having static types that are incompatible (according to the type-flow information) with the static type of the receiving variable.

In previous work [1,13,14], we introduced a (monovariant) type- and control-flow analysis for System F (with recursion). While System F has an expressive type system and has served as a useful core calculus in which to express interesting language features, it only allows abstraction over types and does not allow abstraction over type constructors. Increasingly, researchers are looking at System F_ω, with both term- and type-level abstraction over types of arbitrary kind, as a core calculus in which to explore advanced language features. Hence, we are motivated to define a type- and control-flow analysis for System F_ω that is able to analyze the rich structure of System F_ω types.

In this work, we present a preliminary type- and control-flow analysis for System F_ω (with recursion). As in previous work, we give both a specification-based formulation of the analysis, used to prove soundness of the analysis, and a flow-graph-based formulation, used to guide the implementation of an algorithm. While the macro structure of the development for System F_ω follows that for System F, moving to System F_ω introduces subtle challenges that have left some unanswered questions about the meta-theory. In particular, the decidability of type compatibility defined in terms of System F_ω's definitional type equivalence remains an open question. In order to be computable, our flow-graph-based formulation uses a restricted form of definitional type equivalence and performs a 0CFA at the type-level, yielding an analysis result that is less precise than the "best" (but as of yet, uncomputable) analysis result accepted by the specification-based formulation. Our soundness results have been formalized in the Coq proof assistant.

This work is based in part on the first author's MS thesis [53].

Keywords: Control-flow analysis · Type-flow analysis · System F_ω

1 Introduction

Type- and control-flow analyses are a class of program analyses that combine, in a mutually beneficial manner, a control-flow analysis and a type-flow analysis. Control-flow analyses [26, 28, 34, 47, 48] are themselves a class of program analyses that approximate, at compile time, the flow of first-class functions (and other values) in a program: which first-class functions (and other values) might be bound to a given variable or returned by a given expression at run time. Similarly, type-flow analyses are a class of program analyses that approximate, at compile time, the flow of types in a program: which types might be bound to a given type variable at run time.

Control-flow analyses are an important enabling technology for the compilation and optimization of functional languages [46]. For example, control-flow analyses can be used to guide inlining [4, 29, 49], defunctionalization [6], and the specialization of high-level abstractions [41]. While type-flow analyses are a more recent development, they can similarly be used to guide defunctionalization [7], monomorphisation [24], and the optimization of intensional polymorphism [22].

In a type- and control-flow analysis, each of the underlying flow analyses informs the other. In one direction, the control-flow analysis is used to determine which first-class polymorphic functions (i.e., Λ-expressions) may be applied at a type application (and, therefore, which types may instantiate the Λ-bound type variables). In the other direction, the type-flow analysis is used to filter the values that may be bound to variables by rejecting the flow of values with static types that are incompatible under the type flow with the static type of the receiving variable. Critically, the soundness of a type- and control-flow analysis depends on type soundness and the well-typedness of the program being analyzed. Type soundness and well-typedness ensure that, when a value is bound to a variable at run time, the actual (necessarily closed) type of the value will correspond to the actual (necessarily closed) type of the receiving variable. The type-flow information allows the analysis to over-approximate the set of possible actual (necessarily closed) types for a static (possibly open) type by (repeatedly) mapping any free type variable to one of the types to which it may be bound. Suppose the control-flow analysis proposes that a value flows to a receiving variable, but there is no possible actual type for the value that corresponds to any possible actual type of the receiving variable, in which case the types involved are said to be incompatible. Type soundness ensures that this value will never be bound to this variable at run time and the proposed flow can be rejected.

In previous work [1, 13, 14], we introduced a (monovariant) type- and control-flow analysis for System F (with recursion). The underlying control-flow analysis is 0CFA [34, 49], the classic monovariant control-flow analysis that was formulated for the untyped lambda calculus. The underlying type-flow analysis is novel, but is essentially a straightforward monovariant analysis. We gave both a specification-based formulation of the type- and control-flow analysis [13, 14], used to prove soundness of the analysis, and a flow-graph-based formulation [1], used to guide the implementation of an efficient algorithm.

System F [18,21,39,42], the polymorphic lambda calculus, is an important point in the space of type systems. It, and simple extensions thereof, have been used effectively as typed intermediate languages in compilers for functional languages [36,51]. However, System F has only limited support for polymorphism. While it allows for abstraction over a type, it does not allow for abstraction over a *type constructor*. For example, while we can express the types of the polymorphic and higher-order functions that map over lists (listMap : $\forall \alpha. \forall \beta. (\alpha \to \beta) \to$ List $\alpha \to$ List β) and trees (treeMap : $\forall \alpha. \forall \beta. (\alpha \to \beta) \to$ Tree $\alpha \to$ Tree β), we cannot express the type of a function withMap that accepts a mapping function (either listMap or treeMap) and a data structure containing integers (either List Int or Tree Int) and returns a pair, where the first component is the result of mapping the odd : Int $\to$ Bool predicate and the second component is the result of mapping the inc : Int $\to$ Int function. Such a function wishes to abstract over List or Tree, which are type constructors and not types.

To achieve this level of abstraction, one must turn to System F_ω [18,19,37], the higher-order polymorphic lambda calculus. System F_ω extends System F with both expression-level abstraction over type constructors (generalizing Λ-expressions, type-application expressions, and $\forall$-types) and type-level functions and applications. For example, System F_ω can express the type of the function withMap described above as $\forall c :: \star \Rightarrow \star. (\forall \alpha :: \star. \forall \beta :: \star. (\alpha \to \beta) \to c\, \alpha \to c\, \beta) \to c\,$ Int $\to$ Pair $(c\,$Bool$)\,(c\,$Int$)$, where c is a type variable of *kind* $\star \Rightarrow \star$, meaning that it must be instantiated by a type-level function from (proper) types to (proper) types, while α and β are type variables of *kind* $\star$, which must be instantiated by a (proper) type. Kinds are the "types of types" and ensure that types are used correctly.

The increased expressive power of System F_ω has made it, and various restrictions and extensions thereof, an attractive typed intermediate language for modern functional languages; for example, it can serve as a target language for advanced ML-like module languages [43–45], for a typed store-passing translation of general references [40], and for datatype-generic programming [5]. Thus, we seek to define a type- and control-flow analysis for System F_ω that is able to analyze the rich structure of System F_ω types.

In this work (based on the first author's MS thesis [53]), we present a preliminary type- and control-flow analysis (TCFA) for System F_ω. As in previous work, we give both a specification-based formulation of the analysis, used to prove soundness of the analysis, and a flow-graph-based formulation, used to guide the implementation of an algorithm. While the general structures of the specification-based and the flow-graph-based formulations of the TCFA for System F_ω follow the corresponding formulations of the TCFA for System F, as do the proofs of soundness (via a direct proof for the specification-based formulation and via a correspondence with the specification-based formulation for the flow-graph-based formulation), moving to System F_ω introduces subtle challenges that have left some unanswered questions about the meta-theory. Essentially, the notion of when one type "corresponds" to another (which was intentionally left

$$
\begin{aligned}
Kind \ni \kappa &::= \star \mid \kappa_a \Rightarrow \kappa_r \\
Idx = Nat \ni\ & i,j,k,\ldots \\
ITyVar \ni\ & \mathfrak{a},\mathfrak{b},\ldots \\
TyVar \ni\ & \alpha,\beta,\ldots \\
TyVal \ni \tau &::= \alpha_a \to \alpha_r \mid \forall.\alpha_g \\
&\mid \lambda^{\kappa_a \Rightarrow \kappa_r}\mathfrak{a}.\epsilon_r \mid (\#i,\mathfrak{a})^{\kappa_i} \\
&\mid (\alpha_f\ \alpha_a)^{\kappa_r} \\
TyBnd \ni \psi &::= \mathtt{tlet}\ \alpha :: \kappa_\alpha = \tau \\
TyExp \ni \epsilon &::= \alpha_r \mid \psi\ \mathtt{in}\ \epsilon
\end{aligned}
$$

$$
\begin{aligned}
&TyRes(\cdot) :: TyExp \to TyVar \\
&TyRes(\alpha_r) = \alpha_r \\
&TyRes(\psi\ \mathtt{in}\ \epsilon) = TyRes(\epsilon)
\end{aligned}
$$

$$
\begin{aligned}
Var \ni\ & x,y,z,f,g,\ldots \\
Val \ni v &::= \mu f{:}\alpha_f.\lambda y{:}\alpha_y.e_b \\
&\mid \mu f{:}\alpha_f.\Lambda\beta{::}\kappa_\beta.e_b \\
Rhs \ni r &::= v \mid x_f\ x_a \mid x_f\ [\alpha_a] \\
Bnd \ni b &::= \mathtt{let}\ x : \alpha_x = r \\
Exp \ni e &::= x_r \mid \psi\ \mathtt{in}\ e \mid l\ \mathtt{in}\ e \\
Prog \ni P &::= e
\end{aligned}
$$

$$
\begin{aligned}
&ExpRes(\cdot) :: Exp \to ExpVar \\
&ExpRes(x_r) = x_r \\
&ExpRes(\psi\ \mathtt{in}\ e) = ExpRes(e) \\
&ExpRes(l\ \mathtt{in}\ e) = ExpRes(e)
\end{aligned}
$$

Fig. 1. Syntax of ANF System F_ω (with recursive functions)

vague in the discussion of how a type-flow analysis informs the control-flow analysis) is significantly different in System F and System F_ω. In System F, simple syntactic equality (up to α-equivalence) determines when one type "corresponds" to another and this syntactic equality can be used to define type compatibility, which is used to reject the flow of values with static types that are incompatible with the static type of the receiving variable. But, in System F_ω, *definitional type equivalence* determines when one type "corresponds" to another; type equivalence is a non-trivial relationship, because it must judge an application of a type-level function to a type argument as equivalent to the substitution of the type argument for the function parameter in the body of the function (β-reduction). This definitional type equivalence can be similarly used to define type compatibility, but the decidability of this definition of type compatibility in the specification-based formulation of the TCFA for System F_ω remains an open question (as does the existence of an efficient algorithm). In order to obtain an algorithm, our flow-graph-based formulation of the TCFA for System F_ω uses additional restrictions and over-approximations; while it remains sound (the analysis result obtained by the flow-graph-based formulation is accepted by the specification-based formulation), it applies to fewer programs and can be less precise (there may be "better" analysis results that are accepted by the specification-based formulation). In particular, we restrict the β-reduction used in definitional type equivalence to a class of locally closed types (rejecting as ill-typed some programs that would be accepted as well-typed without the restriction) and we perform a 0CFA at the type-level (introducing imprecision).

2 Language

Syntax. Figure 1 gives the syntax of our object language, which is a variant of System F_ω, extended with recursive functions and recursive type abstractions, using index-type-variable annotated de Bruijn indices for type-level functions, and presented in administrative normal form (ANF). Of note, we use an ANF representation for both expressions and types. The language is Church-style: every bound expression variable is annotated with its type (as a type variable) and every bound type variable is annotated with its kind.

```
tlet Id :: ⋆ ⇒ ⋆ = λt::⋆. t in
let id : ∀a::⋆. a → a = Λα::⋆.λx:α. x in
let k : ∀b::⋆. b → b → b = Λβ::⋆.λy:β.λz:β. y in
let res1 : ∀a::⋆. a → a = id [Id (∀a::⋆. a → a)] id in
let res2 : Id (∀b::⋆. b → b → b) = id [∀b::⋆. b → b → b] k in
res2
```

(a) System F_ω program in (traditional) direct style

```
tlet Id :: ⋆ ⇒ ⋆ = λ⋆⇒⋆t. tlet u01 :: ⋆ = (#0,t)⋆ in
                                  u01 in
tlet u02 :: ⋆ ⇒ ⋆ = λ⋆⇒⋆a. tlet u03 :: ⋆ = (#0,a)⋆ in
                                 tlet u04 :: ⋆ = u03 → u03 in
                                 u04 in
tlet T_id :: ⋆ = ∀.u02 in
let id : T_id = μid_r:T_id.Λα::⋆. tlet u05 :: ⋆ = α → α in
                                    let t01 : u05 = μt02:u05.λx:α. x in
                                    t01 in
tlet u06 :: ⋆ ⇒ ⋆ = λ⋆⇒⋆b. tlet u07 :: ⋆ = (#0,b)⋆ in
                                 tlet u08 :: ⋆ = u07 → u07 in
                                 tlet u09 :: ⋆ = u07 → u08 in
                                 u09 in
tlet T_k :: ⋆ = ∀.u06 in
let k : T_k = μk_r:T_k.Λβ::⋆. tlet u10 :: ⋆ = β → β in
                                tlet u11 :: ⋆ = β → u10 in
                                let t03 : u11 = μt04:u11.λy:β. let t05 : u10 = μt06:u10.λz:β. y in
                                                                 t06 in
                                t03 in
tlet u12 :: ⋆ = (Id T_id)⋆ in
tlet u13 :: ⋆ = u12 → u12 in
let t07 : u13 = id [u12] in
let res1 : T_id = t07 id in
tlet u14 :: ⋆ = T_k → T_k in
let t08 : u14 = id [T_k] in
tlet T_res2 :: ⋆ = (Id T_k)⋆ in
let res1 : T_res2 = t08 k in
res2
```

(b) Equivalent System F_ω program in our ANF variant

Fig. 2. Example System F_ω program

As the language variant may not be familiar, Fig. 2 gives a System F_ω program in the traditional direct-style presentation and then gives the equivalent program in our ANF variant; the program defines the type-level identity function Id on proper types, defines the polymorphic identity function id and the (semi-)polymorphic constant function k (a.k.a, the K combinator), self-applies id (with a type-level application of Id in the type argument passed to id), and applies id to k (with a type-level application of Id in the type annotation of res2). We will use this example program to illustrate and compare the formulations of the TCFA for System F_ω.

A program is simply an expression. An expression is a sequence of tlet-bindings of type variables and let-bindings of expression variables ending with a "result" variable; the function ExpRes(·) extracts the variable that yields the expression's result. A variable may be let-bound to a value (either a recursive function or a recursive type abstraction), a function application, or a type application.

Types in our language have a sophisticated representation, in order to support and simplify our two formulations of the type- and control-flow analysis. Intuitively, a type is either a type variable (bound by an enclosing tlet or Λ), a function type, a universal type, a type-level function, a de Bruijn index [11] ("bound" by an enclosing type-level function), or a type-level application. As in some presentations of System F_ω [19], a universal type is not a binding form; the "body" of a universal type is a type of kind $\kappa_a \Rightarrow \star$, representing the abstraction of a type of kind κ_a over a proper type of kind $\star$ as a type-level function.

We actually use an ANF representation for types, where constituents of function types, universal types, and type-level applications are restricted to type variables. The syntax distinguishes type expressions, which are a sequence of tlet-bindings of type variables ending with a "result" type variable, and type values, which correspond to the different forms of types. As with expressions, the function TyRes($\cdot$) extracts the type variable that yields a type expression's result. We annotate type-level functions, de Bruijn indices, and type-level applications with their kind. This allows the kind of a type value to be determined from the syntax (function types and universal types are always of kind $\star$); the typing rules for type values ensure that the kind annotations are correct.

Using an ANF representation for types allows the flow-graph-based formulation of the TCFA to cache the compatibility of type variables and type values, admitting an efficient work-queue-based algorithm. Moreover, this ANF representation models and promotes sharing of types, leading to a smaller contribution from types to overall program size than with a direct-style representation. For example, the type variables T_{id} and T_k are used to annotate the let-bindings of id and k, in the type applications of id, and in the let-bindings of res1 and res2.

Using de Bruijn indices simplifies the definitions of type equivalence and type compatibility, allowing the bodies of type-level functions to be compared without implicit (e.g., Barendregt convention) or explicit (e.g., introducing a context of "equal" type variables) treatment of "up to α-equivalence". However, our flow-graph-based formulation of the TCFA will introduce a type-level 0CFA, for which a pure de Bruijn representation of type-level functions would introduce unacceptable imprecision; Sect. 4 will discuss this issue in more detail. To support the type-level 0CFA with a "name" for a type-level-function parameter, we introduce a distinct class of *index type variables*; a type-level function $\lambda^{\kappa_a \Rightarrow \kappa_r} \mathfrak{a}.\epsilon_r$ introduces the index type variable $\mathfrak{a}$, which must be used along with the corresponding de Bruijn index $((\#i, \mathfrak{a})^{\kappa_i})$. The typing environment and typing rule for $(\#i, \mathfrak{a})^{\kappa_i}$ will ensure that index type variables are used correctly, allowing type equivalence and type compatibility to ignore index type variables.

We do not assume that all let-, μ-, and λ-bound expression variables, all tlet- and Λ-bound type variables, or all $\lambda^{\kappa_a \Rightarrow \kappa_r}$-bound index type variables in a program are distinct, although the type system will prohibit shadowing of type variables and multiple binding occurrences of the same expression variable, type variable, or index type variable will degrade the precision of the TCFA. Finally, we will use various $\cdot \preceq_{Syn} P$ judgments (Appendix A) to relate a program P

Run-time type values (type closures)	$RTyVal \ni \pi ::= \langle \rho; \tau \rangle$
Run-time values (closures)	$RVal \ni w ::= \langle \rho; v \rangle$
Run-time environments	$REnv \ni \rho ::= \bullet \mid \rho, \alpha \mapsto \pi \mid \rho, x \mapsto w$
Stacks (continuations)	$Stack \ni \varsigma ::= \circ \mid \langle \rho; x; \alpha_x; e \rangle \triangleright \varsigma$
States	$State \ni \Sigma ::= \langle \rho; e; \varsigma \rangle$

$$\boxed{\Sigma \longrightarrow \Sigma'}$$

$$\frac{\rho_r(x_r) = w_r}{\langle \rho_r; x_r; \langle \rho; x; \alpha_x; e \rangle \triangleright \varsigma \rangle \longrightarrow \langle \rho, x \mapsto w_r; e; \varsigma \rangle}$$

$$\frac{}{\langle \rho; \mathtt{tlet}\ \alpha :: \kappa_\alpha = \tau\ \mathtt{in}\ e; \varsigma \rangle \longrightarrow \langle \rho, \alpha \mapsto \langle \rho; \tau \rangle; e; \varsigma \rangle}$$

$$\frac{}{\langle \rho; \mathtt{let}\ x : \alpha_x = v\ \mathtt{in}\ e; \varsigma \rangle \longrightarrow \langle \rho, x \mapsto \langle \rho; v \rangle; e; \varsigma \rangle}$$

$$\frac{\rho(x_f) = w_f \quad w_f = \langle \rho_f; \mu f{:}\alpha_f.\lambda y{:}\alpha_y.e_b \rangle \quad \rho(x_a) = w_a}{\langle \rho; \mathtt{let}\ x : \alpha_x = x_f\ x_a\ \mathtt{in}\ e; \varsigma \rangle \longrightarrow \langle \rho_f, f \mapsto w_f, y \mapsto w_a; e_b; \langle \rho; x; \alpha_x; e \rangle \triangleright \varsigma \rangle}$$

$$\frac{\rho(x_f) = w_f \quad w_f = \langle \rho_f; \mu f{:}\alpha_f.\Lambda\beta{::}\kappa_\beta.e_b \rangle \quad \rho(\alpha_a) = \pi_a}{\langle \rho; \mathtt{let}\ x : \alpha_x = x_f\ [\alpha_a]\ \mathtt{in}\ e; \varsigma \rangle \longrightarrow \langle \rho_f, f \mapsto w_f, \beta \mapsto \pi_a; e_b; \langle \rho; x; \alpha_x; e \rangle \triangleright \varsigma \rangle}$$

Fig. 3. Operational Semantics

to its constituent expressions, binds, right-hand-sides, values, bound expression variables, type expressions, type binds, type values, and bound type variables.

Operational Semantics. The operational semantics for our variant of System F_ω (Fig. 3) is given in the style of the environment- and continuation-based C_aEK abstract machine [12], where a state Σ has three components: a run-time environment, a control expression, and a stack (continuation).

A run-time environment ρ is a map from type variables to run-time type values and from expression variables to run-time values. A run-time type value π is a *type closure*: the pair of a run-time environment and a (possibly open) type value; the run-time environment provides the meanings (as run-time type values) of the free type variables of the type value. A run-time value w is a *closure*: the pair of a run-time environment and a (possibly open) value (either a recursive function or a recursive type abstraction); the run-time environment provides the meanings (as run-time type values and as run-time values) of the free type and expression variables of the value. The use of type closures and an ANF representation for types makes our abstract machine similar to the $\lambda_{\text{gc}}^{\rightarrow\forall}$ abstract machine [31].

A stack is a sequence of frames, each of the form $\langle \rho; x; \alpha_x; e \rangle$, where x is the variable receiving the result run-time value w of a non-tail function application or type application, α_x is the (static) type of x, and e is the expression to be evaluated in the run-time environment ρ extended with x bound to w to yield the result of the frame.

The evaluation rules are straightforward. The first rule resumes execution of the top-most frame of the stack with a result run-time value when the control expression has been reduced to a variable. The second and third rules create run-time types and run-time values and bind them in the run-time environment. The fourth and fifth rules handle a non-tail function application or type application; each extracts a run-time environment ρ_f and body expression e_b from the run-time value w_f of the variable x_f, extend ρ_f with both f mapped to w_f (making the recursive function or recursive type abstraction available to the body expression) and either y mapped to $\rho(x_a)$ (in the case of a function application) or β mapped to $\rho(\alpha_a)$ (in the case of a type application), and pushes a frame onto the stack to receive the result of the body expression.

Type System. A type system for our variant of System F_ω can be given by extending a standard type system for System F_ω [39] with support for type definitions [31,50]. The details are somewhat tedious and mostly relegated to Appendix B. Here, we focus on those aspects that are necessary for the subsequent formulations of the type- and control-flow analysis.

The defining feature of System F_ω is a notion of *definitional type equivalence* that determines when one type "corresponds" to another type for the purpose of classifying values. Rather than expressing definitional type equivalence in terms of the ANF representation for types given above, we introduce *elaborated types* (Fig. 4), which are the direct-style counterparts of the type expressions and type values.

We define two meta-functions on elaborated types to account for substitution using de Bruijn indices: shift(θ, k) increments all of the de Bruijn indices in θ above the cutoff k and open(θ, k, θ') substitutes θ' for index k within θ, while decrementing any de Bruijn indices in θ that are greater than k. When open descends into $\lambda \mathsf{a}{::}\kappa_a.\theta_r$, a shift operation on θ' is required to avoid capturing "free" indices within θ'. There is no renaming of bound index type variables to avoid "capture"; this is because an index type variable must always be used with its corresponding de Bruijn index (which is incremented or decremented appropriately during substitution), thereby uniquely identifying its binding occurrence. The meta-function lclosed(θ, k) determines if θ is *locally closed* with respect to index k, meaning that it does not use any de Bruijn index greater than k.

Definitional type equivalence of θ_1 and θ_2 is established by the $\theta_1 \equiv_{\mathsf{a}\beta} \theta_2$ judgment. It is an equivalence: symmetric and transitive (via the last two rules) and reflexive (via induction). We annotate $\equiv_{\mathsf{a}\beta}$ with $\cdot_\mathsf{a}$, because the relation ignores index type variables (a-equivalence), and with $\cdot_\beta$, because the relation establishes that the type-level application of a type-level function to an argument is equivalent to the substitution of the argument in the body (β-equivalence).

We have judgments for the elaboration and kind checking (including checking that de Bruijn indices are in scope and used with the correct index type variables) of type expressions ($\Gamma \vdash \epsilon \Rightarrow \theta :: \kappa$), type binds ($\Gamma \vdash \psi \Rightarrow \Gamma'$), type values ($\Gamma \vdash \tau \Rightarrow \theta :: \kappa$), and type variables ($\Gamma \vdash \alpha \Rightarrow \theta :: \kappa$). We obtain elaborated types by "expanding" tlet-bound type-variable definitions.

We have judgments for the type checking of expressions ($\Gamma \vdash e : \theta$), binds ($\Gamma \vdash b : \Gamma'$), right-hand sides ($\Gamma \vdash r : \theta$), values ($\Gamma \vdash v : \theta$), and expression vari-

$$EType \ni \theta ::= \alpha \mid \theta_a \to \theta_r \mid \forall.\theta_g \mid \lambda\mathfrak{a}{::}\kappa_a.\theta_r \mid (\#i, \mathfrak{a}) \mid \theta_f\ \theta_a$$

$$\begin{aligned}
\text{shift}(\cdot, \cdot) &:: EType \times Nat \to EType \\
\text{shift}(\alpha, k) &= \alpha \\
\text{shift}(\theta_a \to \theta_r, k) &= \text{shift}(\theta_a, k) \to \text{shift}(\theta_r, k) \\
\text{shift}(\forall.\theta_g, k) &= \forall.\text{shift}(\theta_g, k) \\
\text{shift}(\lambda\mathfrak{a}{::}\kappa_a.\theta_r, k) &= \lambda\mathfrak{a}{::}\kappa_a.\text{shift}(\theta_r, k+1) \\
\text{shift}((\#i, \mathfrak{a}), k) &= \begin{cases} (\#i, \mathfrak{a}) & \text{if } i < k \\ (\#(i+1), \mathfrak{a}) & \text{if } i \geq k \end{cases} \\
\text{shift}(\theta_f\ \theta_a, k) &= \text{shift}(\theta_f, k)\ \text{shift}(\theta_a, k)
\end{aligned}$$

$$\begin{aligned}
\text{open}(\cdot, \cdot, \cdot) &:: EType \times Nat \times EType \to EType \\
\text{open}(\alpha, k, \theta') &= \alpha \\
\text{open}(\theta_a \to \theta_r, k, \theta') &= \text{open}(\theta_a, k, \theta') \to \text{open}(\theta_r, k, \theta') \\
\text{open}(\forall.\theta_g, k, \theta') &= \forall.\text{open}(\theta_g, k, \theta') \\
\text{open}(\lambda\mathfrak{a}{::}\kappa_a.\theta_r, k, \theta') &= \lambda\mathfrak{a}{::}\kappa_a.\text{open}(\theta_r, k+1, \text{shift}(\theta', 0)) \\
\text{open}((\#i, \mathfrak{a}), k, \theta') &= \begin{cases} (\#i, \mathfrak{a}) & \text{if } i < k \\ \theta' & \text{if } i = k \\ (\#(i-1), \mathfrak{a}) & \text{if } i > k \end{cases} \\
\text{open}(\theta_f\ \theta_a, k, \theta') &= \text{open}(\theta_f, k, \theta')\ \text{open}(\theta_a, k, \theta')
\end{aligned}$$

$$\begin{aligned}
\text{lclosed}(\cdot, \cdot) &:: EType \times Nat \to Bool \\
\text{lclosed}(\alpha, k) &= \text{true} \\
\text{lclosed}(\theta_a \to \theta_r, k) &= \text{lclosed}(\theta_a, k) \wedge \text{lclosed}(\theta_r, k) \\
\text{lclosed}(\forall.\theta_g, k) &= \text{lclosed}(\theta_g, k) \\
\text{lclosed}(\lambda\mathfrak{a}{::}\kappa_a.\theta_r, k) &= \text{lclosed}(\theta_r, k+1) \\
\text{lclosed}((\#i, \mathfrak{a}), k) &= i < k \\
\text{lclosed}(\theta_f\ \theta_a, k) &= \text{lclosed}(\theta_f, k) \wedge \text{lclosed}(\theta_a, k)
\end{aligned}$$

$\boxed{\theta_1 \equiv_{\alpha\beta} \theta_2}$

$$\frac{}{\alpha \equiv_{\alpha\beta} \alpha} \qquad \frac{\theta_{a1} \equiv_{\alpha\beta} \theta_{a2} \quad \theta_{r1} \equiv_{\alpha\beta} \theta_{r2}}{\theta_{a1} \to \theta_{r1} \equiv_{\alpha\beta} \theta_{a2} \to \theta_{r2}} \qquad \frac{\theta_{g1} \equiv_{\alpha\beta} \theta_{g2}}{\forall.\theta_{g1} \equiv_{\alpha\beta} \forall.\theta_{g2}}$$

$$\frac{\theta_{r1} \equiv_{\alpha\beta} \theta_{r2}}{\lambda\mathfrak{a}_1{::}\kappa_a.\theta_{r1} \equiv_{\alpha\beta} \lambda\mathfrak{a}_2{::}\kappa_a.\theta_{r2}} \qquad \frac{}{(\#i, \mathfrak{a}_1) \equiv_{\alpha\beta} (\#i, \mathfrak{a}_2)} \qquad \frac{\theta_{f1} \equiv_{\alpha\beta} \theta_{f2} \quad \theta_{a1} \equiv_{\alpha\beta} \theta_{a2}}{\theta_{f1}\ \theta_{a1} \equiv_{\alpha\beta} \theta_{f2}\ \theta_{a2}}$$

$$\frac{}{(\lambda\mathfrak{a}{::}\kappa_a.\theta_r)\ \theta_a \equiv_{\alpha\beta} \text{open}(\theta_r, \theta_a, 0)} \qquad \frac{\theta_2 \equiv_{\alpha\beta} \theta_1}{\theta_1 \equiv_{\alpha\beta} \theta_2} \qquad \frac{\theta_1 \equiv_{\alpha\beta} \theta' \quad \theta' \equiv_{\alpha\beta} \theta_2}{\theta_1 \equiv_{\alpha\beta} \theta_2}$$

Fig. 4. Elaborated Types, Shifting, Opening, Locally Closedness, and Definitional Type Equivalence

ables ($\Gamma \vdash x : \theta$). Rules for these judgments use definitional type equivalence to accommodate differences in the forms of elaborated types. For example, the rule

$$\frac{\Gamma \vdash \alpha_x \rightrightarrows \theta_x :: \star \quad \Gamma \vdash r : \theta_r \quad \theta_x \equiv_{\alpha\beta} \theta_r}{\Gamma \vdash \texttt{let}\ x : \alpha_x = r : \Gamma, x{:}\theta_x}$$

requires only definitional type equivalence (and not syntactic identity) of the elaborated type of x's type annotation and the elaborated type of r.

The type system is sound, via a syntactic proof using entirely standard Progress and Preservation theorems [52].

❦ Theorem 1 (Type Soundness).
If $\bullet \vdash P : \theta$ and $\langle \bullet; P; \circ \rangle \longrightarrow^* \Sigma'$,
then either there exists ρ' and x'_r such that $\Sigma' = \langle x'_r; \rho'; \circ \rangle$
or there exists Σ'' such that $\Sigma' \longrightarrow \Sigma''$.

In addition to the judgments mentioned above, we introduce judgments for checking run-time types ($\vdash \pi \rightrightarrows \theta :: \kappa$), run-time values ($\vdash w : \theta$), run-time environments ($\vdash \rho : \Gamma$), stacks ($\vdash \theta_x : \varsigma : \theta$), and states ($\vdash \Sigma : \theta$). A variety of substitution lemmas are required and the relationship between definitional type equivalence and a parallel-reduction judgment (Appendix B) is used to establish canonical-forms lemmas.

Abstract type values	$ATyVal \ni \hat{\pi} ::= \tau$
Sets of abstract type values	$\mathcal{P}(ATyVal) \ni \hat{\Pi}$
Abstract values	$AVal \ni \hat{w} ::= v$
Sets of abstract values	$\mathcal{P}(AVal) \ni \hat{W}$
Abstract environments	$AEnv = (TyVar \to \mathcal{P}(TyVal)) \times (Var \to \mathcal{P}(Val))$
	$\ni \hat{\rho} ::= (\{\alpha \mapsto \hat{\Pi}_\alpha \mid \alpha \in TyVar\}, \{x \mapsto \hat{W}_x \mid x \in Var\})$
Sets of abstract environments	$\mathcal{P}(AEnv) \ni \hat{R}$

$$\hat{\rho}_1 \sqsubseteq \hat{\rho}_2 \stackrel{\text{def}}{=} \forall \alpha \in TyVar. \hat{\rho}_1(\alpha) \subseteq \hat{\rho}_2(\alpha) \wedge \forall x \in Var. \hat{\rho}_1(x) \subseteq \hat{\rho}_2(x)$$

$$\bigsqcap_{\hat{\rho} \in \hat{R}} \hat{\rho} \stackrel{\text{def}}{=} (\{\alpha \mapsto \bigcap_{\hat{\rho} \in \hat{R}} \hat{\rho}(\alpha) \mid \alpha \in TyVar\}, \{x \mapsto \bigcap_{\hat{\rho} \in \hat{R}} \hat{\rho}(x) \mid x \in Var\})$$

$$\bigsqcup_{\hat{\rho} \in \hat{R}} \hat{\rho} \stackrel{\text{def}}{=} (\{\alpha \mapsto \bigcup_{\hat{\rho} \in \hat{R}} \hat{\rho}(\alpha) \mid \alpha \in TyVar\}, \{x \mapsto \bigcup_{\hat{\rho} \in \hat{R}} \hat{\rho}(x) \mid x \in Var\})$$

$$\top_{\hat{\rho}} \stackrel{\text{def}}{=} \bigsqcap \emptyset = \bigsqcup AEnv = (\{\alpha \mapsto ATyVal \mid \alpha \in TyVar\}, \{x \mapsto AVal \mid x \in Var\})$$

$$\bot_{\hat{\rho}} \stackrel{\text{def}}{=} \bigsqcup \emptyset = \bigsqcap AEnv = (\{\alpha \mapsto \emptyset \mid \alpha \in TyVar\}, \{x \mapsto \emptyset \mid x \in Var\})$$

$$\{\beta \mapsto \hat{\Pi}\}_{\hat{\rho}} \stackrel{\text{def}}{=} \left(\left\{\alpha \mapsto \begin{cases} \hat{\Pi} & \text{if } \alpha = \beta \\ \emptyset & \text{if } \alpha \neq \beta \end{cases} \,\middle|\, \alpha \in TyVar\right\}, \{x \mapsto \emptyset \mid x \in Var\}\right)$$

$$\{y \mapsto \hat{W}\}_{\hat{\rho}} \stackrel{\text{def}}{=} \left(\{\alpha \mapsto \emptyset \mid \alpha \in TyVar\}, \left\{x \mapsto \begin{cases} \hat{W} & \text{if } x = y \\ \emptyset & \text{if } x \neq y \end{cases} \,\middle|\, x \in Var\right\}\right)$$

$$\begin{array}{ll}
|\cdot| :: RTyVal \to ATyVal & |\cdot| :: REnv \to AEnv \\
|\langle \rho; \tau \rangle| = \tau & |\bullet| = \bot_{\hat{\rho}} \\
|\cdot| :: RVal \to AVal & |\rho, \alpha \mapsto \pi| = |\rho| \sqcup \{\alpha \mapsto \{|\pi|\}\}_{\hat{\rho}} \\
|\langle \rho; v \rangle| = v & |\rho, x \mapsto w| = |\rho| \sqcup \{x \mapsto \{|w|\}\}_{\hat{\rho}}
\end{array}$$

Fig. 5. Abstract Environments

3 Specification-Based Formulation

We first give a specification-based formulation of a type- and control-flow analysis for System F_ω. As a specification-based formulation of a program analysis [16, 32–35], it is presented as a set of judgments that assert the various constraints that an acceptable analysis result must satisfy.

For a type- and control-flow analysis, a result is an *abstract environment* (Fig. 5). An abstract environment $\hat{\rho}$ is a pair of a total function from type variables to sets of abstract type values and a total function from expression variables to sets of abstract values, where an abstract type is a (syntactic, possibly open) type value and an abstract value is a (syntactic, possibly open) value.[1] Since an abstract environment is a pair of total functions with disjoint domains, we freely write $\hat{\rho}(\alpha)$ for $(\mathsf{fst}(\hat{\rho}))(\alpha)$ and $\hat{\rho}(x)$ for $(\mathsf{snd}(\hat{\rho}))(x)$. Abstract environments form a complete lattice with the usual definitions for partial order, meet and join (over arbitrary sets of abstract environments, but typically used as binary operators), and greatest and least elements. A "shallow" abstraction function $|\cdot|$ maps run-time environments to abstract environments.[2]

---

[1] In a richer language, abstract values would not necessarily correspond exactly to syntactic values. For example, in a language with integer values, the abstract analogue of an integer value might be a token $\widehat{\mathsf{int}}$ or a subset of $\{-, 0, +\}$ (powerset sign domain) or an interval (interval domain). But, the abstract analogue of a function or type abstraction would typically be the syntax of the function or type abstraction.

[2] This abstraction function is "shallow" in the sense that it does not abstract and join the embedded run-time environments of run-time types and run-time values.

$\boxed{\hat{\rho} \vDash_{\mathsf{S}} \tau}$

$$\overline{\hat{\rho} \vDash_{\mathsf{S}} \alpha_a \to \alpha_r} \qquad \overline{\hat{\rho} \vDash_{\mathsf{S}} \forall.\alpha_g} \qquad \overline{\hat{\rho} \vDash_{\mathsf{S}} (\#i, \mathsf{a})^{\kappa_i}} \qquad \frac{\hat{\rho} \vDash_{\mathsf{S}} \epsilon_r}{\hat{\rho} \vDash_{\mathsf{S}} \lambda^{\kappa_a \Rightarrow \kappa_r} \mathsf{a}.\epsilon_r} \qquad \overline{\hat{\rho} \vDash_{\mathsf{S}} (\alpha_f \ \alpha_a)^{\kappa_r}}$$

$\boxed{\hat{\rho} \vDash_{\mathsf{S}} \psi}$ $\boxed{\hat{\rho} \vDash_{\mathsf{S}} \epsilon}$

$$\frac{\hat{\rho} \vDash_{\mathsf{S}} \tau \quad \boxed{\mathsf{KindOf}(\tau) = \kappa_\alpha \Rightarrow \tau \in \hat{\rho}(\alpha)}}{\hat{\rho} \vDash_{\mathsf{S}} \mathtt{tlet}\ \alpha :: \kappa_\alpha = \tau} \qquad \overline{\hat{\rho} \vDash_{\mathsf{S}} \alpha_r} \qquad \frac{\hat{\rho} \vDash_{\mathsf{S}} \psi \quad \hat{\rho} \vDash_{\mathsf{S}} \epsilon}{\hat{\rho} \vDash_{\mathsf{S}} \psi\ \mathtt{in}\ \epsilon}$$

$\boxed{\hat{\rho} \vDash_{\mathsf{S}} v}$

$$\frac{\hat{\rho} \vDash_{\mathsf{S}} e_b}{\hat{\rho} \vDash_{\mathsf{S}} \mu f{:}\alpha_f.\lambda y{:}\alpha_y.e_b} \qquad \frac{\hat{\rho} \vDash_{\mathsf{S}} e_b}{\hat{\rho} \vDash_{\mathsf{S}} \mu f{:}\alpha_f.\Lambda\beta{::}\kappa_\beta.e_b}$$

$\boxed{\hat{\rho} \vDash_{\mathsf{S}} b}$

$$\frac{\hat{\rho} \vDash_{\mathsf{S}} v \quad \boxed{\hat{\rho} \vDash_{\mathsf{S}} \mathsf{TyOf}(v) \approx \alpha_x :: \star \Rightarrow v \in \hat{\rho}(x)}}{\hat{\rho} \vDash_{\mathsf{S}} \mathtt{let}\ x : \alpha_x = v}$$

$$\frac{\bigwedge_{\mu f{:}\alpha_f.\lambda y{:}\alpha_y.e_r \in \hat{\rho}(x_f)} \begin{pmatrix} \hat{\rho} \vDash_{\mathsf{S}} \mathsf{TyOf}(\mu f{:}\alpha_f.\lambda y{:}\alpha_y.e_r) \approx \alpha_f :: \star \Rightarrow \mu f{:}\alpha_f.\lambda y{:}\alpha_y.e_r \in \hat{\rho}(f) \land \\ \forall \hat{w}_a \in \hat{\rho}(x_a)\ .\ \hat{\rho} \vDash_{\mathsf{S}} \mathsf{TyOf}(\hat{w}_a) \approx \alpha_y :: \star \Rightarrow \hat{w}_a \in \hat{\rho}(y) \land \\ \forall \hat{w}_r \in \hat{\rho}(\mathsf{ExpRes}(e_r))\ .\ \hat{\rho} \vDash_{\mathsf{S}} \mathsf{TyOf}(\hat{w}_r) \approx \alpha_x :: \star \Rightarrow \hat{w}_r \in \hat{\rho}(x) \end{pmatrix}}{\hat{\rho} \vDash_{\mathsf{S}} \mathtt{let}\ x : \alpha_x = x_f\ x_a}$$

$$\frac{\bigwedge_{\mu f{:}\alpha_f.\Lambda\beta{::}\kappa_\beta.e_r \in \hat{\rho}(x_f)} \begin{pmatrix} \hat{\rho} \vDash_{\mathsf{S}} \mathsf{TyOf}(\mu f{:}\alpha_f.\Lambda\beta{::}\kappa_\beta.e_r) \approx \alpha_f :: \star \Rightarrow \mu f{:}\alpha_f.\Lambda\beta{::}\kappa_\beta.e_r \in \hat{\rho}(f) \land \\ \forall \hat{\pi}_a \in \hat{\rho}(\alpha_a)\ .\ \boxed{\mathsf{KindOf}(\hat{\pi}_a) = \kappa_\beta \Rightarrow} \hat{\pi}_a \in \hat{\rho}(\beta) \land \\ \forall \hat{w}_r \in \hat{\rho}(\mathsf{ExpRes}(e_r))\ .\ \hat{\rho} \vDash_{\mathsf{S}} \mathsf{TyOf}(\hat{w}_r) \approx \alpha_x :: \star \Rightarrow \hat{w}_r \in \hat{\rho}(x) \end{pmatrix}}{\hat{\rho} \vDash_{\mathsf{S}} \mathtt{let}\ x : \alpha_x = x_f\ [\alpha_a]}$$

$\boxed{\hat{\rho} \vDash_{\mathsf{S}} e}$

$$\overline{\hat{\rho} \vDash_{\mathsf{S}} x_r} \qquad \frac{\hat{\rho} \vDash_{\mathsf{S}} \psi \quad \hat{\rho} \vDash_{\mathsf{S}} e}{\hat{\rho} \vDash_{\mathsf{S}} \psi\ \mathtt{in}\ e} \qquad \frac{\hat{\rho} \vDash_{\mathsf{S}} b \quad \hat{\rho} \vDash_{\mathsf{S}} e}{\hat{\rho} \vDash_{\mathsf{S}} b\ \mathtt{in}\ e}$$

$$\begin{aligned}
\mathsf{KindOf}(\cdot) &:: ATyVal \to Kind & \mathsf{TyOf}(\cdot) &:: AVal \to TyVar \\
\mathsf{KindOf}(\alpha_a \to \alpha_r) &= \star & \mathsf{TyOf}(\mu f{:}\alpha_f.\lambda y{:}\alpha_y.e_b) &= \alpha_f \\
\mathsf{KindOf}(\forall.\alpha_g) &= \star & \mathsf{TyOf}(\mu f{:}\alpha_f.\Lambda\beta.e_b) &= \alpha_f \\
\mathsf{KindOf}((\#i, \mathsf{a})^{\kappa_i}) &= \kappa_i \\
\mathsf{KindOf}(\lambda^{\kappa_a \Rightarrow \kappa_r} \mathsf{a}.\epsilon_r) &= \kappa_a \Rightarrow \kappa_r \\
\mathsf{KindOf}((\alpha_f \ \alpha_a)^{\kappa_r}) &= \kappa_r
\end{aligned}$$

Fig. 6. Specification-Based TCFA

Our specification-based formulation of a TCFA for System F_ω is given in Fig. 6; it adapts a syntax-directed 0CFA [34, Section 3.3], the classic monovariant (context-insensitive) control-flow analysis for the untyped lambda calculus. Each judgment of the form $\hat{\rho} \vDash_{\mathsf{S}} \cdot$ asserts that the abstract environment $\hat{\rho}$ is an acceptable TCFA result for a particular form of syntax. Intuitively, an acceptable abstract environment for a program is one that (over) approximates every runtime environment that arises during the evaluation of the program.

Ignoring the shaded terms, the judgments and rules are standard for a syntax-directed monovariant control-flow analysis. The interesting rules are those of the $\hat{\rho} \vDash_\mathsf{S} \mathtt{let}\ x : \alpha_x = b$ judgment that assert the presence of abstract values in the abstract environment (i.e., that $\hat{w} \in \hat{\rho}(x)$ for some $\hat{w}$ and x). When b is a value v, we require that v is in $\hat{\rho}(x)$ (corresponding to the $x \mapsto \langle \rho; v \rangle$ binding in the operational semantics). When b is a function application $x_f\ x_a$, we consider each recursive function $\mu f{:}\alpha_f.\lambda y{:}\alpha_y.e_b$ in $\hat{\rho}(x_f)$. We assert that the recursive function is in $\hat{\rho}(f)$ (corresponding to the $f \mapsto w_f$ binding in the operational semantics that makes the recursive function available to the body), that each "argument" abstract value $\hat{w}_a$ in $\hat{\rho}(x_a)$ is also in $\hat{\rho}(y)$ (corresponding to the $y \mapsto w_a$ binding in the operational semantics that makes the actual argument run-time value available to the body as the formal parameter variable), and that each "result" abstract value $\hat{w}_r$ in $\hat{\rho}(\mathsf{ExpRes}(e_b))$ (i.e., in the set of abstract values of the variable that yields the body's result) is also in $\hat{\rho}(x)$ (corresponding to the $x \mapsto w_r$ binding in the operational semantics when a result is returned to the top-most frame of the stack). Finally, when b is a type application $x_f\ [\alpha_a]$, we similarly consider each recursive type abstraction $\mu f{:}\alpha_f.\Lambda\beta{::}\kappa_\beta.e_b$ and assert that the recursive type abstraction is in $\hat{\rho}(f)$ and that each "result" abstract value $\hat{w}_r$ in $\hat{\rho}(\mathsf{ExpRes}(e_b))$ is also in $\hat{\rho}(x)$.

The $\hat{\pi} \in \hat{\rho}(\alpha)$ terms (continuing to ignore the $\kappa_1 = \kappa_2 \Rightarrow$ terms) add the *type-flow analysis*, asserting the presence of abstract type values in the abstract environment. The rule for $\hat{\rho} \vDash_\mathsf{S} \mathtt{tlet}\ \alpha :: \kappa_\alpha = \tau$ asserts that τ is in $\hat{\rho}(\alpha)$ (corresponding to the $\alpha \mapsto \langle \rho; \tau \rangle$ binding in the operational semantics and also to the $\Gamma, \alpha :: (\theta, \kappa)$ binding (with $\Gamma \vdash \tau \rightrightarrows \theta :: \kappa$) in the type system, which records the definition of α in its scope). Similarly, the rule for a type application $\hat{\rho} \vDash_\mathsf{S} \mathtt{let}\ x : \alpha_x = x_f\ [\alpha_a]$ asserts that each "argument" abstract type value $\hat{\pi}_a$ in $\hat{\rho}(\alpha_a)$ is also in $\hat{\rho}(\beta)$ (corresponding to the $\beta \mapsto \pi_a$ binding in the operational semantics that makes the actual argument run-time type value available to the body as the formal parameter type variable).

The $\hat{\rho} \vDash_\mathsf{S} \alpha_1 \approx \alpha_2 :: \kappa \Rightarrow$ terms add the essential feature of a type- *and* control-flow analysis: using the type-flow analysis to improve the control-flow analysis. Each $\hat{\rho} \vDash_\mathsf{S} \mathsf{TyOf}(\hat{w}) \approx \alpha_x :: \star \Rightarrow \hat{w} \in \hat{\rho}(x)$ term asserts that if the static type of the abstract value $\hat{w}$ is compatible with α_x (the static type of x) under the abstract environment $\hat{\rho}$, then $\hat{w}$ must be present in $\hat{\rho}(x)$. If the static type of $\hat{w}$ is *not* compatible with α_x under $\hat{\rho}$, then $\hat{w}$ need not be present in $\hat{\rho}(x)$. The static type of $\hat{w}$ is obtained for recursive functions and type abstractions by taking the type variable of the type annotation of the μ-bound variable.

The judgments and rules for type compatibility under an abstract environment are given in Fig. 7. Two type variables are compatible if they expand to *fully closed* (closed with respect to both type variables and de Bruijn indices) elaborated types that are definitionally type equivalent. The use of definitional type equivalence in type compatibility corresponds to the use of definitional

$$\text{de Bruijn-index environment} \quad IEnv \ni \Delta ::= \bullet \mid \Delta, (\mathfrak{a}, \kappa)$$

$\boxed{\hat{\rho} \vDash_S \alpha_1 \approx \alpha_2 :: \kappa}$

$$\dfrac{\hat{\rho}; \bullet \vDash_S \alpha_1 \rightsquigarrow \theta_1 :: \kappa \quad \hat{\rho}; \bullet \vDash_S \alpha_2 \rightsquigarrow \theta_2 :: \kappa \quad \theta_1 \equiv_{\alpha\beta} \theta_2}{\hat{\rho} \vDash_S \alpha_1 \approx \alpha_2 :: \kappa}$$

$\boxed{\hat{\rho}; \Delta \vDash_S \alpha \rightsquigarrow \theta :: \kappa}$

$$\dfrac{\hat{\pi} \in \hat{\rho}(\alpha) \quad \hat{\rho}; \Delta \vDash_S \hat{\pi} \rightsquigarrow \theta :: \kappa}{\hat{\rho}; \Delta \vDash_S \alpha \rightsquigarrow \theta :: \kappa}$$

$\boxed{\hat{\rho}; \Delta \vDash_S \hat{\pi} \rightsquigarrow \theta :: \kappa}$

$$\dfrac{\hat{\rho}; \Delta \vDash_S \alpha_a \rightsquigarrow \theta_a :: \star \quad \hat{\rho}; \Delta \vDash_S \alpha_r \rightsquigarrow \theta_r :: \star}{\hat{\rho}; \Delta \vDash_S \alpha_a \rightarrow \alpha_r \rightsquigarrow \theta_a \rightarrow \theta_r :: \star} \qquad \dfrac{\hat{\rho}; \Delta \vDash_S \alpha_g \rightsquigarrow \theta_g :: \kappa_a \Rightarrow \star}{\hat{\rho}; \Delta \vDash_S \forall.\alpha_g \rightsquigarrow \forall.\theta_g :: \star}$$

$$\dfrac{\hat{\rho}; \Delta, (\mathfrak{a}, \kappa_a) \vDash_S \mathsf{TyRes}(\epsilon_r) \rightsquigarrow \theta_r :: \kappa_r}{\hat{\rho}; \Delta \vDash_S \lambda^{\kappa_a \Rightarrow \kappa_r} \mathfrak{a}.\epsilon_r \rightsquigarrow \lambda \mathfrak{a}::\kappa_a.\theta_r :: \kappa_a \Rightarrow \kappa_r} \qquad \dfrac{\Delta(i) = (\mathfrak{a}, \kappa_i)}{\hat{\rho}; \Delta \vDash_S (\#i, \mathfrak{a})^{\kappa_i} \rightsquigarrow (\#i, \mathfrak{a}_i) :: \kappa_i}$$

$$\dfrac{\hat{\rho}; \Delta \vDash_S \alpha_f \rightsquigarrow \theta_f :: \kappa_a \Rightarrow \kappa_r \quad \hat{\rho}; \Delta \vDash_S \alpha_a \rightsquigarrow \theta_a :: \kappa_a}{\hat{\rho}; \Delta \vDash_S (\alpha_f \ \alpha_a)^{\kappa_r} \rightsquigarrow \theta_f \ \theta_a :: \kappa_r}$$

✣ **Lemma 2.** *If* $\hat{\rho}; \bullet \vDash_S \alpha \rightsquigarrow \theta :: \kappa$, *then* $\bullet \vdash \theta :: \kappa$

Fig. 7. Specification-Based Type Compatibility

type equivalence in the typing rules.[3] The judgments $\hat{\rho}; \Delta \vDash_S \alpha \rightsquigarrow \theta :: \kappa$ and $\hat{\rho}; \Delta \vDash_S \hat{\pi} \rightsquigarrow \theta :: \kappa$ handle expanding type variables and abstract type values to elaborated types. A de Bruijn-index environment is used to ensure that the expansion of the body of a type-level function uses de Bruijn indices with the correct index type variable and kind; this ensures that expansion always yields a fully closed and well-kinded elaborated type (Lemma 2). Note that when expanding a type variable, the rule is free to choose any abstract type value from the abstract environment's entry for the type variable; when used in the context of the compatibility judgment, this rule must "guess" a satisfying abstract type value from among those in $\hat{\rho}(\alpha)$.

The remaining $\boxed{\kappa_1 = \kappa_2 \Rightarrow}$ terms perform a similar filtering as the $\boxed{\hat{\rho} \vDash_S \alpha_1 \approx \alpha_2 :: \kappa \Rightarrow}$ terms. Each $\boxed{\mathsf{KindOf}(\hat{\pi}) = \kappa_\alpha \Rightarrow}$ $\hat{\pi} \in \hat{\rho}(\alpha)$ asserts that if the kind of the abstract type value $\hat{\pi}$ is compatible with κ_α (the kind of α), then $\hat{\pi}$ must be present in $\hat{\rho}(\alpha)$; note that simple syntactic equality suffices for kind compatibility. The guard in the $\hat{\rho} \vDash_S \mathtt{let}\ x : \alpha_x = x_f\ [\alpha_a]$ rule is meaningful, because this TCFA is monovariant (context-insensitive). If a type variable β has multiple binding occurrences at different kinds in the program being analyzed, then $\hat{\rho}(\beta)$ will have abstract type values of different kinds and the guard can reject (some of) the spurious flows due to conflating all binding

---

[3] This is a critical difference compared to our previous TCFA for System F [13]. In that work, type compatibility simply required the two type variables to expand to fully closed elaborated types that are syntactically equal.

Table 1. Partial flow-analysis results for the System F_ω program given in Fig. 2b via 0CFA, specification-based TCFA, and flow-graph-based TCFA; remaining results are given in Table 2

	0CFA	TCFA$_S$	TCFA$_G$
id	$\{\mu\mathsf{id}_r\colon T_{\mathsf{id}}.\Lambda\alpha\colon\colon\star.\cdot\}$	$\{\mu\mathsf{id}_r\colon T_{\mathsf{id}}.\Lambda\alpha\colon\colon\star.\cdot\}$	$\{\mu\mathsf{id}_r\colon T_{\mathsf{id}}.\Lambda\alpha\colon\colon\star.\cdot\}$
x	$\{\mu\mathsf{id}_r\colon T_{\mathsf{id}}.\Lambda\alpha\colon\colon\star.\cdot,$ $\mu\mathsf{k}_r\colon T_{\mathsf{k}}.\Lambda\beta\colon\colon\star.\cdot\}$	$\{\mu\mathsf{id}_r\colon T_{\mathsf{id}}.\Lambda\alpha\colon\colon\star.\cdot,$ $\mu\mathsf{k}_r\colon T_{\mathsf{k}}.\Lambda\beta\colon\colon\star.\cdot\}$	$\{\mu\mathsf{id}_r\colon T_{\mathsf{id}}.\Lambda\alpha\colon\colon\star.\cdot,$ $\mu\mathsf{k}_r\colon T_{\mathsf{k}}.\Lambda\beta\colon\colon\star.\cdot\}$
k	$\{\mu\mathsf{k}_r\colon T_{\mathsf{k}}.\Lambda\beta\colon\colon\star.\cdot\}$	$\{\mu\mathsf{k}_r\colon T_{\mathsf{k}}.\Lambda\beta\colon\colon\star.\cdot\}$	$\{\mu\mathsf{k}_r\colon T_{\mathsf{k}}.\Lambda\beta\colon\colon\star.\cdot\}$
y	$\{\}$	$\{\}$	$\{\}$
z	$\{\}$	$\{\}$	$\{\}$
res1	$\{\mu\mathsf{id}_r\colon T_{\mathsf{id}}.\Lambda\alpha\colon\colon\star.\cdot,$ $\mu\mathsf{k}_r\colon T_{\mathsf{k}}.\Lambda\beta\colon\colon\star.\cdot\}$	$\{\mu\mathsf{id}_r\colon T_{\mathsf{id}}.\Lambda\alpha\colon\colon\star.\cdot\}$	$\{\mu\mathsf{id}_r\colon T_{\mathsf{id}}.\Lambda\alpha\colon\colon\star.\cdot\}$
res2	$\{\mu\mathsf{id}_r\colon T_{\mathsf{id}}.\Lambda\alpha\colon\colon\star.\cdot,$ $\mu\mathsf{k}_r\colon T_{\mathsf{k}}.\Lambda\beta\colon\colon\star.\cdot\}$	$\{\mu\mathsf{k}_r\colon T_{\mathsf{k}}.\Lambda\beta\colon\colon\star.\cdot\}$	$\{\mu\mathsf{id}_r\colon T_{\mathsf{id}}.\Lambda\alpha\colon\colon\star.\cdot,$ $\mu\mathsf{k}_r\colon T_{\mathsf{k}}.\Lambda\beta\colon\colon\star.\cdot\}$
Id	–	$\{\lambda^{\star\Rightarrow\star}\mathsf{t}.\cdot\}$	$\{\lambda^{\star\Rightarrow\star}\mathsf{t}.\cdot\}$
$u01$	–	$\{(\#0,\mathsf{t})^\star\}$	$\{(\#0,\mathsf{t})^\star, \forall.u02, \forall.u06\}$
T_{id}	–	$\{\forall.u02\}$	$\{\forall.u02\}$
α	–	$\{(Id\ T_{\mathsf{id}})^\star, \forall.u06\}$	$\{(Id\ T_{\mathsf{id}})^\star, \forall.u02, \forall.u06\}$
T_{k}	–	$\{\forall.u06\}$	$\{\forall.u06\}$
β	–	$\{\}$	$\{\}$
$u12$	–	$\{(Id\ T_{\mathsf{id}})^\star\}$	$\{(Id\ T_{\mathsf{id}})^\star, \forall.u02, \forall.u06\}$
T_{res2}	–	$\{(Id\ T_{\mathsf{k}})^\star\}$	$\{(Id\ T_{\mathsf{k}})^\star, \forall.u02, \forall.u06\}$
t	–	–	$\{\forall.u02, \forall.u06\}$
a	–	–	$\{\}$
b	–	–	$\{\}$

occurrences of β. The guard in the $\hat{\rho} \vDash_S$ tlet $\alpha :: \kappa_\alpha = \tau$ rule is redundant (for well-typed programs), but is retained for uniformity.[4]

---

[4] Interestingly, the $\boxed{\hat{\rho} \vDash_S \mathsf{TyOf}(v) \approx \alpha_x :: \star \Rightarrow}$ guard in the $\hat{\rho} \vDash_S$ let $x : \alpha_x = v$ rule is *not* redundant. In a well-typed program, the elaborated type of v must be definitionally type equivalent to the elaborated type of α_x and, therefore, it appears that $\mathsf{TyOf}(v)$ and α_x must be compatible. However, suppose that this binding occurs in the body of a $\mu f{:}\alpha_f.\Lambda\beta{::}\kappa_\beta.e_r$ and that the elaborated types of v and α_x use β. If the type abstraction is never applied, then an acceptable abstract environment can have $\hat{\rho}(\beta) = \emptyset$ and there will be no fully-closed elaborated types to which $\mathsf{TyOf}(v)$ and α_x expand and $\hat{\rho} \vDash_S \mathsf{TyOf}(v) \approx \alpha_x :: \star$ will not be derivable. Thus, we indirectly achieve a weak form of reachability. This occurs with t03 and t05 in Table 2.

Example. Table 1 compares the flow-analysis results for the System F_ω program given in Fig. 2b obtained via "classic" 0CFA, via the specification-based TCFA for System F_ω (using the $\sqsubseteq$-minimal acceptable abstract environment), and via the flow-graph-based TCFA for System F_ω to be discussed in Sect. 4; for now, the final column can be ignored. Note that $\mathsf{TCFA_S}$ is more precise than 0CFA with respect to the expression variables res1 and res2.

Since k is not applied in the program, no abstract type values flow to β and no abstract values flow to y or z (in any of the flow analyses). Since id is type-applied to both $u12$ and T_k, $\mathsf{TCFA_S}$ determines that the abstract type values $(Id\ T_{\mathsf{id}})^\star$ (corresponding to $u12$) and $\forall.u06$ (corresponding to T_k) flow to α. Since id [·] is applied to both id and k, all of the flow analyses determine that the abstract values $\mu\mathsf{id_r}{:}T_{\mathsf{id}}.\Lambda\alpha{::}{\star}.\cdot$ (corresponding to id) and $\mu\mathsf{k_r}{:}T_k.\Lambda\beta{::}{\star}.\cdot$ (corresponding to k) flow to x. Since each of res1 and res2 is bound to the result of id [·] ·, 0CFA determines that all of the abstract values that flow to x also flow to both res1 and res2. However, $\mathsf{TCFA_S}$ uses the type-flow analysis to improve the control-flow analysis. We can reason about res2 as follows. T_{id} (the type annotation of $\mu\mathsf{id_r}{:}T_{\mathsf{id}}.\Lambda\alpha{::}{\star}.\cdot$) is not compatible with T_{res2} (the type annotation of res2) since T_{id} expands (via $\hat{\rho};\bullet \vDash_\mathsf{S} \alpha \rightthreetimes \theta :: \star$) to only $\forall.(\lambda\mathsf{a}{::}{\star}.((\#0,\mathsf{a}) \to (\#0,\mathsf{a})))$ and T_{res2} expands to only $(\lambda\mathsf{t}.(\#0,\mathsf{t}))\ (\forall.(\lambda\mathsf{b}{::}{\star}.(\#0,\mathsf{b}) \to (\#0,\mathsf{b}) \to (\#0,\mathsf{b})))$, which are not definitionally type equivalent. Therefore, $\mu\mathsf{id_r}{:}T_{\mathsf{id}}.\Lambda\alpha{::}{\star}.\cdot$ does not flow to res2. We can reason similarly about res1.

Flow-Analysis Soundness. Soundness of the type- and control-flow analysis asserts that any acceptable abstract environment is an upper bound of the "shallow" abstraction of every run-time environment that arises during evaluation:

❦ Theorem 3 (Flow-Analysis Soundness).
If $\bullet \vdash P : \theta$ *and* $\hat{\rho} \vDash_\mathsf{S} P$ *and* $\langle\bullet; P; \circ\rangle \longrightarrow^* \langle\rho'; e'; \varsigma'\rangle$, *then* $|\rho'| \sqsubseteq \hat{\rho}$.

The main proof is via a Preservation (i.e., subject reduction) lemma. In addition to the judgments given in this section, we introduces judgments (Appendix C) that assert the acceptability of abstract environments with respect to run-time type values ($\hat{\rho} \vDash_\mathsf{S} \pi$), run-time values ($\hat{\rho} \vDash_\mathsf{S} w$), run-time environments ($\hat{\rho} \vDash_\mathsf{S} \rho$), stacks ($\hat{\rho} \vDash_\mathsf{S} \varsigma$), and states ($\hat{\rho} \vDash_\mathsf{S} \Sigma$).

Existence. It is trivial to show $\top_{\hat{\rho}} \vDash_\mathsf{S} P$ for all P. However, this is not a particularly useful type- and control-flow analysis result. The utility of a program analysis lies in its ability to (efficiently) validate or compute a result that gives meaningful information about the program. Given two (comparable) acceptable abstract environments for a program, we would prefer the more precise ($\sqsubseteq$-smaller) one. Indeed, among the (uncountably) infinite number of acceptable abstract environments for a given program, we would most prefer the most precise ($\sqsubseteq$-minimal) one (if such a most precise one exists).

To establish the existence of a minimal TCFA result, we first note that, for a given program P, we can limit our attention to a finite set of abstract environments. In particular, there exists an acceptable abstract environment $\hat{\rho}_\top^P$

A Preliminary Type- and Control-Flow Analysis for System F_ω 175

that maps the finite set of tlet- and Λ-bound type variables of P to the finite set of all type values that occur in P (and all other type variables to the empty set) and that maps the finite set of let-, μ-, and λ-bound variables of P to the finite set of all values that occur in P (and all other variables to the empty set):

❧ **Theorem 4 (Acceptability of $\hat{\rho}_\top^P$).**
If $\hat{\Pi}^P \stackrel{\text{def}}{=} \{\tau \mid \tau \preceq_{TyVal} P\}$ and $\hat{W}^P \stackrel{\text{def}}{=} \{v \mid v \preceq_{Val} P\}$
and $\hat{\rho}_\top^P \stackrel{\text{def}}{=} \left(\left\{ \alpha \mapsto \begin{cases} \hat{\Pi}^P & \text{if } \alpha \preceq_{TyVar} P \\ \emptyset & \text{otherwise} \end{cases} \;\middle|\; \alpha \in TyVar \right\}, \right.$
$\left. \left\{ x \mapsto \begin{cases} \hat{W}^P & \text{if } x \preceq_{Var} P \\ \emptyset & \text{otherwise} \end{cases} \;\middle|\; x \in Var \right\} \right),$
then $\hat{\rho}_\top^P \vDash_S P$.

Also, the meet of two acceptable abstract environments is itself acceptable:

❧ **Theorem 5 (Acceptable Abstract Environments Closed under Meet).**
If $\hat{\rho}_1 \vDash_S P$ and $\hat{\rho}_2 \vDash_S P$, then $\hat{\rho}_1 \sqcap \hat{\rho}_2 \vDash_S P$.

These two facts imply the existence of a minimal TCFA result for a program P. The collection of abstract environments $\sqsubseteq \hat{\rho}_\top^P$ is a non-empty finite set (non-empty since it contains $\hat{\rho}_\top^P$ and finite since $\hat{\rho}_\top^P$ contains only finite sets). Restricting this set to those that are acceptable for P is also a finite non-empty set (non-empty since it still contains $\hat{\rho}_\top^P$ by Theorem 4). Taking the meet over all of these acceptable abstract environments yields an acceptable abstract environment (Theorem 5) that is $\sqsubseteq$ all of them (and equal to one of them). Thus, $\hat{\rho}_*^P \stackrel{\text{def}}{=} \sqcap \{\hat{\rho} \mid \hat{\rho} \sqsubseteq \hat{\rho}_\top^P \wedge \hat{\rho} \vDash_S P\}$ is the minimal TCFA result for the program P.

Decidability(?). A constructive proof that $\hat{\rho}_*^P$ is the minimal TCFA result for the program P requires actually constructing $\hat{\rho}_*^P$; constructing $\hat{\rho}_*^P$ would also be required in order to make use of $\hat{\rho}_*^P$ (e.g., to optimize the program P). Constructing $\{\hat{\rho} \mid \hat{\rho} \sqsubseteq \hat{\rho}_\top^P\}$ is easy, but constructing $\{\hat{\rho} \mid \hat{\rho} \sqsubseteq \hat{\rho}_\top^P \wedge \hat{\rho} \vDash_S P\}$ requires deciding $\hat{\rho} \vDash_S P$ and the decidability of this specification-based formulation of a TCFA for System F_ω remains an open question. The decidability would also be required for other approaches to constructing the minimal TCFA result (e.g., by defining the analysis as a monotone function from abstract environments to abstract environments and using a least fixed point computation [10]).

In order to decide $\hat{\rho} \vDash_S P$, we must decide implications of the form $\forall \hat{w} \in \hat{\rho}(y) . \hat{\rho} \vDash_S \mathsf{TyOf}(\hat{w}) \approx \alpha_x :: \star \Rightarrow \hat{w} \in \hat{\rho}(x)$. Even restricting to abstract environments $\sqsubseteq \hat{\rho}_\top^P$ (with $\hat{\rho}(y)$ and $\hat{\rho}(x)$ finite sets), for each $\hat{w}$ that is in $\hat{\rho}(y)$ but not in $\hat{\rho}(x)$ we must show that $\hat{\rho} \vDash_S \mathsf{TyOf}(\hat{w}) \approx \alpha_x :: \star$ is not derivable.

The real open question is the decidability of the type compatibility rule:

$$\frac{\hat{\rho}; \bullet \vDash_S \alpha_1 \rightleftarrows \theta_1 :: \kappa \qquad \hat{\rho}; \bullet \vDash_S \alpha_2 \rightleftarrows \theta_2 :: \kappa \qquad \theta_1 \equiv_{a\beta} \theta_2}{\hat{\rho} \vDash_S \alpha_1 \approx \alpha_2 :: \kappa}$$

Given θ_1 and θ_2 such that $\hat{\rho}; \bullet \vDash_S \alpha_1 \rightleftarrows \theta_1 :: \kappa$ and $\hat{\rho}; \bullet \vDash_S \alpha_2 \rightleftarrows \theta_2 :: \kappa$, $\theta_1 \equiv_{a\beta} \theta_2$ is decidable (e.g., by reducing θ_1 and θ_2 to β-normal forms, which exist and are unique due to the well-kindness of θ_1 and θ_2 (Lemma 2), and checking α-equivalence); this is the essence of the decidability of type checking of System F_ω.

However, recursive type abstractions (and the lack of other well-formedness constraints on abstract environments) can lead to "recursion" in abstract environments, such that the set $\{\theta \mid \hat{\rho}; \bullet \vDash_S \alpha \approxeq \theta :: \kappa\}$ may be infinite. Therefore, we cannot simply enumerate the expansions of α_1 and α_2 and compare the fully-closed elaborated types for definitional type equivalence. (Note that it may be possible for specific programs, such as the one given in Fig. 2b, which allowed us to obtain the minimal TCFA result given in Table 1).

In our previous type- and control-flow analysis for System F [13], decidability of type compatibility was established by relating it to regular-tree grammars [2,17,30]. A derivation of $\hat{\rho}; \bullet \vDash_S \alpha \approxeq \theta$ is interpreted as a parse tree for the derivation of the ground tree θ from the start non-terminal α in the regular-tree-grammar productions $\hat{\rho}$. The type-compatibility judgment $\hat{\rho} \vDash_S \alpha_1 \approx \alpha_2$ is derivable iff the languages generated by taking α_1 and α_2, respectively, as the start non-terminals in the regular-tree-grammar productions $\hat{\rho}$ have a non-empty intersection. The facts that regular-tree grammars are closed under intersection and that the emptiness of a regular-tree grammar is decidable [2,17,30] implies the decidability of $\hat{\rho} \vDash_S \alpha_1 \approx \alpha_2$ for System F. Note that the intersection of regular-tree grammars is with respect to syntactic equality of the ground trees; hence, this technique is not (directly) applicable to System F_ω, which would need the "intersection" to be with respect to definitional type equivalence.

Although we are cautiously optimistic about the decidability of $\hat{\rho} \vDash_S \alpha_1 \approx \alpha_2 :: \kappa$, we now turn to a graph-based formulation of a TCFA for System F_ω to obtain a *computable* abstract environment that is no worse than (and typically much better than) $\hat{\rho}^P_\top$ (for all programs), though may be worse than $\hat{\rho}^P_*$ (for some programs).

4 Flow-Graph-Based Formulation

Figures 8, 9, and 10 give an alternative flow-graph-based formulation of a TCFA for System F_ω. As a flow-graph-based formulation [23,25], it is presented as a collection of judgments for reachability in an implicit directed graph: source nodes correspond to abstract type values and abstract values appearing in the program under analysis and sink nodes correspond to type variables and expression variables of the program. Although not developed in this paper, a work-queue algorithm can be used to decide the judgments and compute the analysis result. Computability implies that this flow-graph-based TCFA is different from the specification-based TCFA; indeed, the flow-graph-based TCFA performs a 0CFA at the type-level (introducing imprecision) and requires a restriction of the β-reduction rule for definitional type equivalence for soundness.

The judgments yielding the analysis result are $P \vDash_G \hat{w} \rightarrowtail x$, asserting that the abstract value $\hat{w}$ flows to the expression variable x, and $P \vDash_G \hat{\pi} \rightarrowtail \alpha$, asserting that that the abstract type value $\hat{\pi}$ flows to the type variable α.

$\boxed{P \vDash_{\mathsf{G}} \hat{w} \rightarrowtail x}$

VALVAR
$$\frac{P \vDash_{\mathsf{G}} \hat{w} \rightarrowtail^? x : \alpha_x \quad \vDash_{\mathsf{G}} \mathsf{TyOf}(\hat{w}) \approx \alpha_x}{P \vDash_{\mathsf{G}} \hat{w} \rightarrowtail x}$$

$\boxed{P \vDash_{\mathsf{G}} \hat{w} \rightarrowtail^? x : \alpha_x}$

TRANSVAR
$$\frac{P \vDash_{\mathsf{G}} \hat{w} \rightarrowtail x \quad P \vDash_{\mathsf{G}} x \rightarrowtail^? y : \alpha_y}{P \vDash_{\mathsf{G}} \hat{w} \rightarrowtail^? y : \alpha_y}$$

BND
$$\frac{\text{let } x : \alpha_x = v \preceq_{Bnd} P}{P \vDash_{\mathsf{G}} v \rightarrowtail^? x : \alpha_x}$$

APPREC
$$\frac{x_f \; x_a \preceq_{Rhs} P \quad P \vDash_{\mathsf{G}} \mu f{:}\alpha_f.\lambda y{:}\alpha_y.e_b \rightarrowtail x_f}{P \vDash_{\mathsf{G}} \mu f{:}\alpha_f.\lambda y{:}\alpha_y.e_b \rightarrowtail^? f : \alpha_f}$$

TAPPREC
$$\frac{x_f \; [\alpha_a] \preceq_{Rhs} P \quad P \vDash_{\mathsf{G}} \mu f{:}\alpha_f.\Lambda\beta{::}\kappa_\beta.e_b \rightarrowtail x_f}{P \vDash_{\mathsf{G}} \mu f{:}\alpha_f.\Lambda\beta{::}\kappa_\beta.e_b \rightarrowtail^? f : \alpha_f}$$

$\boxed{P \vDash_{\mathsf{G}} y \rightarrowtail^? x : \alpha_x}$

APPARG
$$\frac{x_f \; x_a \preceq_{Rhs} P \quad P \vDash_{\mathsf{G}} \mu f{:}\alpha_f.\lambda y{:}\alpha_y.e_b \rightarrowtail x_f}{P \vDash_{\mathsf{G}} x_a \rightarrowtail^? y : \alpha_y}$$

APPRES
$$\frac{\text{let } x : \alpha_x = x_f \; x_a \preceq_{Bnd} P \quad P \vDash_{\mathsf{G}} \mu f{:}\alpha_f.\lambda y{:}\alpha_y.e_b \rightarrowtail x_f}{P \vDash_{\mathsf{G}} \mathsf{ExpRes}(e_b) \rightarrowtail^? x : \alpha_x}$$

TAPPRES
$$\frac{\text{let } x : \alpha_x = x_f \; [\alpha_a] \preceq_{Bnd} P \quad P \vDash_{\mathsf{G}} \mu f{:}\alpha_f.\Lambda\beta{::}\kappa_\beta.e_b \rightarrowtail x_f}{P \vDash_{\mathsf{G}} \mathsf{ExpRes}(e_b) \rightarrowtail^? x : \alpha_x}$$

Fig. 8. Flow-Graph-Based TCFA (expression variables)

The rules of Fig. 8 perform a monovariant control-flow analysis refined by the type-flow information. The VALVAR rule realizes a conditional flow ($P \vDash_{\mathsf{G}} \hat{w} \rightarrowtail^? x : \alpha_x$) as a confirmed flow when $\mathsf{TyOf}(\hat{w})$ is compatible with α_x. The TRANSVAR rule asserts the transitive flow of an abstract value through an intermediate variable. The BND rule asserts the flow of v to x due to a let $x : \alpha_x = v$ in the program. The APPREC and TAPPREC rules asserts the flow of recursive functions and type abstractions (that flow to an application or type application) to their μ-bound variables. The APPARG and APPRES rules assert the flows due to a let $x : \alpha_x = x_f \; x_a$ in the program for each recursive function that flows to x_f: the actual argument variable x_a flows to the formal parameter variable y and the function result $\mathsf{ExpRes}(e_b)$ flows to x. The TAPPRES rule similarly asserts the flow of a type-abstraction result at a type application.

The judgments and rules for the flow-graph-based formulation of type compatibility are given in Fig. 9. The judgment $P \vDash_{\mathsf{G}} \alpha_1 \approx \alpha_2 :: \kappa$ asserts that the type variables α_1 and α_2 are compatible when there exist abstract type values $\hat{\pi}_1$ and $\hat{\pi}_2$ flowing to α_1 and α_2, respectively, such that $\hat{\pi}_1$ and $\hat{\pi}_2$ are compatible. The judgment $P \vDash_{\mathsf{G}} \hat{\pi}_1 \approx \hat{\pi}_2 :: \kappa$ asserts that the abstract type values $\hat{\pi}_1$ and $\hat{\pi}_2$ are compatible; the rules compare the forms of the abstract type values, requiring corresponding constituent type variables to be compatible.

These rules begin to explain the weakening of the flow-graph-based formulation relative to the specification-based formulation. Although the rules are similar to those for definitional type equivalence (an essential aspect of type compatibility in the specification-based formulation), there

$\boxed{P \vDash_{\mathsf{G}} \alpha_1 \approx \alpha_2 :: \kappa}$

$$\frac{P \vDash_{\mathsf{G}} \hat{\pi}_1 \rightarrowtail \alpha_1 \quad P \vDash_{\mathsf{G}} \hat{\pi}_2 \rightarrowtail \alpha_2 \quad P \vDash_{\mathsf{G}} \hat{\pi}_1 \approx \hat{\pi}_2 :: \kappa}{P \vDash_{\mathsf{G}} \alpha_1 \approx \alpha_2 :: \kappa}$$

$\boxed{P \vDash_{\mathsf{G}} \hat{\pi}_1 \approx \hat{\pi}_2 :: \kappa}$

$$\frac{P \vDash_{\mathsf{G}} \alpha_{a1} \approx \alpha_{a2} :: \star \quad P \vDash_{\mathsf{G}} \alpha_{r1} \approx \alpha_{r2} :: \star}{P \vDash_{\mathsf{G}} \alpha_{a1} \rightarrow \alpha_{r1} \approx \alpha_{a2} \rightarrow \alpha_{r2} :: \star} \qquad \frac{P \vDash_{\mathsf{G}} \alpha_{g1} \approx \alpha_{g2} :: \kappa_a \Rightarrow \star}{P \vDash_{\mathsf{G}} \forall.\alpha_{g1} \approx \forall.\alpha_{g2} :: \star}$$

$$\frac{P \vDash_{\mathsf{G}} \mathsf{TyRes}(\epsilon_{r1}) \approx \mathsf{TyRes}(\epsilon_{r2}) :: \kappa_r}{P \vDash_{\mathsf{G}} \lambda^{\kappa_a \Rightarrow \kappa_r} \mathfrak{a}_1.\epsilon_{r1} \approx \lambda^{\kappa_a \Rightarrow \kappa_r} \mathfrak{a}_2.\epsilon_{r2} :: \kappa_a \Rightarrow \kappa_r} \qquad \overline{P \vDash_{\mathsf{G}} (\#i, \mathfrak{a}_1)^{\kappa_i} \approx (\#i, \mathfrak{a}_2)^{\kappa_i} :: \kappa_i}$$

$$\frac{P \vDash_{\mathsf{G}} \alpha_{f1} \approx \alpha_{f2} :: \kappa_a \Rightarrow \kappa_r \quad P \vDash_{\mathsf{G}} \alpha_{a1} \approx \alpha_{a2} :: \kappa_a}{P \vDash_{\mathsf{G}} (\alpha_{f1}\ \alpha_{a1})^{\kappa_r} \approx (\alpha_{f2}\ \alpha_{a2})^{\kappa_r} :: \kappa_r}$$

Fig. 9. Flow-Graph-Based Type Compatibility

are key differences. First, in the rule for type-level functions, the antecedent $P \vDash_{\mathsf{G}} \mathsf{TyRes}(\epsilon_{r1}) \approx \mathsf{TyRes}(\epsilon_{r2}) :: \kappa_r$ holds if there is *some* result of the first function (for *some* implicit argument) compatible with *some* result of the second function (for *some*, possibly different, implicit argument). This is weaker than the analogous definitional-type-equivalence rule, which asserts that type-level functions are equivalent when they have equivalent behaviors on *all* arguments. Second, notably absent is an analogue of the β-reduction rule for definitional type equivalence. Since type compatibility in the flow-graph-based formulation is based on the flow of abstract type values, we perform a monovariant control-flow analysis (0CFA) *at the type level* to approximate the results of type-level applications. This ensures that (any abstract value flowing to) $\mathsf{TyRes}(\epsilon_r)$ flows to α whenever whenever $\alpha_f\ \alpha_a$ flows to α and some $\lambda^{\kappa_a \Rightarrow \kappa_r}\mathfrak{a}.\epsilon_r$ flows to α_f.

The rules of Fig. 10 perform the monovariant type-flow analysis along with the 0CFA at the type level. The TyValTyVar rule realizes a conditional flow ($P \vDash_{\mathsf{G}} \hat{\pi} \rightarrowtail^? \alpha :: \kappa_\alpha$) as a confirmed flow when $\mathsf{KindOf}(\hat{\pi})$ is compatible with (syntactically equal to) κ_α. The TransTyVar rule asserts the transitive flow of an abstract type value through an intermediate type variable. The TyBnd rule asserts the flow of τ to α due to a tlet $\alpha :: \kappa_\alpha = \tau$ in the program. The TAppArg rule asserts the flow due to a let $x : \alpha_x = x_f\ [\alpha_a]$ in the program for each recursive type abstraction that flows to x_f: the actual argument type variable α_a flows to the formal parameter type variable β.

The remaining rules handle the 0CFA at the type level, asserting the flows due to a tlet $\alpha :: \kappa_\alpha = \alpha_f\ \alpha_a$ in the program for each type-level function $\lambda^{\kappa_a \Rightarrow \kappa_r}\mathfrak{a}.\epsilon_r$ that flows to α_f. The TyAppRes rule, similar to the AppRes and TAppRes rules, asserts the flow of a type-level-function result at a type-level application. The TyAppArg rule, similar to the AppArg and TAppArg rules, assert the flow of an abstract type value from the actual argument type variable α_a to the formal parameter index type variable $\mathfrak{a}$ (when the kind of the abstract type value is

A Preliminary Type- and Control-Flow Analysis for System F_ω 179

$$\boxed{P \vDash_G \hat{\pi} \rightarrowtail \alpha}$$

TYVALTYVAR
$$\frac{P \vDash_G \hat{\pi} \rightarrowtail^? \alpha :: \kappa_\alpha \quad \mathsf{KindOf}(\hat{\pi}) = \kappa_\alpha}{P \vDash_G \hat{\pi} \rightarrowtail \alpha}$$

$$\boxed{P \vDash_G \hat{\pi} \rightarrowtail^? \alpha :: \kappa_\alpha}$$

TRANSTYVAR
$$\frac{P \vDash_G \hat{\pi} \rightarrowtail \alpha \quad P \vDash_G \alpha \rightarrowtail^? \beta :: \kappa_\beta}{P \vDash_G \hat{\pi} \rightarrowtail^? \beta :: \kappa_\beta}$$

TYBND
$$\frac{\text{tlet } \alpha :: \kappa_\alpha = \tau \preceq_{TyBnd} P}{P \vDash_G \tau \rightarrowtail^? \alpha :: \kappa_\alpha}$$

TRANSITYVAR
$$\frac{P \vDash_G \hat{\pi} \rightarrowtail \mathfrak{a} \quad \text{tlet } \alpha :: \kappa_\alpha = (\#i, \mathfrak{a})^{\kappa_i} \preceq_{TyBnd} P}{P \vDash_G \hat{\pi} \rightarrowtail^? \alpha :: \kappa_\alpha}$$

$$\boxed{P \vDash_G \beta \rightarrowtail \alpha :: \kappa_\alpha}$$

TAPPARG
$$\frac{x_f\,[\alpha_a] \preceq_{Rhs} P \quad P \vDash_G \mu f{:}\alpha_f.\Lambda\beta{::}\kappa_\beta.e_b \rightarrowtail x_f}{P \vDash_G \alpha_a \rightarrowtail^? \beta :: \kappa_\beta}$$

TYAPPRES
$$\frac{\text{tlet } \alpha :: \kappa_\alpha = (\alpha_f\,\alpha_a)^{\kappa_r} \preceq_{TyBnd} P \quad P \vDash_G \lambda^{\kappa_a \Rightarrow \kappa_r} \mathfrak{a}.\epsilon_r \rightarrowtail \alpha_f}{P \vDash_G \mathsf{TyRes}(\epsilon_r) \rightarrowtail^? \alpha :: \kappa_\alpha}$$

$$\boxed{P \vDash_G \hat{\pi} \rightarrowtail \mathfrak{a}}$$

TYAPPARG
$$\frac{(\alpha_f\,\alpha_a)^{\kappa_r} \preceq_{TyVal} P \quad P \vDash_G \lambda^{\kappa_a \Rightarrow \kappa_r} \mathfrak{a}.\epsilon_r \rightarrowtail \alpha_f \quad P \vDash_G \hat{\pi} \rightarrowtail \alpha_a \quad \mathsf{KindOf}(\hat{\pi}) = \kappa_a}{P \vDash_G \hat{\pi} \rightarrowtail \mathfrak{a}}$$

Fig. 10. Flow-Graph-Based TCFA (type variables and index type variables)

compatible with the kind of the type-level function's argument). The TRANSITYVAR rule asserts the (conditional) flow of an abstract type value from an index type variable $\mathfrak{a}$ to a type variable α due to a tlet $\alpha :: \kappa_\alpha = (\#i, \mathfrak{a})^{\kappa_i}$ in the program.

It is this 0CFA at the type-level that (finally) motivates the use of index type variables. Since definitional type equivalence ignores index type variables and they play no role in the specification-based formulation of the TCFA, we could have adopted a pure de Bruijn index representation of type-level functions. However, with a pure de Bruijn index representation, the 0CFA at the type-level would be forced to conflate all de Bruijn indices, with a pair of rules like

TYAPPARG-WEAK
$$\frac{(\alpha_f\,\alpha_a)^{\kappa_r} \preceq_{TyVal} P \quad P \vDash_G \lambda^{\kappa_a \Rightarrow \kappa_r} \mathfrak{a}.\epsilon_r \rightarrowtail \alpha_f \quad \mathsf{KindOf}(\hat{\pi}) = \kappa_a}{P \vDash_G \hat{\pi} \rightarrowtail \#}$$

TRANSITYVAR-WEAK
$$\frac{P \vDash_G \hat{\pi} \rightarrowtail \# \quad \text{tlet } \alpha{::}\kappa_\alpha = \#i^{\kappa_i} \preceq_{TyBnd} P}{P \vDash_G \hat{\pi} \rightarrowtail^? \alpha :: \kappa_\alpha}$$

Essentially, without more instrumentation (e.g., a polyvariant analysis), we cannot identify the de Bruijn indices that "belong" to a particular type-level function. Index type variables (and the fact that the type system ensures that they are used correctly) allows us to distinguish the de Bruijn indices that "belong" to different type-level functions. Note, however, that we do not assume that all $\lambda^{\kappa_a \Rightarrow \kappa_r}$-bound index type variables in a program are distinct. Nor does the type system prohibit "shadowing" of index type variables; at a use $(\#i, \mathfrak{a})^{\kappa_i}$, the corresponding de Bruijn index disambiguates. Thus, the type system does not prohibit using a single type index variable throughout the program, in which case the type-level 0CFA devolves to that of the ∗-WEAK rules.

While the 0CFA at the type-level partly handles the missing analogue of the β-reduction rule for definitional type equivalence in the flow-graph-based formulation of type compatibility, there remains a final challenge. The β-reduction rule asserts the equivalence of $(\lambda \mathfrak{a}{::}\kappa_a.\theta_r)\ \theta_a$ and $\mathsf{open}(\theta_r, \theta_a, 0)$. This is problematic for our flow-graph-based formulation: all of the abstract type values that flow through the rules originate from some type value τ appearing in the program, but the adjusting of de Bruijn indices by $\mathsf{open}(\theta_r, \theta_a, 0)$ may yield an elaborated type that cannot be expressed in terms of the type values appearing in the program. One approach would be to again conflate all de Bruijn indices with an axiom asserting $P \vDash_\mathsf{G} (\#i_1, \mathfrak{a}_1)^{\kappa_i} \approx (\#i_2, \mathfrak{a}_2)^{\kappa_i} :: \kappa_i$, but this would significantly weaken the analysis, since it would judge more abstract types as compatible and filter fewer abstract values in the VALVAR rule.

Instead, we adopt a modified definitional type equivalence that restricts the β-reduction rule to locally-closed types:

$$\frac{\mathsf{lclosed}(\lambda \mathfrak{a}{::}\kappa_a.\theta_r, 0) \qquad \mathsf{lclosed}(\theta_a, 0)}{(\lambda \mathfrak{a}{::}\kappa_a.\theta_r)\ \theta_a \equiv_{\mathfrak{a}\beta}^\dagger \mathsf{open}(\theta_r, \theta_a, 0)}$$

On locally-closed types, $\mathsf{open}(\theta_r, \theta_a, 0)$ will not adjust de Bruijn indices. This modified definitional type equivalence induces a modified type system ($\vdash^\dagger P : \theta$) and specification-based formulation of the TCFA ($\hat{\rho} \vDash_\mathsf{S}^\dagger P$).

Example. The fourth column of Table 1 gives the flow-analysis results for the System F_ω program given in Fig. 2b obtained via the flow-graph-based TCFA for System F_ω. Note that $\mathsf{TCFA_G}$ is more precise than 0CFA with respect to the expression variable res1, but is less precise than $\mathsf{TCFA_S}$ with respect to the expression variable res2 and the type variables $u01$, α, $u12$, and T_{res2}. Since Id is applied to T_{id} and T_k, $\mathsf{TCFA_G}$ determines that the abstract type values $\forall.u02$ (corresponding to T_{id}) and $\forall.u06$ (corresponding to T_k) flow to t (TYAPPARG). Since $u01$ is bound to $(\#0, \mathsf{t})^\star$, those values also flow to $u01$ (TRANSITYVAR). Since each of $u12$ and T_{res2} is bound to the result of $Id\ \cdot$, all of the abstract type values that flow to $u01$ (equal to $\mathsf{TyRes}(\lambda^{\star \Rightarrow \star}\mathsf{t}.\cdot)$) also flow to both $u12$ and T_{res2} (TYAPPRES); these abstract type values also flow to α, since $u12$ flows to α (TAPPARG). Now that $\forall.u02$ flows to T_{res2}, T_{id} (the type annotation of $\mu\mathsf{id}_r{:}T_{id}.\Lambda\alpha{::}\star.\cdot$) is compatible with T_{res2} (the type annotation of res2) and $\mu\mathsf{id}_r{:}T_{id}.\Lambda\alpha{::}\star.\cdot$ flows to res2 (VALVAR).

A Preliminary Type- and Control-Flow Analysis for System F_ω 181

Flow-Analysis Soundness. For a program that is well-typed (with the modified type system), the abstract environment defined by the flow-graph-based formulation is acceptable (with the modified specification-based formulation):

❦ **Theorem 6** (Acceptability of Flow-Graph-Defined Abstract Environments).
If $\bullet \vdash^\dagger P : \theta$ and $\hat{\rho}_\mathsf{G}^P \stackrel{\text{def}}{=} (\{\alpha \mapsto \{\hat{\pi} \mid P \vDash_\mathsf{G} \hat{\pi} \rightarrowtail \alpha\} \mid \alpha \in \mathit{TyVar}\},$
$\{x \mapsto \{\hat{w} \mid P \vDash_\mathsf{G} \hat{w} \rightarrowtail x\} \mid x \in \mathit{Var}\}),$
then $\hat{\rho}_\mathsf{G}^P \vDash_\mathsf{S}^\dagger P$.

However, flow soundness is not an immediate corollary. Although $\theta_1 \equiv^\dagger_{\alpha\beta} \theta_2$ implies $\theta_1 \equiv_{\alpha\beta} \theta_2$ and $\bullet \vdash^\dagger P : \theta$ implies $\bullet \vdash P : \theta$, it is *not* the case that $\hat{\rho}_\mathsf{G}^P \vDash_\mathsf{S}^\dagger P$ implies $\hat{\rho}_\mathsf{G}^P \vDash_\mathsf{S} P$, because definitional type equivalence is used *negatively* (as guards via the $\boxed{\hat{\rho} \vDash_\mathsf{S} \alpha_1 \approx \alpha_2 :: \kappa \Rightarrow}$ terms); rather, $\hat{\rho}_\mathsf{G}^P \vDash_\mathsf{S} P$ implies $\hat{\rho}_\mathsf{G}^P \vDash_\mathsf{S}^\dagger P$. Instead, soundness of the modified specification-based formulation of the TCFA can be proven (with a suitably modified proof):

❦ **Theorem 7 (Flow-Analysis† Soundness).**
If $\bullet \vdash^\dagger P : \theta$ and $\hat{\rho} \vDash_\mathsf{S}^\dagger P$ and $\langle \bullet; P; \circ \rangle \longrightarrow^* \langle \rho'; e'; \varsigma' \rangle$, then $|\rho'| \sqsubseteq \hat{\rho}$.

Soundness of the flow-graph-based TCFA now follows as an immediate corollary.

Discussion. Although this flow-graph-based TCFA is sound and computable, it can be less precise, due to the type-level 0CFA, than the specification-based formulation and applies to fewer programs, since the program under analysis must be well-typed using the restricted β-reduction rule for definitional type equivalence. Both of these aspects raise questions about the applicability and effectiveness of this flow-graph-based TCFA to System F_ω programs of interest.

We first consider the impact due to restricting the β-reduction rule for definitional type equivalence to locally-closed types. It is unclear whether or not this restriction makes it significantly more difficult (or even impossible) to write System F_ω programs. Note that the elaborated types in the restricted β-reduction rule only need to be *locally closed*; they can have free tlet- and Λ-bound type variables. It seems that any tlet $\alpha :: \kappa_\alpha = \alpha_f\ \alpha_a$, where α_f elaborates to a type-level function and one or both of α_f and α_a elaborate to locally-open types can be rewritten so that α is bound to the β-reduction (likely requiring the introduction of additional tlet-bound type variables). This would essentially "inline" the type-level function to which α_f elaborates and could be performed as a pre-processing step; such pre-processing is not uncommon as a way to improve the effectiveness of program analyses. We also note that the definitional type equivalence of type-level applications introduced by the typing rules for a recursive type abstraction $\mu f{:}\alpha_f.\Lambda\beta{::}\kappa_\beta.e_b$ and a type application $x_f\ [\alpha_a]$ will only involve locally-closed types and are not directly affected by the restricted β-reduction rule. For example, the System F_ω program in Fig. 2b is well-typed using the restricted β-reduction rule for definitional type equivalence. However, there may yet remain essential uses of β-reduction with locally-open types.

Next, we consider the impact due to the use of a type-level 0CFA. Even with the loss of precision relative to the specification-based TCFA, as demonstrated by the example, the control-flow information obtained by the flow-graph-based TCFA is no less precise, and typically more precise, than that obtained by applying "classic" expression-level 0CFA to the type erasure of a System F_ω program. Moreover, 0CFA is widely accepted as a practical and effective program analysis [3,4,6,41,46] and the flow-graph-based TCFA will be at least as effective. Although we have not yet carefully analyzed the running time of a work-queue algorithm implementing this flow-graph-based TCFA, based on our experience with the corresponding flow-graph-based TCFA for System F, we expect the running time to be (a small) polynomial with respect to program size (at most $O(l^3 + m^5)$, where l is the size of expressions and m is the size of types in the program), making it competitive with "classic" 0CFA's running time of $O(n^3)$. Furthermore, note that these are *worst-case* running-time complexities, which assume that every abstract value flows to every expression variable and every abstract type value flows to every type variable. Type-flow and control-flow analyses are useful because they typically find much smaller flows; a flow-graph-based formulation of a flow analysis performs well in practice, because it only explores the consequences of found flows.

More insight concerning the impact of the type-level 0CFA and the restricted β-reduction rule for definitional type equivalence could be gained with an implementation, which is a direction of future work.

Finally, it is worth briefly considering the impact on the flow-graph-based TCFA if the type compatibility judgment were to be proven decidable. Since the specification-based TCFA, including type compatibility, ignores type index variables entirely, a proof of the decidability of type compatibility would allow type index variables to be eliminated from the language (using a pure de Bruijn index representation of type-level functions) and yet still have an algorithm (constructed directly from the specification-based TCFA) to compute the minimal TCFA result. Nonetheless, one would probably still want to develop a flow-graph-based formulation that incorporates insights from the decidability of type-compatibility, because a flow-graph-based formulation typically has much better running time than the naïve algorithm obtained from the specification-based formulation; the improvement for "classic" 0CFA is from $O(n^5)$ to $O(n^3)$ and for our System F TCFA is from $O(l^5 m^8)$ to $O(l^3 + m^4)$.

5 Mechanization

All of our results are mechanized [15] in the Coq proof assistant [8], using the coq-std++ library [9] for finite maps, finite sets, type classes for common notations, and a solver for goals involving set operations. All of the theorems and lemmas marked with ❦ have a corresponding statement in the mechanization.

One minor difference between the paper presentation and the mechanization is that the mechanization represents an abstract environment as a pair of a *finite* map from type variables to *finite* sets of abstract type values and a *finite* map from expression variables to *finite* sets of abstract values, treated as total functions by returning empty sets for type variables and expression variables outside the domains of the finite maps. Such a representation is only a lattice (rather than a complete lattice), since it does not have a greatest element (and, therefore, we did not state "(Forall P) $\top_{\hat{\rho}} \vDash_S P$" as a theorem).

Another minor difference is that the proposition for definitional type equivalence in the mechanization is parameterized by a boolean flag indicating whether or not the restriction to locally-closed types is in effect and all other propositions that directly or indirectly depend on definitional type equivalence are similarly parameterized. Therefore, we have a single proof of a statement of the form "(Forall b) If $\vdash^b P : \tau$ and $\hat{\rho} \vDash^b_S P$ and $\langle \bullet; P; \circ \rangle \longrightarrow^* \langle \rho'; e'; \varsigma' \rangle$, then $|\rho'| \sqsubseteq \hat{\rho}$" that simultaneously mechanizes both Theorem 3 and Theorem 7.

6 Conclusion

We have developed a preliminary type- and control-flow analysis for System F_ω with recursion, presenting both a declarative specification-based formulation and a computable flow-graph-based formulation (that is less precise and restricted to fewer input programs). In the near term, we intend to investigate the decidability of the $\hat{\rho} \vDash_S \theta_1 \approx \theta_2 :: \kappa$ judgment, evaluate the expressiveness of System F_ω with the restricted β-reduction rule for definitional type equivalence, and implement the flow-graph-based TCFA for a suitable source language. In the long term, we would like extend TCFAs by considering advanced type-system features (e.g., GADTs) and more powerful base analyses (e.g., pushdown control-flow analyses) and by developing novel applications of TCFA for program optimization.

A Language

A.1 Additional Judgments

The various $\cdot \preceq_{Syn} P$ judgments given in Fig. 11 relate a program P to its constituent expressions, binds, right-hand-sides, values, bound expression variables, type expressions, type binds, type values, and bound type variables.

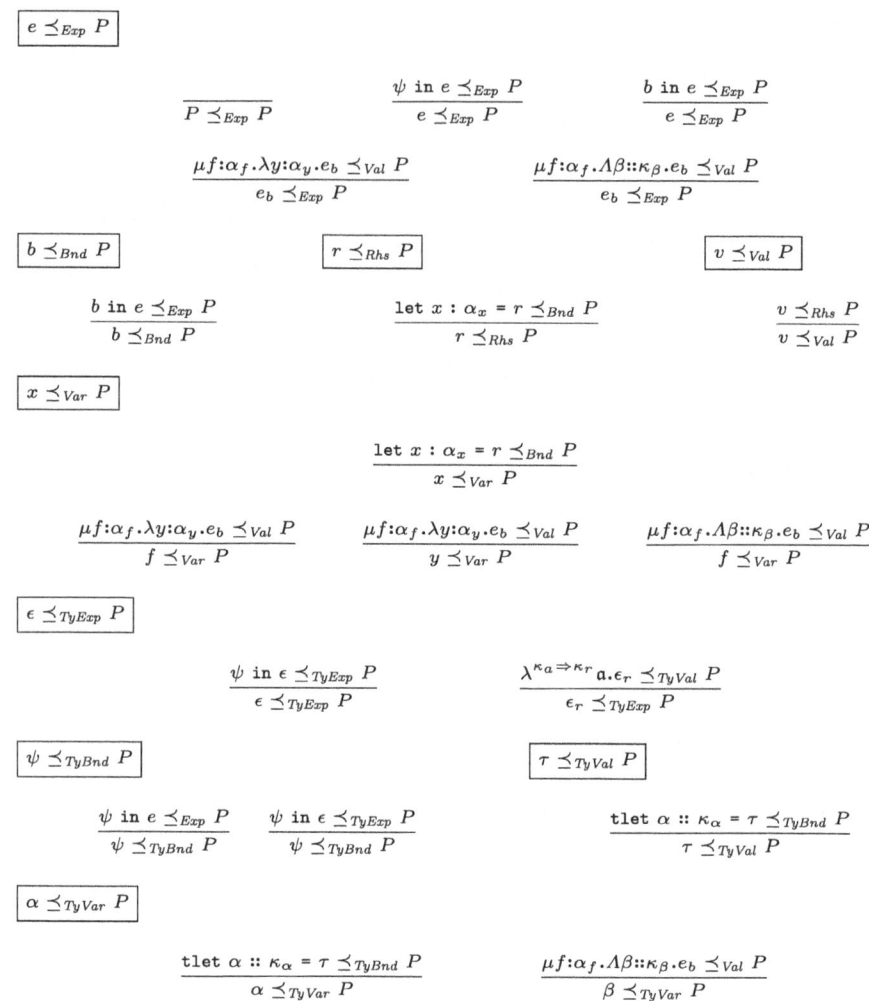

Fig. 11. Constituent Judgments

B Type System

Parallel Reduction and α-Equivalence. Although the definitional-type-equivalence judgment suffices for defining the type system and the two formulations of type- and control-flow analysis for System F_ω, the meta-theory is greatly simplified by the introduction of a *parallel reduction* judgment $\theta \Rrightarrow_\beta \theta'$ (Fig. 12), which is a directed variant of definitional type equivalence. Parallel reduction is "one-way", in the sense that an application of a function to an argument parallel reduces to the substitution, but not vice versa. Parallel reduction also requires that an indexed type variable only parallel reduces to itself (i.e., is not "up to α-

A Preliminary Type- and Control-Flow Analysis for System F_ω 185

equivalence"). To formally relate definitional type equivalence and parallel reduction, we introduce an explicit α-equivalence judgment $\theta_1 \equiv_\alpha \theta_2$ (Fig. 12). The key property is that definitional type equivalence coincides with parallel reduction to α-equivalent reducts:

❦ **Lemma 8.** $\theta_1 \equiv_{\alpha\beta} \theta_2$ *if and only if there exists θ'_1 and θ'_2 such that $\theta_1 \Rightarrow^*_\beta \theta'_1$ and $\theta_2 \Rightarrow^*_\beta \theta'_2$ and $\theta'_1 \equiv_\alpha \theta'_2$.*

$\boxed{\theta \Rightarrow_\beta \theta'}$

$$\dfrac{}{\alpha \Rightarrow_\beta \alpha} \qquad \dfrac{\theta_a \Rightarrow_\beta \theta'_a \quad \theta_r \Rightarrow_\beta \theta'_r}{\theta_a \to \theta_r \Rightarrow_\beta \theta'_a \to \theta'_r} \qquad \dfrac{\theta_g \Rightarrow_\beta \theta'_g}{\forall.\theta_g \Rightarrow_\beta \forall.\theta'_g}$$

$$\dfrac{\theta_r \Rightarrow_\beta \theta'_r}{\lambda\mathfrak{a}::\kappa_a.\theta_r \Rightarrow_\beta \lambda\mathfrak{a}::\kappa_a.\theta'_r} \qquad \dfrac{}{(\#i, \mathfrak{a}) \Rightarrow_\beta (\#i, \mathfrak{a})} \qquad \dfrac{\theta_f \Rightarrow_\beta \theta'_f \quad \theta_a \Rightarrow_\beta \theta'_a}{\theta_f\,\theta_a \Rightarrow_\beta \theta'_f\,\theta'_a}$$

$$\dfrac{\theta_r \Rightarrow_\beta \theta'_r \quad \theta_a \Rightarrow_\beta \theta'_a}{(\lambda\mathfrak{a}::\kappa_a.\theta_r)\,\theta_a \Rightarrow_\beta \mathsf{open}(\theta'_r, 0, \theta'_a)}$$

$\boxed{\theta_1 \equiv_\alpha \theta_2}$

$$\dfrac{}{\alpha \equiv_\alpha \alpha} \qquad \dfrac{\theta_{a1} \equiv_\alpha \theta_{a2} \quad \theta_{r1} \equiv_\alpha \theta_{r2}}{\theta_{a1} \to \theta_{r1} \equiv_\alpha \theta_{a2} \to \theta_{r2}} \qquad \dfrac{\theta_{g1} \equiv_\alpha \theta_{g2}}{\forall.\theta_{g1} \equiv_\alpha \forall.\theta_{g2}}$$

$$\dfrac{\theta_{r1} \equiv_\alpha \theta_{r2}}{\lambda\mathfrak{a}_1::\kappa_a.\theta_{r1} \equiv_\alpha \lambda\mathfrak{a}_2::\kappa_a.\theta_{r2}} \qquad \dfrac{}{(\#i, \mathfrak{a}_1) \equiv_\alpha (\#i, \mathfrak{a}_2)} \qquad \dfrac{\theta_{f1} \equiv_\alpha \theta_{f2} \quad \theta_{a1} \equiv_\alpha \theta_{a2}}{\theta_{f1}\,\theta_{a1} \equiv_\alpha \theta_{f2}\,\theta_{a2}}$$

Fig. 12. Elaborated Type Parallel Reduction and α-Equivalence

Typing Environments and Lookups. A typing environment (Fig. 13) records the index type variables and kinds of de Bruijn indices, maps type variables to an optional elaborated type and a kind, and maps expression variables to elaborated types. A $\beta::(\bot, \kappa_\beta)$ entry corresponds to an abstract type variable, brought into scope by a $\Lambda\beta::\kappa_\beta.e_b$, while an $\alpha::(\theta, \kappa_\alpha)$ entry corresponds to a defined type variable, brought into scope by a `tlet` $\alpha :: \kappa_\alpha = \tau$, where θ is the elaboration of τ. Well-formedness of a typing environment ($\vdash \Gamma$) requires that each elaborated type contained within is well-kinded (with kind $\star$ for an $x{:}\theta$ entry and with kind κ for an $\alpha::(\theta, \kappa)$ entry) with respect to the preceding typing environment, that the elaborated types of expression variables are locally closed (because expression variables are never bound within the body of a type-level function), and that all type variables are distinct. The requirement that all type variables are distinct, which is equivalent to a requirement that no introduced type variable shadows a type variable already in scope, ensures that no type-variable capture occurs when a defined type variable (whose elaborated type makes use of abstract type variables preceding it in the typing environment) is used after the abstract type variables are rebound (possibly with different kinds). For example, in the ill-formed typing environment $\Gamma, \alpha{::}(\bot, \star), \beta{::}(\alpha \to \alpha, \star), \alpha{::}(\bot, \star \Rightarrow \star)$, the type variable β is in scope, yet it's elaborated type $\alpha \to \alpha$ would be ill-kinded with respect to that typing environment.

We have judgments (Fig. 13) for looking up de Bruijn indices ($\Gamma(i) = (\mathfrak{a}, \kappa)$), type variables ($\Gamma(\alpha) = (\theta_\bot, \kappa)$), and expression variables ($\Gamma(x) = \theta$) in a typing environment. Looking up a de Bruijn index i in Γ requires finding the ith $(\mathfrak{a}, \kappa)$ entry of Γ from the head (right) of the typing environment. One final subtlety is that the lookup of a defined type variable fails if it would transport a locally-open elaborated type across an $(\mathfrak{a}, \kappa)$ entry. Again, this ensures that no capture, this time of a de Bruijn index, occurs. For example, in the well-formed typing environment $\Gamma, (\mathfrak{a}, \star), \beta{::}((\#0, \mathfrak{a}) \to (\#0, \mathfrak{a}), \star), (\mathfrak{a}, \star \Rightarrow \star)$, the type variable β is in scope, yet it's elaborated type $(\#0, \mathfrak{a}) \to (\#0, \mathfrak{a})$ would be ill-kinded with respect to that typing environment. This is not restrictive; it simply requires one to tlet-bind de Bruijn-index type values within the body of the innermost type-level function for which they are needed.

$$\textit{Typing environments} \quad TEnv \ni \Gamma ::= \bullet \mid \Gamma, (\mathfrak{a}, \kappa) \mid \Gamma, \alpha{::}(\theta_\bot, \kappa) \mid \Gamma, x{:}\theta$$

$\boxed{\Gamma(i) = (\mathfrak{a}, \kappa)}$

$$\frac{}{(\Gamma, (\mathfrak{a}, \kappa))(0) = (\mathfrak{a}, \kappa)} \qquad \frac{\Gamma(i) = (\mathfrak{a}, \kappa)}{(\Gamma, (\mathfrak{b}, \kappa'))(i{+}1) = (\mathfrak{a}, \kappa)}$$

$$\frac{\Gamma(i) = (\mathfrak{a}, \kappa)}{(\Gamma, \beta{::}(\theta'_\bot, \kappa'))(i) = (\mathfrak{a}, \kappa)} \qquad \frac{\Gamma(i) = (\mathfrak{a}, \kappa)}{(\Gamma, y{:}\theta')(i) = (\mathfrak{a}, \kappa)}$$

$\boxed{\Gamma(\alpha) = (\theta_\bot, \kappa)}$

$$\frac{\Gamma(\alpha) = (\bot, \kappa)}{(\Gamma, (\mathfrak{b}, \kappa'))(\alpha) = (\bot, \kappa)} \qquad \frac{\Gamma(\alpha) = (\theta, \kappa) \quad \textsf{lclosed}(\theta, 0)}{(\Gamma, (\mathfrak{b}, \kappa'))(\alpha) = (\theta, \kappa)}$$

$$\frac{}{(\Gamma, \alpha{::}(\theta_\bot, \kappa))(\alpha) = (\theta_\bot, \kappa)} \qquad \frac{\alpha \neq \beta \quad \Gamma(\alpha) = (\theta_\bot, \kappa)}{(\Gamma, \beta{::}(\theta'_\bot, \kappa'))(\alpha) = (\theta_\bot, \kappa)}$$

$$\frac{\Gamma(\alpha) = (\theta_\bot, \kappa)}{(\Gamma, y{:}\theta')(\alpha) = (\theta_\bot, \kappa)}$$

$\boxed{\Gamma(x) = \theta}$

$$\frac{\Gamma(x) = \theta}{(\Gamma, (\mathfrak{b}, \kappa'))(x) = \theta} \qquad \frac{\Gamma(x) = \theta}{(\Gamma, \beta{::}(\theta'_\bot, \kappa'))(x) = \theta}$$

$$\frac{}{(\Gamma, x{:}\theta)(x) = \theta} \qquad \frac{x \neq y \quad \Gamma(x) = \theta}{(\Gamma, y{:}\theta')(x) = (\theta_\bot, \kappa)}$$

Fig. 13. Typing Environments, de Bruinj-Index Lookups, Type-Variable Lookups, and Expression-Variable Lookups for ANF System F_ω

A Preliminary Type- and Control-Flow Analysis for System F_ω

$\boxed{\vdash \Gamma}$

$$\frac{}{\vdash \bullet} \qquad \frac{\vdash \Gamma}{\vdash \Gamma, (\mathtt{a}, \kappa)} \qquad \frac{\alpha \notin \mathrm{dom}\,\Gamma \quad \vdash \Gamma}{\vdash \Gamma, \alpha::(\bot, \kappa)} \qquad \frac{\alpha \notin \mathrm{dom}\,\Gamma \quad \Gamma \vdash \theta::\kappa}{\vdash \Gamma, \alpha::(\theta, \kappa)} \qquad \frac{\mathrm{lclosed}(\theta, 0) \quad \Gamma \vdash \theta :: \star}{\vdash \Gamma, x{:}\theta}$$

$\boxed{\Gamma \vdash \theta :: \kappa}$

$$\frac{\vdash \Gamma \quad \Gamma(\alpha) = (\bot, \kappa)}{\Gamma \vdash \alpha :: \kappa} \qquad \frac{\Gamma \vdash \theta_a :: \star \quad \Gamma \vdash \theta_r :: \star}{\Gamma \vdash \theta_a \to \theta_r :: \star} \qquad \frac{\Gamma \vdash \theta_g :: \kappa_a \Rightarrow \star}{\Gamma \vdash \forall.\theta_g :: \star} \qquad \frac{\Gamma, (\mathtt{a}, \kappa_a) \vdash \theta_r :: \kappa_r}{\Gamma \vdash \lambda\mathtt{a}{::}\kappa_a.\theta_r :: \kappa_a \Rightarrow \kappa_r}$$

$$\frac{\vdash \Gamma \quad \Gamma(i) = (\mathtt{a}, \kappa_i)}{\Gamma \vdash (\#i, \mathtt{a}) :: \kappa_i} \qquad \frac{\Gamma \vdash \theta_f :: \kappa_a \Rightarrow \kappa_r \quad \Gamma \vdash \theta_a :: \kappa_a}{\Gamma \vdash \theta_f\, \theta_a :: \kappa_r}$$

Fig. 14. Type System for ANF System F_ω (typing environments and elaborated types)

$\boxed{\Gamma \vdash \alpha \Rrightarrow \theta :: \kappa}$

$$\frac{\vdash \Gamma \quad \Gamma(\alpha) = (\bot, \kappa)}{\Gamma \vdash \alpha \Rrightarrow \alpha :: \kappa} \qquad \frac{\vdash \Gamma \quad \Gamma(\alpha) = (\theta, \kappa)}{\Gamma \vdash \alpha \Rrightarrow \theta :: \kappa}$$

$\boxed{\Gamma \vdash \tau \Rrightarrow \theta :: \kappa}$

$$\frac{\Gamma \vdash \alpha_a \Rrightarrow \theta_a :: \star \quad \Gamma \vdash \alpha_r \Rrightarrow \theta_r :: \star}{\Gamma \vdash \alpha_a \to \alpha_r \Rrightarrow \theta_a \to \theta_r :: \star} \qquad \frac{\Gamma \vdash \alpha_g \Rrightarrow \theta_g :: \kappa_a \Rightarrow \star}{\Gamma \vdash \forall.\alpha_g \Rrightarrow \forall.\theta_g :: \star}$$

$$\frac{\Gamma, (\mathtt{a}, \kappa_a) \vdash \epsilon_r \Rrightarrow \theta_r :: \kappa_r}{\Gamma \vdash \lambda^{\kappa_a \Rightarrow \kappa_r} \mathtt{a}.\epsilon_r \Rrightarrow \lambda\mathtt{a}{::}\kappa_a.\theta_r :: \kappa_a \Rightarrow \kappa_r} \qquad \frac{\vdash \Gamma \quad \Gamma(i) = (\mathtt{a}, \kappa_i)}{\Gamma \vdash (\#i, \mathtt{a})^{\kappa_i} \Rrightarrow (\#i, \mathtt{a}) :: \kappa_i}$$

$$\frac{\Gamma \vdash \alpha_f \Rrightarrow \theta_f :: \kappa_a \Rightarrow \kappa_r \quad \Gamma \vdash \alpha_a \Rrightarrow \theta_a :: \kappa_a}{\Gamma \vdash \alpha_f\, \alpha_a \Rrightarrow \theta_f\, \theta_a :: \kappa_r}$$

$\boxed{\Gamma \vdash \psi \Rrightarrow \Gamma'}$

$$\frac{\Gamma \vdash \tau \Rrightarrow \theta_\tau :: \kappa_\alpha}{\Gamma \vdash \mathtt{tlet}\, \alpha :: \kappa_\alpha = \tau \Rrightarrow \Gamma, \alpha{::}(\theta_\tau, \kappa_\alpha)}$$

$\boxed{\Gamma \vdash \epsilon \Rrightarrow \theta :: \kappa}$

$$\frac{\Gamma \vdash \alpha_r \Rrightarrow \theta :: \kappa}{\Gamma \vdash \alpha_r \Rrightarrow \theta :: \kappa} \qquad \frac{\Gamma \vdash \psi \Rrightarrow \Gamma' \quad \Gamma' \vdash \epsilon : \theta}{\Gamma \vdash \psi\, \mathtt{in}\, \epsilon \Rrightarrow \theta :: \kappa}$$

Fig. 15. Type System for ANF System F_ω (type variables, type values, type binds, and type expressions)

Typing Rules (Figures 14, 15, 16, and 17)

$\boxed{\Gamma \vdash x : \theta}$

$$\dfrac{\vdash \Gamma \quad \Gamma(x) = \theta}{\Gamma \vdash x : \theta}$$

$\boxed{\Gamma \vdash v : \theta}$

$$\dfrac{\Gamma \vdash \alpha_f : \theta_f \quad \Gamma \vdash \alpha_y : \theta_y \\ \Gamma, f{:}\theta_f, y{:}\theta_f \vdash e_b : \theta_b \\ \theta_f \equiv_{\alpha\beta} \theta_y \to \theta_b}{\Gamma \vdash \mu f{:}\alpha_f.\lambda y{:}\alpha_y.e_b : \theta_y \to \theta_b} \qquad \dfrac{\Gamma \vdash \alpha_f : \theta_f \\ \Gamma, f{:}\theta_f, \beta{::}(\bot, \kappa_\beta) \vdash e_b : \theta_b \\ \Gamma \vdash \theta_g :: \kappa_\beta \Rightarrow \star \quad \theta_f \equiv_{\alpha\beta} \forall.\theta_g \quad \theta_g\,\beta \equiv_{\alpha\beta} \theta_b}{\Gamma \vdash \mu f{:}\alpha_f.\Lambda\beta{::}\kappa_\beta.e_b : \forall.\theta_g}$$

$\boxed{\Gamma \vdash r : \theta}$

$$\dfrac{\Gamma \vdash v : \theta}{\Gamma \vdash v : \theta} \qquad \dfrac{\Gamma \vdash x_f : \theta_f \quad \Gamma \vdash x_a : \theta_a \\ \Gamma \vdash \theta_r :: \star \quad \theta_f \equiv_{\alpha\beta} \theta_a \to \theta_r}{\Gamma \vdash x_f\,x_a : \theta_r} \qquad \dfrac{\Gamma \vdash x_f : \theta_f \quad \Gamma \vdash \alpha_a \rightrightarrows \theta_a :: \kappa_a \\ \Gamma \vdash \theta_g :: \kappa_a \Rightarrow \star \quad \theta_f \equiv_{\alpha\beta} \forall.\theta_g}{\Gamma \vdash x_f\,[\alpha_a] : \theta_g\,\theta_a}$$

$\boxed{\Gamma \vdash b : \Gamma'}$

$$\dfrac{\Gamma \vdash \alpha_x \rightrightarrows \theta_x :: \star \quad \Gamma \vdash r : \theta_r \quad \theta_x \equiv_{\alpha\beta} \theta_r}{\Gamma \vdash \mathtt{let}\ x : \alpha_x = r : \Gamma, x{:}\theta_x}$$

$\boxed{\Gamma \vdash e : \theta}$

$$\dfrac{\Gamma \vdash x_r : \theta}{\Gamma \vdash x_r : \theta} \qquad \dfrac{\Gamma \vdash \psi \rightrightarrows \Gamma' \quad \Gamma' \vdash e : \theta}{\Gamma \vdash \psi\ \mathtt{in}\ e : \theta} \qquad \dfrac{\Gamma \vdash b : \Gamma' \quad \Gamma' \vdash e : \theta}{\Gamma \vdash b\ \mathtt{in}\ e : \theta}$$

Fig. 16. Type System for ANF System F_ω (variables, values, right-hand sides, binds, and expressions)

$\boxed{\vdash \pi \rightrightarrows \theta :: \kappa}$ $\qquad\qquad$ $\boxed{\vdash w : \theta}$

$$\dfrac{\vdash \rho : \Gamma \quad \Gamma \vdash \tau \rightrightarrows \theta :: \kappa}{\vdash \langle \rho; \tau \rangle \rightrightarrows \theta :: \kappa} \qquad\qquad \dfrac{\vdash \rho : \Gamma \quad \Gamma \vdash v : \theta}{\vdash \langle \rho; v \rangle : \theta}$$

$\boxed{\vdash \rho : \Gamma}$

$$\dfrac{}{\vdash \bullet : \bullet} \qquad \dfrac{\vdash \rho : \Gamma \quad \alpha \notin \mathsf{dom}\,\Gamma \quad \vdash \pi \rightrightarrows \theta :: \kappa}{\vdash \rho, \alpha \mapsto \pi : \Gamma, \alpha{::}(\theta, \kappa)} \qquad \dfrac{\vdash \rho : \Gamma \quad \vdash w \rightrightarrows \theta}{\vdash \rho, x \mapsto w : \Gamma, x{:}\theta}$$

$\boxed{\vdash \theta_r : \varsigma : \theta}$

$$\dfrac{}{\vdash \theta : \circ : \theta} \qquad \dfrac{\vdash \rho : \Gamma \quad \Gamma \vdash \alpha_x \rightrightarrows \theta_x :: \star \quad \theta_r \equiv_{\alpha\beta} \theta_x \quad \Gamma, x{:}\theta_x \vdash e : \theta_e \quad \vdash \theta_e : \varsigma : \theta}{\vdash \theta_r : \langle \rho; x; \alpha_x; e \rangle \triangleright \varsigma : \theta}$$

$\boxed{\vdash \Sigma : \theta}$

$$\dfrac{\vdash \rho : \Gamma \quad \Gamma \vdash e : \theta_e \quad \vdash \theta_e : \varsigma : \theta}{\vdash \langle \rho; e; \varsigma \rangle : \theta}$$

Fig. 17. Type System for ANF System F_ω (run-time type values, run-time values, run-time environments, stacks, and states)

C Specification-Based Formulation of TCFA

C.1 Auxiliary Judgments (Fig. 18)

$\boxed{\hat{\rho} \models_{\mathsf{S}} \pi}$

$$\frac{\hat{\rho} \models_{\mathsf{S}} \pi \quad \hat{\rho} \models_{\mathsf{S}} \tau}{\hat{\rho} \models_{\mathsf{S}} \langle \pi; \tau \rangle}$$

$\boxed{\hat{\rho} \models_{\mathsf{S}} w}$

$$\frac{\hat{\rho} \models_{\mathsf{S}} \pi \quad \hat{\rho} \models_{\mathsf{S}} v}{\hat{\rho} \models_{\mathsf{S}} \langle \pi; v \rangle}$$

$\boxed{\hat{\rho} \models_{\mathsf{S}} \rho}$

$$\frac{}{\hat{\rho} \models_{\mathsf{S}} \bullet} \qquad \frac{\hat{\rho} \models_{\mathsf{S}} \rho \quad \hat{\rho} \models_{\mathsf{S}} \pi \quad |\pi| \in \hat{\rho}(\alpha)}{\hat{\rho} \models_{\mathsf{S}} \rho, \alpha \mapsto \pi} \qquad \frac{\hat{\rho} \models_{\mathsf{S}} \rho \quad \hat{\rho} \models_{\mathsf{S}} w \quad |w| \in \hat{\rho}(x)}{\hat{\rho} \models_{\mathsf{S}} \rho, x \mapsto w}$$

$\boxed{\hat{\rho} \models_{\mathsf{S}} \hat{W} \blacktriangleright \varsigma}$

$$\frac{}{\hat{\rho} \models_{\mathsf{S}} \hat{W} \blacktriangleright \circ} \qquad \frac{\hat{\rho} \models_{\mathsf{S}} \rho \quad \forall \hat{w} \in \hat{W} \,.\, \hat{\rho} \models_{\mathsf{S}} \mathsf{TyOf}(\hat{w}) \approx \alpha_x \Rightarrow \hat{w} \in \hat{\rho}(x) \quad \hat{\rho} \models_{\mathsf{S}} e \quad \hat{\rho} \models_{\mathsf{S}} \hat{\rho}(\mathsf{ExpRes}(e)) \blacktriangleright \varsigma}{\hat{\rho} \models_{\mathsf{S}} \hat{W} \blacktriangleright \langle \rho; x; \alpha_x; e \rangle \triangleright \varsigma}$$

$\boxed{\hat{\rho} \models_{\mathsf{S}} \Sigma}$

$$\frac{\hat{\rho} \models_{\mathsf{S}} \rho \quad \hat{\rho} \models_{\mathsf{S}} e \quad \hat{\rho} \models_{\mathsf{S}} \hat{\rho}(\mathsf{ExpRes}(e)) \blacktriangleright \varsigma}{\hat{\rho} \models_{\mathsf{S}} \langle \rho; e; \varsigma \rangle}$$

Fig. 18. Specification-Based TCFA (auxiliary judgments)

D Example Flow Analyses

Table 2. Remaining flow-analysis results for the System F_ω program given in Fig. 2b via 0CFA, specification-based TCFA, and flow-graph-based TCFA; partial results were given in Table 1

	0CFA	TCFA$_S$	TCFA$_G$
id$_r$	$\{\mu\text{id}_r\colon T_{\text{id}}.\Lambda\alpha\colon\!\!:\!\star..\}$	$\{\mu\text{id}_r\colon T_{\text{id}}.\Lambda\alpha\colon\!\!:\!\star..\}$	$\{\mu\text{id}_r\colon T_{\text{id}}.\Lambda\alpha\colon\!\!:\!\star..\}$
t01	$\{\mu\text{t02}\colon u05.\lambda\text{x}\colon\alpha..\}$	$\{\mu\text{t02}\colon u05.\lambda\text{x}\colon\alpha..\}$	$\{\mu\text{t02}\colon u05.\lambda\text{x}\colon\alpha..\}$
t02	$\{\mu\text{t02}\colon u05.\lambda\text{x}\colon\alpha..\}$	$\{\mu\text{t02}\colon u05.\lambda\text{x}\colon\alpha..\}$	$\{\mu\text{t02}\colon u05.\lambda\text{x}\colon\alpha..\}$
k$_r$	$\{\}$	$\{\}$	$\{\}$
t03	$\{\mu\text{t04}\colon 11.\lambda\text{y}\colon\beta..\}$	$\{\}$	$\{\}$
t04	$\{\}$	$\{\}$	$\{\}$
t05	$\{\mu\text{t06}\colon u10.\lambda\text{z}\colon\beta..\}$	$\{\}$	$\{\}$
t06	$\{\}$	$\{\}$	$\{\}$
t07	$\{\mu\text{t02}\colon u05.\lambda\text{x}\colon\alpha..\}$	$\{\mu\text{t02}\colon u05.\lambda\text{x}\colon\alpha..\}$	$\{\mu\text{t02}\colon u05.\lambda\text{x}\colon\alpha..\}$
t08	$\{\mu\text{t02}\colon u05.\lambda\text{x}\colon\alpha..\}$	$\{\mu\text{t02}\colon u05.\lambda\text{x}\colon\alpha..\}$	$\{\mu\text{t02}\colon u05.\lambda\text{x}\colon\alpha..\}$
$u02$	–	$\{\lambda^{\star\Rightarrow\star}\mathfrak{a}..\}$	$\{\lambda^{\star\Rightarrow\star}\mathfrak{a}..\}$
$u03$	–	$\{(\#0,\mathfrak{a})^\star\}$	$\{(\#0,\mathfrak{a})^\star\}$
$u04$	–	$\{u03 \to u03\}$	$\{u03 \to u03\}$
$u05$	–	$\{\alpha \to \alpha\}$	$\{\alpha \to \alpha\}$
$u06$	–	$\{\lambda^{\star\Rightarrow\star}\mathfrak{b}..\}$	$\{\lambda^{\star\Rightarrow\star}\mathfrak{b}..\}$
$u07$	–	$\{(\#0,\mathfrak{b})^\star\}$	$\{(\#0,\mathfrak{b})^\star\}$
$u08$	–	$\{u07 \to u07\}$	$\{u07 \to u07\}$
$u09$	–	$\{u07 \to u08\}$	$\{u07 \to u08\}$
$u10$	–	$\{\beta \to \beta\}$	$\{\beta \to \beta\}$
$u11$	–	$\{\beta \to u10\}$	$\{\beta \to u10\}$
$u13$	–	$\{u12 \to u12\}$	$\{u12 \to u12\}$
$u14$	–	$\{T_k \to T_k\}$	$\{T_k \to T_k\}$

References

1. Adsit, C., Fluet, M.: An efficient type- and control-flow analysis for System F. In: Tobin-Hochstadt, S. (ed.) IFL 2014: Proceedings of the 26nd International Symposium on Implementation and Application of Functional Languages. Association for Computing Machinery, Boston, MA, USA (2014)
2. Aiken, A., Murphy, B.R.: Implementing regular tree expressions. In: Hughes, J. (ed.) FPCA 1991. LNCS, vol. 523, pp. 427–447. Springer, Heidelberg (1991). https://doi.org/10.1007/3540543961_21
3. Ashley, J.M., Dybvig, R.K.: A practical and flexible flow analysis for higher-order languages. ACM Trans. Program. Lang. Syst. **20**(4), 845–868 (1998)
4. Bergstrom, L., Fluet, M., Le, M., Reppy, J., Sandler, N.: Practical and effective higher-order optimizations. In: Chakravarty, M. (ed.) ICFP 2014: Proceedings of the 19th ACM SIGPLAN International Conference on Functional Programming, pp. 81–93. ACM, Gothenburg, Sweden (2014)
5. Cai, Y., Giarrusso, P.G., Ostermann, K.: System F-Omega with equirecursive types for datatype-generic programming. In: Majumdar, R. (ed.) POPL 2016: Proceedings of the 43rd Annual ACM SIGPLAN-SIGACT Symposium on Principles of Programming Languages, pp. 30–43. Association for Computing Machinery, St. Petersburg, FL, USA (2016)
6. Cejtin, H., Jagannathan, S., Weeks, S.: Flow-directed closure conversion for typed languages. In: Smolka, G. (ed.) ESOP 2000. LNCS, vol. 1782, pp. 56–71. Springer, Heidelberg (2000). https://doi.org/10.1007/3-540-46425-5_4
7. Contractor, M.R., Fluet, M.: Type- and control-flow directed defunctionalization. In: Chitil, O. (ed.) IFL 2020: Proceedings of the 32nd Symposium on Implementation and Application of Functional Languages. Association for Computing Machinery, Canterbury, United Kingdom / virtual (2021)
8. Coq Development Team: Coq proof assistant (2024). https://doi.org/10.5281/zenodo.11551307
9. Coq-std++ Team: Coq-std++: an extended "standard library" for Coq (2024). https://gitlab.mpi-sws.org/iris/stdpp
10. Cousot, P., Cousot, R.: Compositional and inductive semantic definitions in fixpoint, equational, constraint, closure-condition, rule-based and game-theoretic form. In: Wolper, P. (ed.) CAV 1995. LNCS, vol. 939, pp. 293–308. Springer, Heidelberg (1995). https://doi.org/10.1007/3-540-60045-0_58
11. de Bruijn, N.: Lambda calculus notation with nameless dummies, a tool for automatic formula manipulation, with application to the Church-Rosser theorem. Indagationes Mathematicae (Proceedings) **75**(5), 381–392 (1972). https://doi.org/10.1016/1385-7258(72)90034-0, https://www.sciencedirect.com/science/article/pii/1385725872900340
12. Flanagan, C., Sabry, A., Duba, B.F., Felleisen, M.: The essence of compiling with continuations. In: Cartwright, R. (ed.) PLDI 1993: Proceedings of the ACM SIGPLAN 1993 Conference on Programming Languages Design and Implementation, pp. 237–247. ACM, Albuquerque, New Mexico (1993)
13. Fluet, M.: A type- and control-flow analysis for System F. In: Hinze, R. (ed.) IFL 2012. LNCS, vol. 8241, pp. 122–139. Springer, Heidelberg (2013). https://doi.org/10.1007/978-3-642-41582-1_8
14. Fluet, M.: A type- and control-flow analysis for System F. Tech. rep., Rochester Institute of Technology (2013). https://ritdml.rit.edu/handle/1850/15920

15. Fluet, M.: A preliminary type- and control-flow analysis for System F_ω (Coq mechanization) (2024). https://doi.org/10.5281/zenodo.11583328, https://www.cs.rit.edu/~mtf/research/tcfa/TFP24/coq_tcfa_sysfw.tgz
16. Gasser, K.L.S., Nielson, F., Nielson, H.R.: Systematic realisation of control flow analyses for CML. In: Tofte, M. (ed.) ICFP 1997: Proceedings of the Second ACM SIGPLAN International Conference on Functional Programming, pp. 38–51. Association for Computing Machinery, Amsterdam, The Netherlands (1997)
17. Gecseg, F., Steinby, M.: Tree Automata. Akademiai Kiado, Budapest, Hungary (1984)
18. Girard, J.Y.: Une extension de l'interprétation de Gödel à l'analyse, et son application à l'élimination des coupures dans l'analyse et la théorie des types. In: Fenstad, J.E. (ed.) Proceedings of the 2nd Scandinavian Logic Symposium. Studies in Logic and the Foundations of Mathematics, vol. 63, pp. 63–92. Elsevier, Amsterdam, Netherlands (1971)
19. Harper, R.: Higher Kinds, chap. 18. In: Harper [20] (2016)
20. Harper, R.: Practical Foundations for Programming Languages, 2nd edn. Cambridge University Press (2016)
21. Harper, R.: System F of Polymorphic Types, chap. 16. In: Harper [20] (2016)
22. Harper, R., Morrisett, G.: Compiling polymorphism using intensional type analysis. In: Lee [27], pp. 130–141
23. Heintze, N., McAllester, D.: On the cubic bottleneck in subtyping and flow analysis. In: Winskel, G. (ed.) Proceedings of the 12th Annual IEEE Symposium on Logic in Computer Science (LICS 1997), pp. 342–351. Warsaw, Poland (1997)
24. Hoang, T., Trunov, A., Lampropoulos, L., Sergey, I.: Random testing of a higher-order blockchain language (experience report). Proc. ACM on Program. Lang. **6**(ICFP) (2022). https://doi.org/10.1145/3547653
25. Jagannathan, S., Weeks, S.: A unified treatment of flow analysis in higher-order languages. In: Lee [27], pp. 393–407
26. Jones, N.D.: Flow analysis of lambda expressions. In: Even, S., Kariv, O. (eds.) ICALP 1981. LNCS, vol. 115, pp. 114–128. Springer, Heidelberg (1981). https://doi.org/10.1007/3-540-10843-2_10
27. Lee, P. (ed.): POPL 1995: Proceedings of the 22nd Annual ACM SIGPLAN-SIGACT Symposium on Principles of Programming Languages. Association for Computing Machinery, San Francisco, California (1995)
28. Midtgaard, J.: Control-flow analysis of functional programs. ACM Comput. Surv. **44**(3), 10:1–10:33 (2012)
29. Might, M., Shivers, O.: Environmental analysis via ΔCFA. In: Peyton Jones, S. (ed.) POPL 2006: Proceedings of the 33rd Annual ACM SIGPLAN-SIGACT Symposium on Principles of Programming Languages, pp. 127–140. Association for Computing Machinery, Charleston, South Carolina (2006)
30. Mishra, P., Reddy, U.S.: Declaration-free type checking. In: Van Deusen, M.S., Galil, Z., Reid, B.K. (eds.) POPL 1885: Proceedings of the Twelfth Annual ACM SIGPLAN-SIGACT Symposium on Principles of Programming Languages, pp. 7–21. ACM, ACM, New Orleans, Louisiana (1985)
31. Morrisett, G., Harper, R.: Semantics of memory management for polymorphic languages. In: Gordon, A.D., Pitts, A.M. (eds.) Higher-Order Operational Techniques in Semantics, pp. 175–226. Publications of the Newton Institute, Cambridge University Press (1998)
32. Nielson, F., Nielson, H.R.: Infinitary control flow analysis: a collecting semantics for closure analysis. In: Jones, N.D. (ed.) POPL 1997: Proceedings of the 24th Annual

ACM SIGPLAN-SIGACT Symposium on Principles of Programming Languages, pp. 332–345. Association for Computing Machinery, Paris, France (1997)
33. Nielson, F., Nielson, H.R.: Interprocedural control flow analysis. In: Swierstra, S.D. (ed.) ESOP 1999. LNCS, vol. 1576, pp. 20–39. Springer, Heidelberg (1999). https://doi.org/10.1007/3-540-49099-X_3
34. Nielson, F., Nielson, H.R., Hankin, C.: Principles of Program Analysis. Springer-Verlag (1999). https://doi.org/10.1007/978-3-662-03811-6
35. Nielson, H.R., Nielson, F.: Flow logics for constraint based analysis. In: Koskimies, K. (ed.) CC 1998. LNCS, vol. 1383, pp. 109–127. Springer, Heidelberg (1998). https://doi.org/10.1007/BFb0026426
36. Jones, S.L.P.: Compiling Haskell by program transformation: a report from the trenches. In: Nielson, H.R. (ed.) ESOP 1996. LNCS, vol. 1058, pp. 18–44. Springer, Heidelberg (1996). https://doi.org/10.1007/3-540-61055-3_27
37. Pierce, B.C.: Higher-Order Polymorphism, chap. 30. In: Pierce [38] (2002)
38. Pierce, B.C.: Types and Programming Languages. The MIT Press (2002)
39. Pierce, B.C.: Universal Types, chap. 23. In: Pierce [38] (2002)
40. Pottier, F.: A typed store-passing translation for general references. In: Sagiv, M. (ed.) POPL 2011: Proceedings of the 38th Annual ACM SIGPLAN-SIGACT Symposium on Principles of Programming Languages, pp. 147–158. Association for Computing Machinery, London, United Kingdom (2011)
41. Reppy, J., Xiao, Y.: Specialization of CML message-passing primitives. In: Felleisen, M. (ed.) POPL 2007: Proceedings of the 34th Annual ACM SIGPLAN-SIGACT Symposium on Principles of Programming Languages, pp. 315–326. Association for Computing Machinery, Nice, France (2007)
42. Reynolds, J.C.: Towards a theory of type structure. In: Robinet, B. (ed.) Programming Symposium. LNCS, vol. 19, pp. 408–425. Springer, Heidelberg (1974). https://doi.org/10.1007/3-540-06859-7_148
43. Rossberg, A.: 1ML – core and modules united (F-ing first-class modules). In: Reppy, J. (ed.) ICFP 2015: Proceedings of the 20th ACM SIGPLAN International Conference on Functional Programming, pp. 35–47. ACM, Vancouver, BC, Canada (2015)
44. Rossberg, A.: 1ML - core and modules united. J. Funct. Program. **28**, e22 (2018)
45. Rossberg, A., Russo, C., Dreyer, D.: F-ing modules. In: Benton, N. (ed.) TLDI 2010: Proceedings of the Fifth ACM SIGPLAN Workshop on Types in Language Design and Implementation, pp. 89–102. Madrid, Spain (2010)
46. Serrano, M.: Control flow analysis: a functional languages compilation paradigm. In: George, K.M., Carroll, J., Oppenheim, D. (eds.) SAC 1995: Proceedings of the 1995 ACM Symposium on Applied Computing, pp. 118–122. Association for Computing Machinery, Nashville, Tennessee (Feb 1995)
47. Sestoft, P.: Replacing function parameters by global variables. In: Stoy, J.E. (ed.) FPCA 1989: Proceedings of the Fourth International Conference on Functional Programming Languages and Computer Architecture, pp. 39–53. Association for Computing Machinery, London, England (1989)
48. Shivers, O.: Control-flow analysis in Scheme. In: Schwartz, M.D. (ed.) PLDI 1988: Proceedings of the ACM SIGPLAN 1988 Conference on Programming Languages Design and Implementation, pp. 164–174. Association for Computing Machinery, Atlanta, Georgia (1988)
49. Shivers, O.: Control-flow analysis of higher-order languages or taming lambda. Ph.D. thesis, School of Computer Science, Carnegie Mellon University, Pittsburgh, Pennsylvania (1991), Technical Report CMU-CS-91-145

50. Stone, C.A.: Type definitions. In: Pierce, B.C. (ed.) Advanced Types and Programming Languages. The MIT Press (2005)
51. Tarditi, D., Morrisett, G., Cheng, P., Stone, C., Harper, R., Lee, P.: TIL: a type-directed optimizing compiler for ML. In: Fischer, C. (ed.) PLDI 1996: Proceedings of the ACM SIGPLAN 1996 Conference on Programming Languages Design and Implementation, pp. 181–192. ACM, Philadelphia, Pennsylvania (1996)
52. Wright, A.K., Felleisen, M.: A syntactic approach to type soundness. Inf. Comput. **115**(1), 38–94 (1994)
53. Wu, D.: A type- and control-flow analysis for System F_ω. Master's thesis, Rochester Institute of Technology, Rochester, NY (2023). https://www.proquest.com/docview/2884521850

Error Messages for Students Taught Using a Systematic Program Design Curriculum

Shamil Dzhatdoyev[1], Josephine A. Des Rosiers[2], and Marco T. Morazán[3(✉)]

[1] Axoni, New York, USA
[2] IBM Global Business Services Inc., New York, USA
[3] Seton Hall University, South Orange, USA
morazanm@shu.edu

Abstract. To make a Formal Languages and Automata Theory course more palatable to Computer Science students, a new trend has emerged that integrates the program-by-design methodology. Such courses are being successfully delivered, but have revealed that students need error messages that they comprehend and that reinforce the design steps when errors are thrown. This article describes a novel contract-based error messaging system that exploits blame assignment and message customization to help students advance their programming efforts. The described system has two novel features. The first is that the error messaging system is tightly-coupled with the steps of a design recipe for state machines. Error messages always include the step of the design recipe not successfully completed. The second is integrated support for testing, which reduces the amount of repeated code written for unit testing. The programmer optionally specifies words that ought and that ought not be in the machine's language. An error is thrown when there are words for which the expected behavior is not achieved and machine construction fails.

1 Introduction

In a Formal Languages and Automata Theory (`FLAT`) course, students are asked to construct (deterministic/nondeterministic) finite-state automata (`dfa`s/`ndfa`s), pushdown automata (`pda`s), Turing machines (`tm`s), and multi-tape Turing machines (`mttm`s). In most courses, these machines are implemented by pencil and paper or, in some cases, by using a `GUI`-based system like `JFLAP` [43,44]. Typically, these approaches expect students to learn by presenting them with examples which, in theory, they can emulate to solve problems on their own. In practice, however, many students struggle to design machines and, like any `FLAT` instructor can attest to, it is often very difficult to tease out the design of machines students submit for grading.

A new emerging trend in `FLAT` education (e.g., adopted at Seton Hall University and at Worcester Polytechnic Institute) borrows from the well-known designed-based approach pioneered by Felleisen et al. for a first course in programming [11] and from the work done to extend this pioneering approach to the first two programming courses for beginners [28,29]. It takes a programming-based approach that presents students with a design recipe to implement machines [30]. The design recipe is a series of steps that defines a systematic process to design and implement machines. By following the steps of the design recipe, a student reasons about each component needed to build a machine. For instance, students attach meaning to each state before developing a transition relation. The instruction language is FSM (Functional State Machines) [31,33], which is a domain-specific language for the FLAT classroom embedded in Racket [12]. By adopting a programming-based approach, of course, we inherit all the challenges associated with programming like, for example, learning an API, syntax errors, and type errors.

To help students overcome these challenges, in our experience, a design recipe is not enough for the bulk of the students. The top students usually are disciplined and make sure to successfully complete all the steps of the design recipe. Less disciplined students, however, may be careless and not pay careful attention to correctly completing the design recipe steps. This leads them to become frustrated when constructor misuse throws an error or when a constructed machine does not work as they expect. For instance, it is common for some students to write transition rules using states that are not part of the set of states they define. Another stumbling block for some students is the amount of repeated syntax they must write to thoroughly test a machine. More often than not, this leads them to write insufficient tests and not discover errors in the set of words accepted/rejected by a machine. We note that when a student does not follow the steps of the design recipe, it is challenging to discern why a machine works or does not work. Thus, making it difficult for instructors to grade a submission.

To address such problems, we have developed language support that helps students to successfully use machine constructors and to navigate the design recipe for machines. Specifically, the customized error messaging system described goes beyond reporting type errors. It is the first error messaging system to be tightly-coupled with the steps of a design recipe. That is, error messages indicate which step of the design recipe has not been successfully completed. To this end, contracts are ideal to develop such a system by exploiting their support for blame assignment and for customizable error messages. In this article, we put forth a novel first-order contract-based error-messaging system designed and implemented for FSM. It replaces an exception-based error messaging system that is not tightly-coupled with design recipe steps and that presents students with (sometimes very long) error messages reporting all problems found at once.

To tightly-couple error messages and the steps of the design recipe for state machines, we exploit contracts to assign blame and produce customized error messages. The new error messaging system presents the programmer with short well-focused messages one argument at a time. Every error message indicates which step of the design recipe has not been successfully completed. Thus, one of the contributions of this article is to illustrate that contracts are well-suited to support a program-by-design methodology. Although the implementation described uses Racket, the approach is not Racket-specific and the presented approach may be replicated in other programming languages. The error messaging system, in part, plays the role of a tutor that provides immediate feedback. As is well-known, providing immediate feedback and comprehensible error messages is essential in a learning context [40]. In addition, the error messages are crafted with the important characteristic of not being prescriptive [24,25]. That is, they do not suggest to the programmer the solution to the error detected. Another contribution of this article is to combine contracts and testing–an essential design recipe step. In addition to supporting the design process, this feature reduces the amount of repeated code a student needs to write. Syntax is provided for the programmer to supply a list of words that ought to be accepted and a list of words that ought to be rejected by the constructed machine. If there is a failure for any word in either list then an error is thrown and the machine constructor fails. This feature also allows instructors to easily run a test suite of their choice as they grade assignments.

The article is organized as follows. Section 2 presents a brief overview of contracts. Section 3 provides an outline to programming and designing using FSM. Section 4 discusses the principles followed to design the described error messaging system. Section 5 discusses FSM contracts for machine constructors. Section 6 presents how testing is incorporated with contracts. Section 7 compares and contrasts with related work. Finally, concluding remarks and directions for future work are presented in Sect. 8.

2 A Brief Overview of Racket Contracts

This section presents an overview of contracts in Racket. The goal is not to provide an exhaustive presentation of Racket contracts. Instead, the goal is to present enough information to help readers unfamiliar with such contracts to navigate this article.

Contracts are extensively used to build more reliable software [26,27]. They provide three desirable features to develop an error-messaging system. The first is that contracts help guarantee that the caller provides appropriate arguments and that the callee returns an appropriate value. In essence, contracts place assertions on the input and on the output, which are known as preconditions and postcondition. The caller is obliged to satisfy the precondition for each argument and the callee is obliged to satisfy the postcondition. The second is that contracts assign blame for errors more effectively than exceptions [21,38]. The third is that contracts allow a great deal of flexibility for customizing error messages.

To illustrate how contracts improve error messages, consider the following function:

```
(define (addlist lst)
   (foldl (λ (n acc) (+ n acc)) 0 lst))
```

Observe that a contract for `addlist` is not defined. In contrast, built-in Racket functions, like +, have contracts on them. Assess misusing the function as follows: `(addlist '(1 2 c))`. The error thrown is:

```
+: contract violation
expected: number?
given: 'c
```

This error is manifested where it is caught as input to + (by Racket's contract on +). This, however, is rather inaccurate and of little help to the programmer. The real blame for the error lies with the argument provided to `addlist`. To obtain a more robust error message, a contract may be placed on `addlist` as follows:

```
(define/contract (addlist lst)
  (-> (listof number?) number?)
  (foldl (λ (n acc) (+ n acc)) 0 lst))
```

The contract combinator, ->, states that the input must satisfy the contract (`listof number?`) and the returned value must satisfy the contract `number?`. These types of contracts are known as flat[1] contracts–they are fully checked immediately for a given value and are, in essence, predicates [12, Chapter 8]. Evaluating (`addlist '(1 2 c)`) yields:

```
addlist: contract violation
expected: number?
given: 'c
in: an element of
    the 1st argument of
    (-> (listof number?) number?)
contract from: (function addlist)
blaming: C:\Users\...
```

Although verbose, the error message now correctly blames the error on the argument provided to `addlist`.

The verbosity of the error message may be trimmed by defining a flat contract with a *projection function* for the behavior of applying the contract. A projection function is a curried function that consumes two arguments, a blame object and a value to protect, and that may format the error message. It tests the value to protect. If an error is not encountered the value is returned. Otherwise, a blame error is raised using the formatted error message. For example, a flat contract to test if an argument is a list of numbers may be defined as displayed in Fig. 1. The protected value, x, is tested to determine if it is a list of numbers. If it is a list of numbers then no error is raised. Otherwise, a blame error is raised that requires as input the blame object, the value protected, and a customized message (in our example, a string containing the name of the function). The formatting function given to `current-blame-format`, in this example, ignores the blame object and constructs an error message using the other two arguments. The function `addlist` may now be rewritten as follows:

---

[1] Here, "flat" should not be confused with the abbreviation, **FLAT**, for Formal Languages and Automata Theory.

```
(define/contract (addlist lst)
  (-> is-lon? number?)
  (foldl (λ (n acc) (+ n acc)) 0 lst))
```

Observe that the contract for `addlist` now combines: `is-lon?` and `number?`. Evaluating `(addlist '(1 2 c))` yields:

```
addlist: expected a list of numbers but got (1 2 c)
```

As the reader may appreciate, the error message is concise and informative. The blame for the error is better communicated to the programmer. We exploit the support for customizable messages to implement the presented system.

```
(define is-lon?
  (make-flat-contract
    #:projection
    (λ (blame)
      (λ (x)
        (current-blame-format
          (λ (blame x msg)
            (format "~a: expected a list of numbers but got ~a" msg x)))
        (if (and (list? x) (andmap number? x))
            x
            (raise-blame-error blame x "addlist"))))))
```

Fig. 1. Flat contract with a projection function for a list of numbers.

Racket provides a myriad of contract combinators. Of these, this article makes extensive use of the following three:

- and/c Produces a contract that takes as input an arbitrary number of contracts and accepts any value that satisfies all the given contracts [12, Section 8.2]
- -> Produces a contract for a function. It takes as input an arbitrary number of contracts such that the last contract is for the value returned and the rest are for the input values. The contracts for the input are applied when the function is called. The contract for the value returned is called after the function is applied to the arguments [12, Section 7.2].
- ->i As ->, produces a contract for a function. It allows expressing dependencies between arguments and results [12, Section 8.2]. Each argument and each result may be named and, subsequently, used in subcontracts. It provides support for required, optional, and keyword parameters. For each argument, there is a stanza containing the argument's name, an optional list of dependencies, and a contract that must be satisfied.

3 Introduction to FSM and the Machine Design Process

FSM provides an extensive interface to construct, access, execute, test, and visualize machines, grammars, and regular expressions[2]. Our focus is on the machine constructors: `make-dfa`, `make-ndfa`, `make-ndpda`[3], `make-tm`, and `make-mttm`. Presented in this section is an overview of input properties tested for these constructors (Sect. 3.1), the design recipe tightly-coupled with our error-messaging system (Sect. 3.2), and an illustrative example of programming in FSM (Sect. 3.3).

3.1 State Machine Construction in FSM

The argument types needed to construct state machines in FSM may be partitioned into two sets: non-dependent types and dependent types. The following descriptions summarize the properties tested by our error messaging system. The non-dependent types are described as follows:

- K: A list of distinct states, where each state is a symbol denoting an uppercase letter in the Roman alphabet.
- Σ A list of distinct symbols representing an input alphabet, where each symbol denotes a lowercase letter in the Roman alphabet.
- Γ: A list of distinct symbols representing a stack alphabet, where each symbol denotes an uppercase/lowercase letter in the Roman alphabet (only needed to build `pdas`).
- n: A positive integer for the number of tapes in a multitape Turing machine.

The dependent types are described as follows:

- S: The starting state such that S∈K.
- F: A list representing the set of distinct final states such that F⊆K
- R: A list of transition rules (described below)
- Y: An optional argument, Y∈F, that denotes the accept state for a Turing machine or a multitape Turing machine that decides or semidecides a language.

For `dfas`, R must be a transition function. For nondeterministic machines, R only needs to be a relation. This relation may be empty (e.g., for a machine that only halts). The transition rules depend on K, Σ, and Γ as follows:

```
    dfa: (K Σ K)
   ndfa: (K {Σ ∪ {ε}} K)
    pda: ((K {Σ ∪ {ε}} Γ*) (K Γ*))
     tm: ((K {Σ ∪ {@ _}}) (K {Σ ∪ {L R _}}))
   mttm: ((K {Σ ∪ {@ _}}ⁱ) (K {Σ ∪ {L R _}}ⁱ))
```

---

[2] For a complete description, the reader is referred to the FSM documentation: https://morazanm.github.io/fsm/fsm/index.html.

[3] This constructor name, instead of `make-pda`, is used to emphasize to students that `pdas` may be nondeterministic. We have found this is helpful when `pdas` are introduced in lectures.

1. Name the machine and specify alphabets
2. Write unit tests
3. Identify conditions that must be tracked as input is consumed, associate a state with each condition, and determine the start and final states
4. Formulate the transition relation
5. Implement the machine
6. Test the machine and, if necessary, redesign
7. Design, implement, and test an invariant predicate for each state
8. Prove L = L(M)

Fig. 2. The design recipe for state machines.

Each transition is a list that has a source state, an element to read (which may be empty), and a destination state. In addition, pda-rules specify the elements to pop and push, tm-rules the action to take on the tape, and mttm-rules specify the element to read on each tape and an equal number of actions to take on each tape[4].

3.2 Design Recipe for State Machines

The design recipe for state machines presented to students is displayed in Fig. 2 [30]. The steps relevant for the described error messaging system are steps 1 (to test the alphabet value), 2 (to write a valid list of testing words), 3 (to test the states, start state, and final states values), 4 (to test the transition relation value), and 6 (to determine if expected behavior is observed).

When an argument provided to a constructor does not satisfy its contract, an error is thrown. In addition to describing the error, the message highlights the design recipe step, 1–4 or 6, that has not been successfully completed.

3.3 Illustrative Example

Consider designing a pda to decide L = $a^n b^{2n}$. From the problem statement, a student can determine the needed input alphabet, {a b}, to partly satisfy Step 1 of the design recipe. Having defined the alphabet, a student can proceed to write tests to satisfy step 2 with words such as '(), '(a b b) and '(a a b b b b) that ought to be accepted and words such as '(b a) and '(a a a) that ought to be rejected. This development is helpful to satisfy step 3 by thinking about the properties words in the language have and about the steps necessary to decide if a word is in the language. In this example, for step 3, students realize that all as must be read before the bs and that for every a read two as are pushed onto the stack to be matched with every b read. This suggests, for example, that two states are needed and their roles may be defined as follows (where c_i denotes the consumed input):

---

[4] The symbols @, _, L, and R, respectively, denote the left-end marker, a blank, moving the head left, and moving the head right.

1. S is the starting state used to read and push as such that $c_i = a^i \wedge$ stack $= a^{2i}$
2. F is the only final state and is used to match every read b with an a on the stack such that $c_i = a^i b^j \wedge$ stack $= a^{2i-j}$

Based on the state roles, a student identifies the needed transition rules to satisfy step 4. For the state roles identified above, a student determines that the machine can loop on S by reading an a and pushing two as onto the stack, and can loop on F by reading a b and popping an a. Finally, the machine may nondeterministically transition from S to F. This suggests the following transitions are needed:

((S a ϵ) (S (a a)))   ((S ϵ ϵ) (F ϵ))   ((F b (a)) (F ϵ))

Based on the answers to the previous steps of the design recipe, a student implements the machine as displayed in Fig. 3a. Observe that the conditions outlined in Sect. 3.1 are satisfied by the arguments to the constructor. Thus, the machine is successfully constructed. At this point, a student can run the unit tests as part of step 6. In addition, a student can use FSM to generate a graphic for the machine's transition diagram as displayed in Fig. 3b or can visualize its execution [33].

For step 7, a student implements a predicate to validate each state's role identified in step 3. For step 8, a student proves by induction that the predicates hold during a computation and based on this that the language of the machine is correct. In the interest of brevity, these steps are not outlined given that the described error messaging system does not play a role.

Observe that writing unit tests requires a significant amount of repetition. This makes writing unit tests an error-prone process for some students. Finally, observe that it is easy to see the correspondence between the FSM implementation and the transition diagram[5]. The ease with which a diagram is translated to an FSM program and vice versa provides a low extraneous cognitive load for students learning to program in FSM.

4 Design Principles for the Error Messaging System

This section outlines the general design principles followed to develop the described error messaging system. We categorize these in three categories: composition, content, and reporting time. The composition of the error messages have the following characteristics:

1. Jargon-free vocabulary
2. Vocabulary familiar to students from classroom lectures and the textbook
3. Positive non-blaming tone
4. Full sentences used in the prose

---

[5] The FSM primitive, sm-graph, is used to automatically generate transition diagram graphics.

```
#lang fsm

;; L = a^nb^2n
(define P (make-ndpda
            '(S F)
            '(a b)
            '(a)
            'S
            '(F)
            `(((S a ,)  (S (a a)))
              ((S , ,) (F ,))
              ((F b (a)) (F ,)))))

(check-equal? (sm-apply P '(b a)) 'reject)
(check-equal? (sm-apply P '(a a a)) 'reject)
(check-equal? (sm-apply P '(a b b a a b b b b))
              'reject)
(check-equal? (sm-apply P '()) 'accept)
(check-equal? (sm-apply P '(a a b b b b))
              'accept)
```

(a) FSM implementation. (b) Transition diagram.

Fig. 3. A pda for $L = a^n b^{2n}$.

These characteristics aim to ensure that students understand the message reported and that students are not intimidated. The use of jargon-free familiar vocabulary and full sentences is especially important for students whose native language is not English.

The content of the error messages have the following characteristics:

1. State the machine component for which the error is thrown
2. State the value that led to the thrown error
3. Concretely state the reason the value provided is an error
4. State the step of the design recipe that has not been successfully completed
5. Only reports one error (regardless of the existence of multiple errors)
6. Only contains information relevant to the reported error
7. Prescriptive solutions are not offered

These characteristics aim to help students comprehend the reason behind the error and keep the cognitive load low. By reporting only one error at a time, students are encouraged to reason and solve one error instead of multiple errors at once. Logical argumentation is used to state the reason for an error to help students find a solution. By not offering possible solution, we aim to ensure that students are not misled to follow an unfruitful path to bug resolution.

The reporting time of the error messages are organized as follows:

1. Non-dependent type errors are reported first
2. Dependent type errors are reported only when no non-dependent type errors are detected
3. Detected errors for required arguments are reported before detected errors for optional arguments
4. Detected errors for optional testing arguments are reported last

The choice to report non-dependent type errors first is based on the observation that an error in such an argument can lead to errors in a dependent type. For instance, providing (m T) as states is an error that also makes the rule (M a T) an error (i.e., M is not in the provided list of states). Observe that correcting the non-dependent type error first resolves the error in the dependent type. Therefore, FSM reports non-dependent types first. Reporting errors for required arguments before optional arguments is necessary, because all optional arguments depend on required arguments. Finally, errors for optional testing arguments are reported last given that machines must be successfully constructed before testing can be performed.

Observe that the reporting time characteristics help guarantee that error messages properly identify the step of the design recipe that has not been successfully completed. For instance, reporting non-dependent type errors first, one at a time, means that either Step 1 of the design recipe has not been successfully completed (i.e., a bug detected with the provided argument for the input or the stack alphabet) or Step 3 of the design recipe has not been successfully completed (i.e., a bug detected with the provided argument for the states). If no errors are detected with the non-dependent types, then errors for the dependent types are reported. This means, for instance, that an error in the argument for the final states means that Step 3 of the design recipe has not been successfully completed and that an error in the argument for the transition relation means that Step 4 of the design recipe has not been successfully completed. The resolution of an error, of course, depends on the student's design. For instance, an error in a transition rule may be resolved by editing the rule or by editing arguments it depends on (i.e., the arguments for states and for alphabets).

We note that this framework does not report errors in the same order that corresponds to the order in which the steps of the design recipe are listed. For instance, errors for Step 2 (i.e., testing) are not reported before errors for Step 4 (i.e., transition relation). Simply stated, it is impossible to report testing failures until the machine is successfully constructed. To the extent possible, however, an effort is made to report errors detected following the order of the design step not successfully completed. For instance, errors in the argument provided for the input alphabet, associated with Step 1, are reported before errors in any subsequent step and errors in the argument provided for the final states, associated with Step 3, are reported after errors in any previous step except for Step 2.

5 FSM Contracts

This section outlines machine-constructor contracts. First, a general outline of contract design is presented. Second, contract sharing across arguments is described. Third, contract implementation for non-dependent types is outlined. Fourth, contract implementation for dependent types is presented.

5.1 General Design

In general, a machine-constructor contract combines contracts for each argument. The ->i contract combinator is used given that machine constructors expect arguments that depend on other arguments. The general structure of a machine-constructor contract is outlined as follows:

```
(->i (;; required arguments
      [states <contract>]
      [sigma  <contract>]
      [gamma  <contract>]    ;; for make-ndpda
      [start  (<dependencies>) <contract>]
      [finals (<dependencies>) <contract>]
      [rules  (<dependencies>) <contract>]
      [num-tapes <contract>]) ;; for make-mttm
     ;; optional arguments
     ([accept (<dependencies>) <contract>]  ;; for make-tm/mttm
      #:accepts [accepts (<dependencies>) <contract>]
      #:rejects [rejects (<dependencies>) <contract>])
     ;; result
     [result <contract>])
```

For each argument, there is a stanza that names said argument and associates a contract with it. The first stanzas are for required arguments and the stanzas for the optional arguments are provided in a sublist. For a dependent type, the arguments it depends on are listed in a list after the parameter's name. Any given machine constructor does not contain all the possible stanzas described above. For instance, the constructor for ndfas does not utilize contracts for a stack alphabet, the number of mttm tapes, nor an accept tm/mttm state.

The returned contract applies the given contracts from top to bottom and returns an error for the first contract that fails. As described in Sect. 4, this is important, because fixing a bug in the argument for a non-dependent type may resolve a bug in an argument with a dependency and, therefore, the programmer is never unnecessarily burdened with an error message targeting the dependent type. We observe that the reverse is not true. For instance, consider (A b C D) being the argument for states and (B a D) being part of the argument for rules. We can observe that b is a bug in the first and that (with the given argument for states) B is a bug in the second. Resolving the bug in states by changing b to B resolves the bug in the transition rule. In contrast, resolving the bug in the transition rule does not resolve the bug in the argument for `states`. Therefore, we want the first failing contract, if any, to be for non-dependent arguments as outlined above.

To outline the syntax in practice, consider the header for the `dfa` constructor:

```
(define/contract (make-dfa states sigma start finals rules
                 #:accepts [accepts '()]
                 #:rejects [rejects '()])
```

For a required non-dependent parameter, like `states`, its stanza outline is:

```
[states (and/c ...)]
```

The ... contain a contract for each property tested and they are combined using `and/c` given that all must hold for the argument given for `states` to be valid. For a dependent argument, like `finals`, its stanza is outlined as follows:

```
[finals (states) (and/c ...)]
```

This stanza lists `states` as the only value it depends on. The contracts provided to `and/c` may refer to `states`. For keyword parameters, the keyword must appear before its contract stanza. For instance, the stanza for a list of words that ought to be accepted may be outlined as follows:

```
#:accepts [accepts (states sigma start finals rules)
          (and/c ...)]
```

The list of words that ought to be accepted depends on all arguments needed for the machine under construction given that the machine must be built to apply it to each word. We note that if the contract for `accepts` is evaluated then it is safe to build the machine given that all the previous contracts are satisfied.

5.2 Contract Sharing

The contracts for several arguments have checks in common. For instance, the arguments for `states` and `finals` must be lists. A contract may be shared to perform this test. Sharing contracts requires providing an argument that identifies the argument tested and/or an argument that identifies the design recipe step that is not successfully completed when an error is thrown.

To illustrate the implementation of such a contract, consider the contract to test if an argument is a list displayed in Fig. 4[6]. This contract is used, for example, to test the argument given for `states`, for `finals`, and for `rules`. These are different arguments tested and a failure indicates not successfully completing, respectively, steps 3, 3, and 4 of the design recipe. Thus, this contract requires both an argument identifying the value tested and the step of the design recipe that may not be successfully completed. Consider providing the arguments `"final states"` and `"three"`. When an error is thrown, the error message specifies that step `three` of the design recipe is not successfully completed and that the argument for the `final states` must be a list.

---

[6] By convention, the name ends in `/c` to identify it as a contract.

```
;; string string --> contract
;; Purpose: A flat contract that checks if the input is a list.
(define (is-a-list/c field-name drstep)
  (make-flat-contract
   #:name 'is-a-list/c
   #:first-order (λ (x) (list? x))
   #:projection
    (λ (blame)
      (λ (x)
        (current-blame-format format-error)
        (raise-blame-error
          blame
          x
          (format "Step ~a of the design recipe has not been
                   successfully completed.\n The given ~a must
                   be a list."
           drstep
           field-name))))))
```

Fig. 4. The shared contract to test if an argument is a list.

5.3 Contracts for Non-dependent Types

These contracts test properties of the given argument without regard for other arguments. For instance, the argument provided for the states is tested to determine that the argument is a list, that each element is valid (as defined in Sect. 3.1), and that there are no duplicates. The states stanza is implemented as follows for all machine types:

```
[states (and/c (is-a-list/c "machine states" "three")
               (valid-listof/c valid-state?
                               "machine state"
                               "list of machine states"
                               #:rule "three")
               (no-duplicates/c "states"))]
```

The contract is-a-list/c is described in Sect. 5.2. The second contract, valid-listof/c, tests if the content of a list is valid. It takes as input a predicate to apply to each list element, and three strings to build the error message: the type of element tested (e.g., machine state), the argument that fails (e.g., list of machine states), and the design recipe rule that is not successfully completed (e.g., rule three). In addition, this contract accumulates all the elements that do not satisfy the predicate to build the error message. Finally, the last flat contract checks for duplicates and takes as input a string identifying, if necessary, the argument whose contract fails[7]. In this manner, when an error is thrown, the

---

[7] We note that no-duplicates/c does not take as input an argument for the design recipe step, because the step is easily inferred from the value received for the argu-

error is identified, blame is assigned, and the step of the design recipe violated is provided.

To illustrate this contract in practice, consider the following use of the constructor for `dfas`:

```
(make-dfa '(A B B C A)
          '(a b c D 1)
          'A
          '(B C)
          `((A b C)  (A c C)  (B c B)  (B a B))
          #t)
```

When the expression is evaluated, the reported error is:

```
Step three of the design recipe has not been successfully
completed. The following states, (A B), are duplicated
in the given states: (A B B C A).
```

Observe that the error and the design recipe step not successfully completed are clearly identified without prescribing a solution. Upon correcting the state list and calling the `dfa` constructor again, the following error is reported:

```
Step one of the design recipe was not successfully
completed. The following: (D 1) are not valid
lowercase alphabet letters in the given input
alphabet: (a b c D 1).
```

Upon correcting this error, all the (sub)contracts are satisfied and the machine is constructed.

5.4 Dependent Type Contracts

These contracts check conditions that require the value of other arguments. The transition rules for all machines, for example, depend on the states and input alphabet provided. In addition, they may depend on other arguments. For instance, the `mttm` transition rules also depend on the number of tapes and the `pda` transition rules depend on the stack alphabet.

To illustrate how such a contract is written for our error messaging system, consider the contract for `mttm` rules:

```
[rules (states sigma num-tapes)
       (and/c (is-a-list/c "machine rules" "four")
              (correct-mttm-rule-structures/c num-tapes)
              (correct-mttm-rules/c states sigma)
              (no-duplicates/c "rules"))]
```

---

ment tested (e.g., upon failure, `"states"` means step three of the design recipe is not successfully completed).

```
(make-mttm '(S A T U V H)
           `(i)
           'S
           '(H)
           `(((S (,BLANK ,BLANK ,BLANK)) (A (R R)))
             ((A (i ,BLANK ,BLANK)) (A (,BLANK i ,BLANK)))
             ((A (,BLANK i ,BLANK)) (A (R R ,BLANK)))
             ((A (,BLANK ,BLANK ,BLANK)) (T (R ,BLANK ,BLANK)))
             ((T (i ,BLANK ,BLANK)) (T (,BLANK ,BLANK i)))
             ((T (,BLANK ,BLANK i)) (T (R ,BLANK R)))
             ((T (,BLANK ,BLANK ,BLANK)) (Q (L ,BLANK ,BLANK)))
             ((Q (,BLANK ,BLANK ,BLANK)) (U (L L L)))
             ((U (,BLANK i i)) (U (i i ,BLANK)))
             ((U (i i ,BLANK)) (U (L i L)))
             ((U (,BLANK i ,BLANK)) (V (,BLANK I ,BLANK)))
             ((V (,BLANK i ,BLANK)) (V (i ,BLANK ,BLANK)))
             ((V (i ,BLANK ,BLANK)) (V (L L ,BLANK)))
             ((V (,BLANK ,BLANK ,BLANK)) (H (,BLANK ,BLANK ,BLANK))))
           3)
```

Fig. 5. A proposed mttm to add two natural numbers in unary notation.

The contract is constructed using and/c to combine 4 (sub)contracts. The first checks that the given argument is a list as described in Sect. 5.2. The second uses the number of tapes to verify the structure of the argument for the rules: the first tuple contains num-tapes + 1 symbols (i.e., a state and num-tapes elements to read) and the second tuple has the same number of symbols (i.e., a state and an action for each tape). The third uses states and sigma to verify that the contents of each transition rule is valid. The fourth checks that there are no duplicate rules (a common error among students that copy and paste a rule to write the next rule). The second and third (sub)contracts do not take arguments for the component to blame nor the design recipe step violated upon failure, because they are exclusively used to check mttm rules.

To illustrate a transition relation contract in action, consider building a 3-tape mttm to add two numbers in unary notation as displayed in Fig. 5. The first reported error informs the programmer that the first transition rule is not properly structured:

```
Step four of the design recipe was not successfully completed.
The following rule has structural errors:
  Rule ((S (_ _ _)) (A (R R))):
    The second element in the second part of the rule, (R R),
    is not a list of 3 symbols.
```

In this case, for one of the tapes there is a missing action: R. Upon adding it, the following error reported is:

```
Step four of the design recipe was not successfully completed.
The following rule has error, which makes it invalid.
   Rule: ((T (_ _ _)) (Q (L _ _))):
   The to-state, Q, is not in the given list of states.
```

Upon adding Q to the list of states, the following error is reported:

```
Step four of the design recipe was not successfully completed.
The following rule has errors, which make it invalid.
   Rule: ((U (_ i _)) (V (_ I _))):
   The action I on tape 1 must be in the given input alphabet
   or be L, R, or _.
```

Upon changing I to i, no more errors are reported and the machine successfully builds.

6 Contracts for Testing

To assist students and instructors to more easily validate machines, contracts are leveraged to easily test the expected result for given words. The syntax for machine constructors is expanded to allow for two keyword parameters: a list of words that ought to be rejected and a list of words that ought to be accepted. The contracts for these parameters are listed last and, therefore, only report an error, if any, after the contracts for all other machine components are satisfied. This approach results in three advantages. First, this mechanism may be used to collect words for which the wrong result is obtained. In this manner, instead of getting multiple failed tests reports, the user gets one error message listing the words that do not produce the expected result. Second, it cuts down on the amount of coding required by the programmer. In lieu of writing multiple tests using check-equal?, a programmer simply lists the words that ought to be tested in the proper list. Third, it simplifies how instructors may use their own test suites during grading.

For all machine types, the contracts for both keyword parameters follow the same general design based on three (sub)contracts. The first tests that the argument is a list of words and takes as input a string identifying if the tests are for accepts or for rejects. The second tests that the given words only contains elements in sigma. In this manner, students are explicitly warned about invalid testing words. The third, builds the machine and accumulates words that do not produce the expected result to build the error message. It takes as input a symbol identifying if words ought to be accepted or rejected.

For example, the #accepts contract for ndfas is implemented as follows:

```
#:accepts
  [accepts
    (states sigma start finals rules)
    (and/c (listof-words/c "accepts")
           (words-in-sigma/c sigma 'accepts)
           (ndfa-input/c states sigma start finals rules #t))]
```

The dependencies include all the elements needed to built the ndfa. The contracts that are combined take as input an argument to identify that words that ought to be accepted are being processed. For instance, ndfa-input/c takes #t as input for this purpose. The contract for #rejects is built in a similar fashion substituting "accepts" with "rejects", 'accept with 'reject, and #t with #f.

To illustrate the contract behavior, consider the following attempt to build a dfa to decide a*:

```
(make-dfa '(A B)
          '(a b)
          'A
          '(A)
          '((A a A) (A b B) (B b B) (B a B))
          #:accepts '((a a a a a) (b))
          #:rejects '((a a a) (a s a a b a)))
```

Upon evaluating this expression, the following error is reported:

```
Step six of the design recipe has not been successfully
completed. The constructed machine does not accept the
following words: ((b)).
```

Observe that the error clearly indicates that testing (step six of the design recipe) has not been properly completed. In this case, a word that is rejected appears in the accepts argument. The student must now decide if the bug is in the machine or in the test. Upon moving '(b) to the rejects argument and reevaluating, the following error is reported:

```
Step two of the design recipe has not been successfully
completed. The following words the machine should reject
contain symbols not included in sigma: ((a s a a b a)).
```

Observe that the message clearly indicates that Step 2 (i.e., writing tests) is not successfully completed.The listed word is not valid given that it contains an element not in the input alphabet (i.e., s). Upon making the listed word valid by changing the s to and a and reevaluating, the following error is reported:

```
Step six of the design recipe has not been successfully
completed. The constructed machine does not reject the
following words: ((a a a)).
```

Once again, we see that the design recipe's testing step is not successfully completed. In this case, a word that ought to be accepted appears in the rejects argument. Upon moving this word to the accepts argument, the machine is successfully constructed and tested.

7 Related Work

7.1 Error Message Design

For decades, the development of useful error messages has been the focus of many research efforts (e.g., [1–6,8,10,13,15,18–20,22,23,34,41,46]). Such a long-lasting focus is justified given that over the same time period error messages have been described as cryptic and inadequate [1–5,8,18,20,22,34,46], frustrating [6,13], and an impediment to making progress during software development [5,6,23]. Given that programmers read error messages [2,39], poor error messages have significant repercussions on programmers. For instance, programmers find reading error messages as difficult as reading code. Consequently,the completion of programming tasks is made more challenging requiring a significant time investment to understand error messages [2]. This all means that the interaction with poor error messages is inefficient and costly [4].

In 2019, an ITiCSE working group report put forth guidelines to address the shortcomings mentioned above [4]. These include:

- Making error messages comprehensible by using a positive tone and jargon-free familiar vocabulary
- Reduce the cognitive load in programmers by including relevant information in error messages and reduce repetition
- Provide context for the error such as code location and symbols/identifiers involved in the error
- Use logical argumentation to make concrete claims that help the programmer understand the reason behind the error

In addition, the report suggests that the error messaging systems should not break the abstraction barrier expected by the programmer. That is, error messages need to refer to the program under development and not to the implementation of the programming language.

The described error messaging system for FSM makes an effort to address the issues and adopt the guidelines outlined above. In this regard, error messages are phrased in jargon-free language using vocabulary used in both the classroom and in the textbook. In addition, they help the programmer to make progress by pinpointing the source of the problem and reducing redundant repetition. Redundant information is reduced by reporting one type of error at a time (instead of an error and all the derivative errors it causes) and reporting non-dependent type errors before any dependent type errors are reported.

7.2 Error Messages for Students

There is a large body work describing research on designing error messages for students, which agrees on error messages being one of the most important tools offered to students [4,5,9,17,24,25,35,36,39,47]. These efforts suggest that the error messages for students need to be jargon-free [4,9], use complete sentences [9], use simple vocabulary [9,25], reduce redundant information [17], report one error at a time [47], and be concise [4,9]. In addition, the literature suggests that students need to start corrections by addressing the first error [6,35]. There is some division on whether longer/enhanced error messages are more beneficial than shorter error messages. One study found that longer error messages are not more effective [36] while another study was inconclusive [37]. Others, however, have found that such messages help students understand and fix errors [39].

Programming languages developed for beginning students like the Racket student languages [11] and Helium [16] include customized error messaging systems. In the Racket teaching languages, error messages assist students to understand the reason for an error and to make progress towards a working program. To this end, error messages are not prescriptive and use vocabulary that is aligned with the curriculum used for instruction. In contrast, Helium suggests (i.e., prescribes) improvements using a wide range of heuristics. Although the authors report success with this system, the effectiveness of a prescribing error messaging system remains unclear at best. A study by Hartmann, for example, found a useful suggestion rate of only 47% [14]

The described FSM error messaging system is designed to help students advance their program development while at the same time assist them to understand their error. To this end, error messages are not prescriptive, employ the language used in the textbook and in the classroom, help match errors with code, and align with the curriculum's content. In contrast, the system described in this article goes a step further to help students understand their errors by indicating the design recipe step not successfully completed. In this manner, students are encouraged to think about design to understand the error message generated. That is, the error messages are intended to pull students away from a "start making code changes to fix the problems" mentality to a mentality where they must pull back from making code changes to think about their design.

7.3 The Former FSM Messaging System

Another consideration that influenced our design choices is the impact that the length of an error message can have on students. This was a source of frustration for a significant number of students that used the former FSM error messaging system [32]. In that system, multiple errors were provided at once partitioned in two by error type. The first partition reported errors on non-dependent arguments and the second reported errors on the dependent arguments. The goal was to provide an informative global view of constructor misuse. For instance, consider the following misuse of the dfa constructor:

```
(make-dfa '(A B C)
          '(a b c)
          'a
          '(B C D)
          '((A b D) (A a c) (B b B) (B a c))))
```

The error reported by the former error messaging system is:

```
-STARTING states CONTENT ERROR:
  Starting state a is not in the list of states (A B C)
-FINAL STATES CONTENT ERRORS:
  The final states (D) are not contained in the list of
  states (A B C)
-RULE CONTENT ERRORS:
  The following symbols are not defined in your list of
  states or alphabet: (D).
- THE RHS OF THE FOLLOWING RULES ARE NOT VALID:
   (A b D)
   (A a c)
   (B a c)
Check above message for errors
```

Observe that errors for multiple arguments are reported at once. In practice, such an approach revealed significant drawbacks. This approach works well for top students that take the time to read and understand all the error messages. Other students, unfortunately, are frustrated by the length of the error message and, typically, interpret that all the error messages are related to each other (when they may not). This observation guided our decision to report errors one argument at a time and to keep the error messages short. In this manner and in conjunction with coupling errors with design recipe steps, students are helped to focus on one error at a time with information that relates to the design process.

7.4 Design in FLAT Textbooks

The presented work builds on the design recipe put forth by the only **FLAT** textbook that employs a design-based and programming-based methodology [30]. This textbook applies its design recipe for state machines to the development of every `dfa`, `ndfa`, `pda`, `tm`, and `mttm` it presents. Furthermore, all machine development exercises ask students to follow the steps of the design recipe. Students reason about state machine development just as they reason about program development as advocated in the textbooks for beginners by Felleisen et al. [11], Morazán [28,29], Bloch [7], and Sperber [45]. It quickly became evident that the designed- and programming-based approach required a tailor-made error messaging system that is tightly-coupled with the design recipe.

The lack of a design-based methodology in **FLAT** textbooks/courses is not entirely surprising, because the program-by-design methodology has not yet been vertically integrated into most Computer Science curricula. The sole mention of design the authors are aware of is found in Rich's textbook [42]. This textbook asks the reader to think about the following two questions:

What do the machine states need to record?

If the language is infinite, what strings take the machine to the same state?

The first question is tantamount to the third step of the design recipe for state machines (i.e., the conditions that must be tracked). The second question is part of the fourth step of the design recipe for state machines (i.e., formulating the transition relation). Rich, however, presents no systematic way to answer these questions.

8 Concluding Remarks

This article presents a novel contract-based error messaging system for FSM–a domain specific language embedded in Racket for the Automata Theory classroom–that is tightly-coupled with state-machine design and development. The purpose is to two-fold. The first is to help students design and implement machines by associating an error message with a design-recipe step that is not successfully completed. The second is to make machine testing easier for students and instructors alike. The described system has well-known desirable features such as concise, understandable, and nonprescriptive error messages. In this manner, students are encouraged to focus on design to correctly implement their machines.

Future work includes two goals. On the one hand, we wish to collect empirical data from the students. We will measure student perceptions as well as the usefulness of the error messages. On the other hand, we plan to extend the described system to grammar constructors (i.e., regular, context-free, and context-sensitive) and to regular expression constructors. The goal is to help students always reason systematically about errors in terms of design steps.

Acknowledgements. The authors thank Tijana Minić, Oliwia Kempinski, and Joshua Schappel for their feedback during the design and the development of the presented error messaging system. In addition, the authors thank our TFP reviewers and Andrés Maldonado for their constructive feedback on previous versions of this manuscript.

References

1. Algaraibeh, S.M.: Techniques for enhancing compiler error messages. In: Proceedings of the 2022 ACM Conference on International Computing Education Research - Volume 2, ICER 2022, pp. 1–2. Association for Computing Machinery, New York (2022). https://doi.org/10.1145/3501709.3544292
2. Barik, T., et al.: Do developers read compiler error messages? In: Proceedings of the 39th International Conference on Software Engineering, ICSE 2017. pp. 575–585. IEEE, New York City(2017). https://doi.org/10.1109/ICSE.2017.59
3. Becker, B.A.: An effective approach to enhancing compiler error messages. In: Proceedings of the 47th ACM Technical Symposium on Computing Science Education, SIGCSE 2016, pp. 126–131. Association for Computing Machinery, New York (2016). https://doi.org/10.1145/2839509.2844584

4. Becker, B.A., et al.: Compiler error messages considered unhelpful: the landscape of text-based programming error message research. In: Proceedings of the Working Group Reports on Innovation and Technology in Computer Science Education, ITiCSE-WGR 2019, pp. 177–210. Association for Computing Machinery, New York (2019). https://doi.org/10.1145/3344429.3372508
5. Becker, B.A., Glanville, G., Iwashima, R., McDonnell, C., Goslin, K., Mooney, C.: Effective compiler error message enhancement for novice programming students. Comput. Sci. Educ. **26**(2–3), 148–175 (2016). https://doi.org/10.1080/08993408.2016.1225464
6. Becker, B.A., Murray, C., Tao, T., Song, C., McCartney, R., Sanders, K.: Fix the first, ignore the rest: dealing with multiple compiler error messages. In: Proceedings of the 49th ACM Technical Symposium on Computer Science Education, SIGCSE 2018, pp. 634–639. Association for Computing Machinery, New York (2018). https://doi.org/10.1145/3159450.3159453
7. Bloch, S.: Picturing Programs: An Introduction to Computer Programming, Texts in Computing, vol. 13. College Publications, Rickmansworth, UK, August 2010
8. Brown, P.J.: Error messages: the neglected area of the man/machine interface. Commun. ACM **26**(4), 246–249 (1983). https://doi.org/10.1145/2163.358083
9. Denny, P., et al.: On designing programming error messages for novices: readability and its constituent factors. In: Proceedings of the 2021 CHI Conference on Human Factors in Computing Systems, CHI 2021, Association for Computing Machinery, New York (2021). https://doi.org/10.1145/3411764.3445696
10. Eremondi, J., Swierstra, W., Hage, J.: A Framework for Improving Error Messages in Dependently-Typed Languages. Open Computer Science **9**(1), 1–32 (2019). https://doi.org/10.1515/comp-2019-0001
11. Felleisen, M., Findler, R.B., Flatt, M., Krishnamurthi, S.: How to Design Programs: An Introduction to Programming and Computing, 2nd edn. MIT Press, Cambridge (2018)
12. Flatt, M., PLT: The Racket Reference, https://docs.racket-lang.org/reference/index.html, last accessed: June 2024
13. Flowers, T., Carver, C., Jackson, J.: Empowering students and building confidence in novice programmers through gauntlet. In: 34th Annual Frontiers in Education, 2004. FIE 2004, pp. T3H/10–T3H/13 Vol. 1. IEEE, New York City (2004). https://doi.org/10.1109/FIE.2004.1408551
14. Hartmann, B., MacDougall, D., Brandt, J., Klemmer, S.R.: What would other programmers do: suggesting solutions to error messages. In: Proceedings of the SIGCHI Conference on Human Factors in Computing Systems. p. 1019-1028. CHI '10, Association for Computing Machinery, New York (2010). https://doi.org/10.1145/1753326.1753478
15. Heemskerk, B.: The Error that is the Error Message: Comparing Information Expectations of Novice Programmers Against the Information in Python Error Messages. Master's thesis, Delft University of Technology, Delft, The Netherlands (2020)
16. Heeren, B., Leijen, D., van IJzendoorn, A.: Helium, for learning haskell. In: Proceedings of the 2003 ACM SIGPLAN Workshop on Haskell, Haskell 2003, pp. 62–71. Association for Computing Machinery, New York (2003). https://doi.org/10.1145/871895.871902
17. Hundhausen, C.D., Olivares, D.M., Carter, A.S.: IDE-based learning analytics for computing education: a process model, critical review, and research agenda. ACM Trans. Comput. Educ. **17**(3) (2017). https://doi.org/10.1145/3105759

18. Jadud, M.C.: An Exploration of Novice Compilation Behaviour in Blue J. Ph.d. thesis, University of Kent at Canterbury, Cantebury, UK, October 2006
19. Kelleher, C., Cosgrove, D., Culyba, D.: Alice2: Programming Without Syntax Errors. In: User Interface Software and Technology - UIST 2002, vol. 2, pp. 35–36. ACM, New York, October 2002. https://uist.acm.org/archive/adjunct/2002/pdf/demos/p35-kelleher.pdf
20. Kohn, T.: The error behind the message: finding the cause of error messages in python. In: Proceedings of the 50th ACM Technical Symposium on Computer Science Education, SIGCSE 2019, pp. 524–530. Association for Computing Machinery, New York (2019). https://doi.org/10.1145/3287324.3287381
21. Lazarek, L., Greenman, B., Felleisen, M., Dimoulas, C.: How to Evaluate Blame for Gradual Types, Part 2. Proc. ACM Program. Lang. **7**(ICFP), August 2023. https://doi.org/10.1145/3607836
22. Leinonen, J., Hellas, A., Sarsa, S., Reeves, B., Denny, P., Prather, J., Becker, B.A.: Using Large Language Models to Enhance Programming Error Messages. In: Proceedings of the 54th ACM Technical Symposium on Computer Science Education V. 1, SIGCSE 2023, pp. 563–569. Association for Computing Machinery, New York (2023). https://doi.org/10.1145/3545945.3569770
23. Luxton-Reilly, A., et al.: Introductory programming: a systematic literature review. In: Proceedings Companion of the 23rd Annual ACM Conference on Innovation and Technology in Computer Science Education, ITiCSE 2018 Companion, pp. 55–106. Association for Computing Machinery, New York (2018). https://doi.org/10.1145/3293881.3295779
24. Marceau, G., Fisler, K., Krishnamurthi, S.: Measuring the effectiveness of error messages designed for novice programmers. In: Proceedings of the 42nd ACM Technical Symposium on Computer Science Education, SIGCSE 2011, pp. 499–504. Association for Computing Machinery, New York (2011). https://doi.org/10.1145/1953163.1953308
25. Marceau, G., Fisler, K., Krishnamurthi, S.: Mind your language: on novices' interactions with error messages. In: Proceedings of the 10th SIGPLAN Symposium on New Ideas, New Paradigms, and Reflections on Programming and Software, pp. 3–18. Onward! 2011. ACM, New York (2011). https://doi.org/10.1145/2048237.2048241
26. Meyer, B.: Advances in Object-Oriented Software Engineering, chap. Design by Contract, pp. 1–50. Object-Oriented series, Prentice Hall (1992)
27. Meyer, B.: Applying design by contract. Computer **25**(10), 40–51 (1992). https://doi.org/10.1109/2.161279
28. Morazán, M.T.: Animated Problem Solving - An Introduction to Program Design Using Video Game Development. Texts in Computer Science. Springer (2022). https://doi.org/10.1007/978-3-030-85091-3
29. Morazán, M.T.: Animated Program Design - Intermediate Program Design Using Video Game Development. Texts in Computer Science, Springer (2022).https://doi.org/10.1007/978-3-031-04317-8
30. Morazán, M.T.: Programming-Based Formal Languages and Automata Theory - Design, Implement, Validate, and Prove. Texts in Computer Science. Springer (2024). https://doi.org/10.1007/978-3-031-43973-5
31. Morazán, M.T., Antunez, R.: Functional automata–formal languages for computer science students. In: Caldwell, J.L., Hölzenspies, P.K.F., Achten, P. (eds.) Proceedings 3rd International Workshop on Trends in Functional Programming in Education, TFPIE 2014, Soesterberg, The Netherlands, 25th May 2014. EPTCS, vol. 170, pp. 19–32 (2014). https://doi.org/10.4204/EPTCS.170.2

32. Morazán, M.T., Rosiers, J.A.D.: FSM error messages. In: Achten, P., Miller, H. (eds.) Proceedings Seventh International Workshop on Trends in Functional Programming in Education, TFPIE@TFP 2018, Chalmers University, Gothenburg, Sweden, 14th June 2018. EPTCS, vol. 295, pp. 1–16 (2018). https://doi.org/10.4204/EPTCS.295.1
33. Morazán, M.T., Schappel, J.M., Mahashabde, S.: Visual Designing and Debugging of Deterministic Finite-State Machines in FSM. Electronic Proceedings in Theoretical Computer Science **321**, 55–77 (2020). https://doi.org/10.4204/eptcs.321.4
34. Moulton, P.G., Muller, M.E.: DITRAN-a compiler emphasizing diagnostics. Commun. ACM **10**(1), 45–52 (1967). https://doi.org/10.1145/363018.363060
35. Munson, J.P., Schilling, E.A.: Analyzing novice programmers' response to compiler error messages. J. Comput. Sci. Coll. **31**(3), 53–61 (2016). https://doi.org/10.5555/2835377.2835386
36. Nienaltowski, M.H., Pedroni, M., Meyer, B.: Compiler error messages: what can help novices? In: Proceedings of the 39th SIGCSE Technical Symposium on Computer Science Education, SIGCSE 2008, pp. 168–172. Association for Computing Machinery, New York (2008). https://doi.org/10.1145/1352135.1352192
37. Pettit, R.S., Homer, J., Gee, R.: Do enhanced compiler error messages help students? results inconclusive. In: Proceedings of the 2017 ACM SIGCSE Technical Symposium on Computer Science Education, SIGCSE 2017, pp. 465–470. Association for Computing Machinery, New York (2017). https://doi.org/10.1145/3017680.3017768
38. Plösch, R.: Design by contract for python. In: 4th Asia-Pacific Software Engineering and International Computer Science Conference (APSEC '97 / ICSC '97), 2-5 December 1997, Clear Water Bay, Hong Kong, pp. 213–219. IEEE Computer Society (1997). https://doi.org/10.1109/APSEC.1997.640178
39. Prather, J., et al.: On novices' interaction with compiler error messages: a human factors approach. In: Proceedings of the 2017 ACM Conference on International Computing Education Research, ICER 2017, pp. 74–82. Association for Computing Machinery, New York (2017). https://doi.org/10.1145/3105726.3106169
40. Race, P.: Using Feedback to Help Students Learn, January 2005. https://www.heacademy.ac.uk/knowledge-hub/using-feedback-help-students-learn
41. Randell, B., Russell, L.J.: Algol-60 Implementation. Academic Press Inc., USA (1964)
42. Rich, E.: Automata, Computability and Complexity: Theory and Applications. Pearson Prentice Hall (2019)
43. Rodger, S.H.: JFLAP: An Interactive Formal Languages and Automata Package. Jones and Bartlett Publishers Inc., USA (2006)
44. Rodger, S.H., Bressler, B., Finley, T., Reading, S.: Turning automata theory into a hands-on course. In: Baldwin, D., Tymann, P.T., Haller, S.M., Russell, I. (eds.) Proceedings of the 37th SIGCSE Technical Symposium on Computer Science Education, SIGCSE 2006, Houston, Texas, USA, March 3–5, 2006, pp. 379–383. ACM (2006). https://doi.org/10.1145/1121341.1121459
45. Sperber, M., Klaeren, H.: Schreibe Dein Programm! April 2024. https://github.com/deinprogramm/schreibe-dein-programm/releases/download/2024-04-05-print-2/i1.pdf. Accessed June 2024

46. Traver, V.J.: On Compiler Error Messages: What They Say and What They Mean. Adv. in Hum.-Comp. Int. **2010** (jan 2010). https://doi.org/10.1155/2010/602570
47. Wrenn, J., Krishnamurthi, S.: Error messages are classifiers: a process to design and evaluate error messages. In: Proceedings of the 2017 ACM SIGPLAN International Symposium on New Ideas, New Paradigms, and Reflections on Programming and Software, pp. 134–147. Onward! 2017. Association for Computing Machinery, New York (2017). https://doi.org/10.1145/3133850.3133862

Flattening Combinations of Arrays and Records

Reg Huijben, Jordy Aaldering(✉)[iD], Peter Achten[iD], and Sven-Bodo Scholz[iD]

Radboud University, Nijmegen, Netherlands
{Reg.Huijben,Jordy.Aaldering,Peter.Achten,SvenBodo.Scholz}@ru.nl

Abstract. Flattening is known to be a performance-boosting technique to orchestrate parallel computations on arbitrarily deeply nested arrays. In this paper, we propose a flattening transformation that deals with nested data structures that are composed of combinations of arrays and records. We choose the functional array programming language SaC as basis for this work, as it already supports flattening of homogeneously nested arrays, i.e. arrays in which all elements have the same shape. We propose an extension of SaC's syntax for records that allows records and arrays to be used in homogeneously nested form, and provide an implementation of this record transformation in the SaC compiler. Based on that extension, we show how any legal program that operates with such data structures can be transformed into an equivalent one that does not require any records at runtime.

Keywords: nested data structures · records · array programming · program transformation

1 Introduction

Nested data structures usually impose a performance and memory management challenge. A straightforward implementation allocates memory for each level of such data structures, leading to situations where the components of a data structure are spread out over a wide region of memory. This introduces several challenges in terms of runtime efficiency. Many small allocations tax memory management and reference counting, and bulk operations on such data suffer from poor memory locality.

Functional programming languages such as Haskell, Clean, and ML all use algebraic data types as one of their main ways of constructing data. To keep the memory management overhead at bay, these languages typically use garbage collection schemes like mark-and-sweep [6] or more sophisticated versions thereof such as generational garbage collection [15]. More recently, work in the context of Koka [14,16] tackles the memory management overhead by statically identifying reuse opportunities. While these techniques help deal with the memory management overhead, they usually do not improve memory locality.

Dealing with locality, in particular when aiming at bulk-synchronous parallel operations, is most effective for data that is stored in a flat way in memory. To achieve this, arrays are better suited: they lead to larger grain allocations and they allow for better data locality through the use of a flattened notation instead of a nested one. To further improve these aspects when creating nested arrays, performance oriented languages typically apply some form of flattening. Languages such as Accelerate [5], Futhark [9] and SaC [7,8] aim at purely flattened memory representations for nested arrays at runtime.

Once we add records to these languages, we run the risk of losing the advantages of a flattened representation, in particular when creating several layers of nested structures such as arrays of records that contain further arrays within their fields. A naive implementation would result in a large amount of small allocations, not to mention the loss of locality when accessing elements of fields in neighbouring records. Instead, we would like to reduce the number of allocations to only a single allocation for each field. The key idea is to enable flattening "through" records. To achieve this, we rewrite records into separate arrays; a vector of records that contain two vectors each thus turns into two two-dimensional arrays. Not only does this resolve the overhead due to allocations and the consequent loss of locality, it also implies that we no longer need to support records at runtime at all. The record extension that is described in this paper works for all uses of non-recursive records and in which all fields have known size. The extension has been implemented in SaC as of version 1.3.3-1175-1 and can be downloaded from https://sac-home.org/download:main.

The contributions of this paper are:

- A syntax for records, constructors and accessors that introduces immutable records while preserving compliance with an imperative specificational style.
- A transformation scheme that translates programs that operate on potentially nested record structures into programs that do without.
- Optimisations for eliding unused arguments and unmodified return values from function applications, respectively, and
- A real-world example showing how the presented techniques cooperatively transform nested arrays of records into record-free multi-dimensional arrays.

2 Single Assignment C

Since we use the functional array language Single assignment C (SaC) [7,8] as implementation vehicle for our proposed flattening, we provide a quick overview of the key features that we use throughout the paper. For a more in-depth introduction we refer the reader to papers such as [7,8] or the online material available on https://sac-home.org/docs:main.

SaC combines a syntax very close to the imperative language C with a purely side-effect-free semantics. This is achieved by the addition of multi-dimensional, immutable arrays to the language core, paired with an exclusion of pointers.

2.1 Arrays in SaC

Arrays in SaC are multi-dimensional; each array has a dimensionality (also referred to as *rank*) and a *shape* which describes the legal index-space of the array. This enables computations on multi-dimensional arrays to inspect and manipulate not only the data of an array but also its rank and shape. Table 1 shows a few examples for arrays in SaC. The left-most column provides an abstract / mathematical representation, the middle column contains a corresponding definition in SaC and in the right column we see the three conceptual components of these arrays: their rank (an integer value), their shape (a vector of natural numbers), and their data (a vector of the values of the array).

Table 1. Array representation in SaC

$\begin{pmatrix} 1 & 2 & 3 \\ 4 & 5 & 6 \\ 7 & 8 & 9 \end{pmatrix}$	`[[1,2,3], [4,5,6], [7,8,9]]`	rank: 2 shape: [3,3] data: [1,2,3,4,5,6,7,8,9]
$\begin{pmatrix} 1, 2, 3, -4, -5 \end{pmatrix}$	`[1,2,3,-4,-5]`	rank: 1 shape: [5] data: [1,2,3,-4,-5]
$\left(\left(true, false, true\right)\right)$	`[[true, false, true]]`	rank: 2 shape: [1,3] data: [true,false,true]
0.5	`0.5`	rank: 0 shape: [ ] data: [0.5]

From this table, we can observe that all elements of any given array ultimately can be represented as a *flat* data vector in memory. While the SaC syntax in the middle column may suggest to the programmer that some arrays indeed are nested, in fact, they are not; in SaC, nesting inherently is indistinguishable from higher-dimensional arrays. This contrasts starkly with the idea of arrays prevalent in most non-array languages, where arrays are considered inherently one dimensional and where higher dimensional arrays are mimicked through nesting. As a consequence of SaC's choice to support higher-dimensional arrays in combination with a vector for representing the shape, nested notations in SaC are restricted to the homogeneous case, i.e. all inner expressions must have the same shape. An expression of the form `[[1], [2,3]]` is not admissible in SaC.

2.2 Tensor Comprehensions

The key language construct of SaC for defining arrays from other arrays is the *Tensor Comprehension* [19,22]. A tensor comprehension is essentially a mapping of index vectors to values. For example, the tensor comprehension

```
{ iv -> arr[iv] * 2  |   iv < shape(arr) }
```

defines an array of the same shape as array `arr`, whose value in each index position `iv` equates to twice the value of `arr` at the given position. Note here that the index variable `iv` denotes an index vector with as many elements as the array `arr` has dimensions. The ability to express such operations that operate on arrays of arbitrary rank is referred to as *rank polymorphism*. If a fixed rank is expected, an explicit vector of indices can be used instead. For example,

```
{ [i,j] -> mat[j,i]  |  [i,j] < reverse(shape(mat)) }
```

transposes the two dimensional array `mat`. Despite having a fixed-rank index space, this tensor comprehension can be turned into a rank polymorphic operation by a small change into

```
{ [i,j] -> mat[j,i]  |  [i,j] < reverse(take([2], shape(mat))) }
```

The rank polymorphism of this expression is achieved through two measures. Firstly, selections in SaC select entire subarrays if there are fewer indices than the rank of the array to be selected from. Secondly, the specification of the upper bound through `reverse(take([2], shape(mat)))` ensures a two element vector as upper bound, even if the rank of the array `mat` is higher than 2.

2.3 Function Definitions, Types, and Type Patterns

Function definition in SaC look like their C counterparts. The main difference is the types that are supported in SaC. All types in SaC consist of an element type followed by a shape specification. If the shape specification is omitted, scalar arrays are expected. For example, the simple transpose can be defined as:

```
double[n,m] transpose(double[m,n] mat)
{
    return { [i,j] -> mat[j,i]  |  [i,j] < reverse(shape(mat)) };
}
```

Note here that the shape variables `m` and `n` define scalar integer values that can be referred to in the function body. This allows for a specification of the upper bound as `[n,m]` instead of `reverse(shape(mat))`.

```
double[n,m] transpose(double[m,n] mat)
{
    return { [i,j] -> mat[j,i]  |  [i,j] < [n,m] };
}
```

The dual use of shape variables for describing domain constraints as well as for capturing these values are referred to as *type patterns* [1].

3 A Syntax for Records in SaC

We try to match the syntax for records to that of C, following the overall syntactic approach of SaC. The required syntactic extensions are shown in Fig. 1.

Record type declarations `<record-decl>` start with the **struct** keyword, followed by the name of the record type. Such a record can contain any positive number of fields, where each field can be of arbitrary type as long as the shapes of

```
<record-decl>     ::= 'struct' <id> '{' (<field-type> <id> ';')+ '}'
<field-type>      ::= <type> <static-shp>?
                    | 'struct' <id> <static-shp>?
<static-shp>      ::= '[' <int> (',' <int>)* ']'
<record-type>     ::= 'struct' <id> <shp>?
<record-field>    ::= <expr> '.' <id>
<full-constr>     ::= <id> '{' <expr> (',' <expr>)* '}'
<default-constr>  ::= <id> '{' '}'
<explicit-constr> ::= <id> '{' <explicit-set> (',' <explicit-set>)* '}'
<explicit-set>    ::= '.' <id> '=' <expr>
```

Fig. 1. EBNF for SaC record syntax.

these field-types are statically fixed. This includes record types as well, provided that there is no recursive use.

Record types `<record-type>` extend the set of basic types[1] in SaC. They can occur in all positions where basic types are admissible such as function signatures, variable declarations, or type assertions. Similar to record type declarations, record types start with the **struct** keyword followed by the name of the record type. Note here that the restriction to statically fixed shapes only applies to record fields, not the construction of record types. A vector of statically unknown length of records **struct T** can be denoted by the type **struct T[.]**.

Fields of records `<record-field>` can be accessed by using a dot-symbol in infix notation. Similar to the modification of array elements, we support the use of such infix-dot-symbols on the left hand side of assignments as well.

We provide three ways for constructing record values as reflected by the last non-terminals in the syntax extension all of which constitute expressions in SaC. First, `<full-constr>` constructs a record value by enumerating a value for every field of the record, in the same order as those fields are defined in the corresponding record type declaration. Second, `<default-constr>` constructs a record value using default values for each of the fields. Examples of default values are 0 for numbers and *false* for booleans. The default value for an array is an array of the given shape, filled with the corresponding default values. Third, `<explicit-constr>` assigns values to selected fields and assigns the default value to the non mentioned fields.

4 Example

As a running real-world example we consider the *naive n-body problem*, which is concerned with predicting the individual motions of a group of celestial bodies. We define a record **Body** to keep track of these celestial bodies, as well as a **Vector3** record for the position of this body. Using these we define a function that

---

[1] **byte, short, int, long, longlong, ubyte, ushort, uint, ulong, ulonglong, bool, char, float, double**.

computes the acceleration one body imposes on another, along with a function that computes the acceleration imposed on each body by all other bodies.

```
struct Vector3 {
    double x;
    double y;
    double z;
};
struct Body {
    struct Vector3 pos;
    double mass;
};
struct Vector3
acc(struct Body b1, struct Body b2)
{
    dir = b2.pos - b1.pos;
    factor = l2norm(dir) == 0.0
        ? 0.0 : b2.mass / pow3(l2norm(dir));
    return factor * dir;
}
struct Body[n]
acc_v(struct Body[n] bodies)
{
    return { [i] -> rsum(1, { [j] -> acc(bodies[i], bodies[j])
                            | [j] < shape(bodies) })
           | [i] < shape(bodies) };
}
```

With these acceleration functions we can define a function that computes the updated positions of all bodies after some given delta time dt. For this each body additionally requires a velocity field, which we can add to the record without requiring modifications to the acceleration function, highlighting one of the benefits of using records.

```
struct Body {
    struct Vector3 pos;
    double[3] vel;
    double mass;
};
struct Body[n]
timestep(struct Body[n] bodies, double dt)
{
    acceleration = acc_v(bodies);
    bodies.pos += bodies.vel * dt;
    bodies.vel += acceleration * dt;
    return bodies;
}
```

5 Key Idea

In a typical naively nested memory layout for arrays of records (Fig. 2) each element in the array is a pointer to a single record object, where each of those objects has a single value for each field of that record. In the case that these fields are arrays or nested records, they are yet again pointers to that array or record object respectively. Such a naive nesting requires a large amount of memory allocations, and consequently results in a blowup in the amount of reference counting operations that is required. Furthermore this naive nesting has a negative impact on the memory locality of these objects; adjacent record fields in an array of records are no longer adjacent in memory. This limits the applicability of vectorization of operations on arrays of records.

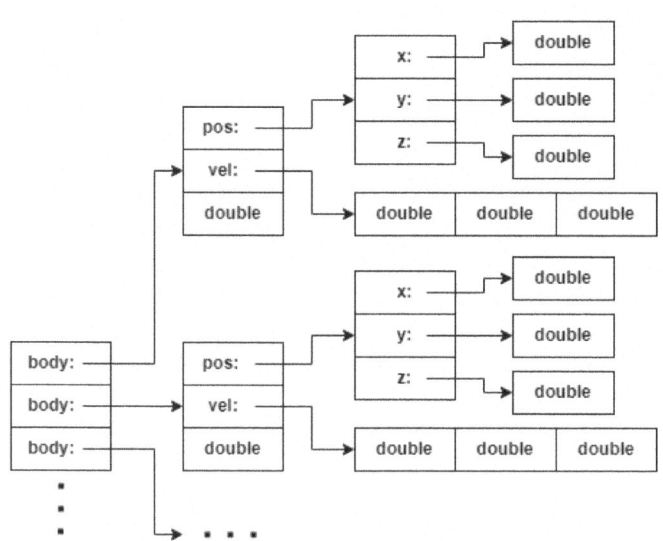

Fig. 2. Naively nested memory layout of the Body record.

In order to combat these drawbacks we rewrite records into a flattened array representation, where each base-type field is defined by a single array. Nested records are recursively flattened until only base-types remain. In the proposed flattened representation, only a single allocation is required for each base-type field of a record. Consequently this also decreases the amount of reference counting operations that is required, and opens the door to vectorization of operations on these arrays.

This transformation from arrays of records to flattened arrays additionally requires a rewrite of the rest of a program. Programs need to be rewritten to operate on multiple arrays, instead of on singular arrays of records. In the case of the n-body example, the record declaration is removed and the acceleration and timestep functions are rewritten to operate on arrays instead. These functions now require additional arguments and return multiple return values, instead of only a single record. Unused record fields are removed from these rewritten function definitions. Below we show the result of the rewriting process on the acceleration functions from the example.

```
double, double, double
acc(double x1, double y1, double z1,
    double x2, double y2, double z2,
    double mass2)
```

```
{
    xdir = x2 - x1;
    ydir = y2 - y1;
    zdir = z2 - z1;
    factor = l2norm(xdir, ydir, zdir) == 0.0
        ? 0.0 : m / pow3(l2norm(xdir, ydir, zdir));
    return (xdir * factor, ydir * factor, zdir * factor);
}

double[n], double[n], double[n]
acc_v(double[n] xs, double[n] ys, double[n] zs, double[n] masses)
{
    return { [i] -> rsum(1, { [j] -> acc(xs[i], ys[i], zs[i],
                                         xs[j], ys[j], zs[j],
                                         masses[j])
                              | [j] < [n] })
             | [i] < [n] };
}
```

The example shows that the transformation is not trivial. When arrays and records are combined and nested, the transformation to the required homogeneous arrays by SaC can become complex. To ensure that arrays of records can be transformed into homogeneous arrays we disallow (mutual) recursion and we require that array fields in records are of a statically known and fixed shape.

Additional effort is required for primitive functions, in order for those to be able to operate on record types. For example, it should be possible to get the dimensionality or shape of an array of records, or to select one of its elements, without the need for a special syntax. Similarly we need to ensure that tensor comprehensions and other array constructors are able to operate on multiple arguments. Already in the n-body example we see that often not all fields defined in a record are used by a function, and that not all fields of a record need to be returned. In order to limit the overhead introduced by an increase in the amount of arguments, and to maximise optimisation potential, two more optimisations are required to remove these unused arguments and return values.

6 Transformation

Similarly to earlier approaches (Homann et al. [11], Jubertie et al. [12], Kofler et al. [13]) we aim to improve the runtime performance of programs with records by transforming arrays of records into records of arrays. However, we go one step further and remove records from programs entirely. As discussed in Sect. 5 this transformation decreases the number of allocations and reference counting operations, as well as improving memory locality. An additional benefit is that removing records from programs in their entirety decreases the implementation effort of adding records to the language, since no modifications to the type system and other existing compiler phases are necessary. Especially in a large-scale project such as SaC, with many compiler phases that would require modifications to support records, such a transformation is paramount for a feasible implementation effort.

After the record transformation has been applied to a program, that program will no longer contain any record types. Instead, all record arguments and variable declarations are replaced by distinct arrays. Record constructors and field accessors and mutators are transformed into functions that operate on arrays instead. Any user-defined functions and primitive operations on records are similarly transformed into operations on arrays.

In the case of SaC this record transformation is actually split up into two separate phases. During the parsing phase we replace records by a temporary "external" type, which is only fully removed after the type checking phase. This ensures that error messages generated by the type checker still pertain to record types without having to add support for records to the type checker, and that these error messages remain consistent with the pre-existing error messages. For example we get the following error message if we try to add a body to a string.

```
No definition found for a function "ArrayArith::+" that accepts
an argument of type "_MAIN::_struct_Body" as parameter no 1.
Full argument types are "( _MAIN::_struct_Body, String::string)".
```

However had records already been transformed into distinct arrays, the error message would look as follows and the relation between the error and the actual written code would be lost.

```
No definition found for a function "Array::+" that
expects 4 argument(s) and yields 1 return value(s)
```

For the sake of brevity however, we omit this additional step in the following transformation rules because it is specific to SaC and is not relevant to the actual transformation of records to arrays.

6.1 Constructors, Accessors, and Mutators

The first step in transforming programs with records into programs without records is to replace record constructors, accessors, and mutators by generated function definitions. For each record type in a program we generate a full constructor and a default constructor function, as well as accessor and mutator functions for every field of that record. Any record constructors, accessors, and mutators in the program are then replaced by applications of the corresponding generated functions.

Accessors and Mutators. Normally an infix dot symbol is used to access or mutate the field of a record type, e.g. `bodies.pos`. In order to access or mutate a nested field, multiple accessors or mutators may be chained. However after programs have been transformed there will no longer be any records, and such a selection is no longer applicable. Instead we generate accessor and mutator functions for every field occurring in a record type. To access and mutate the position field of the body record, for example, these would be `body_set_pos` and `body_get_pos` respectively. For a record type with n fields, we generate an accessor and a mutator function for every field $i \in [1, n]$:

```
type₁[shp₁], ..., typeₙ[shpₙ]
rt_get_idᵢ(type₁[shp₁] id₁, ..., typeₙ[shpₙ] idₙ)
{
```

```
        return id_i;
}
type_1[shp_1], ..., type_n[shp_n]
rt_set_id_i(type_i[shp_i] value, type_1[shp_1] id_1, ..., type_n[shp_n] id_n)
{
        return (id_1, ..., id_{i-1}, value, id_{i+1}, ..., id_n);
}
```

Note that the argument and return types in these generated functions can still be records at this point. We expand these records at a later step, along with the expansion of records in user-defined functions.

Accessors and mutators through field selection can now be replaced by applications of these generated functions. For a field selection `id = x.y` on the right-hand-side of a let-expression we apply the accessor function `id = rt_get_y(x)`, whereas if on the left-hand-side there occurs a field selection `x.y = expr`, the mutator function is applied `rt_set_y(expr, x)`.

Constructors. Syntactically there are three kinds of record constructors: a full constructor that expects a value for each field in order, a default constructor that takes no arguments and assigns a default (zero) value to each field, and an explicit constructor with only the values for some fields explicitly defined. For every record type `rt` in the program we generate a new function definition for both the full and the default constructor:

```
type_1[shp_1], ..., type_n[shp_n]
new_rt(type_1[shp_1] id_1, ..., type_n[shp_n] id_n)
{
        return (id_1, ..., id_n);
}
type_1[shp_1], ..., type_n[shp_n]
zero(type_1[*] id_1, ..., type_n[*] id_n)
{
        return new_rt(genarray([shp_1], zero([:type_1]))
                      ...
                      genarray([shp_n], zero([:type_n])));
}
```

Where `[:type]` is an empty array of the given type. This ensures that the correct overload of the `zero` function is applied, returning the default value for that type.

Now whenever we encounter a full constructor of the form `rt{expr_1, ..., expr_n}` we replace it by `new_rt(expr_1, ..., expr_n)`, and whenever we encounter a default constructor of the form `rt{}` we replace it by `zero([:rt])`. Finally, if we encounter an explicit constructor of the form

`rt{.field_q = value_q, ..., .field_r = value_r}`

we first apply the default constructor, followed by a chain of mutator functions for the explicitly given fields.

```
rt_set_id_r(value_r,
        ...
        rt_set_id_q(value_q, zero([:rt])));
```

6.2 Expanding Records to Base Types

After record-specific syntax has been replaced by function applications, we must ensure that those and all other functions no longer contain any record types and record variables. To achieve this we replace those record types and variables by the fields of those records instead. We look at the l2norm function as an example:

```
double
l2norm(struct Vector3 v)
{
    vx = vector3_get_x(v);
    vy = vector3_get_y(v);
    vz = vector3_get_z(v);
    return sqrt(vx * vx + vy * vy + vz * vz);
}
```

We aim to transform this function into one without any record types.

```
double
l2norm(double x, double y, double z)
{
    vx = vector3_get_x(x, y, z);
    vy = vector3_get_y(x, y, z);
    vz = vector3_get_z(x, y, z);
    return sqrt(vx * vx + vy * vy + vz * vz);
}
```

In this example we see how the record argument struct Vector3 v is separated into three distinct arguments x, y, and z; corresponding to the three fields of the Vector3 record. Furthermore, all occurrences of this argument v are also replaced by the same three variables instead.

In the case where records and arrays are nested, this tranformation becomes non-trivial. Consider the signature of the timestep function from the example. Here the given record type is an array instead of a scalar value, furthermore it contains the nested Vector3 record for the position, and an array double[3] for the velocity.

```
struct Body[n]
timestep(struct Body[n] bodies, double dt)
```

After expanding the Body record, and the nested Vector3 record, we expect the function signature to look like:

```
double[n], double[n], double[n],   /* pos  */
double[n,3],                       /* vel  */
double[n]                          /* mass */
timestep(double[n] x, double[n] y, double[n] z,
         double[n,3] vel, double[n] mass,
         double dt)
```

This example highlights multiple interesting cases. Firstly, although the mass field of the body record is a scalar double, after expansion we expect it to become an array of type double[n] since struct Body[n] denotes an array of records instead of a scalar record, which consequently applies to all fields of the record. Secondly, the body record contains a nested Vector3 record, which itself is then expanded into its three distinct x, y, and z fields. Similarly to the mass field, here we must also ensure that these fields become arrays of type double[n]. Finally there is the velocity field, which itself is already an array of type `double[3]`. In this case, the shape of the bodies array must be concatenated with the shape of the velocity field, resulting in the type `double[n,3]`.

6.3 Denesting Fields of Nested Records

In order to be able to apply this transformation we need to have a mapping of record types to the fully denested fields and expanded shapes. We call this mapping σ, and allow it to be indexed by a record type to get the expanded fields of that record. In the case of the `Vector3` record, this would look as follows:

$$\sigma[\texttt{Vector3}] = \{\, \texttt{x} : \texttt{double},\ \texttt{y} : \texttt{double},\ \texttt{z} : \texttt{double} \,\}$$

whereas for the `Body[n]` array of records we expect the following:

$$\sigma[\texttt{Body[n]}] = \{\, \texttt{x} : \texttt{double[n]},\ \texttt{y} : \texttt{double[n]},\ \texttt{z} : \texttt{double[n]}$$
$$\texttt{vel} : \texttt{double[n,3]},\ \texttt{mass} : \texttt{double[n]} \,\}$$

Note that this environment does not contain the `pos` field, and instead has already expanded that record into its nested x, y, and z fields.

Denesting Records. We populate this environment using a function called $\texttt{Denest}_{\texttt{rt}}$. This function expects a record declaration as its first argument, and the (initially empty) accumulated environment σ as its second argument. All fields of this record are then denested separately using a function $\texttt{Denest}_{\texttt{f}}$, whose resulting environments are combined to form the mapping σ of the record type. We apply this denesting function to all record types in a program, from top to bottom.

$$\texttt{Denest}_{rt} \begin{pmatrix} \texttt{struct rt \{} \\ \quad \texttt{type}_1\,\texttt{[shp}_1\texttt{]} : \texttt{id}_1; \\ \quad \ldots \\ \quad \texttt{type}_n\,\texttt{[shp}_n\texttt{]} : \texttt{id}_n; \\ \texttt{\};} \end{pmatrix}, \sigma = \cup \begin{array}{l} \texttt{Denest}_f(\texttt{type}_1,\,\texttt{shp}_1,\,\texttt{id}_1,\,\sigma) \\ \ldots \\ \cup\,\texttt{Denest}_f(\texttt{type}_n,\,\texttt{shp}_n,\,\texttt{id}_n,\,\sigma) \end{array}$$

Because from this point on this record may be used in a nested fashion in all following record declarations, we add this record to the environment.

Denesting Fields. The main body of work lies in the $\texttt{Denest}_{\texttt{f}}$ function. Given a field name *id* and its corresponding type and shape, this function computes the environment σ' of that shape. Additionally this function requires the thus far accumulated environment σ, which is required when looking up the environment of a previously defined record type in the case that *type* is a record type. We distinguish between base-type fields and record type fields. In the case that we encounter a base-type field *id*, be it a scalar or an array, a mapping can immediately be added to the environment without additional work.

$$\texttt{Denest}_f(basetype,\ [\,],\ id,\ \sigma) = \{\, id : basetype \,\}$$
$$\texttt{Denest}_f(basetype,\ shp,\ id,\ \sigma) = \{\, id : basetype[shp] \,\}$$

If instead *id* is a scalar record type, we lookup the previously computed environment of that record type. Since this field does not have a shape, there is nothing more to do and we can copy the environment as is. Because we require that records are defined top-to-bottom, this environment must exist at this point. Otherwise an incorrect program was provided and we can raise an error.

$$\texttt{Denest}_f(recordtype,\ [\,],\ id,\ \sigma) = \sigma[recordtype]$$

As we have seen in the example, we need to do some additional work in the case that *id* is an array of a record type. Not only does that record type need to be denested, but the shape of *id* must be prepended to all fields of the denested record type as well, for which we use a new function: prepend.

$$\texttt{Denest}_f(recordtype,\ shp,\ id,\ \sigma) = \texttt{prepend}(shp,\ \sigma[recordtype])$$

Following is the prepend function. Its first argument is the shape we want to prepend, and the second argument is the environment of the record type to which we want to prepend this shape. For every field in this environment, we then prepend the given shape to the previous shape, resulting in a new environment that has the same identifiers and types as the given argument, but now with expanded shapes.

$$\texttt{prepend}(shp_{rt},\ \sigma_{rt}) = \begin{cases} id_1 : type_1[shp_{rt} :: shp_1], \\ \ldots, \\ id_n : type_n[shp_{rt} :: shp_n] \end{cases}$$

where $\sigma_{rt} = \{\, id_1 : type_1[shp_1],\ \ldots,\ id_n : type_n[shp_n]\,\}$

No case distinction is needed for scalar fields, since their shape is the empty list (as seen in Sect. 2), and thus the concatenation $shp::[]$ will act as an identity on shp. Additionally we do not need to worry about nested records at this point, as they have already been denested and thus at this point we only have basetypes.

Using this environment we can now actually apply the transformation proposed in Sect. 6.2. Whenever we encounter a record type, a record argument, or a record identifier we replace it by the expanded base-types and identifiers accordingly.

6.4 Primitive Functions

This record argument expansion applies to both the formal arguments of a function definition, and the actual arguments of applications of those functions. Consequently, the number of formal arguments and the number of actual arguments of user-defined functions will remain equal after the record transformation. Because of this no additional work is required for user-defined functions.

However in the case of primitive functions this leads to a problem. The actual record arguments of primitive function applications will have been expanded into multiple arguments, but since these functions are defined as compiler primitives they do not have a corresponding function definition in the program. As a result, the number of actual arguments and the number of expected arguments for these primitive functions will no longer be the same. Since we expose record types to users as primitive types, we should also ensure that primitive operations on records are also possible. Namely, we must ensure that it is possible to get the dimensionality and shape of a record array, and it should be possible to select into this array. Additional work is required with regards to primitive function applications in order to ensure that they remain valid after the record transformation.

Consider the built-in `shape` primitive that we use in the running example to find the upper bound of the tensor comprehension. Given a single array, this primitive function returns the shape of that array. Such primitive functions should be applicable to arrays of records as well, for example to get the shape of an array of bodies. After the transformation, records arguments will have been expanded into multiple arguments, leading to incorrect applications of these primitive functions. For example,

```
shp = shape(bodies);
```

will be transformed into an application without records

```
shp = shape(bodies_pos, bodies_vel, bodies_mass);
```

This transformed code is no longer valid. The shape primitive expects only a single argument, however it now receives three arguments. To resolve this we might decide to arbitrarily take the first field of the record, in this case `bodies_pos`, and use only that value in primitive functions instead. However, this field might already have a shape within the record itself. Such is the case with `bodies_pos`, where `pos` itself is already a three-element integer vector. After transformation, this shape will then be [n,3], whereas given the definition of `bodies` in the argument `struct Body[n] bodies`, we would expect its shape to be [n].

Here we can rely on the fact that record fields are always arrays of a statically known shape. Because we know that `pos` is a one-dimensional vector, we can statically decide that the last element of the resulting shape vector ([3]) should be dropped from the resulting shape.

```
shp = drop(-1, shape(bodies_pos));
```

We apply a similar approach to the remaining primitive functions that require modification, such as `dim` (dimensionality) and `sel` (selection). However for the sake of brevity we omit those cases here.

6.5 Tensor Comprehension

Whereas tensor comprehensions on records previously operated on only that single record value, after the record expansion these tensor comprehensions operate on and return multiple values. For example, a tensor comprehension that generates a list of bodies

```
bodies = { iv -> Body{} | iv < [N] };
```
is transformed into a tensor comprehension that returns three values:
```
pos, vel, mass = { iv -> ([0,0,0], [0,0,0], 0) | iv < [N] };
```
This requires that tensor comprehensions, and similar constructions such as with-loops, are able to operate on and return multiple values. In the case of SaC, this is already supported [22].

7 Unused Argument Removal

After applying the record transformation to the acceleration function from the running example, the fields of all record arguments are expanded into separate arguments, which leads to the following intermediate function definition:
```
double[n], double[n], double[n]
acc_v(double[n] xs, double[n] ys, double[n] zs,
      double[n,3] vels, double[n] masses)
{
    return { [i] -> rsum(1, { [j] -> acc(xs[i], ys[i], zs[i],
                                         xs[j], ys[j], zs[j],
                                         masses[j])
                              | [j] < [n] })
             | [i] < [n] };
}
```
However the velocity field is not used within the body of this function. Typically the number of arguments quickly explodes when expanding records, which has a negative effect on the compilation time of programs, this would especially be the case for the timestep function for example. Furthermore, calling sites of these functions are not able to apply optimisations such as dead code removal on these unused arguments, limiting further optimisation potential. Removing these unused arguments from function signatures and corresponding function applications would not only improve compilation times, but also opens the door to better optimisation of those calling sites. In certain cases this may make it possible to remove some flattened fields entirely, avoiding the need for unnecessary memory allocation of those unused fields.

After applying this unused argument removal optimisation any calling sites of the accelerate function will only pass the required arguments instead of also including the velocity field, and the function signature becomes:
```
double, double, double
double[n], double[n], double[n]
acc_v(double[n] xs, double[n] ys, double[n] zs, double[n] masses)
```
Naively applying this unused argument removal optimisation only once is not sufficient. After applying the optimisation once, it may expose additional arguments that have become unused. Therefore this optimisation is applied iteratively in the optimisation cycle, which repeatedly applies a suite of program optimisations.

8 Unused Return Removal

Typically when a function expects a record and returns a modified version of that record, only some of the fields of that record will actually have been changed. This occurs in the `timestep` function from the running example, which returns a modified lists of bodies without changing their masses.

```
            double[n], double[n], double[n], double[n,3], double[n]
timestep(double[n] x, double[n] y, double[n] z, double[n,3] vel,
         double[n] mass, double dt)
{
    ...
    return (x, y, z, vel, mass);
}
```

Here only the positions and velocities of the given bodies are changed, whereas the mass remains unchanged and is still equal to the value of the given argument after returning. Ideally, we would remove this mass from the return type to increase the potential for further optimisations. I.e., after removing the mass from the return types unused argument removal is able to remove this mass from the arguments as well, which as discussed previously opens the door for other optimisations.

Because overloaded functions must always have the same number of return types, we require a different approach compared to unused argument removal. This restriction however actually leads to a very simple implementation. During the optimisation cycle we annotate return types that remain unchanged with respect to one of the arguments, similarly to the annotation done by unused argument removal. However since we cannot change the return types of this function, we instead update calling sites of this function during the optimisation cycle. If we encounter an application that assigns an identifier whose corresponding return type is marked as unchanged, we replace any following occurrences of that identifier by the argument instead.

```
x2, y2, z2, vel2, mass2 = timestep(x, y, z, vel, mass, dt);
x3, y3, z3, vel3, mass3 = timestep(x2, y2, z2, vel2, mass2, dt);
x4, y4, z4, vel4, mass4 = timestep(x3, y3, z3, vel3, mass3, dt);
```

Since `timestep` does not change the value of `mass`, the returned value is thrown away and all following occurrences of `mass2` and `mass3` are replaced by `mass`.

```
x2, y2, z2, vel2, _ = timestep(x, y, z, vel, mass, dt);
x3, y3, z3, vel3, _ = timestep(x2, y2, z2, vel2, mass, dt);
x4, y4, z4, vel4, _ = timestep(x3, y3, z3, vel3, mass, dt);
```

9 Runtime Performance

We investigate whether the record flattening transformation introduces any significant overhead compared to hand-optimised code by benchmarking two implementations of the n-body algorithm: a hand-optimised version without records, and a version that makes use of records. In order to make optimal use of vectorization, the hand-optimised version operates on seven distinct arrays; three arrays for the x, y, and z coordinates, three arrays for the x, y, and z velocities, and a single array for the masses.

The record implementation from the example already does this through the use of the `Vector3` record, which highlights how without much effort we can play around with the memory layout. We do however modify the velocity field to also use a `Vector3` instead of a `double[3]`. The only necessary change then is to replace occurrences of `double[3]` types for velocities by `Vector3` types.

We benchmark these two implementations on 50,000 bodies, applying the timestep iteration 10 times. These benchmarks are repeated ten times on a Dell PowerEdge R7525 rack server containing two AMD EPYC 7313 CPUs, which have 16 cores running at 3.7GHz. Figure 3 plots the results of these benchmarks, which shows that the record version with `Vector3`s performs similarly to the hand-optimised version.

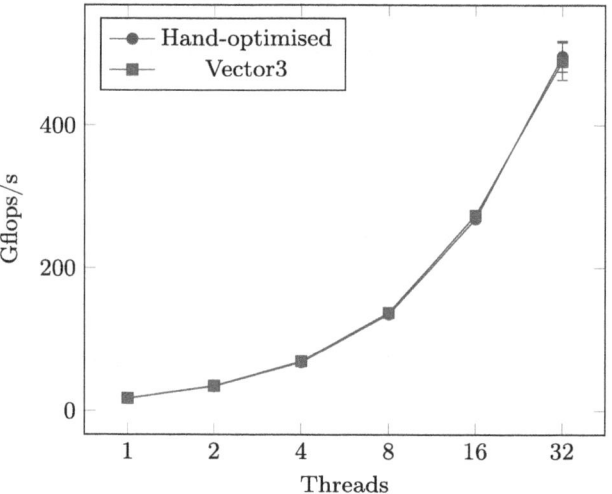

Fig. 3. Compute rate in GFLOP/s.

10 Related Work

This work expands upon previous work in the context of SaC [17], which explores how records can be added to the language. We extend on that work to fully support arbitrary non-recursive nesting of arrays and records, including all array operations on records as well as on tensor comprehensions and with-loops for constructing arrays of records.

The idea of converting the nesting structure of records and arrays is by no means new. Several papers investigate the performance gains of such rearrangements. In particular the performance benefits from records of arrays over arrays of records are well established. It has manifested itself in various software design strategies as, for example, the data-oriented design, which is applied in the context of game development [3].

However, it is also widely recognised that arrays of records for many application areas quite naturally lend themselves for specifying algorithms. For example, Homann et al. [11] discuss this ambiguity: they show the specificational benefits of arrays of records and demonstrate the performance benefits of converting arrays of records into records of arrays. As a potential solution, they propose a new data structure based on C++ templates that provides a programming interface similar to arrays of records yet results in code with records of arrays. Jubertie et al. [12] and Kofler et al. [13] further improve on that idea. They suggest a more flexible interface that enables a decoupling of data specification and the layout that ultimately is being generated for the execution.

The main differences between that line of research and ours is that in our work the conversion from arrays of records is fully compiler-driven. There is no need for the programmer to create any specific scaffolding or to make decisions about the layout. There is not even a need for the programmer to be aware of the conversion. By converting all records to arrays, our approach goes even one step further: the resulting programs no longer contain any records.

Further related work suggests library [4,21] or DSL [20] based approaches for converting records to arrays. Similar to the template-based approaches, these require developers to actively consider the performance of their programs. By instead making this transformation a core part of the SaC language, we allow developers to focus on the "what" of their program instead of on the "how".

The two new optimisations this paper proposes, unused argument removal and unused return removal, bear quite some relation to standard optimisations found in the context of functional programming languages as well as optimising compilers in general. Unused Argument Removal can be seen as a dual to strictness analysis [18,23]. Instead of identifying function arguments that are guaranteed to be evaluated, we identify arguments that are guaranteed not to be needed. This allows us to eliminate these arguments, effectively avoiding the corresponding beta-reductions when applying the functions. Unused Return Removal also avoids redexes by forwarding values within the calling context. This can be seen as a special form of variable propagation, a standard optimisation in compilers (e.g. [2]). The main difference here is that we propagate the arguments to functions where we statically find out that the correponding parameter is directly propagated into one of the results. The identification of such functions, by itself, can be seen as a special form of program slicing [24]. However, instead of computing the slices, we only identify these trivial slices for applying the propagation.

11 Conclusion

This paper proposes an extensions of the array language SaC by records. As with any other basic type in SaC, all records are implicitly n-dimensional arrays of records; a scalar record has dimensionality 0 and an empty shape. As records are normal expressions, all array constructing operations of SaC can be applied to records as well.

The key contribution of this paper is a transformation that systematically transforms all arrays of records into records of arrays. As a consequence, any non-recursive nesting of arrays and records can be transformed into records that appear as scalar records on the top level only and, thus, can be replaced by their fields entirely. Meaning that there is no need to support records at runtime at all. This not only reduces the implementation effort but it also avoids the overhead of nested memory allocations entirely.

The price that needs to be paid for getting rid of all records at runtime is an increase in function arguments and return values. To counter this effect, we also propose two optimisations that identify those arguments and return values that do not contribute to the actual computations within functions that operate on records. This reduces the increase of function signatures that results from our transformation to the necessary minimum.

To be able to perform the proposed transformation in all cases, we need to impose two restrictions. Firstly, we have to restrict arrays in record fields to be of a fixed shape. This restriction is a consequence of SaC's limitation to homogeneously nested arrays. In array languages without this restriction, arbitrarily shaped record fields would be directly possible, using the same transformation scheme as proposed in the paper.

Secondly, we have to restrict records to be defined in a non-recursive manner. This is a fundamental limitation of the proposed flattening approach. As the memory size of flattened arrays needs to be known prior to computing array values, recursively defined records cannot be flattened away as proposed in the paper. However, for most compute intensive applications such recursion is not needed. Language support for such recursion surely is possible and would constitute an extension of the language capabilities of SaC, but it would be orthogonal to the transformation work presented here. Our current implementation in the SaC compiler at www.sac-home.org does not support such recursion.

While our records do not support methods as part of the records, the function overloading of SaC provides the programmer with the opportunity to define record-type-specific functionalities. Even though no subtyping relation between record types is supported in SaC, it does support subtyping in array types [10] in general. Extending this to records as they are suggested in this paper might be interesting future work.

Acknowledgements. The authors thank Thomas Koopman for his help with optimising and benchmarking the record implementation in the SaC compiler, and the anonymous reviewers for their constructive feedback.

References

1. Aaldering, J., Scholz, S.B., Van Gastel, B.: Type patterns: pattern matching on shape-carrying array types. In: Proceedings of the 35st Symposium on Implementation and Application of Functional Languages. IFL 2023, Association for Computing Machinery, New York, NY, USA (2024). https://doi.org/10.1145/3652561.3652572
2. Aho, A., Sethi, R., Ullman, J.: Compilers – Principles, Techniques, and Tools. Addison-Wesley (1986). iSBN 0-201-10194-7
3. Bayliss, J.D.: Developing games with data-oriented design. In: Proceedings of the 6th International ICSE Workshop on Games and Software Engineering: Engineering Fun, Inspiration, and Motivation, pp. 30–36. GAS 2022, Association for Computing Machinery, New York, NY, USA (2022). https://doi.org/10.1145/3524494.3527626
4. Bell, N., Hoberock, J.: Thrust: a productivity-oriented library for CUDA. In: mei W. Hwu, W. (ed.) GPU Computing Gems Jade Edition, pp. 359–371. Applications of GPU Computing Series, Morgan Kaufmann, Boston (2012). https://doi.org/10.1016/B978-0-12-385963-1.00026-5
5. Chakravarty, M.M., Keller, G., Lee, S., McDonell, T.L., Grover, V.: Accelerating Haskell array codes with multicore GPUs, pp. 3–14. DAMP 2011, Association for Computing Machinery, New York, NY, USA (2011). https://doi.org/10.1145/1926354.1926358
6. Dijkstra, E.W., Lamport, L., Martin, A.J., Scholten, C.S., Steffens, E.F.M.: On-the-fly garbage collection: an exercise in cooperation. Commun. ACM **21**(11), 966–975 (1978). https://doi.org/10.1145/359642.359655
7. Zsók, V., Horváth, Z., Plasmeijer, R. (eds.): CEFP 2011. LNCS, vol. 7241. Springer, Heidelberg (2012). https://doi.org/10.1007/978-3-642-32096-5
8. Grelck, C., Scholz, S.B.: SaC - A functional array language for efficient multi-threaded execution. Int. J. Parallel Prog. **34**(4), 383–427 (2006). https://doi.org/10.1007/s10766-006-0018-x
9. Henriksen, T., Serup, N.G.W., Elsman, M., Henglein, F., Oancea, C.E.: Futhark: Purely functional GPU-programming with nested parallelism and in-place array updates. SIGPLAN Not. **52**(6), 556–571 (2017). https://doi.org/10.1145/3140587.3062354
10. Herhut, S., Scholz, S.B.: Generic programming on the structure of homogeneously nested arrays (2006). https://sac-home.org/_media/publications:pdf:gpotsohna.pdf
11. Homann, H., Laenen, F.: SoAx: a generic C++ structure of arrays for handling particles in HPC codes. Comput. Phys. Commun. **224**, 325–332 (2018). https://doi.org/10.1016/j.cpc.2017.11.015
12. Jubertie, S., Masliah, I., Falcou, J.: Data layout and SIMD abstraction layers: decoupling interfaces from implementations. In: 2018 International Conference on High Performance Computing & Simulation (HPCS), pp. 531–538 (2018). https://doi.org/10.1109/HPCS.2018.00089
13. Kofler, K., Cosenza, B., Fahringer, T.: Automatic data layout optimizations for GPUs. In: Träff, J.L., Hunold, S., Versaci, F. (eds.) Euro-Par 2015. LNCS, vol. 9233, pp. 263–274. Springer, Heidelberg (2015). https://doi.org/10.1007/978-3-662-48096-0_21
14. Leijen, D.: Koka: Programming with row polymorphic effect types. Electron. Proc. Theor. Comput. Sci. **153**, 100–126 (2014). https://doi.org/10.4204/eptcs.153.8

15. Lieberman, H., Hewitt, C.: A real-time garbage collector based on the lifetimes of objects. Commun. ACM **26**(6), 419–429 (1983). https://doi.org/10.1145/358141.358147
16. Lorenzen, A., Leijen, D., Swierstra, W.: FP^2: Fully in-place functional programming. Proc. ACM Program. Lang. **7**(ICFP) (2023). https://doi.org/10.1145/3607840
17. Luyat, H.: A lightweight implementation of records in functional array language SaC (2009), bachelor thesis, University of Amsterdam (2009)
18. Mycroft, A.: The theory and practice of transforming call-by-need into call-by-value. In: Robinet, B. (ed.) Programming 1980. LNCS, vol. 83, pp. 269–281. Springer, Heidelberg (1980). https://doi.org/10.1007/3-540-09981-6_19
19. Scholz, S.B., Šinkarovs, A.: Tensor comprehensions in SaC. In: Proceedings of the 31st Symposium on Implementation and Application of Functional Languages. IFL 2019, Association for Computing Machinery, New York, NY, USA (2021). https://doi.org/10.1145/3412932.3412947
20. Springer, M., Masuhara, H.: Ikra-Cpp: A C++/CUDA DSL for object-oriented programming with structure-of-arrays layout. In: Proceedings of the 2018 4th Workshop on Programming Models for SIMD/Vector Processing. WPMVP 2018, Association for Computing Machinery, New York, NY, USA (2018). https://doi.org/10.1145/3178433.3178439
21. Strzodka, R.: Abstraction for AoS and SoA layout in C++. In: mei W. Hwu, W. (ed.) GPU Computing Gems Jade Edition, pp. 429–441. Applications of GPU Computing Series, Morgan Kaufmann, Boston (2012). https://doi.org/10.1016/B978-0-12-385963-1.00031-9
22. Šinkarovs, A., Scholz, S.B.: Parallel scan as a multidimensional array problem. In: Proceedings of the 8th ACM SIGPLAN International Workshop on Libraries, Languages and Compilers for Array Programming, pp. 1–11. ARRAY 2022, Association for Computing Machinery, New York, NY, USA (2022). https://doi.org/10.1145/3520306.3534500
23. Wadler, P., Hughes, R.J.M.: Projections for strictness analysis. In: Proceedings of the Functional Programming Languages and Computer Architecture, pp. 385–407. Springer-Verlag, Heidelberg (1987). https://doi.org/10.1007/3-540-18317-5_21
24. Weiser, M.: Program slicing. IEEE Trans. Softw. Eng. **SE-10**(4), 352–357 (1984). https://doi.org/10.1109/TSE.1984.5010248

Author Index

A
Aaldering, Jordy 220
Achten, Peter 75, 220

B
Barwell, Adam D. 1
Brown, Christopher 1

C
Chang, Mun See 1
Chen, Adam 134

D
Dzhatdoyev, Shamil 195

F
Fluet, Matthew 160

G
Gibbons, Jeremy 55

H
Hartmann, Johannes 55
Huijben, Reg 220

K
Koopman, Pieter 75
Kudasov, Nikolai 22

L
Lötters, Björn 112

M
Morazán, Marco T. 195

O
Omar, Cyrus 134

P
Porter, Thomas 134

R
Rosiers, Josephine A. Des 195

S
Scholz, Sven-Bodo 220
Schrijvers, Tom 55
Šefl, Vít 92

T
Theocharis, Constantine 1
Thompson, Simon 1

W
Wu, Dongyu 160

The manufacturer's authorised representative in the EU is Springer Nature Customer Service Centre GmbH, Europaplatz 3, 69115 Heidelberg, Germany. If you have any concerns regarding our products, please contact ProductSafety@springernature.com

Printed and bound by CPI Group (UK) Ltd, Croydon, CR0 4YY

26/03/2026

02078962-0005